Safeguarding Vulnerable Adults and the Law

Michael Mandelstam

Jessica Kingsley Publishers
London and Philadelphia

First published in 2009
by Jessica Kingsley Publishers
116 Pentonville Road
London N1 9JB, UK
and
400 Market Street, Suite 400
Philadelphia, PA 19106, USA

www.jkp.com

Library of Congress Cataloging in Publication Data
Mandelstam, Michael, 1956-
   Safeguarding vulnerable adults and the law / Michael Mandelstam.
      p. cm.
   ISBN 978-1-84310-692-0 (pb : alk. paper) 1. People with disabilities--Legal status, laws, etc.--Great Britain. 2. People with disabilities--Abuse of--Great Britain--Prevention.. 3. Community health services--Law and legislation--Great Britain. 4. National health services--Great Britain. 5. Social service--Great Britain. I. Title.
   KD737.M38 2009
   362.941--dc22

                                                2008043856

British Library Cataloguing in Publication Data
A CIP catalogue record for this book is available from the British Library

ISBN 978 1 84310 692 0

Printed and bound in Great Britain by
MPG Books Group, Cornwall

CONTENTS

AUTHOR'S NOTE

In a book of this size and complexity, there will inevitably be some mistakes. I would be grateful for any observations or comments in this respect (michael.mandelstam@ btinternet.com).

Otherwise, I owe huge thanks to Jessica Kingsley for her unstinting support and encouragement, and to her staff who have worked so hard, quickly, efficiently and patiently.

Michael Mandelstam, September 2008

Introduction

This book attempts to outline what has come to be known as adult protection or safeguarding adults. It seeks to do this in two main ways. First, it uses many examples to illustrate the harm which vulnerable adults may suffer, generally through conduct comprising abuse, neglect or omission. Second, it sets these in a legal context.

The sort of matter with which it deals covers a wide range. Agency staff not turning up and vulnerable older people having accidents in their homes and dying as a result. People with learning disabilities suffering abuse or neglect, because the local authority has forgotten about them or refuses to find the money to meet the needs which it has a duty to meet. Older, sick and ill people being charged large sums of money by local authorities for care home placements when legally those placements should be free of charge. Or people, clearly in need, being told by local authorities that they are not needy enough to receive that help; and accidents, self-neglect and undermining of dignity occurring as a result. The vulnerable person with learning disabilities, grossly exploited and shortly to be murdered, who might be deemed ineligible for help. Or those, eligible for help, left without adequate safeguarding support – in the name of choice, control and independence. A local authority failing to invoke its emergency rehousing procedure for a couple with learning disabilities (and their children) known to be at significant risk, with the result that the couple are subject to a weekend of horrific torture by a group of youths who had been exploiting the couple.

Systematic and deliberate shortcuts in infection control contributing to scores of deaths in a hospital; NHS chief executives concealing the problem and making it worse. Understaffing leading to gross lapses in standards of care. Overcrowded hospitals with older people being moved from ward to ward to their clinical detriment. Mental health wards running at an occupancy rate of up to 135 per cent. Dying patients being nursed in the dining room while other patients eat. Hospital discharge of elderly inpatients taking place unplanned in the middle of the night. Patients not being helped with eating and drinking when they need help. Malnourishment in hospitals. Patients told to relieve their bladder and bowel in bed. Soiled clothing and bedding not being changed for hours. People tied up in wheelchairs or on commodes for extended periods.

Care home workers who kick, push, shove, beat, handle roughly, verbally abuse, neglect, deceive and steal. Managers of care homes standing back and doing nothing even when receiving reports about this. 89-year old men left to die in an upstairs care home room, with suppurating pressure sores down to the bone, the care home owner hacking off rotting flesh with a pair of scissors, wearing gloves with which he had just scooped faeces off the sheets. Care workers who force medication down people's throats, so that they have to swallow to stop from choking, throw residents across the room, pinch them. The care home worker who taunts and distresses residents with learning disabilities. Or who sleeps when she is meant to be on duty – during which time a resident catches his head between the headboard and rails of his bed, suffers brain damage and dies – and then falsifies the night time record.

Carers wilfully neglecting people with severe learning disabilities by leaving them locked up in a car on a hot day for hours while the manager and his assistant go to a betting shop. Professionals engaging in improper and indeed unlawful relationships with mentally vulnerable service users.

Financial abuse on a large scale involving a whole range of people in positions of trust, close family members, health care workers, social services care managers, solicitors, clergy, carers, bank staff. Theft, forgery, fraud, false accounting, robbery, burglary committed by those (a) already in a longstanding position of trust, (b) who have very recently but rapidly gained the victim's trust, or (c) who have deliberately targeted vulnerable, often older but also younger, adults. A nurse stealing money from a patient, a war hero, dying in hospital. Carers, trusted absolutely and treated like daughters, stealing from 76-year old blind women. Families driven to installing hidden surveillance cameras in pink teddy bears, so as to catch NHS primary care trust health care assistants stealing money in the home of 75-year old women suffering from leukaemia. A man of low intelligence taken by his carer to the building society every day for six months until he has transferred to the carer £60,000, his inheritance from this father. A friendly neighbour taking an interest in the vulnerable, elderly man next door exercising 'undue influence' and relieving him in a short space of time of £300,000, 90 per cent of his liquid assets.

Vicars forging the wills of parishioners while on their death bed in hospital. An old friend getting a mentally incapacitated person to change her will – in favour of the old friend. Mother and daughter carers in a private capacity from the next village getting a mentally incapacitated woman to sign over her £300,000 house to them, thereby depriving a children's hospital (to which she had left the house in her will). A former senior civil servant, suffering from Alzheimer's disease and cancer, being tricked fraudulently out of his £500,000 life savings by a builder. Cold calling, bogus tradespersons getting an older person to agree to roofing work that is not needed, sitting on the roof all morning, then driving the person to the bank to be paid hundreds of pounds.

It is practices and occurrences such as these that lie at the heart of the book.

1.1 DEPARTMENT OF HEALTH GUIDANCE

During the 1990s concern grew about the abuse of vulnerable adults. For example, in 1992, the Social Services Inspectorate had published *Confronting elder abuse* (SSI 1992) followed by some practice guidelines called *No longer afraid* (SSI 1993).

In 2000, the Department of Health published guidance, called *No secrets*, aimed primarily, but not only, at local social services authorities, and concerned with protecting vulnerable adults from abuse. It gave those authorities the lead in adult protection, and in coordinating other local agencies including the NHS, the police, housing providers etc. (DH 2000).

The term 'adult protection', or 'protecting vulnerable adults' began to be widely used. By 2007, that term was in turn being replaced by another, 'safeguarding adults'. In Scotland, the term adult protection remains and is now embodied in legislation. This book uses the two terms generally interchangeably. Both are in essence concerned with vulnerable adults, not just any adult.

1.1.1 VULNERABLE ADULT

The *No secrets* guidance defines a vulnerable adult as a person 'who is or may be in need of community care services by reason of mental or other disability, age or illness; and who is or may be unable to take care of him- or herself, or unable to protect him- or herself against significant harm or exploitation.'

1.1.2 ABUSE

The guidance refers to abuse as taking various forms, including physical, sexual, psychological, financial or material, neglect and acts of omission, discriminatory, and institutional. It states that some abuse will also constitute potentially a criminal offence, for instance in relation to physical assault, sexual assault and rape, theft, fraud, etc.

1.2 SCOPE OF WHAT IS MEANT BY ADULT PROTECTION OR SAFEGUARDING ADULTS

Despite the *No secrets* guidance, the scope of what is meant by protecting and safeguarding vulnerable adults is ill-defined. This is partly because there is no specific legislation in England setting out either definitions or statutory duties and powers of intervention. There is no equivalent of the Children Act 1989, which gives local authorities in England and Wales clear powers of intervention to protect children who are at risk of significant harm. This situation contrasts with Scotland, which passed an Adult Support and Protection Act in 2007 (currently in the process of being brought into force), providing statutory definitions and conferring on Scottish local authorities just such powers of intervention. This followed one particular investigation into abuse of people with learning disabilities in Scotland (SWSI 2004).

1.2.1 VULNERABILITY TO HARM

In selecting examples and relevant law, the book has used to full extent the definition of harm and abuse given in the *No secrets* guidance – in particular taking account of the reference to acts of omission or neglect and to institutional abuse. Heed has also been paid to the Adult Support and Protection (Scotland) Act 2007; it has of course no direct legal application to England, but usefully sets out definitions of harm, vulnerability, and adults at risk.

The book therefore adopts a broad if selective approach. For instance, at one extreme, it includes the harm perpetrated by neglectful, reckless, sadistic, bullying or dishonest individuals, whether known to the victim or strangers. Equally, it considers the systemic harm – in term of neglect and acts of omission – sometimes perpetrated or tolerated by institutions and organisations, including NHS bodies, local authorities and care providers generally.

1.3 LEGAL PERSPECTIVE

The book considers the protection and safeguarding of vulnerable adults in legal perspective. Not least for intervention to take place, a legal underpinning of some sort may often be essential. Law is not necessarily a magic wand in this respect but it serves as an additional, and sometimes essential, tool with which to intervene.

Law can be viewed as having a preventative, ameliorative, remedial or punitive role. For instance, preventatively, assessment of vulnerable people and their informal carers by local authorities under community care legislation may result in social services providing assistance and reducing stress in a caring situation – which is beginning to tip into possible abuse or neglect.

If matters have already deteriorated, a compulsory (ameliorative or remedial) intervention might be possible – for instance, under the Mental Capacity Act 2005 if a vulnerable person lacks capacity to take relevant decisions to protect himself or herself from serious harm. If, unfortunately, the situation nevertheless results in a criminal offence being committed, then the criminal law may provide a punitive measure in response, for example, to theft, assault, wilful neglect etc.

1.3.1 BREADTH OF LAW RELEVANT TO SAFEGUARDING ADULTS

The breadth of law considered in the book is wide and includes, for example, social services and NHS functions, regulation of health and social care providers, the banning and barring of people from working with vulnerable adults, mental capacity, mental disorder, human rights, environmental health, civil torts (negligence, trespass to the person, false imprisonment), the civil equitable remedy associated with 'undue influence', assault and battery, the giving of evidence by vulnerable people in court, manslaughter, murder, assisted suicide, theft, fraud, false accounting, sexual offences, the wilful neglect or ill-treatment of people with a mental disorder or mental incapacity, and information disclosure and confidentiality.

However, this is clearly not, neither is it intended to be, a detailed legal textbook. To cover all these areas of law in depth would make the book unwieldy and lose focus. Instead, it illustrates this law by picking out particular principles and legal cases relevant to vulnerable adults. These legal cases are deployed extensively in the book, in order both to illustrate the law in practical terms as well as to depict the plight in which vulnerable people may find themselves.

Furthermore, because the nature of adult protection is precisely so ill-defined, in terms of both law and practice, the book can lay no claim to having covered all that could or should be covered. In one sense, it is exploratory only, in an embryonic field of law and practice.

1.4 APPROACH OF BOOK

The book takes no moral standpoint; it attempts simply to identify harm that befalls certain groups of people because of their greater vulnerability, and then to set this in legal context. Equally, however, there are no sacred cows.

Thus, the harm which one individual, in a position of trust, may inflict on another can make painful reading. But it was ever so; individuals have always inflicted harm upon one another, in a sometimes despicable manner. Perhaps more noteworthy, therefore, is the harm caused – directly and indirectly – by the conduct of public bodies such as the NHS or local social services authorities. We are told by politicians that we have modern, enlightened and even world class health and welfare services. Yet these are sometimes implicated, directly or indirectly, in some of the very harm to vulnerable adults which forms the subject matter of this book. This is disconcerting because they are the public welfare services which are meant, with public money, to provide care for us all and to be taking a lead in adult protection and safeguarding activities. And behind NHS bodies and local authorities at local level lies central government; it would seem that inadvertently the latter's policies are to some extent contributing to, or at least associated with, the harm befalling vulnerable adults.

The book also carries reminders that, important though safeguarding and protecting vulnerable adults is, balance and proportionality are required in both identifying and responding to abuse.

1.5 APPLICATION TO UNITED KINGDOM

The book concentrates on England, although much of the law discussed is either the same, or has its equivalent, in the rest of the United Kingdom. Some specific reference is made to Scotland, which not only has passed adult protection and support legislation, but also brought mental capacity legislation into force some years ago. In both cases, it has stolen a march on England.

1.6. SUMMARY OF BOOK

Chapter 2 considers the policy background and definitions – for example, what is meant by terms such as abuse, harm, vulnerable adult and how these are applied in practice to the work of local authorities and other statutory agencies involved in adult protection and safeguarding work.

Chapter 3 outlines the statutory basis for the activity of local social services authorities and the range of assistance and intervention they can provide under community care legislation. It also considers, however, the extent to which local authorities themselves sometimes contribute to, or are associated with, the harm suffered by vulnerable people. Such contribution includes improper and unlawful charging for services, failing to monitor the provision of care for highly vulnerable people and the sometime fatal consequences, the imposition of ever stricter eligibility rules and assistance for fewer and fewer people (with resulting harm in some cases), failure to meet the needs of people where a clear duty to do so exists (again with very serious consequences in some cases), and the impact of 'self-directed' care on vulnerable adults who may be left with insufficient protection as a result.

Chapter 4 concentrates in particular on the NHS and the range of practices which have been exposed by the Healthcare Commission, particularly in respect of older people and people with learning disabilities. On any view, they constitute serious harm and abuse, especially since in extreme cases such practices have been associated with scores of patient deaths in one hospital alone. They include serious lapses in basic standards of care, lack of dignity, degrading management of continence, malnutrition, poor infection control, and overcrowded and understaffed hospitals.

Chapter 5 considers the regulatory legal framework designed to maintain standards generally in the provision of care, as well the Protection of Vulnerable Adults (POVA) list and the system of criminal record certificates – both aimed to stop unsuitable people from working with vulnerable adults. In particular it digests a number of cases heard by the

Care Standards Tribunal about people's suitability to work with vulnerable adults. The cases reveal at one extreme the obvious, such as blatant financial, physical or sexual abuse; at another the danger of mistaken allegations being made, the importance of evidence and the existence of the Tribunal as a safeguard for the 'innocent'; and, in the middle, the sometimes many shades of grey as to what constitutes misconduct and unsuitability to work with vulnerable adults.

The Mental Capacity Act 2005 is set out in some detail in Chapter 6 because, by definition, adults lacking mental capacity to take decisions about their everyday welfare and finances are likely to be more vulnerable. Furthermore, the Act has both protective and empowering roles which should complement one another but a tension between the two may sometimes emerge in everyday practice. A number of key issues are covered and illustrated with case law, including the definition of capacity, unwise decisions, acting in a person's best interests, restraint, depriving people of their liberty, lasting powers of attorney, Court of Protection interventions to safeguard vulnerable adults lacking capacity, advance refusals of medical treatment, independent mental capacity advocacy (IMCA) – and a new offence of ill-treatment or wilful neglect.

Chapter 7 covers a range of legally based interventions which might assist in protecting and safeguarding vulnerable adults. These include removing people from their home under the National Assistance Act 1948, environmental health law, interventions under the Mental Health Act 1983 including guardianship, court orders (related to harassment, non-molestation, occupation and anti-social behaviour). Multi-agency public protection arrangements (MAPPA) are summarised. Lastly, protection for 'whistle-blowers' under the Public Interest Disclosure Act 1998 is also covered.

Physical and sexual harm and abuse is outlined in Chapter 8 in terms of a range of criminal offences including assault and battery, other forms of bodily harm, manslaughter, murder, attempted murder, assisted suicide, ill-treatment or wilful neglect, causing the death of a vulnerable adult, sexual offences, and health and safety at work offences.

Chapter 9 looks at financial harm and abuse and legal remedies both civil and criminal. These include the equitable principle of undue influence, which the courts have identified as a growing issue, indeed a social trend, in respect of older people – as well as criminal offences such as theft, fraud and forgery.

The disclosure or non-disclosure of personal (and other) information may be a key issue in safeguarding and protecting vulnerable adults. Agencies may need to share information in order to protect people; equally people who believe they have been wrongly vilified may wish to have access to information held about them. And sometimes when harm (including death) has come to their relative, family members may do their own investigating to try to find out what happened or is still happening (e.g. in a hospital or care home) and to disinter relevant information. Legally, this bring into play various laws, including the common law of confidentiality, Human Rights Act 1998, Data Protection Act 1998 and the Freedom of Information Act 2000. Chapter 10 summarises some key legal 'rules', illustrating them with a range of cases from the courts, the Information Commissioner and the Information Tribunal.

Lastly, Chapter 11 deals with what it calls procedural aspects of protecting and safeguarding vulnerable adults. This includes the importance of supporting evidence and proportionate responses to suspected harm and abuse, factors considered by the Crown Prosecution Service in whether to prosecute, the provision of 'appropriate adults' for vulnerable suspects in police stations, special measures and other support for vulnerable witnesses from initial interview right through to giving evidence in court, and admissibility of evidence.

CHAPTER 2

Background: policy, definition and prevalence

KEY POINTS

In the absence of explicit, comprehensive legislation on adult protection, Department of Health guidance instead defines vulnerable adults, characterises different forms of abuse and sets out a framework, within which local social services authorities are expected to take the lead in protecting and safeguarding adults.

2.1 ADULT PROTECTION AND SAFEGUARDING ADULTS: LEGAL DEFINITION

Adult protection, or safeguarding adults, has only relatively recently been identified as a concern and area of work in its own right. Its boundaries are unclear; it is ill-defined. In England it is recognised only piecemeal in legislation. Nonetheless, it is a fast-growing activity for local social services authorities, the bodies to which central government – through policy and guidance rather than legislation – has given the lead in dealing with the issue.

Legally pinpointing and defining adult protection is therefore made all the harder by the absence of dedicated, comprehensive legislation. There is nothing equivalent to the child protection provisions contained in the Children Act 1989. Indeed, central government has failed to adopt proposals made by the Law Commission (1995) that local authorities in England should be given such statutory protective powers for adults. This lacuna in England now contrasts with that in Scotland, where the Adult Support and Protection (Scotland) Act 2007 will, when in force, give Scottish local authorities explicit powers of intervention. The Commission for Social Care Inspection has pointed out that the absence of clear definitions about the meaning of terms such as 'safeguarding', 'abuse', 'harm', 'vulnerable', contributes to a lack of clarity about roles and responsibilities (CSCI 2008a, p.7).

At the same time, given the breadth of what is meant by adult protection or safeguarding adults, there is inevitably a wide range of specific legal interventions which are nonetheless relevant (Kalaga and Kingston 2007). Yet, it has also been pointed out, following a national survey of prevalence of abuse and neglect of older people, that greater priority and more resources are required to prevent and respond to elder abuse, that these should not necessarily centre exclusively on adult protection and that legal reform would not be the only answer (Manthorpe *et al.* 2008).

2.2 *NO SECRETS*: DEPARTMENT OF HEALTH GUIDANCE AND ITS IMPLICATIONS

In the absence of legislation, the Department of Health published policy guidance in 2000 under s.7 of the Local Authority Social Services Act 1970. Entitled *No secrets*, it stated that local authority social services departments should take the lead in inter-agency working to combat such abuse of vulnerable adults. It set out a framework only, on which local authorities could base more detailed local policies and procedures (DH 2000).

Although only guidance, as opposed to legislation, it is sometimes referred to as statutory guidance. This is because s.7 of the 1970 Act requires a local authority to act under such guidance, and substantial deviation from it may result in the authority acting unlawfully (*R v Islington LBC, ex p Rixon*). However, the guidance is generally broad-brush in approach; for example, it suggests that local authorities may wish to set up adult protection committees, but does not require this. So, the potential force of the guidance is to some extent limited. Furthermore, the statutory nature of such guidance applies in any case only to local social services authorities; it does not have such status in respect of other local agencies referred to in the guidance as having a role in adult protection – for example, NHS bodies, the police and housing providers.

2.2.1 DEFINITION OF VULNERABLE ADULT

The guidance states that it is concerned with the protection from abuse of vulnerable adults. A vulnerable adult is defined as a person 'who is or may be in need of community care services by reason of mental or other disability, age or illness; and who is or may be unable to take care of him- or herself, or unable to protect him- or herself against significant harm or exploitation' (DH 2000, p.8).

Part of this definition, referring to possible need for community care services, has been taken directly from s.47 of the NHS and Community Care Act 1990 which governs the duty of local authorities to assess people's needs for community care services. This is significant because, as the courts have pointed out, the safeguarding work of local authorities remains grounded in the community care legislation (*Re Z*). Nevertheless, the House of Commons Health Committee has recommended that the definition of 'elder abuse' be extended to 'to include those individuals who do not require community care services, for example older people living in their own homes without the support of health and social care services, and those who can take care of themselves' (HCHC 2004, p.9).

Whether such changes in definition are – strictly speaking at least – necessary is open to question, since an older person who was being abused, or at risk of abuse, would arguably qualify for community care services in any case. This is because, first, older people generally (i.e. even without an obvious physical, mental or sensory disability) come within the ambit of community care under s.45 of the Health Services and Public Health Act 1968. Second, support, information and advice are all community care services – even if the person is not actually receiving any other assistance.

Third, statutory guidance on 'fair access to care' states that abuse and neglect, serious or otherwise, constitute critical or substantial community care needs for the purpose of local authority intervention (LAC(2002)13). All local authorities regard people in critical need as eligible for assistance, and the vast majority – at the moment at least – will also assist people deemed to be in substantial need. It is true, however, that the 1968 Act is weakened by the fact that local authorities have only a power, rather than a duty, under it to arrange services for older people.

2.2.1.1 Adults at risk (Scotland)

By way of comparison with the English guidance, the Adult Support and Protection (Scotland) Act 2007 refers to 'adults at risk', although vulnerability is a key part of the definition.

These are defined as people who (a) are unable to safeguard their own well-being, property, rights or other interests; (b) are at risk of harm; and (c) because they are affected by disability, mental disorder, illness or physical or mental infirmity, are more vulnerable to being harmed than adults who are not so affected (s.3). The draft code of practice to the Scottish Act notes that the presence of a particular condition does not automatically mean that the adult is at risk. This is because a person might have a disability but be perfectly well able to safeguard his or her well-being. So all three elements of the definition are required; it is the aggregate of the person's particular circumstances that might combine to make them more vulnerable than other people (Scottish Executive 2008, p.12).

Risk of harm in turn is defined to mean that (a) another person's conduct is causing (or is likely to cause) the adult to be harmed; or (b) the adult is engaging (or is likely to engage) in conduct which causes (or is likely to cause) self-harm (s.3).

The Act defines harm as including all 'harmful conduct', including (a) conduct which causes physical harm; (b) conduct which causes psychological harm (for example: by causing fear, alarm or distress); (c) unlawful conduct which appropriates or adversely affects property, rights or interests (for example: theft, fraud, embezzlement or extortion); and (d) conduct which causes self-harm.

2.2.2 HARM: ABUSE, NEGLECT, ACTS OF OMISSION

Abuse is characterised by the Department of Health guidance as physical, sexual, psychological, financial or material, neglect and acts of omission, discriminatory, institutional. Some forms of abuse are criminal offences, for example physical assault, sexual assault and rape, fraud, etc. (DH 2000, p.9).

Taking their cue from the Department of Health's guidance, many local authority social services departments seem to talk only in terms of protecting people from 'abuse'. Terms such as neglect and acts of omission are not so explicitly emphasised in the guidance, although in principle they are clearly covered by the overall term, abuse. The import of the English guidance appears to be that self-neglect is not deemed to be part of safeguarding or adult protection work. By way of contrast it would appear that the Adult Support and Protection (Scotland) Act 2007, at least on its face, confers powers on Scottish local authorities in relation to self-neglect, as well as to neglect or abuse by other people (see 2.2.1.1 above).

One particular aspect of abuse about which there is growing concern is that of improper 'chemical restraint'; that is the inappropriate use of medication to control care home residents with conditions such as Alzheimer's disease. It has been suggested that abusive prescribing of these drugs can lead to premature death, and could constitute in some circumstances a criminal offence of assault, ill-treatment or wilful neglect (Burstow 2008).

2.2.2.1 Relationship between harm and abuse

In contrast to the English guidance the Scottish legislation, the Adult Protection and Support (Scotland) Act 2007, does not contain the term abuse.

There may be an important distinction in this differing use of language between the English guidance and the Scottish legislation. The dictionary meanings of abuse tend to import not just the notion of harm, but also of ill-motivation and moral fault on the part of the perpetrator. For example, the Chambers Dictionary (1998) refers to the word as entailing: making bad use of, taking undue advantage of, betraying (e.g. a confidence), misrepresenting, deceiving, reviling, maltreating, violating (especially sexually). This does not have quite the same ring as the more neutral concept of conduct causing harm; the same dictionary refers to harm as meaning injury which may be physical, mental or moral. Neither singly nor in combination do the words, conduct or harm, suggest necessarily blatant moral fault on the part of any perpetrator.

The *No secrets* guidance does in fact go on to refer to harm, when it considers what degree of abuse justifies intervention. It quotes the Law Commission which referred to harm as including not only ill-treatment (including sexual abuse and forms of ill-treatment which are not physical), but also the impairment of, or an avoidable deterioration in, physical or mental health; and the impairment of physical, intellectual, emotional, social or behavioural development. (DH 2000, para 2.18)

Even so, the import of the guidance would seem to suggest that such harm is only relevant if it flows from abuse which, in turn, carries clear moral fault. This may make it more difficult to label at least some institutional or organisational harm as a safeguarding and protection issue – if that harm is not flowing from ill-motivated individuals or groups of individuals. Clearly, all abuse encompasses (potential) harm, but not all harm encompasses abuse. The problem would seem to lie in identifying when harm warrants the safeguarding and adult protection label.

2.2.2.2 Institutional neglect and omissions

It may be then that the distinction in use of language between the English guidance and the Scottish legislation is more than merely theoretical or academic.

For instance, at least some English local social services authorities tend in practice, it appears, to understand adult protection as about identifying and responding to abuse of a vulnerable adult by another individual or individuals (who may tend, though not necessarily, to be ill-motivated). Whereas, sometimes harm in a wider sense – typically institutional and with less discernible ill-motivation – seems to be less easily recognised and even to occupy a blind spot.

For instance, it may be easy enough to invoke adult protection procedures in respect of the care home assistant who is physically rough with residents and is suspected also of stealing their personal property. It becomes more problematic, however, in the example of an NHS trust which, struggling in good faith to meet performance and financial targets, loses sight systematically and thoroughly of standards of care and infection control. The result may be loss of dignity and even of life. Yet, it would seem that local authorities, in their safeguarding and adult protection role, are at present singularly ill-equipped either (a) to recognise the latter as an adult protection issue; or (b) to do anything about it. NHS trusts, in their role as partner agency of local authorities in adult protection, seem in general even less able to put their own house in order.

Likewise, when local authorities are themselves, institutionally, breaching rules about the 'topping up' of care home fees by families, the impropriety and unlawfulness are seldom even recognised, let alone treated as an adult protection issue in those authorities. And, it is only belatedly that local authorities have begun to wake up to the fact that for a decade or more they have, with relatively little protest, forced many people to use up their savings and sell their houses – to pay for nursing home care that should have been provided free of charge by the NHS. All this has involved local authorities relieving vulnerable people and their relatives of considerable sums of money both improperly and unlawfully (see 3.3.1.3). This constitutes significant financial harm; given the vulnerability of the people involved, it is difficult to see why it should not be viewed as a safeguarding and adult protection matter.

2.2.2.3 Institutional neglect: a blind spot

Thus it seems that if the test of individual ill-motivation is applied, adult protection concerns seem more likely to be triggered by the example of a dishonest care home assistant, than by the example of the NHS trust that has lost perspective on basic, humane care. But if the test of conduct causing harm is applied, the actions of the NHS trust as a whole should not only trigger adult protection procedures, but arguably demand a far greater priority of response than the individual care assistant. The overall focus should presumably be on protecting vulnerable adults from harm, rather than on the ill intent or motivation of the perpetrator. And, presumably, the degree of harm should determine the priority.

All that said, the problem of course in tackling the example of the NHS trust is at least fourfold. First, the problem is typically institutional in scale, and so much more difficult to grapple with.

Second, local authorities are charged politically and legally with working cooperatively with the NHS and find it hard to challenge the health service. The greater ease with which local authorities raise issues about individuals rather than organisations is sometimes only too evident. For example, in one case, a local authority went to court seeking an order to remove an elderly man lacking mental capacity from his daughter and granddaughter. Amongst the grounds argued by the local authority was that the latter were irresponsible in what food they gave him, given that he had diabetes. It turned out that this allegation was in fact unfounded (*LLBC v TG*). Yet, in contrast, one is not aware of adult protection alerts being raised around the country by local authorities (through their hospital social workers) about the widespread failure to help elderly hospital inpatients – with or without mental capacity – with their food and drink, and about the resulting poor nutrition (see 4.2.2).

Some hospital social workers say that if they were to raise issues about dignity, nutrition, continence management and hygiene of patients, whenever they came across them in acute hospitals, they would never get any work done. Local authorities may believe that it would do no good to rock the boat; besides which it would make working with NHS colleagues difficult. Yet, if they do not raise these matters, not only does it seem that they unwittingly become complicit, but they compound the problem; the poor practice becomes accepted to the point where it is considered no longer remarkable and certainly not a cause for formal concern.

Third, it is less easy to pinpoint the cause and blame; there is a distinct dearth of accountability if things go wrong systemically in a large organisation such as the NHS. This is particularly so, when the actions and priorities of an NHS trust, which lead to poor standards of care, are inextricably linked to central government policies and targets. For instance, nurses may be forced into neglecting their patients because of systematic cuts in staffing, over-occupancy of beds and management's view of patients first and foremost as financial units and statistics. What, or who, is the cause then if patients subsequently die from infection or are cared for in a degrading manner? Is it the frontline nurses, senior management, or even, ultimately, government ministers for their unsung contribution to a NHS climate of fear and stress amongst staff, and neglect of older patients? All will argue that they are acting in good faith and have no wish to harm the very patients they are, in fact, harming.

Fourth, local authorities have no legal remit to investigate other organisations, the NHS or any other. In fact, in relation to the NHS, it is the Healthcare Commission which has consistently identified high profile examples of neglect, harm and abuse. It is not by and large the NHS trusts themselves that have done so, even though they are meant to be an integral part of local adult protection work. Even then, it is unclear how effective the Healthcare Commission has been in improving practices.

2.2.2.4 Central government policies

Some of the issues raised immediately above inevitably lead to a consideration of central government policy in England. Certainly, it has recognised the issue of adult protection and safeguarding; its guidance is testimony to this. Yet only belatedly has it begun to think about the sort of protective legislation which the Scottish Parliament had already passed.

Indeed, some of what emerges in this book clearly points to government policy as inadvertently contributing to some of the harm that befalls vulnerable people. For instance, within the NHS there is often a ruthless imposition of financial and performance targets which, as the Healthcare Commission has found, are given greater priority than patient care. This can lead to patients being counted as financial units rather than people in need, and in some instances to the appalling standards of health care provided for older people detailed in Chapter 4.

It is likewise central government policy that has lain behind what some have called the scandal of NHS continuing health care, whereby tens of thousands of older people have used up savings and had to sell their homes, in order to pay for nursing home care that should have been provided free of charge. This is certainly financial harm; contributors to a BBC *Panorama* programme characterised it, perhaps not unreasonably, as 'state sponsored theft'. It is also central government that has facilitated the imposition of ever stricter 'eligibility criteria' by local authorities. This has the result of leaving ever more people unassisted and vulnerable to harm.

Most recently, a tension has emerged between central government's view that users of health and social services should be given ever more choice, control and independence. It sees them as active consumers in a 'market' model of health and social care. But it is by no means clear that such a model, applied over-simplistically and crudely, will sufficiently protect and safeguard all those who are vulnerable. Central government will retort that local authorities and the NHS should give added support to those who are more vulnerable and need additional help to achieve this control, choice and independence. Given, however, the general shortage of resources to cope with demand in health and social care, this may be wishful thinking. Government has recently stated that there is no place for a paternalistic welfare state (HMG 2007). One question is whether this dislike of paternalism will in some circumstances militate against adequate safeguarding. The government maintains that 'self-care' will enable people to have 'maximum choice and control' and that the State and its agencies will be 'more active and enabling, less controlling' (Skills for Care 2008, p.2). This sounds attractive; but in practice it carries the undoubted danger that vulnerable people in need may be – in the hurly burly and financially harassed world of social and health care – be left to sink or swim, with minimal intervention and assistance.

For example, government is pursuing a policy of 'self-directed social care' involving 'individual budgets' and 'community care direct payments'. Briefly, this involves people to a greater extent assessing their own community care needs and deciding how those needs should be met. Direct payments then involve the local authority giving people a certain amount of money to purchase their own care or daily living equipment – rather than have them arranged by the local authority. Hitherto, one safeguard has been that direct payments could only be legally be made if the community care recipient (a) gave (and therefore had the mental capacity to) consent to the payment, and (b) had the ability to manage it with or without assistance (Health and Social Care Act 2001, s.57). This rule is to be amended by s.146 of the Health and Social Care Act 2008, which will allow for other 'suitable' people to consent to, to receive and to manage direct payments, where the disabled person lacks the capacity to do so himself or herself. On the one hand this allows those without capacity to benefit, as other people do, from the same flexibility afforded by direct payments. On the other, it arguably creates additional risk of financial or other exploitation. Regulations are still to be made as to how suitability will be established with adequate safeguards.

2.2.3 WHEN TO INTERVENE

The Department of Health guidance considers when a local authority should appropriately intervene in relation to the seriousness or extensiveness of abuse. It states that the following factors should be considered: the vulnerability of the individual, the nature and extent of the abuse, the length of time it has been occurring, the impact on the individual, and the risk of repeated or increasingly serious acts involving the vulnerable adult or other vulnerable adults (DH 2000, para 2.19).

2.2.4 INTER-AGENCY APPROACH TO ADULT PROTECTION

Department of Health guidance stresses the importance of inter-agency working including the NHS and social services, sheltered and supported housing providers, regulators of services, police and Crown Prosecution Service, voluntary and private sector agencies, local authority housing and education departments, probation service, DSS benefit agencies, carer support groups, user groups and user-led services, advocacy and advisory services, community safety partnerships, legal advice and representation services, and so on (DH 2000, p.20).

The guidance states that collaboration needs to take place at all levels involving operational staff, supervisory line management, senior management staff, different parts of the local authority (i.e. corporately), chief officers/chief executives, and local authority members. In particular, the director of adult social services will have a particularly important role to play (DH 2000, pp.16–17).

It suggests the formation of adult protection committees, but does not make this a requirement, stating instead that agencies 'may consider there are merits to establishing a multi-agency management committee (adult protection) which is a standing committee of lead officers' (DH 2000, para 3.4). This is in contrast to the local safeguarding children's boards which were made obligatory by the Children Act 2004.

The lack of statutory obligation placed upon local authorities and other agencies has been criticised. For example, in the case of the NHS, the chair of the serious case review into the murder of a man with learning disabilities made a number of points, which in her view may have underlain the apparent failure of the NHS in that case. She noted that there was no requirement that the NHS have a lead officer for adult protection, was no guidance on expenditure of resources in making sure NHS staff are properly trained, was an apparent lack of monitoring and scrutiny of safeguarding processes in NHS trusts – and that there were questions about whether safeguarding was integral to all contracting arrangement of primary care trusts, and whether GPs were charging for submitting evidence to and for attending strategy meetings (and, if so, who should pay) (Flynn 2008).

2.2.5 INFORMATION SHARING

The Department of Health guidance emphasises that, as part of inter-agency working, agreement on the sharing of information will be required, in order to balance on the one hand confidentiality, and on the other the importance of sharing information (even in the absence of a person's consent). The guidance summarises the principles of sharing confidential information as follows (DH 2000, p.24):

- Information must be shared on a 'need to know' basis only.
- Confidentiality should not be confused with secrecy.
- Informed consent should be obtained but, if this is not possible and other vulnerable adults are at risk, it might be necessary to override this requirement.
- Assurances of absolute confidentiality should not be given where there are concerns about abuse.
- Principles of confidentiality designed to safeguard and promote the interests of service users and patients should not be confused with those designed to protect the management interests of an organisation.

It also goes on to state that principles of confidentiality designed to safeguard and promote the interests of service users should not be confused with those 'designed to protect the management interests of an organisation' (DH 2000, p.22).

In fact, this comment could usefully be taken to apply not only to personal information (disclosure of which is regulated under the Data Protection Act 1998), but also more general information concerning the policies, and their implications for vulnerable adults, of public bodies (disclosure of which is regulated under the Freedom of Information Act 2000). Arguably, the latter type of information becomes all the more important given the prevalence of concealment and disingenuousness, which may be highly damaging to vulnerable adults. For instance, the Healthcare Commission uncovered concealment of the facts by executive members of NHS trust boards during the lethal outbreaks of infection in Buckinghamshire and Kent – concealment that arguably contributed to the effects of the outbreaks (see Chapter 4 of this book).

Generally, local authorities, NHS trusts, police forces etc. may receive a range of request for information, relevant to safeguarding adults, under both the 1998 and 2000 Acts.

2.3 OTHER GUIDANCE

Five years on from the Department of Health guidance, the Association of Directors of Social Services (ADSS) issued a national framework of standards for 'safeguarding adults', a term it preferred to 'adult protection'. The standards cover issues of partnership between organisations, preventing abuse and neglect in the community, preventing abuse and neglect within service delivery, training standards, human rights, joint systems, partner agency systems, procedures, access to safeguarding services, engaging citizens.

The framework was to cover 'all work which enables an adult who is or may be eligible for community care services to retain independence, well-being and choice and to access their human right to live a life that is free from abuse and neglect. This definition specifically includes those people who are assessed as being able to purchase all or part of their community care services, as well as those who are eligible for community care services but whose need – in relation to safeguarding – is for access to mainstream services such as the police' (ADSS 2005, p.5).

The Commission for Social Care Inspection (CSCI) has also published a protocol in relation to working with other agencies, outlining basic principles, limits to CSCI's role, information sharing, initial response to notifications or alerts, assessment strategy, strategy meetings, investigation strategies, safeguarding plans, collection of data about safeguarding activities, safeguarding adults partnerships boards, serious case reviews, quality assurance, definitions and types of abuse (CSCI 2007).

2.4 PREVALENCE OF ABUSE OR NEGLECT OF VULNERABLE ADULTS

Given the hazy definitions surrounding adult protection and safeguarding adults, information about the prevalence of relevant harm, abuse and neglect is also sketchy. Likewise it seems uncertain whether there is an increasing problem in society, or whether people are now simply talking about it more.

As already pointed out, there is also a difference between identifying abuse taken in a narrow, almost moralistic, sense, and taking the wider approach of conduct leading to harm. For instance, one major study surveyed some 2100 people in the United Kingdom living in private households, aged 66 years or over. On the basis of this sample, it concluded that, in the past year, some 227,000 people (2.6% of the relevant population) had suffered neglect or abuse. The categories of abuse used in the study were financial, psychological, physical and sexual. Neglect was also included. However, this study did not cover what it termed 'stranger abuse' or institutional abuse – since care homes and hospitals were excluded, although sheltered accommodation was included (O'Keefe et al. 2007, pp.3–15).

Whilst such exclusions may have been expedient in terms of that particular study, they mean that part of the equation is missing. The potential level of harm, through abuse and neglect, in care homes and hospitals is considerable. Furthermore, it is clear that certain groups of people may be more vulnerable to harm even if it emanates not from people known to them, but from 'strangers'. For instance, in 2003 a burglar was jailed having raided 600 homes and targeted in particular elderly people in their nineties and concentrating in particular on people who were blind, deaf or partially sighted (Bird 2003). Certainly, Crown Prosecution Service draft guidance on crimes against older persons, for example, does not limit its view of their aggravating nature to crimes committed only by those in a position of trust or known to the person. It notes that there a 'number of cases of crimes against older people, such as theft, robbery, burglary and obtaining property by deception, which highlight the aggravating nature of targeting an older or vulnerable victim' (CPS 2007, para 11.1).

Thus, the logic of excluding such harm from the ambit of adult protection concerns simply because it involves a stranger is questionable. It may in any case beg the question as to when the perpetrator is deemed to be a stranger, and when he or she is no longer so. And a local strategy, involving local authority and police, to protect vulnerable older people from 'cold calling' bogus tradesmen and workmen, is precisely about protecting them for strangers. But it may be a legitimate and useful part of adult protection; indeed some councils now set up 'no cold calling zones', in response to criminals who target homes with visible clues such as hand rails, wheelchair ramps or who even have scanned the obituary columns to identify the recently bereaved (LGA 2007).

In 2004, Action on Elder Abuse stated that it could not say whether abuse was increasing or was of epidemic proportions, but that it was certainly being more widely recognised. It identified inadequate care as an issue of great concern. This was on the basis of calls to its helpline. It, too, excluded stranger, but not institutional, abuse. It defined elder abuse as 'a single or repeated act or lack of appropriate action occurring within any relationship where there is an expectation of trust, which causes harm or distress to an older person' (Action on Elder Abuse 2004, pp.11,16).

2.4.1 BALANCED APPROACH TO IDENTIFYING ABUSE AND SAFEGUARDING

Local authorities and other agencies tread a fine and sometimes undoubtedly difficult line. The identification of abuse and safeguarding needs to be taken seriously, but at the same time a proportionate and balanced approach to identification and intervention is required. For example, over-zealousness must be guarded against.

Reminders of this are to be found, for instance, (a) in cases concerning the banning of carers from working with vulnerable adults where the evidence is scanty or non-existent; (b) the weighing up under article 8 of the European Convention on Human Rights as to whether an intervention (such as removing a person lacking capacity from the family home) is justifiable and proportionate – and ensuring that such intervention does not end up exposing a vulnerable person to abusive consequences at the hands of the State; (c) local authority applications to the courts to protect vulnerable, incapacitated adults but made without the requisite evidence; (d) excessive retention of sensitive personal information; or (e) the disproportionate invoking of adult protection procedures (e.g. by a regulatory body such as the Commission for Social Care Inspection). Indeed, unbalanced interventions may not only be unfair to any alleged perpetrator of abuse or neglect but not be in the best interests of service users and even lead to positive harm. The Commission for Social Care Inspection, perhaps with over simple interventions in mind, refers to the need to acknowledge the 'shades of grey' that can arise 'from complex family relationships and situations which may impact on interventions' (CSCI 2008a, p.22).

Furthermore, there might be a danger, in the light of the Care Standards Tribunal decisions (see chapter 5) or theft cases (see 9.4), to take a jaundiced view of care workers. However, it should be noted that (a) the vast majority are honest and genuinely caring, (b) they care for vulnerable people and thus carry an immense amount of responsibility, (c) a range of not inconsiderable caring skills are involved, (d) they carry out tasks that are none too pleasant, for example, not infrequently dealing with both urinary and faecal incontinence, and (e) they are arguably underpaid in respect of such responsible work. Supervision, training, organisation and staffing levels are not necessarily adequate in every care agency, local authority or NHS trust - leading to additional stresses and strains on staff and those being cared for, and sometimes to things going wrong.

When vulnerable people are being cared for in their own homes, it is wholly unsurprising that boundaries are sometimes crossed, and that care workers should end up providing help and support outside of care plans and in a personal capacity. In some instances, in the real world, if they did not do so, nobody else would. For isolated elderly people, struggling both physically and mentally (either cognitively or with stress or both), the daily carer may not only be the natural person to turn to, but the only one. This is against a backdrop of the Commission for Social Care Inspection reporting local authorities (a) in retreat from assisting many older people by imposing every stricter criteria governing eligibility for assistance (Henwood and Hudson 2008), and (b) providing inadequate services even for those people supposedly eligible (Forder 2007, pp.5–7). Of course, the crossing of boundaries may well raise safeguarding suspicions and, certainly beyond a certain point, should not happen under regulatory legislation and 'national minimum standards' (see 5.4). Such boundary crossing may amount to misconduct (see 5.1.6). Nevertheless, it must be recalled that many carers may be acting from the best of motives – helpfulness and kindness.

2.5 HUMAN RIGHTS

Closely allied to the protection of vulnerable adults are human rights. It is beyond the scope of this book to set out in detail the Human Rights Act 1998, together with the underpinning European Convention on Human Rights. However, in sum, the human rights under the European Convention obviously relevant to the protection of vulnerable adults include the:

- right to life (article 2)
- right not to be subjected to torture or to inhuman or degrading treatment or punishment (article 3)
- right not to be deprived of liberty other than in specified circumstances and only then in accordance with legal procedures (article 5)
- right to respect for a person's home, private and family life. However, interference with this may be justified if it is in accordance with the law and is necessary in a democratic society. In addition it must be (a) in the interests of national security, public safety or the economic well-being of the country; (b) for the prevention of disorder or crime; (c) for the protection of health or morals; or (d) for the protection of the rights and freedom of others (article 8)

- right to marry (article 12)
- right not to suffer discrimination (article 14).

Only public bodies, or other bodies carrying out functions of a public nature, directly have human rights obligations. For example, in the past the courts have stated that a resident of a *local authority care home* could legally argue a human rights case against the authority in its role of care home owner. However, the resident of an *independent care home* could not bring a human rights case directly against the care home, even if the resident had been placed there by the local authority. This was because the care home was deemed not to be carrying out functions of a public nature (*YL v Birmingham CC*). However, s.145 of the Health and Social Care Act 2008 (not yet in force) changes the effect of this legal ruling by stating that care homes are, after all, deemed to be carrying out functions of a public nature – and are thus subject to the Human Rights Act 1998 – but only in respect of residents placed by local authorities under ss.21 and 26 of the National Assistance Act 1948.

Thus, this legislative amendment does not confer on vulnerable adults human rights, where those adults (a) are placed in an independent care home by the NHS, (b) are placed by local authorities and the NHS in an independent care home under s.117 of the Mental Health Act 1983, (c) are self-funding residents who have their own contractual arrangements with the independent care home, or (d) who receive services in their own home from independent domiciliary care agencies (rather than from the local authority). Central government maintains in the case of the NHS that human rights would automatically apply; but this does not seem necessarily to be so, given the reasoning of the courts in the *YL* case.

The link between human rights and adult protection seems clear enough. For instance, the Parliamentary Joint Committee on Human Rights has drawn attention to a wide range of concerns about the poor treatment of older people in health care, much of it in the context of care and treatment directly provided or commissioned by the NHS. The Committee associated aspects of this poor treatment with particular rights under the European Convention. There appears to be a close correlation between this list and what would be considered adult safeguarding matters, involving harm, abuse and neglect. The list set out by the Committee included:

- malnutrition and dehydration (articles 2,3,8)
- abuse and rough treatment (articles 3,8)
- lack of privacy in mixed sex wards (article 8)
- lapses in confidentiality (article 8)
- neglect and poor hygiene (articles 3,8)
- inappropriate medication and physical restraint (article 8)
- inadequate assessment of a person's needs (articles 2,3,8)
- over-hasty discharge from hospital (article 8)
- bullying and patronising attitudes (articles 3,8)
- discrimination on basis of age, disability or race (article 14)

- communication difficulties particularly for people with dementia (articles 8,14)
- fear of making complaints (article 8)
- eviction from care homes (article 8) (JCHR 2007a, p.9).

There are many examples throughout this book involving actual, or potential, breach of people's human rights – where public bodies, either by action or omission, directly put those rights in jeopardy.

2.5.1 RIGHT TO LIFE

Article 2 (the right to life) demands that the state take reasonable steps positively to safeguard people's right to life. Part of this involves setting up independent enquiries in certain circumstances where people have died in connection with the acts or omissions of public bodies. For instance, had the Healthcare Commission not independently investigated the scores of deaths from *Clostridium difficile* in Buckinghamshire and Kent (HC 2006; HC 2007a), an article 2 challenge could possibly have been made. Thus, in a 2008 case, the European Court of Human Rights pointed out the following in a case involving the disappearance of a person with dementia from a nursing home:

Disappearance of man's mother from nursing home: human organ gang possibly involved. The European Court states that there was an obligation to 'make regulations compelling hospitals, whether public or private, to adopt appropriate measures for the protection of their patients' lives and to set up an effective independent judicial system so that the cause of death of patients in the care of the medical profession, whether in the public or private sector, can be determined and those responsible made accountable'. In a case involving the disappearance and (presumed – she was never found) death of a woman with Alzheimer's from a nursing home, the European Court interpreted this requirement broadly and as applicable to the circumstances. Her son suspected abduction by a criminal gang trading in human organs. Although legal remedies, disciplinary, civil and criminal were in principle available, in practice they had not been used to 'secure an effective possibility to establish the facts surrounding the disappearance' (*Dodov v Bulgaria*).

2.5.2 INHUMAN OR DEGRADING TREATMENT

The courts normally regard article 3 as setting a high threshold; in other words it is not easily breached. The European Court of Human Rights has stated that inhuman or degrading treatment means that the ill-treatment in question must reach a minimum level of severity, and involve actual bodily injury or intense physical or mental suffering. Degrading treatment could occur if it 'humiliates or debases an individual showing a lack of respect for, or diminishing, his or her human dignity or arouses feelings of fear, anguish or inferiority capable of breaking an individual's moral and physical resistance' (*Pretty v United Kingdom*).

The European Court of Human Rights found a breach of article 3 in relation to the distress and hardship caused to a heroin addict in prison who subsequently died there. Amongst the key reasons for this finding were the inability accurately to record her weight loss (through dehydration and vomiting), a gap in monitoring by doctors, failure to admit the person to hospital to ensure medication and fluid intake, and failure to obtain more expert assistance to control the vomiting (*McGlinchey v United Kingdom*). It was a breach also in the case of a severely physically disabled person subjected to degrading treatment in a police cell:

Degrading treatment of severely disabled woman in police cell. A severely physically disabled person had been sent to prison for contempt of court. She had failed to disclose her assets in a debt case. In the police cell she was unable to use the bed and had to sleep in her wheelchair where she became very cold. When she reached the prison hospital, she could not use the toilet herself, the female duty officer could not manage to move her alone, and male prison officers had to assist. The European Court concluded that to detain a severely disabled person – in conditions where she is dangerously cold, risks developing pressure sores because her bed is too hard or unreachable, and is unable to go to the toilet or keep clean without the greatest difficulty – constituted degrading treatment contrary to article 3. Damages of £4500 were awarded (*Price v United Kingdom*).

The unnecessary use of handcuffs on a prisoner receiving chemotherapy treatment in a civilian hospital has been held to be degrading, inhumane and a breach of article 3 – where there was no adequately founded risk of escape or harm to the public (*R(Graham) v Secretary of State for Justice*).

The following examples, identified in the context of the NHS, were not taken to court as human rights cases, but arguably involved possible breach of article 3 rights. The right not to be subjected to inhuman or degrading treatment may arguably be engaged if a person with learning disabilities is restrained excessively in a wheelchair for 16 hours a day (HC and CSCI 2006), if hospital patients are told to relieve their bowels and bladder in bed and then left for hours in wet or soiled bedding (HC 2007a), if a dying man is nursed in the hospital dining room in front of other patients eating their meals (MHAC 2008), and if hospital patients are tied to commodes for extended periods and given their meals on them (CHI 2000).

2.5.3 UNLAWFUL DEPRIVATION OF A PERSON'S LIBERTY

If a local authority deprives a person of his liberty, by placing him in a care home or hospital and preventing him returning to his own home, without following a lawful procedure, it will breach article 5 (*JE v DE; HL v United Kingdom*).

2.5.4 RIGHT TO RESPECT FOR A PERSON'S HOME, PRIVATE AND FAMILY LIFE

Article 8 demands respect for a person's home, private and family life. However, it then allows interference with these by a public body if certain conditions are met. These are that the interference be (a) in accordance with the law; (b) necessary in a democratic society; and (c) for a specified purpose, including for the protection of health or morals, for the protection of the rights of other people, for the economic well-being of the country, for the prevention of crime. The courts have held that respect for private life includes physical and psychological integrity.

For example, it was a breach of article 8 when a local authority failed to act for two years to alleviate the dire state of a physically disabled woman, with a family of six

(*R(Bernard) v Enfield LBC*). Similarly, there was a breach when a local authority carried out a massively flawed and defective assessment about where a 95-year-old woman should live – the court pointed out that the consequences of such a lapse could be fatal and so engage article 8 (*R(Goldsmith) v Wandsworth LBC*).

Equally, however, if adult protection measures involve interference in home, private and family life, article 8 may provide the justification for that interference. For instance, a local authority may wish to protect a vulnerable adult lacking capacity, by removing him or her from the family home. It will not necessarily be acting contrary to article 8 as a whole, if it can show that certain conditions are met, even though it might clearly be interfering with the right to respect for private life. First, it needs to show that it is acting in accordance with the law, such as the NHS and Community Care Act 1990 or Mental Capacity Act 2005. Second, that the intervention is 'necessary in a democratic society', that is, the authority is taking steps that are proportionate in respect of the problem and risk; in effect, that it is not taking a sledgehammer to crack a nut. Third, it would need to indicate the purpose justifying the intervention; for instance, to protect a person's health or to prevent a crime.

The right to respect for private life also encompasses the question of confidentiality, but interference with confidentiality is permitted if there is sufficient justification on the same basis: in accordance with the law, necessary and for a particular purpose (e.g. protection of health or prevention of crime). It is about balancing the competing interests of confidentiality as opposed to disclosure (e.g. *R v Plymouth CC v Stevens*).

2.6 REVIEW OF ADULT PROTECTION AND SAFEGUARDING GUIDANCE

In October 2008, the Department of Health, the Department of Criminal Justice and the Home Office published a consultation document on the review of the No secrets guidance. It put forward a number of questions about whether or not new legislation was required, which would put on a statutory footing: (a) adult safeguarding boards, (b) multi-agency cooperation and information sharing, (c) the duties and powers of the different agencies involved in safeguarding, and (d) the definition of terms such as 'safeguarding', 'vulnerability', 'people at risk'. In addition it asked whether social workers should have a right of entry to assess and remove a vulnerable adult from his or her own home – or to bar other people from the home – even if the vulnerable adult does not want this. A separate, related, issue was whether police officers should have extended powers, perhaps under s.17 of the Police and Criminal Evidence Act 1984, to enter people's homes in case of suspected abuse (DH, MJ, Home Office 2008, Chapter 8).

CHAPTER 3

Local authority social services

KEY POINTS

When central government issued its *No secrets* guidance, giving local social services authorities the lead in local adult protection and safeguarding work, it did not accompany this responsibility with any new legislative powers for those authorities. Thus, adult protection work by local authorities rests primarily on existing community care legislation. This accounts for the reference in the guidance to a vulnerable adult having to be a person who may be in need of community care services. It is a direct reference to the same condition in s.47 of the NHS and Community Care Act 1990, which is the legal trigger for community care assessment of a person's needs.

Nonetheless, community care legislation is directly relevant to adult protection, in terms of the duties to assess and to provide services. For the most part, use of this legislation is associated with the ability of local authorities to assist, protect and safeguard vulnerable adults. However, there is an underbelly. Acting ostensibly under social services legislation, local authorities sometimes behave in such a way so as directly or indirectly to put vulnerable people at risk of harm. To the extent that this is so, the situation is a curious one; the gamekeeper acting also as poacher.

First, there is evidence of vulnerable people suffering financial harm when local authorities are acting in clear and systematic breach of legal rules about charging for services. Second, the failure on the part of a local authority to monitor and review care providers, to whom they contract out care services, can lead to serious harm and some-times even to the death of service users. Third, local authorities are progressively applying more restrictive eligibility criteria, thus assisting fewer vulnerable people and potentially exposing them to arguably unacceptable risk of harm. Fourth, the failure sometimes to recognise a clear statutory duty to meet a vulnerable person's needs either at all or in the appropriate manner, can also lead to severe detriment and, if not necessarily to abuse, then to highly inappropriate alternative care and to harm. Fifth, current government social (and health) care policy is awash with the mantra of giving people more control, choice and independence. There appears already to be a danger that such a policy will be indis-criminate in practice, irrespective of the vulnerability of some of the adults to whom it is applied.

3.1 COMMUNITY CARE ASSESSMENT

Local authorities have a duty to assess people who appear to may be in need of commu-nity care services (NHS and Community Care Act 1990, s.47).

Central government has passed a considerable amount of guidance concerning this duty. Some of this guidance is of the strong variety, made under s.7 of the Local Authority Social Services Act 1970. Such guidance must be generally followed by local authorities, unless there are cogent reasons for not doing so. One such set of statutory guidance concerns a policy known as 'fair access to care services', often abbreviated to FACS. This guidance sets out four categories of risks to people's independence, or need, which the local authority must assess for: critical, substantial, moderate or low. When people are assessed, the risks to their independence and their needs are allocated to one or more of the categories. Each council has to decide, by weighing up its limited resources in the light of local needs, which categories of need it will meet (LAC(2002)13). For instance, the policy of many councils is to meet critical and substantial, but not moderate or low, needs.

Within the critical and substantial categories, the guidance makes explicit reference to abuse and neglect. The critical category refers to serious or abuse neglect that has occurred or will occur; the substantial category refers to abuse or neglect only, without it necessarily being serious (LAC(2002)13, para 16). Thus, the assessment of abuse and neglect is embedded in the community care assessment duty of local authorities.

Nonetheless, the absence of any specific adult protection legislation giving local authorities explicit powers and duties has been recognised by the courts. In one adult pro-tection case (concerning an assisted suicide), whilst acknowledging the *No secrets* guidance, the judge held that a local authority's duties were limited to addressing the community care needs of the particular person as assessed by the authority. Any common law duties that it might owe 'did not extend the scope of the statutory duties' under the relevant community care legislation. Furthermore, such duties were not 'all-embracing' in the ways provided for children under Part 3 of the Children Act 1989 (*Re Z*).

3.2 COMMUNITY CARE SERVICES

Community care legislation contains a wide variety of services that local authorities can potentially arrange for people – and which may be relevant in the context of safeguarding adults. For instance, they might place a person in a care home under s.21 of the National Assistance Act 1948. A care home placement might represent a place of safety for a person lacking mental capacity who was otherwise subject to alleged abuse or neglect in their own home (*LLBC v TG*).

Alternatively, authorities have duties and powers to provide a wide range of non-residential services. These include practical assistance in a person's own home, day services and centres, travel, recreational activities, meals, assistive equipment, adaptations to the home – as well as advice, support and visiting services, and so on. Such services, provided adequately and timeously, may play a crucial role in preventing or ameliorating highly stressful caring situations which, in some circumstances, might otherwise tip into neglect or abuse.

Such non-residential services are available for disabled people under the National Assistance Act 1948 (s.29) and the Chronically Sick and Disabled Persons Act 1970 (s.2). They are also available for older people generally, who are not disabled, under the Health Service and Public Health Act 1968 (s.45). One such example of a service, designed to safeguard vulnerable adults, provided possibly under the 1968 Act, was reported to the author as follows:

Gardening services to prevent crime. In one particular area, 'con men' were targeting older people by means of unkempt front gardens. Where the householder did turn out to be elderly and vulnerable, they were performing small amounts of gardening and charging extortionate amounts of money. In consultation with the police, the local authority arranged for a gardening service for older people in that particular area, in order to remove the indicator (the unkempt garden).

Indeed in 1993, the Social Services Inspectorate suggested in its report, *No longer afraid*, that the 1968 Act would be a key statute for preventative strategies in respect of the abuse of older people (SSI 1993, p.5). A range of other non-residential services are available under schedule 20 of the NHS Act 2006, including for illness generally, mental disorder in particular – as well as home help and laundry services for households where somebody is ill, lying in, an expectant mother, aged or disabled.

3.2.1 ASSESSMENT AND SERVICES FOR INFORMAL CARERS: ROLE IN ADULT PROTECTION

Local authorities are subject also to duties and powers in relation to people's informal carers. In summary, this legislation places a duty on local authorities to assess informal carers in their own right if (a) they are caring for a person who may in need of community care services; (b) they are providing substantial care on a regular basis; and c) they request an assessment. The assessment must be about the person's ability to care, and also take account of their involvement in work, education, training and leisure activities. The legislation goes on to give a local authority a power, although seemingly not a duty, to arrange services for an informal carer. If the local authority asks the NHS to assist in respect of providing for carers, the NHS has a duty to give due consideration to the request. The relevant legislation comprises the Carers (Recognition and Services) Act 1995, Carers and Disabled Children Act 2000, and Carers (Equal Opportunities) Act 2004.

The current policy pursued by both local authorities and the NHS, of more care in people's own homes rather than institutional care, inevitably places a greater burden on families and informal carers. A build-up of physical and mental stress can sometimes lead to situations that threaten to descend into abuse or neglect by informal carers, or at any rate to harm suffered by the vulnerable, cared for person. The carers' legislation, as well as the community care legislation, can be used to assess and to prevent, defuse, or avoid a repeat of, stress leading to harm. In the protection and safeguarding of vulnerable adults, it is arguably essential legislation. There has been a hint, in several safeguarding legal cases, of possible local authority failure to provide adequate support for carers of vulnerable adults lacking capacity – and of such failings may be contributed to the eventual crisis which precipitated the legal disputes (e.g. *Newham LBC v BS; Re S (Adult Patient); B Borough Council v Mrs S*).

The stresses on carers should not be underestimated. In an article in *The Times* newspaper a daughter revealed her feelings about the relentless care she was providing for her 98-year-old mother – though there was no suggestion of any abuse or neglect. It was a catalogue of bitterness, anger and despair; a 'living hell', exhaustion, depression, isolation, resentment felt toward 'this dreadful old crone'. Yet her conscience could not allow her to place in the strange environment of a care home her mother, who had failing hearing and eyesight, together with physical and mental frailties (*The Times* 2007).

The author of *The selfish pig's guide to caring* notes that anyone who has cared for somebody else long-term can understand the temptation to lash out verbally if not physically. He relates a conversation with a nurse from a care home, a good carer, who was cheerful, open, voluble and compassionate. She jokingly states how the residents drove her mad and that the only reason she hadn't pushed them down the stairs was that she would be found out. He wanted to ask her how serious she was being, but didn't dare – because he knew exactly what she meant, in relation to caring for his own wife (Marriott 2003, p.189).

3.3 PROTECTION OF VULNERABLE PEOPLE FROM LOCAL AUTHORITY PRACTICES

Central government has given local social services authorities the lead in protecting and safeguarding vulnerable adults. As outlined immediately above, a substantial body of community care legislation underpins the ability of authorities to act.

Nonetheless, owing to the pressures placed on local authorities, they sometimes find themselves in situations where, far from protecting vulnerable people from harm of various sorts, they are themselves implicated to greater or lesser degree in that harm.

Harm can come to vulnerable adults at the hands of local authorities in, for example, terms of (a) the imposition of unlawful charges for care; (b) failure of local authorities to monitor the care provided for highly vulnerable people; (c) application of strict criteria of eligibility so as to exclude vulnerable adults from assistance; (d) failure to carry out their duty to meet a person's assessed needs; and (e) indiscriminate application of the mantra of 'independence, choice and control' in the context of 'self-directed care' – thus leaving some vulnerable adults at sometimes serious risk.

Perhaps an illustration of the understandable difficulty that local authorities may have in looking inward - that is, investigating their own activities - came in a case involving warden-controlled sheltered housing, owned and run by the local authority. Serious complaints, supported by cogent evidence, were made by two residents about persistent bullying and harassment by the warden. The council's response was inadequate. The complainants ultimately had to resort to the local government ombudsman. She found that the council had failed to follow its own adult protection procedures and did not launch a full investigation into the allegations against the warden. This was maladministration. One of the local authority officers, providing information to the ombudsman, explained that he had pressed for a comprehensive investigation at the first adult protection strategy meeting about the case, but had been refused permission. He stated that in any other case there would have been a full adult protection investigation, but an exception had been made in this case because it was a scheme owned and run by the council itself (*South Tyneside Metropolitan Borough Council 2008*).

3.3.1 LOCAL AUTHORITIES LINKED TO FINANCIAL HARM

The following paragraphs consider local authority charging in terms of the topping up of care home fees, mental health aftercare services and NHS continuing health care. When this has gone badly and systematically wrong, as it has in some places, it is difficult to describe it as anything other than a form of financial harm being perpetrated against vulnerable people – by the very type of body that is meant to be protecting them from such harm. On the face of it, there appears little reason not to categorise it – certainly in more egregious instances – as a form of financial abuse.

3.3.1.1 Care home charges: unlawfully making people and their families pay extra care home fees

There is evidence that suggests some, possibly many, local authorities are systematically – to greater or lesser extent – breaching rules about care home charges.

Under s.21 of the National Assistance Act 1948, local authorities place people in care homes. If a person wishes to go to a more expensive care home than the local authority is offering, he or she can do so – but only if a third party (typically a family member) agrees to 'top up' the difference between the amount the local authority is prepared to pay and the actual care home fees. In other words, topping up is envisaged, and is lawful, under the rules, if a person chooses to go to more expensive accommodation – that is, over the usual cost that the local authority is prepared to pay to meet certain levels of need. But for there to be choice in this respect, there obviously must be a cheaper care home, charging a fee within the local authority's 'usual cost level', which could meet the needs of the person (including, for instance, the need to be near close relatives). Otherwise, logically, there could be no choice involved.

However, if a person ends up being placed by the local authority in a care home which is more expensive than the authority's usual cost level – because there is no other cheaper care home place available and suitable for meeting the person's assessed needs – then it is unlawful for a local authority to demand a top-up. It is equally unlawful, under the rules, for the local authority to turn a blind eye by allowing the care home to extract a top-up in these circumstances. This is because the local authority must remain contractually responsible for the whole of the fee.

All this is made quite clear under the regulations, directions and guidance (SI 2001/3441, LAC(92)27 directions, and LAC(2004)20).

In the late 1990s, 14 per cent of residents funded by local authorities received third-party top-ups; by 2004, this had risen to 33 per cent. In addition, 40 per cent of local authorities believe that more top-ups are being paid than they know about, because they were being negotiated directly between the home and the relatives. This is a practice which appears to be consistent neither with the legal rules nor with the Department of Health's guidance. In short, this pattern seems to indicate 'widespread illegal conduct' (CCC 2007, pp.4, 17). In 2008, the Commission for Social Care Inspection found that older people lacked adequate information about top-ups, and that the prevalence of top-ups appeared closely related to the local care market. Where care home places were limited, up to 75 per cent of people placed by local authorities had to pay a top-up (CSCI 2007a, p.5).

Since, where care home places are so limited, it is much less likely that people would have been exercising a choice to be in a more expensive home, this figure would almost certainly represent extensive and unlawful behaviour by the local authorities concerned. Indeed, CSCI confirmed in addition that councils felt constrained to keep fee rates (usual cost levels) as low as possible (p.5).

In some instances, this situation seems to mean that in whichever home a person chooses to have his or her assessed needs met, it will be more expensive than the council is prepared to pay. Once again, in these circumstances, it is unlawful for the local authority either to demand, or to allow the care home to demand, a top-up. At the very least, it was clear to CSCI that vulnerable older people and their families were bereft of information about top-up fees; indeed such guidance was 'almost non-existent'. This opened the path to arbitrary decisions being made (CSCI 2007a, p.78).

In sum, the rules about care home fees and topping up are fairly clear. They are meant to be applied by public bodies charged with protecting vulnerable people. Local authorities should know and adhere to the rules. Yet it seems many vulnerable people, through their families, are (a) being deprived of crucial information about the rules and options; and (b) being asked, sometimes effectively forced, improperly and unlawfully to pay care home fees that are properly the responsibility of the local authority. This results in clear financial harm; it is not clear why, at least in some circumstances, it should not be labelled financial abuse. It is equally not clear that any local authority has labelled it as such.

3.3.1.2 Charges for mental health aftercare

Local authority demands have also been under scrutiny for payment for aftercare services provided under s.117 of the Mental Health Act 1983. These services are provided for people who have previously been detained under certain sections of the Mental Health Act 1983. There was clearly in the past some genuine lack of clarity about just what the rules under s.117 really were; and even when local authorities levied unlawful charges, it would be harsh to characterise this past conduct as financial propriety, although it clearly constituted financial harm.

However, even since the law was clarified, cases continue to come to light which are suggestive of a cavalier approach to the rules and to people's money – always remembering the degree of vulnerability of the people concerned. Some local authorities have continued to persist with legally dubious attempts to find a way of charging people for services which should be free under s.117.

For instance, local authorities may maintain that, because s.117 services being provided have been successful in stabilising the person in the community – such that there is little risk of readmission to hospital – they no longer need to be provided under s.117. Instead, they argue, the very same services can be provided under other community care legislation which allows charging – even though the very reason for the stability is those s.117 services. The courts have disapproved of this approach (*R v Manchester CC, ex p Stennett*, High Court) as have the local government ombudsmen (*Clwyd CC 1997; Bath and North East Somerset Council 2007*).

Alternatively, a local authority may claim, sometimes retrospectively, to have properly discharged a person from s.117; it is just that it didn't tell anyone at the time – and failed to consult with the person and carer as demanded by central government guidance (HSC

2000/3) and the Mental Health Act code of practice (DH 1999a, now superseded by a revised code: DH 2008a). The local ombudsmen have underlined the importance of this procedural safeguard, so that local authorities do not casually re-categorise services being provided under s.117 as suddenly coming under other community care legislation, with a view to imposing financial charges (which are barred under s.117).

The ombudsmen have therefore criticised those local authorities that have attempted to discharge s.117 in retrospect, in order to justify charging, but have failed to consult properly at the relevant time. Such cases are all too suggestive of attempts by local authorities to get hold of large sums of money improperly and of an unconcern with the legal rules. Such attempts are condemned as maladministration by the local ombudsman (*Wiltshire CC 1999*, and *Leicestershire CC 2001*). Nor are the sums at stake paltry; in the *Wiltshire* case the ombudsman recommended the council repay £60,000. In another case, £264,000 was found owing to one person (CLAE 2004, p.7).

In a further case, the local authority attempted to place a woman in a cheaper care home that would not meet her assessed needs and the requirements of her care plan. If she wished to go into the more expensive home, she was told she would have to top up. The local ombudsman found maladministration; the authority was obliged to cover the cost of a care home that would meet her needs (*North Yorkshire CC 2007*). Another local authority, astonishingly, persuaded the patient to sign away her statutory right to free placement under s.117 in a care home – telling her that unless she did so she might have to wait 12 months before the council could place her. The ombudsman found maladministration (*York CC 2006*).

3.3.1.3 NHS continuing health care

For some 14 years or more, many people with what are termed 'NHS continuing health care needs' have been charged by local authorities for care that should have been funded free of charge by the NHS. The health service ombudsman has been investigating this pattern since at least 1994. This investigation culminated in a highly critical, overview report issued in 2003 (HSO 2003). It resulted in the Department of Health, reluctantly, having to repay between £180–200 million to people or their families unlawfully charged for nursing home care (Womack 2008).

However, although it is the NHS and Department of Health that has borne the main brunt of the criticism for this state of affairs, it is often overlooked that it is local authorities that have been actually charging unlawfully the people affected. Unlawfully because, as the law courts have pointed out, it is not just a case of what the NHS should have been paying for, it is about what local authorities are not legally permitted to do – namely, place people in nursing homes who have primary health needs which are of the continuing care variety (*R v North East Devon HA, ex p Coughlan; R(Grogan) v Bexley NHS Care Trust*). Indeed, in the *Grogan* case, the judge lamented the absence of the local authority as a party to the proceeding, since in his view the local authority was key. Arguably, the local authority's absence from that case was symptomatic of the passivity and detachment of local authorities generally on this whole issue.

Nobody would accuse local authorities of having set out deliberately and unlawfully to cause financial harm to people in this way. Indeed, they would argue that they were merely acting in a humane and socially responsible manner by picking up the pieces improperly discarded by the NHS. But, until the end of 2007, when the Association of Directors of Adult Social Services (ADASS 2007) issued guidance urging local authorities to be more assertive on the issue, local authorities were both individually and collectively silent for well over a decade. The consequence was that, by their inaction and readiness to take substantial sums from highly vulnerable people, they were complicit in conduct that caused significant financial harm to many – perhaps tens of thousands of people over this period – including the loss of their savings and homes in order to pay for care that should have been free of charge.

In this respect, it is notable that in one investigation, the local ombudsman (as opposed to the health service ombudsman) found maladministration when a local authority social worker stood back and allowed a vulnerable service user to be unlawfully charged for a nursing home placement (*Hertfordshire CC 2003*).

3.3.1.4 Legal remedies for unlawful charging for services

There are some obvious legal remedies for such unlawful charging by a public body. Complaints can be made to local authorities and, if necessary, to the independent local government ombudsmen. The local ombudsmen can include compensation in their recommendations, following a finding of maladministration causing injustice. Alternatively, a judicial review legal case may also be possible, although the court would not normally award financial compensation directly.

If local authority senior managers could be shown knowingly to have (a) flouted the law; and (b) therefore deprived the family of money dishonestly, then in principle at least, this could amount not just to maladministration, but also possibly to fraud. The fact that they might have acted with best possible of intentions – for example, to make the local authority's scarce resources go further – would arguably be irrelevant. However, in practice, it is certainly difficult to see such a case being brought, let alone succeed.

It might also be possible in principle, but with a highly doubtful chance of success in practice, to bring a civil tort case involving what is called misfeasance in public office. This involves a public officer exercising public functions as follows:

Misfeasance in public office. The case law reveals two different forms of liability for misfeasance in public office. First there is the case of targeted malice by a public officer, i.e. conduct specifically intended to injure a person or persons. This type of case involves bad faith in the sense of the exercise of public power for an improper or ulterior motive. The second form is where a public officer acts knowing that he has no power to do the act complained of and that the act will probably injure the plaintiff. It involves bad faith inasmuch as the public officer does not have an honest belief that his act is lawful (*Three Rivers DC v Bank of England*).

3.3.2 FAILING TO MONITOR AND REVIEW CONTRACTUAL ARRANGEMENTS

Increasingly, local social services authorities commission community care services from the independent sector, rather than providing them directly. They do so by means of contracts, held with a range of care providers, including care homes, domiciliary care providers and day centres. Although the services are contracted out, local authorities retain at least a twofold responsibility.

First, they retain the duty, under the NHS and Community Care Act 1990, ultimately to ensure that people's assessed needs are met adequately. Second, they are spending public money on contracts, the efficacy of which they should be ensuring. This responsibility becomes all the more acute, when one considers that local authorities deal with highly vulnerable people. And it is this latter consideration of vulnerability which has led the local government ombudsman to make findings of maladministration against local authorities when they fail to discharge this twofold responsibility. For such failure, the ombudsman has pinned local authorities with a significant degree of blame for consequent detriment to – including the death of – service users. Clearly, such a level of detriment becomes a safeguarding and adult protection matter. Typically, it involves omissions and neglect.

If a local authority has known full well about a care provider's failings, but failed to act or acted inadequately, the ombudsman will fix the local authority with maladministration. The following case involved the death of a highly vulnerable service user:

Woman's death following council's apparent indifference to the fate of elderly people. The complainant's elderly parents were both in their nineties when they began to receive services provided by care agencies on behalf of the council. Even before his father died, he had been complaining to the council that agency staff frequently missed calls, or arrived late – in which case, many elderly people like his mother tried to get up to make their own meals, putting their health in danger. On one occasion, his mother fell in the bedroom at 12.30 pm. She was unable to get up, but expected a lunch-time visit, so lay on the floor waiting for the carer. After an hour, she realised nobody was coming. She then used her alarm. A few days later there was no breakfast-time call; she managed to get herself up, but she went without breakfast or medication.

Carer arriving with no torch: woman startled and falls and dies. Finally, a home help made a tea-time call in January. She did not have a torch, which she was meant to have, to illuminate the door entry key pad. So she banged on the living room window. The woman was startled. As she tried to hurry into the kitchen to switch on the light, she fell on to the corner of a table. The home help let herself in, got the woman off the floor, made her a cup of tea and sandwich, wrote up the daily log without mentioning the fall, and left. Two later, the woman's son arrived to find his mother slumped in her chair unable to move. A doctor was called. She suffered eight broken ribs as a result of the fall. The doctor made an incorrect diagnosis; appropriate treatment was delayed. She died two weeks later after the onset of pneumonia. The carer was dismissed for failing to report the incident.

Failure of council to respond to reports of missed or late calls: routine contract compliance checks not enough. The ombudsman was scathing. She stated that 'councils must respond to reports of missed or late calls by agency staff and follow up complaints by or on behalf of vulnerable service users as a matter of urgency. It cannot be left to routine contract compliance checks to find out whether planned services are really being delivered. It can never be acceptable for elderly people whose care is the responsibility of the Council to wait long periods of time for the next meal or for their medication to be given.' The council's failure promptly to take up complaints of missed calls was mal-administration; likewise its failure to consider whether to make alternative arrangements. When an agency is failing, the council 'must simultaneously look and act in two directions at the same time – to the contractor to improve performance and to the client to assess and respond to the risk posed to them by the contractor's failures.'

Furthermore, the way in which the complaint was then handled – including a failure to coordi-nate papers for the review panel stage – contributed to the complainant's impression that the council was merely going through the motions and that it 'did not care what was happening to its elderly and vulnerable clients' (*Sheffield CC 2007*).

In another case, the agency carers failed to turn up, resulting in the complainant's aunt lying all day on the floor and subsequently dying:

Council fails to do anything about an inadequate care agency: elderly woman lies on the floor all day and dies. The woman, 79 years old, used a wheelchair having had both legs amputated. She had generalised arthritis, diabetes controlled by diet and a hearing impairment. She was highly dependent and required daily contact. On one particular day in March 2003, the care agency con-tracted to provide care failed to visit in the morning. The carer, who had decided not to work that day, had not informed the agency. The early evening visit did not take place either. Later that evening, she was found on the floor and admitted to hospital. During the period she lay on the floor, she had suffered a stroke, a heart attack and hypothermia. She died eight days later. The time the aunt spent on the floor before she was helped was some 13 hours after the time set for the morning visit. She was without food or water. The cause of the accident was probably because of the failure of the carers to visit her. 'She was badly let down by the Council and its provider.'

Known inadequacies of care agency. However, the inadequacies of the care agency on that particular day were not uncharacteristic. They were already well known to the council and included inappropri-ate and untrained staff, a failure to log in and out or report to the office, failure of the back-up tele-phone system, and failure to ensure all carers had access to a care plan explaining entry and emergency arrangements. In addition, a significant number of complaints had been made in the past about missed or late visits. These problems had existed for nine months, from the start of a block contract the council had with the care agency; yet the council's interventions had failed to protect service users.

Given the background of complaints during 2002 about the care agency involved, the council 'failed to understand that it was dealing with a provider that was acting dangerously towards some service users. It failed to understand the random nature of the problem. The Council failed to monitor the reports of missed visits.'

Previous survey revealing serious shortcomings in agency. By January 2003, an audit of the care agency had revealed that, of a survey of 20 service users, 75 per cent did not have care plans, 60 per cent lacked a written assessment by the provider, and 60 per cent had received no risk assessment. Of 20 staff files reviewed, there was no evidence that the company employed as many people as it claimed to, and staff were averaging considerably more than 48 hours per week of work. There was no evidence of induction training; no training schedule was in place. Complaints made by service users were not recorded on their files. For 25 of 43 visits surveyed, carers provided less than 25 per cent of the time they had been commissioned to spend.

Inadequate investigation of incident. In addition, the council's investigation of the incident involving the death of the woman was inadequate. It lacked a sense of urgency, and the responsible officer was content to leave matters largely with the company and to correspond with it over a number of months. The information the council did obtain showed that, in the week before the incident, the aunt had experienced the same failings experienced by other service users including a lack of continuity in care because of different carers' involvement, truncated visits, possible missed visits, and use of inappropriate staff. The inappropriate staff comprised one who had been banned from working with service users, and another who, in January (so the agency had informed the council), had been sacked for misconduct. All this was maladministration.

Maladministration: and ombudsman's recommendations. Overall, the council failed to consider what measures to take to safeguard service users. It was clearly maladministration. The ombudsman recommended that the council should:

- waive the outstanding home care charge still being asked by the council of the niece (who administering her aunt's estate)
- apologise to the niece and pay her £500 for her time and trouble in complaining
- make a payment of £1000 to the aunt's estate to recognise the failure in service
- offer the niece a form of tribute or memorial to her aunt
- adopt at Member level a policy to ensure risks to individual service users are assessed
- ensure that the contracts unit had adequate resources to monitor contract performance
- review complaints procedures and staff training to ensure a customer care culture which recognizes the difficulty and fears that vulnerable service users may have about complaining
- consider, at Member level, annually, information about the performance of care providers
- review all adult service users with critical and substantial needs and ensure that a care plan is available for all service users (*Blackpool BC 2006*).

In similar vein, national press coverage was given to the following example of serious shortcuts being taken, with potentially serious consequences:

Allegations that carers had falsified a log of daily visits made to the home of an 83-year-old woman. For nine days after the woman had been admitted to hospital, the carers let themselves into her home and signed the log saying they had seen and checked her, and that she was fine in bed – for example: 'Again staying in bed. Cat fed and watered.' It was only on the ninth day that a carer checked the bedroom to find that the woman was not there, and recorded this. Devon County Council, which commissioned services from the carer agency involved, and the Commission for Social Care Inspection were informed (Morris and Brindle 2008).

Local authorities may make half-hearted efforts to act but, under pressure, fail to act adequately. For instance, at a care home in the Portsmouth area, serious concerns had arisen – a care worker was jailed for abusing five elderly residents there. The authority suspended placements there but then lifted the suspension four months later even though the Commission for Social Care Inspection had continued to voice concerns. In fact matters didn't improve until the police had become involved, by which time residents had been slapped, punched and bullied (*File on Four* 2007).

3.3.2.1 Contracting failures: remedies for failing to protect service users from harm

Remedies other than the local government ombudsman might be possible. For instance, the Health and Safety Executive has in the past prosecuted a local authority for poor contracting arrangements – which led to a substandard contractor being used and to injuries to the contractor's employees. The contractor was of course itself prosecuted also for poor health and safety practices (*HSE v Barnet LBC*).

There would seem no reason at all why such a prosecution could not also cover harm to vulnerable service users (as opposed to paid staff), and lie against both the local authority and the contractor. It might also be possible, in some circumstances at least, similarly to argue a civil negligence case brought to seek financial compensation, against both contractor and local authority. This would of course depend on the degree of blame (legally, the extent of any breach of duty of care) and being able to show that this had directly caused the harm alleged (see 8.12.1).

Furthermore, if the harm suffered by a person – either in an isolated case or an ongoing basis – amounted to a breach of human rights, then a case might lie against the local authority. This might be possible if the local authority knew, or clearly should have known, that a person's human rights were being, or would be likely to be, breached. (The human rights case could also lie against the independent contractor in limited circumstances: see 2.5 above).

3.3.3 APPLICATION OF STRICT THRESHOLD OF ELIGIBILITY FOR ASSISTANCE

Owing to a considerable mismatch between the demands made upon them and available resources, local social services authorities have a continual struggle to reconcile these limited resources with their ability to meet people's needs. In the light of this, they commonly apply an eligibility threshold in order to establish what level of needs they are obliged to meet and which not. If this threshold becomes too restrictive, vulnerable adults are not assisted and may be put at risk of harm.

Typically, local authorities, under government guidance (LAC(2002)13), adopt policies to meet needs if they are deemed 'critical' or 'substantial', but not if they are 'moderate' or 'low' only. However, there is considerable variation between local authorities. Government guidance has stated that, if necessary, this could entail raising the threshold so high, that only people in critical need would qualify for services (DH 2003b). A few local authorities have done so; others are contemplating doing so. However, there are direct consequences in relation to safeguarding adults. The government guidance on eligibility, what it calls 'fair access to care' includes 'serious abuse or neglect' in the critical category, and just 'abuse or neglect' in the substantial category. If the guidance is taken at face value, the imposition of a threshold set at the critical level would result in a local authority not responding to abuse or neglect, unless it were serious. (The National Assembly for Wales avoided this particular problem, by defining all abuse as a critical issue, in its equivalent guidance; see NAFWC 9/02).

That this sort of issue is not hypothetical is clear, even when a local authority's eligibility threshold is set lower, at the substantial level. For instance, the serious case review into the torture and murder of a man with learning disabilities in Cornwall noted that a question had to be asked about why the ever tightening eligibility criteria of services were rendering vulnerable men and women so unprotected (Flynn 2007). It transpired that, although he had requested a discontinuation of local authority support, he would probably have lost his service anyway. This was because, had he been reviewed by social services at the time, he might not anyway have been eligible under the local authority's fair access to care eligibility threshold. At the time this had been set at the substantial level (Cornwall Adult Protection Committee 2007, p.9).

More generally, the Commission for Social Care Inspection (CSCI) has outlined the adverse consequences of this approach for increasing numbers of older people, in terms of physical accidents, self-respect, mental health, emotional well-being and dignity (2008). It is not too difficult to see that situations of harm and neglect could arise. For instance, a second report from CSCI report noted how low-level needs – deemed ineligible for assistance – might escalate, accidents might occur as people struggled to cope alone, and experiences might be dismal and very poor. The eligibility decisions of local authorities might fail 'utterly to meet people's needs for dignity and self-respect'. With some understatement, it records how a local authority visited a woman at home, assessed her as managing her own personal care and closed the case – having first recorded that she was unkempt, her knickers were around her knees, there was evidence of faeces on the floor and she was not taking her medication (Henwood and Hudson 2008, pp.8–12).

Somewhere here, a line is crossed, at which point vulnerable people are being directly or indirectly being placed at risk of harm by the omission to assist – notwithstanding that local authorities are acting in good faith and subject to competing demands with limited resources.

3.3.4 HARM ARISING FROM A FAILURE OF LOCAL AUTHORITIES TO MEET PEOPLE'S NEEDS

If a person is judged to have eligible needs, that is, coming over the eligibility threshold, then legally the local authority will have a duty to meet that person's needs. But there are situations, where a local authority has in principle taken – or should legally have taken – responsibility for meeting a person's care needs, but has failed to do so – with adult protection issues resulting.

The local government ombudsmen have investigated a number of cases in which local authorities have refused to carry out their legal duty to meet a person's assessed needs on the grounds of lack of resources. These cases typically involved vulnerable younger adults with learning disabilities or autism and high needs. In one case, the local authority's failure to pay for a suitable placement with the National Autistic Society led to the person being detained under the Mental Health Act 1983 compulsorily and inappropriately in a locked psychiatric ward (*Bolton MBC 2004*).

In another, the social worker had found a suitable placement for a man with learning disabilities and autism. The social worker's recommendations were overruled by a manager on grounds of cost; instead the person was placed in an alternative care home at half the cost even though this conflicted with the findings of the assessment. The placement broke down, his condition deteriorated seriously and he was then detained under the Mental Health Act for some eight months in a psychiatric ward, where he was sedated with medication. The ombudsman was highly critical (*Southend on Sea BC 2005*).

A third case warrants recounting in slightly more detail, leading as it did to neglect and abuse of a woman with learning disabilities. Once again, the ombudsman found the local authority had acted with maladministration:

Woman wrongly kept in hospital for ten years. At the age of 18 years, a woman with severe learning difficulties was received into guardianship by the local authority; she resided at a care home. Following concerns about her behaviour, she was admitted in March 1990 to hospital under s.3 of the Mental Health Act 1983; this compulsory detention replaced the guardianship order. Six months later in September 1990, the consultant psychiatrist wrote to the local authority, stating that a further stay in hospital was not warranted; the s.3 detention ceased. However, the local authority failed to put in place any plan for discharge because it was concerned about the cost of any such placement, and also argued with the NHS about who should be responsible for the funding.

The woman finally left hospital in 2001, having spent over ten years as an informal, compliant but incapacitated, patient. As a consequence, aftercare duties under s.117 of the 1983 Act were never triggered and the local authority was never tested on its potential duties under s.117. The ombudsman concluded that if it had been, the authority would have 'fallen far short' of its responsibilities.

The evidence suggested that the woman did not need to be a long-stay patient. A consequence of this unnecessary stay in hospital was that the local authority had neither investigated, nor prevented, the abuse the woman suffered at the hands of other patients during her inappropriate hospital stay. For example, as early as 1991, a local authority mental health management officer wrote to the director of social services about the woman's deteriorating welfare, bites on her legs inflicted by another patient, and her shoddy clothing.

The ombudsman found that the local authority had failed in its duties, notwithstanding legal uncertainties during some of the period about NHS 'continuing care' responsibilities; and recommended £20,000 compensation (*Wakefield MDC 2003*).

A fourth case focused, on the surface at least, on the failure to assess, review, supervise and manage the foster placement of a woman with learning disabilities. Underneath, however, lay a local authority learning disabilities team, with one in three posts unfilled, and a massive overspend. The consequences for the woman were dire and gave rise, belatedly, to an adult protection investigation:

Adult protection investigation arising from woefully inadequate management of woman with learning disabilities in foster placement. The council had failed over a period of many years to assess, review the needs of a woman with learning disabilities in a foster placement, and ensure those needs were met. The woman's welfare suffered, such as ultimately to give rise to an adult protection investigation. She had been obstructed by the foster family from having contact with her previous foster family, was not allowed to use sign language (although this was her preferred means of communication), was deprived of batteries for hearing aids, was treated like a child (being sent to bed at 7 pm), was forced to share a bedroom, was prevented from developing a relationship with a young man at her work placement and was instead encouraged to form an inappropriate relationship with an older man acquainted with the family.

As a baby she had been abandoned on park bench. As a child, she had then been fostered by the council. When she was 18, she remained with her previous foster family who, however, were not registered, as they should have been, for eight years. They were only approved as foster carers for children. She was not reviewed between 1998 and 2004. No assessment of her needs was undertaken until social services launched an adult protection investigation at the end of 2004. The council failed to respond to expressions of concern received from MENCAP and the mother. It did not respond when she lost her placement at a day centre. It delayed in providing funding for advocacy to help find a new centre. Following a complaint, it delayed for seven months in responding to the review panel's recommendations and then took no effective action on a number of points. When she was provided with a new placement, the court failed to review it within the 28 days specified in the council's own policy. It failed to involve a signer or the mother in a review in 2006; the review was also unclear and the council failed to maintain a record of it. The learning disabilities team was unable to function as it should have done, with two out of three established posts vacant and a major overspend. The ombudsman was concerned about 'how such a crisis could develop and endure for so long and on how the council, as corporate body and a social services authority, responds in such situations.'

This was all maladministration; it was 'woefully inadequate' management and supervision (*Birmingham CC* 2008).

Remedies for such aberrations include potentially complaints to the local ombudsmen (who might recommend award financial compensation and recommend actions by the local authority), or judicial review legal cases to show the local authority is in breach of its duty. If significant harm has been suffered directly, a civil negligence case may be contemplated, although might be difficult to win; obstacles to overcome would lie in showing the extent or even existence of the local authority's duty of care, a breach in that duty, and the causation of the specific harm (see 8.12.1).

3.3.5 IMPACT OF SELF-DIRECTED CARE

Department of Health community care policy talks currently and explicitly about greater choice, control and independence for people. To this end its policy is that people should increasingly be assessing their own needs, and should have the freedom to choose (a) how those needs will be met, and (b) how to spend a sum of money that is allocated to them by local authorities. The amount of money is to be determined by the apparent level and type of need (self-assessed or otherwise) that a person has.

Roughly, this summarises a policy which has come to be known variously as concerned with 'self-directed care', and 'individual' or 'personalised' budgets (see e.g. LAC(DH)(2008)1). In addition, s.146 of the Health and Social Care Act 2008 will amend the direct payment provisions in s.57 of the Health and Social Care Act 2001. The intention is to make more people eligible to receive direct payments, by allowing other 'suitable' people to consent and receive the payment on the disabled person's behalf. This has not been legally possible in the past (although it appears to have been going on in practice in some local authorities – with, on some occasions, safeguarding concerns arising as a result). However, such increased flexibility increases the risk of precisely unsuitable people receiving the money and misusing it. Donees of a lasting power of attorney or deputies appointed by the Court of Protection will automatically be deemed, as representatives of the person lacking capacity, to be suitable. However, the amended legislation will also allow other 'suitable' people to receive the payment; these others may or may not be family members or friends already involved in providing care for the person lacking capacity. Draft regulations propose that a criminal records check would be necessary where the proposed suitable person was not a family member or friend providing care (DH 2008).

There may, however, be a tension between this notion of people as active consumers of social care services and safeguarding adults. For instance, the serious case review conducted into the murder of a man with learning disabilities in Cornwall tackled this tension head-on. In this case, nearly a year before he was killed, the man had requested that his service from the local authority be discontinued. This duly happened. The review quoted from the White Paper about people with disabilities, *Valuing people*, which talked about independence but which also stated that 'independence in this context does not mean doing everything unaided' (DH 2001, p.23).

The review pointed out that his decision to terminate services was not discussed with him, even though such a choice might be compounding his vulnerability, and might be made on the basis of inappropriate information or coercion from third parties. The review noted the danger of policies about choice being translated into an attitude of admitting no restraints, adoption of an attitude of indifference and the promotion of unfettered independence. In any case, in the particular circumstances, with social services receding into the background, the opposite outcome had in fact been achieved, as the police report had made clear. It found that the man had lost all control of his own life within his own home, had no say, choice or control over who stayed or visited him, no voice or influence over what happened to him – and had lost the little ability he had to make his own choices and decisions.

The review went on to be quite blunt about the lessons emerging from the man's murder. It challenged the dogma about 'choice' for adults who are apparently 'able', and stated that there were 'profound implications for the support of vulnerable adults in our communities' (Flynn 2007, p.25). The Commission for Social Care Inspection has warned that in the 'policy environment of personalisation, choice and control, it is important not to be over-protective or to prevent adults from living ordinary lives – but that this must be weighed against individuals' fundamental right to expect to be safe, and to be protected and safeguarded from harm' (CSCI 2008a, p.11).

Perhaps in similar vein, the Mental Health Act Commission quoted, from the *Wandsworth Guardian*, a coroner investigating the death of a schizophrenic woman who had been detained under s.2 of the Mental Health Act 1983 and then discharged into the care of a relative who also had mental health problems. She died of hypothermia in a freezing room. The coroner noted that 'time was when a person like this would have been cared for in a safe warm environment. But there has been a change, where people are not kept in institutions but are cared for in the community' (MHAC 2008, p.25).

As ever, it seems to be about a balance, not minimising risk at all costs but still protecting people. For example, in one case, the question arose about a local authority's care plan for a highly vulnerable woman with mental health problems and learning disabilities. The question was about whether the local authority's care plan should allow continuation of a sexual relationship (to which she could consent) with her longstanding partner. This would be a clear benefit to her, but it would also carry a number of risks in relation to her mental health and to other matters about which she lacked the capacity to decide. The court stated:

Wrapping up people in cotton wool: physical health and safety, happiness and manageable risk. 'The fact is that all life involves risk, and the young, the elderly and the vulnerable are exposed to additional risks and to risks they are less well equipped to cope with. But just as wise parents resist the temptation to keep their children metaphorically wrapped up in cotton wool, so too we must avoid the temptation always to put physical health and safety of the elderly and the vulnerable before everything else. Often it will be appropriate to do so, but not always. Physical health and safety can sometimes be bought at too high a price in happiness and emotional welfare. The emphasis must be on sensible risk appraisal, not striving to avoid all risk, whatever the price, but instead seeking a proper balance and being willing to tolerate manageable or acceptable risks as the price appropriately to be paid in order to achieve some other good – in particular to achieve the vital good of the elderly or vulnerable person's happiness. What good is it making someone safer if it merely makes them miserable?' (*Local Authority X v MM*)

The judge's reference to management of risk in this case was not superfluous. Concrete risks had indeed been identified – relevant to adult protection and on the basis of past events – that might arise from her having contact with her partner. These included the compromising of her compliance with medication and support, resulting deterioration in her mental health (and possible hospitalisation), homelessness – and domestic violence leaving bruising, marks and, on one occasion being stabbed in the leg (her partner had been sentenced to four months' imprisonment for this wounding).

CHAPTER 4

National Health Service legislation

4.1   NHS care legislation
4.2   Protection of vulnerable people from NHS practices
    4.2.1   Dignity
    4.2.2   Malnutrition
    4.2.3   Poor standards of care, infection control, high bed occupancy, low staffing levels, finance and performance targets
    4.2.3.1   Stoke Mandeville Hospital: poor standards of care, deaths from infection, performance and finance targets, low levels of staffing, high bed occupancy
    4.2.3.2   Maidstone and Tunbridge Wells: poor standards of care, deaths from infection, performance and finance targets, low levels of staffing, high bed occupancy
    4.2.3.3   East Kent: overcrowding, poor standards or care, patients put at risk
    4.2.3.4   Mid-Cheshire: attempted murder, finance and performance targets, basic standards of care abandoned, short staffing
    4.2.4   Discharge from hospital
    4.2.5   Active abuse of older people in hospital and poor standard of care
    4.2.5.1   Manchester, Rowan Ward: physical and emotional abuse
    4.2.5.2   Portsmouth: poor administration of pain-relieving medication, suspicious deaths, poor standards of care
    4.2.5.3   North Lakelands: unprofessional, degrading and cruel practices
    4.2.6   Mental health services: safety, dignity, privacy, high bed occupancy, staff shortages
    4.2.7   Care of people with learning disabilities: poor standards of care, restrictive care regimes, impoverished environments, restraint
    4.2.7.1   Cornwall: physical, emotional, environmental abuse
    4.2.7.2   Sutton and Merton: restrictive care for people with learning disabilities
    4.2.8   Lack of transparency
    4.2.9   Social services response to abuse and neglect in the NHS
    4.2.10   Accountability of NHS for harm caused to vulnerable patients through institutional practices
    4.2.11   Legal remedies

KEY POINTS

The NHS has broad duties to meet health care needs. It has no explicit duty to engage in adult protection and safeguarding activity, nor has any specific guidance been issued to the NHS detailing its responsibilities.

However, a series of reports, including a number by the Healthcare Commission as well as various other bodies, have revealed practices in the NHS which are both systematic and cause considerable and direct harm to NHS patients including death. These practices include serious lapses in basic care, dignity and infection control. It would seem clear, that if adult protection is at the very least about trying to prevent and respond to conduct causing serious harm to vulnerable adults, then these practices should be considered as safeguarding matters. They would seem clearly to fall into the category of institutional abuse, often in the form of neglect and omissions to act and to care.

4.1 NHS CARE LEGISLATION

Legally, the NHS has a number of general duties under the NHS Act 2006 to provide medical, nursing, ambulance, aftercare services etc. These duties are vague and broad in nature but, ultimately, underpin the whole range of health services provided by the NHS.

As with local authorities, there is no legislation that directly places adult protection responsibilities on the NHS. The *No secrets* guidance was issued to local authorities under s.7 of the Local Authority Social Services Act 1970, which makes it so called statutory guidance carrying considerable legal weight. However, s.7 of that Act does not apply to the NHS; the guidance states only that it is 'commended' to the NHS.

Thus, unlike the case of local authorities, central government has issued no explicit guidance to the NHS on safeguarding adults. However, NHS bodies are amongst those which, according to the guidance, should be participating in local inter-agency adult protection work, headed up by local authorities. This means that, according to the guidance at least, NHS bodies should have some sort of procedure in order to coordinate and act upon reports of incidents relevant to adult protection. The guidance states that in each local agency, including the NHS, roles and responsibilities need to be clear at a number of levels: supervisory line management, senior management staff, corporate/cross authority, chief officers/chief executives (DH 2000, para 3.9).

Certainly the health service ombudsman has found fault when an NHS trust reacted to complaints without a proper awareness of adult protection:

Rough handling. An elderly woman was admitted to hospital for repair of a fractured hip. She told her daughter that on Christmas Day a member of the night staff treated her roughly when attending to her because of vomiting and diarrhoea. Now she was frightened. The daughter made an oral complaint. The ward manager investigated and interviewed the staff member, but did not tell the daughter of the result of the investigation. The daughter then made a formal complaint; the trust apologised for not telling mother and daughter the outcome of the investigation.

The health service ombudsman found that the trust's complaints procedures and documentation were deficient; and that the trust had failed to realise that the mother and daughter viewed the incident as an assault. As such, the trust had not responded sufficiently robustly, and should review its complaints policy in the light of the Department of Health's guidance *No secrets* (*Warrington Hospital NHS Trust 2001*).

4.2 PROTECTION OF VULNERABLE PEOPLE FROM NHS PRACTICES

In the recent past, a plethora of reports have emerged about systemic practices in the NHS which, on any reasonable view, suggest conduct causing harm, sometimes very serious, to vulnerable people. Furthermore, the predisposing factors which have come to light in these cases tend to be common across the NHS. In part, they seem to be an unintended, though not unpredictable, consequence of central government policy which tends to place a greater priority on financial, performance and political targets, than on humane and dignified care. These harmful practices include:

- serious neglect of infection control measures contributing to scores of deaths (in one hospital alone) from *Clostridium difficile*
- premature hospital discharges which can be distressing and put patients at significant risk
- the detrimental moving of patients from bed to bed and ward to ward for non-clinical reasons resulting in clinical detriment
- not giving people adequate help with eating and drinking
- not helping people get to the toilet, telling people to empty their bladder and bowel in hospital beds
- not changing soiled clothing and bedding for hours, tying people up in wheelchairs or on commodes for extended periods of time – and so on.

In sum, these are practices concerned with people's fundamental health, welfare, dignity and – in some circumstances – very life. It would seem incontrovertible that vulnerable people need protecting and safeguarding protecting from such practices.

It is unsurprising, in the light of these practices, that the Healthcare Commission found in 2008 that the most frequently raised complaints against hospitals related to the standard of clinical care. Of these, nearly a third concerned the 'fundamentals of nursing care, such as hygiene, communication, privacy and dignity, and nutrition' (HC 2008, p.7). At the same time, the Commission reported on a survey of staff, finding that in some NHS trusts, up to 65 per cent of staff strongly disagreed that their trust regarded patients as the top priority (HC 2008a).

Because, therefore, such practices appear to have become rooted and institutional within the NHS, the following paragraphs recount in some detail the gist of the evidence, as uncovered by organisations such as the Healthcare Commission, Commission for Health Improvement, Mental Health Act Commission, Age Concern England and Help the Aged.

4.2.1 DIGNITY

The Healthcare Commission has highlighted common examples relating to dignity generally, on the basis of complaints received. These included patients not being spoken to in an appropriate manner, not being given proper information, consent not being sought, being left in soiled clothes, being exposed in an embarrassing manner, not being given appropriate food or help with eating and drinking, being placed in mixed-sex accommodation, being left in pain, being in a noisy nocturnal environment causing lack of sleep, using premises that are unclean and noisome (toilets and wards), suffering lack of protection of personal property including personal aids (hearing and visual), being subjected to abuse and violent behaviour (HC 2007, p.14).

Dignity, in whatever care setting, has become an increasing concern. The organisation, Help the Aged has identified a number of factors contributing to dignity, including personal hygiene, eating and nutrition, privacy, communication, pain, autonomy, personal care, end of life, and social inclusion. It pointed out the following:

Dignity in care. Ten years ago, as a basis for its 'dignity on the ward' campaign, Help the Aged had 'uncovered a quiet outrage, of modern hospitals delivering archaic care, of professional care workers acting in an uncaring and inhuman way, of sophisticated health services not even delivering on the basics of toileting, mealtimes and communication... So now, after ten years of initiatives, plans, targets and frameworks, where do we stand...surely we have moved beyond the basics, the mere minimum entitlement in any decent society. Too often the answer is no...' (Levenson 2007, p.4).

In May 2006, the Healthcare Commission, Audit Commission and Commission for Social Care Inspection published a report called *Living well in later life*. Amongst its findings was evidence of ageism towards older people across all services. This included 'patronising and thoughtless treatment from staff', failure to take needs and aspirations of older people seriously, lack of dignity, lack of respect, poor standards of care on general hospital wards, being repeatedly moved between wards for non-clinical reasons, being cared for in mixed-sex bays or wards, having meals taken away from before they could eat them due to a lack of assistance, abuse and neglect. In addition, older people were concerned about access to health in rural areas. And so on (HC, AC, CSCI 2006, summary).

Against such a backdrop it seems no longer noteworthy that a senior nurse, running an acute medical unit, should state that performance targets and the drive to free up beds lead to an undermining of professionalism. They lead to the hurrying of relatives out of the ward while they are at the bedside of their just deceased relative – and the nurse telling the beds manager to 'fuck off' when she is asked how long it will take to clean the excrement and blood from the dead body. The nurse points out that the fundamentals of nursing are concerned with clean, comfortable, well-fed, nourished, valued and respected patients; but these are not achievable with the imposition of targets and the idea that everything can be done at top speed (Moffat 2006).

4.2.2 MALNUTRITION

It has been reported that six out of ten patients in hospital risk becoming malnourished or their existing malnutrition getting worse; in particular there is too often a lack of appropriate food or an absence of help with eating and drinking for people who are unable to manage it for themselves (Age Concern England 2006, p.4). In 2007, the Healthcare Commission noted that in nearly half of NHS trusts, improvements were required in relation to nutrition, particularly in respect of (a) patchy implementation of policies and practices including protected mealtimes; (b) lack of formal arrangements to identify those who needed assistance with eating and drinking and to provide it; and (c) a lack of formal systems of monitoring (HC 2007d, p.6).

4.2.3 POOR STANDARDS OF CARE, INFECTION CONTROL, HIGH BED OCCUPANCY, LOW STAFFING LEVELS, FINANCE AND PERFORMANCE TARGETS

In 2006 and 2007, the Healthcare Commission issued two reports concerning outbreaks of the bacterium, *Clostridium difficile*, in Buckinghamshire and in Kent. In the former, poor infection control was associated with nearly 40 deaths; in the latter with nearly 90 deaths. What concerned the Healthcare Commission was that in both NHS trusts it appeared that, at board and chief executive level, the preoccupation was with finance and performance rather than infection control. This led to tardy and ineffective measures to control the infection once it had taken hold – including explicit disregarding of the advice offered by the infection control team.

More generally, this preoccupation with performance and finance led also to the factors which laid the ground for the infection to take such hold. These factors included running the hospitals with very high bed occupancy, moving patients from ward to ward for non-clinical reasons in order to meet accident and emergency targets (such moves spread infection and are clinically counter-indicated), reduced staffing levels, an autocratic style of management, staff frightened to speak out, stressed staff and managers, staff shortages, broken cleaning equipment, contaminated bedpans and commodes, lack of time to clean beds and mattresses, not taking patients to the lavatory, and leaving patients in wet and soiled bedding for hours.

Although the two reports concerning Buckinghamshire and Kent received considerable publicity, they should have come as no surprise. Previous reports had highlighted precisely the same type of issue, for example, in East Kent and Cheshire. Indeed, the problem was widespread. In 2005, the *Clostridium difficile* and MRSA infections in England were responsible for more than 5400 deaths. Between 2001 and 2005, death rates from MRSA doubled, those from *Clostridium difficile*, trebled. Furthermore, the link between high bed occupancy had been made; in July 2006, a leaked report from the Department of Health blamed government targets on waiting lists for increasing the risk of infection. Hospitals with more than 90 per cent bed occupancy boasted an MRSA incidence running at 42 per cent above average (Laurance 2007).

Notwithstanding the clear link between over-emphasis on targets at the expense of basic care and even patients' lives, a poll conducted in 2008 by the Health Service Journal suggested that most trust boards continued to prioritise finance and targets ahead of infection control (Santry 2008). Yet the research continues to show that overcrowding of patients and understaffing in hospitals undermine infection control measures. This increases infection, which in turn leads to increased length of patient stay, bed blocking, worse overcrowding and pressure on staff – and thus to a vicious circle (Clements *et al.* 2008).

In 2005, a total of 3807 people died of *Clostridium difficile*, which was an increase of 69 per cent in 12 months. An infection expert at the Health Protection Agency stated that 85 per cent bed occupancy would make a considerable difference; yet despite government claims to the contrary, a Royal College of Nursing survey suggested that the average bed occupancy rate of acute hospitals was 97 per cent, with more than half of wards running at 100 per cent (Fleming 2007).

The wider point about these two investigations is not just about fatalities and infection control, but about the more general lapses in dignified care for patients. In other words, even without the infection and deaths, the way in which patients were treated in those hospitals is not only a cause for concern, but a safeguarding and protection issue.

4.2.3.1 Stoke Mandeville Hospital: poor standards of care, deaths from infection, performance and finance targets, low levels of staffing, high bed occupancy

Stoke Mandeville Hospital suffered two outbreaks of *Clostridium difficile*. The Healthcare Commission eventually investigated.

Nearly 40 deaths, poor standards of care. During the first outbreak (October 2003–June 2004), 174 cases of *Colstridium* were recorded, with 19 deaths resulting. The outbreak was due to a failure to isolate patients with the infection, against the advice of the infection control team. A second outbreak (October 2004–June 2005) involved 160 cases and 19 further deaths definitely or probably due to the infection.

Resisting infection control advice. Even during the second infection, senior managers resisted the advice and recommendations of the infection control team. Finally, when the infection became known at the Department of Health and received national publicity, priority was given by the trust to containing the infection. This was in 'stark contrast' to what had gone before. The Commission concluded that the trust had only changed its approach because of the involvement of the Department of Health and 'more particularly, national publicity'.

Isolation sacrificed in order to meet targets for elective, non-emergency surgery. The trust failed to isolate patients because of the use of side rooms, the reconfiguration of wards and the ring-fencing of beds – not for infection control purposes, but in order to ensure shorter waiting times for non-emergency surgery patients. This determination to hit accident and emergency waiting time targets led to patients with diarrhoea being left on open wards instead of in isolation.

Nurses contribute to spread of infection because of short-staffing. Shortage of nursing staff contributed to the spread of infection because they were too rushed to wash their hands, wear aprons and gloves consistently, empty commodes promptly, and clean mattresses and equipment properly. They were also too busy to answer call bells, wake patients to give them antibiotics, complete fluid balance charts, and supervise confused, wandering patients. Patients and relatives reported dirty wards, toilets and commodes, faeces on bed rails, dirty areas under beds, urine and mop water emptied down a sink on the ward, urine spillages cleared up neither promptly nor properly.

There were particularly low numbers of nurses on some wards, a ban on agency of staff – and vacancies and illness were not covered.

Priority given to targets, not to clinical risk. At corporate level, 'the achievement of the Government's targets was seen as more important than the management of the clinical risk inherent in the outbreaks.' Even at the height of the second outbreak, and despite the advice of the infection control team, the trust board decided to continue to pursue the accident and emergency target. This had a blunt effect. For instance, a non-infected patient in accident and emergency might be moved to a side room in preference to a patient who required isolation. Likewise, an infected patient in accident and emergency would be moved on to an open ward, if no side room was available, in order to avoid breach of the target.

High bed occupancy, inappropriate movement of patients. The high bed occupancy also meant that patients were moved inappropriately between, and were nursed on the wrong, wards. This was to their clinical detriment as well as conducive to the spread of infection. Patients were moved at night, sometimes several times, to their detriment. For example, one patient with diarrhoea was moved six times.

Oppressive and intolerant senior executive team. The executive team at the trust was considered oppressive and intolerant; staff were frightened to speak openly. The Healthcare Commission was concerned at the degree of stress suffered by managers, both clinical and non-clinical. The chief executive, approached directly by clinical staff, failed to act.

Overall problem of performance and financial targets. Overall, the Healthcare Commission was clear where the fault lay: 'These operational problems arose out of "must do" objectives, including the control of finance, the reconfiguration of services, and meeting targets for waiting times. It is our conclusion that the approach taken by the Trust compromised the control of infection and hence the safety of patients. This was a significant failing, and we would reiterate to NHS boards that the safety of patients is not to be compromised under any circumstances.'

Common tensions across the NHS. Notably, the Commission was clear that the problems faced by the NHS trust involved were not peculiar to it. It warned of the continuing tensions between control of infection and other national priorities, a conflict which all acute trusts faced, not just the Buckinghamshire NHS Trust (HC 2006, pp.4–9 and generally).

4.2.3.2 Maidstone and Tunbridge Wells: poor standards of care, deaths from infection, performance and finance targets, low levels of staffing, high bed occupancy

In the Maidstone and Tunbridge Wells areas of Kent, the observation of the Healthcare Commission – that the problems identified at Stoke Mandeville were not to be viewed in isolation – was borne out. Once again, an outbreak of *Clostridium difficile* was at the heart, accompanied by an associated range of failings in basic health care standards:

Failure to isolate patients: 90 patients dying from infection. Overall, the NHS trust had insufficient guidelines on the importance of isolating infected patients. The infection control team was keen on such isolation, but the scarcity of side rooms hindered this. Whilst some infected patients were grouped together in bays on wards, others were not; this resulted in other patients being infected. It took four months to establish an isolation ward; the delay was partly due to the trust's desire to meet performance targets. Some patients were prescribed the wrong antibiotics and died even though they had been expected to make a full recovery from the original condition for which they had been admitted to hospital. The Commission estimated that, of the 345 patients infected with *Clostridium difficile* who had died in the relevant period between March 2004 and April 2006, 90 or so patients had died primarily from the infection. However, the Commission stated that some of these might have died anyway of other illnesses and some would still have died of the infection even had they received better care.

Telling patients to empty bladder and bowel in bed. As was the case at Stoke Mandeville, poor infection control was associated with a range of poor care practices. It was reported that nurses sometimes told patients to relieve their bladder or bowels in their beds, because they had not time to take patients to the toilet. The patients might then be left for hours in wet or soiled sheets, putting them at increased risk of pressure sores. Help with eating and drinking was not given. Patients claimed that medication and nutritional supplements were not given on time, if at all. Wards, bathrooms and commodes were not clean and patients had to share walking frames, which were not cleaned between use by different patients.

Short-staffed nurses spreading infection and in despair. The shortage of nurses contributed to the spread of infection because they were too rushed to undertake hand hygiene, to empty and clean and commodes, to clean mattresses and equipment properly, and to wear aprons and gloves appropriately and consistently. Nurses were reported to be in despair, with their heads in their hands. The shortage of nurses, together with high bed occupancy, also meant that patients were placed on inappropriate wards – where, for example, rehabilitation nurses would be faced with acutely ill patients for whose care they lacked the appropriate skills.

Worn, dirty equipment; 98 per cent of commodes soiled. The Commission also found a catalogue of broken and worn equipment. Eight bedpan macerators were in poor condition, dirty, rusty and leaking. Bedpan washers were not working, so bedpans that had been washed still showed visible signs of faeces. In September 2006, the trust found 98 per cent of its commodes were soiled on 16 wards, and that 48 per cent of its commodes needed replacing. It undertook to do this. By the Commission's next visit in 2007, the condemned commodes were still in use.

Excessively high bed occupancy sometimes over 100 per cent. Bed occupancy was running at an average of over 90 per cent. This was 'extremely high' as the Healthcare Commission pointed out. Some wards ran at over 100 per cent for several months. Patients were on this account moved from one ward to another; some patients had multiple moves, even those who were infected. Apart from undermining infection control, this had the effect of causing distress to patients and their families, and could result in the appropriate doctor not seeing the patient for several days. Because of the high bed occupancy, escalation areas, often unsuitable, had to be opened up for extra beds.

Information repeatedly provided sparingly, belatedly or misleadingly. As if all this were not enough, the Healthcare Commission was concerned with the fact that the trust repeatedly provided information sparingly, misleadingly or belatedly – to the trust's own board, the public including relatives of patients, the press, and to the Commission itself.

Autocratic drive to hit targets, management and staff stressed and downtrodden. The shared perception of staff was that the trust was 'strongly driven by the achievement of financial balance and targets.' The chief executive was described as autocratic and dictatorial; she was difficult to challenge. Managers reported high levels of stress and a fear of losing their jobs. Failure to achieve financial and other targets 'led to threats of disciplinary action'. Such possible action was recorded in the executive team's minutes of a meeting. Ward staff and middle managers were described to the Commission as 'exhausted and downtrodden'.

Focus on finance greater than on quality of care. Senior staff believed that the overwhelming priority was finance; the Commission concluded that the focus on finance was greater than that on quality of care. The accident and emergency target was described by staff as the main reason why patients were moved from ward to ward inappropriately with increased risk of infection – and as causing chaos elsewhere in the hospital. As one senior manager put it, 'if anyone at the top says that the top priorities aren't money and targets, they're lying.'

Failure of PCT and reduction of beds. To make matters worse, the primary care trust, which commissioned services from the NHS trust, was also 'preoccupied with the numbers of patients treated and the cost, and had given little attention to the quality of care or the control of infection.' Furthermore, the trust had reduced the number of beds before the PCT had put in place alternative measures which would reduce the number of hospital admissions. This put additional pressure on the NHS trust (HC 2007a, generally).

When the chairman subsequently resigned he stated in a letter to the Secretary of State that the trust's board had had 'to devote an inordinate amount of time' to targets and finances at the expense of managing infection control (Rose 2007). The chief executive was allowed to leave four days before publication of the Healthcare Commission's report. Three months later, she was reported as having rejected a pay-off of £75,000, arguing that she should receive more (Stephens 2008).

4.2.3.3 East Kent: overcrowding, poor standards or care, patients put at risk

In 2002, the problem of high bed occupancy and overcrowding had already been identified by the Commission for Health Improvement. Quite apart from infection control, this was clearly detrimental to the health and welfare of patients.

Reporting on East Kent, the Commission found that overcrowding in the hospital's accident and emergency department put patients at clinical risk and staff under unremitting pressure. Patients were simply admitted to any bed, 'causing staff to care for patients they may not have the skills or training to care for and forcing doctors to seek out their patients throughout the hospital.'

The overcrowding and pressure resulted in other compromises in care. Trays regularly came to the ward with dirty cutlery. Food was often cold. There were insufficient toilets and washing facilities for the number of patients, who were sometimes physically examined in open areas. Patients might be left in corridors for days rather than hours. It was difficult for doctors to get to outlying wards; this caused delays in ordering treatments, obtaining drugs and discharging patients; one patient waited over 14 hours to have a cannula replaced because of difficulty getting in touch with the responsible doctor (CHI 2002).

4.2.3.4 Mid-Cheshire: attempted murder, finance and performance targets, basic standards of care abandoned, short staffing

Following the conviction of a ward sister on two counts of attempted murder, the Healthcare Commission investigated the Mid-Cheshire Hospitals NHS Trust. Its findings were various; clearly the circumstances surrounding the attempted murders were part of a much broader picture.

Medication and pain relief were inadequate, and staff shortages affected adversely patient care which was described as generally sloppy. The management of beds focused primarily on the hitting of government-set targets, the system was not working in the interests of patients, and patients were moved to inappropriate wards to their clinical detriment. It was a culture of 'nurses who were rushed, short-staffed, stretched and not delivering basic standards of care.'

All this meant, for instance, that even after a serious incident resulting in a diabetic patient's death arising from staff shortage, the level of nursing staff was not increased – in fact it decreased. Drug rounds might be two hours late because of staff shortage, and medication simply left at patients' bedsides where it was either not taken or taken late. Nutritional drinks were likewise left, becoming warm and undrinkable. Crash trolleys were not properly stocked and even after the Healthcare Commission had raised this issue, the problem persisted seven weeks later.

Assistance with eating and drinking was provided only 50 per cent of the time it was needed. Call bells would be out of reach or not answered by staff. Patients could not get to the bathroom, commode or bedpan in time. Only about half of patients were cared for on appropriate wards; those on the wrong wards would be called outliers. They often did not get to see the appropriate specialist doctor. The allocation of beds was determined by the four-hour accident and emergency waiting time target or by red alerts, when the hospital was over-occupied. Nurses were under pressure to move patients who were not fit to be moved. They would move families grieving at the bedside of a just deceased relative. Patients were being moved throughout the evening, sometimes after midnight. These movements, for non-clinical reasons, contributed to the spread of infection, in the form of MRSA and *Clostridium difficile* (HC 2006a).

4.2.4 DISCHARGE FROM HOSPITAL

Associated closely with finance and performance targets, high bed occupancy and overcrowding in acute hospitals – all depicted immediately above – is premature and inappropriate discharge of people from hospital. Clearly, there is a fine line between timely and untimely discharge; after all, it is not in people's interests to remain in acute hospitals unnecessarily. However, the argument sometimes used by hospitals, that people should leave quickly because of infection risk and inappropriate environment, may become self-serving. The infection risk and inappropriate environment often only arise because of the way the trust is running, or being forced to run, the hospital.

Nonetheless, whilst not every premature discharge should give rise to adult protection concerns, there are some discharge practices which do – depending on the degree to which they are systematic, frequent or harm, or put at risk of harm, an individual (or group of patients) at risk. Generally, premature discharge can lead to emergency readmissions; and statistics seem to show that whilst hospitals are clearing beds more quickly, so too are their readmissions rising (Taylor 2007).

For instance, an 84-year-old woman felt obliged to lay a complaint against Hereford County Hospital, after being discharged from hospital in the middle of the night. She had been admitted on the evening of New Year's Day for a leg injury. She had to pay £80 for a taxi to take her home (*BBC News* 2008). At Ipswich NHS Trust, which was under acute pressure from the Suffolk Primary Care Trust, discharges in the middle of the night seemed to take hold during 2007 (Barnes 2007). At that hospital, shortly before Christmas, a group of patients was woken in the middle of the night and simply sent home (Bond 2007).

In Warrington, an 83-year-old woman was sent home in the middle of the night from hospital after she had attended for shoulder pains that evening. She was found dead later that day at home. The hospital accepted that it should have informed the family, given the woman's age and vulnerability (Tozer 2007). In similar vein, in Bath, an 80-year-old man was reported to have been sent home by bus 24 hours after an operation, when he was still drowsy from the anaesthetic and had a drainage bag attached. He was wrapped up in a blanket, wheeled to the discharge area, had to wait a considerable period for the bus, and then endure a one-and-a-half hour journey home – at the end of which he was sick. A nurse explained that his bed was needed (Williams 2008).

4.2.5 ACTIVE ABUSE OF OLDER PEOPLE IN HOSPITAL AND POOR STANDARD OF CARE

Sometimes, in addition to poor standards of care as depicted above, more active abuse of older people in hospital takes place.

4.2.5.1 Manchester, Rowan Ward: physical and emotional abuse

In Manchester, the Commission for Health Improvement investigated physical and emotional abuse on a particular mental health ward for older people. This appeared to have taken place over several years, and to have taken the form of hitting, slapping, stamping on feet, thumb twisting, intimidatory language – and emotional abuse by restricting food and playing on the known anxieties of patients. The Commission found that the Rowan ward service had many of the known risk factors for abuse: poor and institutionalised environment, low staffing levels, high use of bank and agency staff, little staff development, poor supervision, lack of incident reporting, inward-looking culture, weak management at ward and locality level (CHI 2003, pp.2,4).

4.2.5.2 Portsmouth: poor administration of pain-relieving medication, suspicious deaths, poor standards of care

In Portsmouth, the Commission for Health Improvement found inadequate safeguards for the prescribing of medicines for older people, such that concerns had arisen about the deaths of a number of patients. There was no evidence of a policy to ensure appropriate prescription and dose escalation of powerful pain-relieving drugs. Experts commissioned by the police had serious concerns about anticipatory prescribing. There was inappropriate combined subcutaneous administration of diamorphine, midazolam and haloperidol which risked excessive sedation and respiratory depression leading to death. No clear guidelines were available for staff, to guard against their making assumptions that patients had been admitted for palliative rather than rehabilitative care. Staff failed to recognise potential adverse effects of prescribed medicines. Clinical managers failed routinely to monitor and supervise care on the ward.

As seems to be the case in reports of this type, major failings in one aspect of care were found to be indicative of others. Wider concerns about care included continence management and claims by relatives that patients were automatically catheterised to save nursing time, patients not being dressed in their own clothes (despite these having been clearly labelled), and physical transfers from one hospital to another involving lengthy waits, inadequate clothing and cover during the journey, and one patient being carried on nothing more than a sheet (CHI 2002a, pp.12–13, 22–23).

4.2.5.3 North Lakelands: unprofessional, degrading and cruel practices

In 2000, the Commission for Health Improvement published a report into the care of older people with mental health problems in one particular NHS Trust. Physical abuse of patients had become evident following complaints by two nurses about what they had witnessed. Three staff received disciplinary warnings, one was dismissed, one resigned. An external review panel had identified a range of what it called unprofessional, counter-therapeutic and degrading – even cruel – practices. These included brusque and uncaring attitudes on the part of staff, patients being sworn at, rough manhandling of patients, patients being fed while on the toilet or commode, restraint of patients on commodes, denial of ordinary food in favour of pureed food even when this was not recommended, and withholding of adequate clothing and blankets. It was alleged, though not ultimately confirmed, that the occupational therapy department had made the wooden board and harness device that was used to restrain and keep patients on commodes (CHI 2000, paras 2.12, 5.24).

4.2.6 MENTAL HEALTH SERVICES: SAFETY, DIGNITY, PRIVACY, HIGH BED OCCUPANCY, STAFF SHORTAGES

In its final biennial report, before its dissolution, the Mental Health Act Commission reported in 2008 how bed pressure and over-occupancy of acute services had exerted a deleterious effect on the care of patients detained under the Mental Health Act 1983 – at their most vulnerable time. Key issues raised included safety, dignity and privacy.

Continuity of care was affected by the movement of patients within hospitals and wards; staff morale was also harmed. It noted that 'in a service which is running under extreme pressures, there is an ever-present danger of the cursory or careless exercise of power, which might barely register in the mind of the mental health professional but deeply scar the patient concerned.'

It found a range of unacceptable practices including, for instance, restrictions on bathing because of staff shortages, inappropriate restraint, a dying man being nursed in the dining room while other patients were having lunch because of staff shortages, vulnerable women housed with predatory men, blinds to patients' rooms being kept open permanently for staff convenience, seclusion rooms with no privacy to use the toilet, new acute wards being run at 135 per cent bed occupancy with patients sleeping in day rooms and staff run off their feet, inappropriate use of closed circuit television, a woman in seclusion deprived of sanitary protection whilst menstruating – and so on (MHAC 2008, pp.17–29).

The National Patient Safety Agency published a report recording 122 sexual safety incidents reported to it in a two-year period; after reluctance from the Department of Health, it emerged in the public domain after it had been leaked to a newspaper (NPSA 2006).

4.2.7 CARE OF PEOPLE WITH LEARNING DISABILITIES: POOR STANDARDS OF CARE, RESTRICTIVE CARE REGIMES, IMPOVERISHED ENVIRONMENTS, RESTRAINT

The Healthcare Commission published in 2007 the findings of a national inspection of NHS services for people with learning disabilities. It found evidence of many shortcomings, including poor procedures for safeguarding people, poor care planning, lack of stimulating activities, doubtful use of PRN (*pro re nata*, as needed) medication to control behaviour, and care that is excessively institutionalised and restrictive (HC 2007b, chapter 6). These general points emerged from more specific inspections which had thrown up examples raising adult protection concerns.

4.2.7.1 Cornwall: physical, emotional, environmental abuse

In Cornwall, for example, the Healthcare Commission (with the Commission for Social Care Inspection) investigated the Cornwall Partnership NHS Trust and its care of people with learning disabilities. It found a range of what it described as physical, emotional and environmental abuse. This included one person who suffered multiple injuries over time, including a fractured skull, at the hands of another service user; another person tied up in a wheelchair for 16 hours a day, a culture of locked doors, the removal of taps and light fittings, and inappropriate pooling of patients' money.

Generally, people were prevented from exercising rights to independence, choice and inclusion. Care planning was poor, physical restraint was used illegally, and *pro re nata* (PRN) medication, to control unacceptable behaviour, was used excessively (HC and CSCI 2006, pp.4–6).

4.2.7.2 Sutton and Merton: restrictive care for people with learning disabilities

In Sutton and Merton NHS Primary Care Trust, the Healthcare Commission investigated NHS services for people with learning disabilities at Orchard Hill Hospital. It found that the way in which people were cared for reflected convenience for the service providers rather than the needs of individual service users.

Regimented meal times, including universal teapot. People had their shoulders wrapped in a large sheet of blue tissue paper at meal times, before being fed at a speed which would preclude any enjoyment of the food. This was after they had been lined up around a table waiting to be fed in a queue. There was little choice of food and drinks were mostly limited to meal times. Special dietary requirements were not always met. In one of the houses, drinks were all made in one large pot and thus everyone appeared to have the same amount of milk and sugar.

Unsuitable accommodation and equipment. Most of the houses people lived in were unsuitable and created particular difficulties for those requiring use of wheelchair and hoists. One person had been waiting for a new wheelchair for six years; two service users had to share one wheelchair which meant they could not go out at the same time. Bathing areas lacked privacy.

Inappropriate restraint. The lack of a system to monitor restraint meant that one woman had experienced restraint for many years. This was in the form of a splint on her arm, seemingly throughout the day, to stop her putting her hand into her mouth. Yet subsequent assessment showed that such prolonged use of the splint had been unnecessary; it was eventually used only for three hours a day.

Staff. Many of the staff had themselves been working at the hospital for many years and the long-term relationships between staff and patients made it difficult for the latter to promote choice and independence. The former talked of adults as girls or children and sometimes viewed them as babies. The Commission was concerned that adequate consideration had not been given as to which of the service users should have been sectioned under the Mental Health Act 1983, under which they would have had certain statutory rights.

Serious incidents. There were also serious incidents, such as a member of staff being convicted of sexual activity with a woman unable to give consent under the Sexual Offences Act 2003 – as well as other allegations of sexual assault by staff members. There were also incidents involving service users being attacked by other service users, or allegations of staff physically assaulting service users.

Inadequate staffing levels, training, risk management. Unsurprisingly, the Commission found historically low levels of staffing, high rates of sickness, inadequate training, lack of appraisals, poor risk management, deficiencies in the PCT's governance of the hospital and more concern about a judicial review legal case than about the quality of the service (HC 2007).

4.2.8 LACK OF TRANSPARENCY

A key additional factor, which underlines the need to protect and safeguard vulnerable people from some of the NHS practices outlined in the paragraphs immediately above, is the lack of transparency that seems to afflict the NHS. This lack of transparency exacerbates the harm being perpetrated, making recognition, prevention and protection all the harder.

For example, at Stoke Mandeville Hospital, the Healthcare Commission found that – despite the two very serious outbreaks of *Clostridium difficile* – the NHS trust board had consistently resisted the recommendations of its infection control team, and had not publicly owned up to what was going on. The Commission found that the trust changed its approach only when the Department of Health found out and, more particularly, following a leak to the press (HC 2006).

In Maidstone and Tunbridge, the Healthcare Commission uncovered a catalogue of incomplete, misleading and belated information given by the trust and, in particular, the chief executive – to the public, the press and to the Commission itself. The chief executive even deprived her own trust board of relevant information. The Commission also found that while the board was making statements about how patient safety was a priority, the

Trust's actual practice was almost diametrically opposed to this. The statement was meaningless. Managers referred to the 'positive spin' employed by the chief executive:

Catalogue of incomplete, misleading and belated information given by NHS Trust, while 90 people died of infection. The Healthcare Commission recorded its considerable concern at a catalogue of information – incomplete, misleading and belated – provided by the Maidstone and Tunbridge Wells NHS Trust, and in particular by the chief executive. As already described above, two outbreaks of the infection, *Clostridium difficile*, occurred with an associated 90 deaths. The first occurred in the autumn of 2005, the second in early 2006. Despite this, the trust declared itself at the relevant time in 2005, to the Healthcare Commission's annual health check operation, to be in compliance with the control of infection. In 2006, it only issued a press statement about the infection in July, two months after it had begun (in April), and then only in response to a press enquiry.

The outbreak was not discussed at board level until July. On several occasions, the board and patients' relatives who attended the meetings were given inaccurate information or simply no information at all. The number of deaths was under-reported. The board stated that the safety of patients was its top priority, but the PCT's practice belied the policy. The chief executive misled her own board and the Healthcare Commission on a number of occasions; she was also described by senior clinicians and managers as using a significant degree of 'positive spin'.

The Commission was particularly concerned, for example, at the delay in a press release, the inaccurate inference that the outbreak was due to patients admitted who were already infected rather than having acquired it after admission, premature statements about the outbreak being over, playing down of the disagreements between the trust and the Health Protection Unit, limited counting of deaths, the claim to the Commission that no patient had died of the infection in the relevant period, the claim that the Trust had instigated the investigation. Even after a first meeting with the trust, and the Commission's request that it be informed of further outbreaks, such outbreaks were not subsequently reported to the Commission.

Furthermore, the trust failed to adhere to an agreement with the Commission to share press releases about the infection outbreak (HC 2007a).

In the following example, the NHS trust concerned was determined not to concede that anything might be wrong:

Waking people up and sending them home, unplanned, in the middle of the night. At Ipswich Hospital, a state of blue alert had been declared at the hospital shortly before Christmas. The crisis was such that patients were being woken up and discharged unplanned, in the middle of the night. Given that the hospital had anyway been on black alert for some while, and so would not have retained patients who did not need to be there, the statement from the hospital is inexplicable: 'Some of the patients had to be woken up so they could be discharged, but there were very sick people who needed to come in. Those who went home were all ready and happy to leave and we organised transport for them' (Bond 2007).

Discharging vulnerable, older patients – unplanned – in the middle of the night is clearly, potentially, an adult protection and safeguarding issue. Euphemistic statements made by hospitals make it even more so, because they represent a denial that anything is wrong.

The inevitable conclusion is that the lack of transparency derives from policy, and ultimately, the political imperatives concerning performance and financial targets. The resulting fear and stress that permeates the system – from government ministers, through strategic health authorities, primary care trust and NHS trust management right down to frontline staff – has a corrosive effect. For instance, a survey of 97 chief executives from such trusts found opinion overwhelmingly that the government blamed trusts and their managers for its own financial problems, and that inflexible targets were a root problem. Disingenuousness, dishonesty, blind panic and incompetence on the part of central government also emerged as opinions (Vaughan 2007).

4.2.9 SOCIAL SERVICES RESPONSE TO ABUSE AND NEGLECT IN THE NHS
With such apparently widespread, poor, abusive and neglectful treatment of vulnerable patients within the NHS, a question remains as to how local social services authorities, with the lead in safeguarding adults, are responding. It would appear, generally speaking, that they are not or, at best, are finding it difficult to do so.

By way of example, the Healthcare Commission, having found serious failures in NHS services for people with learning disabilities in Cornwall, criticised social services. This was for having failed adequately to coordinate inter-agency adult protection arrangements, including referrals. The local authority was 'too willing to accept the opinion of staff at the [NHS] trust without challenge' (HC, CSCI 2006, p.6).

The solutions to what has been described above are by no means easy. Pinpointing the exact causes of why things go so badly wrong, who is accountable and how to implement remedies, would clearly be a challenge for local authorities. First, they tend to view the NHS as an organisation and with which they cannot readily interfere and with which they have to work cooperatively. There is a general reluctance to rock the boat. Second, they tend in practice to be more comfortable viewing adult protection as involving abuse by individuals against other individuals, not as involving large organisational issues. Third, bereft of direct legal powers of intervention, they may feel there is little they can anyway achieve. Whatever the reasons, it is noteworthy that notwithstanding the close involvement of social services with groups of vulnerable hospital patients, hospital social workers appear not to have been triggering widespread adult protection and safeguarding enquiries concerning the NHS.

4.2.10 ACCOUNTABILTY OF NHS FOR HARM CAUSED TO VULNERABLE PATIENTS THROUGH INSTITUTIONAL PRACTICES
Hitherto, the NHS has been less accountable for poor institutional care practices, and not subject to the degree of registration and inspection applied, for example, to the social care sector.

The implications of this are illustrated in the Mental Capacity Act Code of Practice, in the chapter on protecting from abuse people who lack capacity. It runs through the courses of action to take if concerns arise about abuse. In every case, the advice is to contact an external agency, except in the case of the NHS. Thus it lists the topics of concern and the agency to contact in each case: appointeeship (Jobcentre Plus), attorney or deputy under the Mental Capacity Act (Public Guardian), possible criminal offence (police), ill-treatment or wilful neglect (local authority), care home or domiciliary care (local authority or Commission for Social Care Inspection). But when it comes to the NHS, it simply refers to NHS managers as the contact (Lord Chancellor 2007, p.243). Evidence about what is happening in the NHS does not suggest that NHS managers, often themselves overseeing poor care practices in the single-minded pursuit of financial and performance targets, are necessarily the right port of call.

4.2.11 LEGAL REMEDIES

Where the safety of NHS patients is put at risk by poor practice, the Health and Safety Executive could consider prosecution under, for example, s.3 of the Health and Safety at Work Act 1974 (see section 8.11 in this book). There are indeed many prosecutions in the case of individual mishaps, such as patients falling from windows, being scalded on radiators or dying when caught in bed rails. One might not categorise one-off incidents as coming within adult protection, but might do if they recur with regularity and vulnerable people are particularly at risk.

It is perhaps noteworthy, however, that prosecutions appear not to have followed when health and safety breaches have been wholesale – for example, systematic abandonment of good standards of care and infection control.

Where death has resulted from grossly negligent or reckless practice, manslaughter charges may be possible (see 8.3). When injury or death has resulted, civil negligence cases may also be possible, if the poor practice can be shown to have been at least a substantial cause (see 8.12). And some of what is described in the paragraphs above might suggest clear human rights issues – for instance, under article 3 of the European Convention (inhuman and degrading treatment) and article 8 (right to respect for private life, including physical and psychological integrity; see 2.4).

CHAPTER 5

Regulation of care provision for vulnerable adults

KEY POINTS

Regulation of health and social care providers, as well as of professionals working in the field, has in principle a key role to play in protecting and safeguarding vulnerable adults.

Regulation, in the form of registration and inspection, under the Care Standards Act 2000, covers children's homes, independent hospitals, independent clinics, care homes, residential family centres, independent medical centres, domiciliary care agencies, fostering agencies, nurse agencies, voluntary adoption agencies and adult placement schemes. Furthermore, local authorities acting as care providers are covered in the same way as providers in the independent sector. The NHS is monitored and investigated by the Healthcare Commission under the Health and Social Care (Community Health and Standards) Act 2003. This legislation is due for replacement by a different set of regulatory provisions under the umbrella of a new Health and Social Care Act 2008, which will create Care Quality Commission and a more uniform system of regulation across both health care (including the NHS) and social care.

The 2000 Act also includes provisions relating to legal requirements and standards in services, to the registration and inspection of care providers (including the functions of regulatory bodies), and to a system of listing people who are prohibited from working with vulnerable adults. This involves a Protection of Vulnerable Adults (POVA) list, held by the Secretary of State. It is a list of care workers judged unsuitable, and not permitted, to work with vulnerable adults – because of misconduct that harmed or placed at risk of harm such an adult. In late 2009, the POVA list scheme is due to be replaced by a new 'barring' scheme under the Safeguarding Vulnerable Groups Act 2006.

Appeals against inclusion on the POVA list are heard by the Care Standards Tribunal. These cases illustrate the type of issue that arises concerning misconduct, harm to a vulnerable adult, and unsuitability of a care worker to work with vulnerable adults. There are the obvious cases but also those involving shades of grey.

In parallel to the POVA list and, in future, the barring scheme, is a system of criminal record certificates operated by the Criminal Records Bureau.

In addition, professional bodies regulate professional groups in health and social care, having the power to suspend or strike off those who harm vulnerable adults.

5.1 PROTECTION OF VULNERABLE ADULTS LIST

Under the Care Standards Act 2000, there is a duty on the Secretary of State to keep a list of care workers who are considered unsuitable to work with vulnerable adults because they have, through misconduct, harmed, or placed at risk of harm, a vulnerable adult – and the employer has, or would have, dismissed the person, or transferred him or her to a non-care position (s.81). The protection of vulnerable adults (POVA) list was started in July 2004. It has not covered NHS staff. The POVA list scheme is due to be replaced by a new barring and monitoring system, probably from October 2009, under the Safeguarding Vulnerable Groups Act 2006 (see 5.2 below).

5.1.1 DEFINITION OF CARE WORKER AND VULNERABLE ADULT

Care workers have been defined as (Care Standards Act 2000, s.80):

- people who are or have been employed in a position giving them regular contact in the course of their duties with adults to whom accommodation is provided at a care home
- people with similar contact where prescribed services are provided by an independent hospital, independent clinic, independent medical agency or NHS body
- people who are or have been employed in a position concerned with the provision of personal care for persons in their own home who by reason of illness, infirmity or disability are unable to provide it for themselves without assistance
- people who have entered an agreement to provide support, care or accommodation by way of employment, for an adult (who is not a relative) [i.e. under an adult placement scheme].

Department of Health guidance has pointed out that 'regular contact' should be given its 'ordinary everyday meaning', but that it implies contact with a constant or definite pattern, or which recurs at short uniform intervals or on several occasions during short periods of time such as a week (DH 2004, para 9). Thus, care workers could include managers, care assistants, voluntary workers, ancillary workers (such as cooks, gardeners or cleaners), workers supplied by employment agencies or businesses – and visiting practitioners such as chiropodists, hairdressers, therapists, priests and other religious leaders (Barnes 2006, p.26). Vulnerable adult means (Care Standards Act 2000, s.80):

- a person for whom accommodation and nursing or personal care are provided in a care home

- a person for whom personal care is provided in his or her own home by a domiciliary care agency
- a person for whom prescribed services are provided by an independent hospital, independent clinic, independent medical agency or NHS body
- a person provided with support, care or accommodation under and adult placement scheme.

Harm means (Care Standards Act 2000, s.120):
- in the case of an adult who is not mentally impaired – ill-treatment or impairment of health
- in the case of an adult who is mentally impaired – ill-treatment, or the impairment of health or development.

5.1.2 DUTY OF REFERRAL FOR INCLUSION ON LIST

There is a wide-ranging duty of referral placed on care home providers and domiciliary care providers (and on employment agencies and employment businesses). This is whether or not they are run for profit (Care Standards Act 2000, s.121).

Such providers of care for vulnerable adults have a duty to refer a worker (paid or voluntary) to the Secretary of State for Health if the care provider has dismissed or transferred to a non-care position that worker on the grounds of misconduct that harmed or placed at risk of harm a vulnerable adult. The duty of referral has applied even where there is only a suspension or provisional transfer on these grounds (Care Standards Act 2000, s.82).

The duty to refer applies if such a dismissal or transfer would have occurred, or the care provider would have considered those steps, had the worker not already resigned, retired or been made redundant. Likewise if (a) the care provider has dismissed the worker, or the worker has resigned or retired or has been transferred to a non-care position; (b) information not available at the time of the dismissal, resignation, retirement or transfer has since become available; (c) the provider is of the view that, if that information had been available at that time, the provider would have dismissed him/her or considered doing so, on such grounds as mentioned above (harm or risk of harm to vulnerable adult (Care Standards Act 2000, s.82). Corresponding duties are placed on employment agencies and employment businesses (s.83).

Registration authorities (i.e. the Commission for Social Care Inspection) have the power to refer a care worker if they consider that he or she is guilty of the relevant misconduct and has not been referred to the Secretary of State (s.84).

5.1.3 INCLUSION OF WORKER ON THE LIST

The Secretary of State has to consider the reference and information submitted and, if it seems that it may be appropriate to include the individual on the list, place the person on it provisionally. The person must then be invited to make observations. The Secretary of State must then either confirm inclusion on the list or remove the person from the list (ss.81–82). The courts have held that the provisional listing provisions under the Act were unfair and that at least in some cases, care workers had to be allowed to make representations before they were included on the list, even provisionally:

POVA list: unfair and unlawful referral system. The case revolved around care workers being referred to the Secretary of State and placed provisionally on the list for periods of nine months or longer.

High Court. Care workers did not have a fair hearing within a reasonable period of time, with a prohibition for a period of nine months on applications to the Care Standards Tribunal (s.86). The Secretary of State was taking this amount of time and longer to decide whether to confirm a person on the list, or remove him or her. This was not compatible with article 6 of the European Convention on Human Rights (right to a fair hearing). The court saw no reason why the procedure should not be akin to the system available to other health care professionals, involving independent judicial scrutiny. This was an unjustified interference with the right of access to the courts. Furthermore, article 8 of the European Convention was engaged and breached, because the interests of the care workers were not adequately safeguarded. The provisional listing procedures constituted a disproportionate approach.

One of the examples given in the case (although not one of the particular claimants) was a psychiatric nurse who had won an award for innovation and excellence in dementia care. After she was provisionally included on the list in February 2006, she launched judicial review proceedings in June 2006, and in the same month won an employment tribunal case for unfair dismissal. In July 2006, she was removed from the list. However, by this time she had been unable to work and to keep up her mortgage payments, with the result that she had lost her home (*R(Wright) v Secretary of State for Health*).

Court of Appeal: referral was of drastic character, seriously detrimental and could cause irreversible prejudice. The Court of Appeal upheld the High Court's judgment, although did not find it necessary to rule on article 8 of the European Convention, because article 6 had clearly been breached. The court pointed out that the consequences of a provisional listing could be 'seriously detrimental' to a care worker, and constituted a decision of a 'drastic character' which could cause 'irreversible prejudice' to the worker. It concluded that the failure to allow the care worker to make representations before being included on the list breached article 6.

The three safeguards argued by the Secretary of State (application to the Secretary of State at any time to remove the worker, judicial review, and right of appeal after nine months) were not sufficient to remedy the defect. This was because the failure to allow representations before inclusion was not just a technical breach but a denial of a fundamental element of the right to a fair determination of a person's civil rights – namely, the right to be heard. The denial was total. However, article 6 was about proportionality. So the problem was not that representations were denied in some circumstances (for example, those that appeared the most serious) but in all.

Rather than declare the Act incompatible with the Human Rights Act, the court held that s.82(4) could be read so as to require the Secretary of State to allow workers the right to make representations before being included provisionally on the POVA list – unless he or she considers the delay would place a vulnerable adult at risk of harm (*R(Wright) v Secretary of State for Health*).

A worker included on the list (other than provisionally) has a right of appeal to the Care Standards Tribunal (s.86). The Tribunal has to allow the appeal if it was not satisfied either that the individual was guilty of the misconduct, or that the individual was unsuitable to work with vulnerable adults.

In addition, a person can apply to the Tribunal for removal from the list if he or she has been on the list for ten years (or five years if placed on the list when he or she was under 18 years old) and has not made such an application during that time. However, the Tribunal cannot give permission for the application to be made unless during that time the individual's circumstances have changed and the change is such that permission should be given (ss.87–88).

Cross-referral between the POVA list and the Protection of Children Act 1999 (POCA) list can be made (s.92).

5.1.4 DUTY TO CHECK POVA LIST

From 26 July 2004, care providers have had a duty to check the POVA list, and cannot offer employment if the prospective employee was included on the list (whether or not provisionally). This duty also covers existing employees who are moving or being transferred from a non-care to a care position. If the employer has discovered that an existing employee was on the list, the employer must cease to employ the person in that care position (Care Standards Act 2000, s.89; DH 2004, para 29).

The original intention was that when application for criminal record certificates under the Police Act 1997 was made to the Criminal Records Bureau (CRB), then the CRB would automatically check against the POVA list as well (Police Act 1997, ss.113(3C), 115(6B)). However, regulatory changes meant that, exceptionally, new staff have been able to start work in advance of a full CRB check, but only after a check has been made against the POVA list. This exceptional POVA check is referred to as a 'POVA First' check; it is intended that it be used only so that care providers can recruit staff quickly in order to ensure that statutory staffing requirements are met (DH 2004, paras 40, 46).

It is an offence for a person on the POVA list (unless the inclusion is provisional only) to apply for, offer to do, accept or do any work in a care position.

The duty of referral applies only in respect of dismissals, resignations or other departures that occur after the POVA's scheme inception, on 26 July 2004. However, guidance states that care providers may (but are not obliged to) refer care workers in respect of such occurrences before that date, but would have to supply the necessary supporting information (DH 2004, paras 56–57). The guidance goes on to set out a list of the various information that is required to support a referral to the Secretary of State (DH 2004, para 68).

5.1.5 PROOF OF MISCONDUCT, HARM, UNSUITABILITY TO WORK WITH VULNERABLE ADULTS

The role of the Care Standards Tribunal, on hearing appeals, is to determine whether there was misconduct which caused harm or risk of harm to a vulnerable adult, and whether the person is unsuitable to work with vulnerable adults. If the Tribunal is not satisfied about the misconduct causing harm (or risk of harm) and unsuitability – then it must direct that the person be removed from the POVA list (s.86).

5.1.5.1 Standard of proof and burden of evidence

The Care Standards Tribunal has consistently confirmed that the standard of proof, required to demonstrate misconduct, is the civil standard. This means proof on the balance of probabilities (*EK v Secretary of State*). However, the more serious the allegation, the stronger should the evidence be (*AB v Secretary of State for Education and Skills*; and *R(N) v Mental Health Review Tribunal (Northern Region)*). It is still the civil standard of proof but the cogency and probative value of the evidence must be in proportion to the nature of the finding sought and the gravity of the consequences (*NJ v Secretary of State for Health*).

The burden of proof lies on the person making the allegation. However, once misconduct and harm have been established, then the burden shifts to the person to satisfy the Tribunal that he or she is suitable to work with vulnerable adults (*SM v Secretary of State; KM v Secretary of State for Health*).

5.1.5.2 Misconduct and harm

Misconduct is not defined in the legislation. The Tribunal has stated misconduct:

- need not be serious or gross
- can arise from acts of commission or omission
- need not involve dishonesty or disgracefulness
- does not arise if the person was unable to avoid the impropriety
- is capable of mitigation
- might not be made out in circumstances of overwork, shortness of time, or lack of support – but only where such extenuating circumstances make proper performance of a duty impossible as opposed to more difficult
- can be considered without restriction by the Tribunal (*EK v Secretary of State for Health*).

Harm is defined as ill-treatment or impairment of health to a vulnerable adult or to a child (Care Standards Act 2000, s.121). The Tribunal has stated that 'all links in the chain of causation between misconduct and the harm or potential harm' to a vulnerable adult must be intact.' However, in considering misconduct by omission, 'it is necessary to consider the professional responsibilities of the person listed and whether, if those responsibilities had been properly discharged, there is a real and substantive likelihood that such harm or risk would have been prevented or materially lessened' (*EK v Secretary of State*).

The Tribunal has further stated that not all misconduct will mean that a person is unsuitable to work with vulnerable adults or children: a 'finding of a less serious nature will not generally lead to finding of unsuitability without more. Conversely an individual guilty of relatively trivial misconduct could be shown to be wholly unsuitable' (*EK v Secretary of State*).

The courts have confirmed that, in deciding whether a person is suitable to work with vulnerable adults, the Care Standards Tribunal is not confined to considering the misconduct originally reported by the person's employer to the Secretary of State. It has instead a wide discretion to consider other misconduct that may have come to light by the time of the appeal hearing. This issue arose in a case involving the barring of a lounge door in the dementia unit of a care home, so that the nurse and a colleague could sleep there, leaving residents neglected. However, at the appeal, other matters were raised including administration of medication, an unsecured door, and hygiene on the unit. The Tribunal had confirmed the nurse's inclusion on the POVA list; the court did not interfere with that decision (*Joyce v Secretary of State for Health*).

5.1.5.3 Unsuitability to work with vulnerable adults

Judgement about unsuitability will involve questions of character, disposition, capacity and ability of the individual concerned, including ability to act properly in difficult or frustrating circumstances, past performance, nature and extent of misconduct. The following matters, not exclusive, need to be considered:

- number of incidents constituting the misconduct established
- gravity of misconduct
- time elapsed since misconduct
- timing and degree of recognition by person that the conduct was misconduct and had the potential to harm
- steps taken by person to minimise the possibility of a recurrence of that, or similar misconduct
- extenuating circumstances.

The Tribunal has noted that one incident of misconduct can suffice to establish unsuitability to work with vulnerable adults. Equally, however, 'such a finding, as matter of common sense, demands caution because no career is without its low points and few are wholly without any instances at all of human error. The gravity of the misconduct, the circumstances and, in particular, the probability of repetition are crucial factors' (*Matswairo v Secretary of State for Health*).

An assessment of risk is also required. The test of suitability is not evidential but the exercise of discretion by the Tribunal, applying its experience to evidential matters considered in establishing misconduct and harm (*EK v Secretary of State*).

5.1.6 CARE STANDARDS TRIBUNAL: APPEALS CASES

Appeal to the Care Standards Tribunal is the process has been intended as a safeguard, to ensure that decisions to place, or not to place, people on the POVA list are correct. The following examples of such appeals are instructive on a number of counts, in respect of a balance being struck. They illustrate a firm, though not a one-sided approach, intended to protect vulnerable people. They reveal, too, not only black and white cases, but also many shades of grey. Although the following case summaries relate to the POVA scheme under the Care Standards Act 2000, which is due to be replaced (see 5.2 below), nonetheless they give insight into the sort of issue arising in relation to care workers and the safe-guarding of vulnerable adults.

5.1.6.1 Cases involving money

Not being a 'bad person' does not necessarily mean that a person is suitable to work with vulnerable adults, having stolen money from an 88-year old woman:

Stealing money: not a 'bad person'. Allegations were made that money had been stolen from a resident in her eighties in her flat. The police were informed and they installed a covert camera. The care worker concerned eventually pleaded guilty to theft, and received a community punishment order. She was referred to the POVA list. The resident concerned was 88 years of age. The theft had a huge impact on her, and she no longer trusted her carers. The care worker argued that her name should be removed from the POVA list because she had, as she explained, 'put her hands up to that, walked out on her job, paid the lady back, did some community service and hung her head in shame for years.'

The Tribunal concluded that 'although we warmed to her as an individual and have some empathy with her, her lack of insight of the effect of her actions on the victim and the failure to understand that her integrity has been affected, do not help us conclude she is now suitable...We do appreciate that, in her words, she is "not a bad person" but, again, that does not mean she is suitable to work with vulnerable adults' (DG v Secretary of State).

In another case, a depressed local authority care worker stole a sum of money, returned it anonymously and expressed deep regret:

Care worker with mental health problems stealing money, returning it, expressing deep regret. A care worker stole a sum of £240 from the home of a service user. Some months later, an envelope was found at the service user's home with the same amount of money and an anonymous note apologising for the theft. The carer was taking medication for depression and for schizophrenia. The Tribunal found both misconduct and actual harm, since the theft would have had an effect on the woman's well-being and have caused anxiety, as well undermining confidence in services provided by the local authority. The Tribunal accepted that the carer deeply regretted her actions, but was not satisfied she would not do the same again. Her rationalisation of why she committed the theft, together with her failure to disclose past theft and fraud offences, meant she was unsuitable to work with vulnerable adults (SM v Secretary of State).

More straightforwardly, another case about money involved an agency care worker in a person's own home who, having fraudulently written out a cheque to herself, then tried to make the service user feel guilty:

Fraudulent use of cheque made out for £2500. The service user, who was severely disabled through multiple sclerosis, paid the agency using direct payments received from the local authority. The carer told the woman that she had lost her glasses, the woman wrote out a blank cheque so the carer could buy some new ones. The carer made out the cheque to herself for £2500. She subsequently apologised, paid back £2000 with a promise of repaying the rest. Nobody from the agency ever visited the woman even after the misconduct had come to light (something the Tribunal subsequently criticised).

The Tribunal took the view that the carer had not lost her glasses, the plan was premeditated, and she only apologised after the fraud came to light when the bank phoned to say that the woman had become overdrawn (the carer had miscalculated how much money was in the account). Even then, the carer had persuaded the woman not to report it.

The Tribunal noted that the woman was 'trapped in her house at the mercy of a live-in carer. She must have felt very frightened and angry.' It was surprised that the agency had not visited and apologised, wondered what checks had been carried out and hoped that the agency had significantly improved its recruiting and training procedures. The carer had had a five-minute interview before being taken on by the agency. She was clearly unsuitable to work with vulnerable adults (*Nkala v Secretary of State for Health*).

Other cases are much more opaque. For instance, suspicion is one thing, proof and evidence quite another. In the following case, involving a domiciliary care worker, there were 12 alleged incidents of theft; ten were discounted, and although the other two involved taking money, the Tribunal found they did not amount to theft:

Twelve incidents of alleged theft: no misconduct. A domiciliary care worker had been included on the POVA list as result of allegations of theft on 12 occasions. The Tribunal responded as follows.

Missing money, handbag, purse. An allegation about missing money from a man's flat was dismissed, since there was no evidence that money was in fact missing. In another instance, a woman had been unable to find her handbag and purse, but no specific allegation was made that the care worker had taken it. A third allegation was made to a neighbour about theft of a purse, but considerable doubt was cast on whether it was stolen (as opposed to mislaid) by the woman's godson and there was no evidence of its having been stolen by the care worker.

Missing money, missing watch, borrowing money. In another instance of alleged missing money, there was insufficient evidence; it was unclear when the money went missing, and other carers visited as well the care worker in question. Another allegation was withdrawn concerning pound coins going missing from a couple's house; it transpired that a carer had made this observation, but no accusation had been made against the care worker. The next allegation involved the taking of a watch; the care worker said she had taken it for mending; there was no evidence that she had intended to take the watch permanently. It was further alleged that the care worker had borrowed £135 (there was no evidence for this) and that her husband had decorated the service user's house and been paid £100 (the care worker stated this had been requested of her husband by a mutual friend of his and of the service user).

Money missing from purse, duvet, toilet rolls. Another service user alleged the theft of £60 from her purse. This was investigated by the police, who had noted that she had numerous carers visiting her and there was no evidence that the care worker was responsible. Another allegation that the care worker had retained for herself a duvet she was meant to take to a charity shop was not made out. The care worker should have obtained a receipt, but at that time her employer's procedures and policies did not specify the obtaining of receipts for goods. Yet another allegation concerning the theft of toilet rolls and sums of £10 and £30 were discounted; there was no direct evidence and up to ten other carers were also visiting the service user at the relevant time.

Cashing pension of sister of service user. The two allegations of most potential substance were as follows. The care worker took the sister of a service user (they lived together) to the Post Office to cash her pension, which produced a sum of over £1000. The care worker reported this to the office and also that she had been given a plant by the service user. Subsequently, a large proportion of this money went missing. The care worker was a suspect because she knew the money was in the house. The Tribunal noted that the care worker had gone beyond what was expected of her, but the company manager did state that it was not unusual for carers to look out for the interests of the partners of service users. The care worker faced criminal charges on this allegation but was acquitted.

Although the Tribunal worked to a lower standard of proof (balance of probability only), it was not minded to find this allegation proven. The time the money went missing was unknown and there were other visitors to the house. Furthermore, reporting to her employer about the cashing of the pension and the large sum of money in the house seemed inconsistent with an intention to steal. At a later date, the care worker was found with the sister's (who was herself now a service user as well as the first sister) pension book in her possession (without a receipt having been given), but there was no evidence that she intended to retain it and obtain cash for herself.

Entrapment of care worker. Lastly, was the allegation that she had taken £10 from a service user's house, money which had been planted by the company to entrap the care worker. She had been found with it on the dash board of her car; she argued that she had taken it buy food for the service user. The Tribunal did not accept that she intended to steal the money, but felt the matter came to a failure to give a receipt – which she had not given because, on the evidence, she was in a rush.

No misconduct. The Tribunal concluded that there was no misconduct, which harmed or placed at risk of harm a vulnerable adult; thus it did not have to consider whether the care worker was unsuitable to work with vulnerable adults. Her appeal succeeded (*Pain v Secretary of State*).

5.1.6.2 Physical and other mistreatment cases

Tribunal decisions might be relatively straightforward, as in the case of proven allegations of sexual assault on clients in residential settings with mental disabilities – and non-disclosure of previous convictions (*McNish v Secretary of State for Health*). Similarly, the taking of objectively obscene photographs of elderly residents by a care worker, apparently formerly a medical doctor in Bulgaria – compounded by disingenuousness and the fact that he was an intelligent man with professional medical training – meant this was misconduct and he was unsuitable to work with vulnerable adults or children (*Kalchev v Secretary of State for Education and Skills*). It might simply be assault:

Bending back the thumbs of residents. A care assistant working in a nursing home had been found guilty of assault of beating, following allegations that she had bent back the thumbs of residents. Aggravating features were that the actions had been premeditated against elderly, mentally ill residents. She had not appealed against her inclusion on the POVA list, but contested her inclusion on the POCA list. The Tribunal rejected her appeal (*Mwaura v Secretary of State for Health*).

The fact that a care worker had spent most of her life caring, and had troubled to improve her skills to achieve senior status may not be enough:

Force-feeding by senior care worker. A senior carer had tried to force food into elderly residents' mouths. One was able to say whether she had had enough, the other had a poor swallow reflex and could have choked if the food had been pushed in any further. Despite the fact that the care worker had spent most of her life working in the care sector, had gone to the trouble of getting qualifications and had achieved senior care status, the Tribunal found both misconduct and unsuitability to work with vulnerable adults or children (*Jackson v Secretary of State for Health*).

The issue may simply be evidential, one person's word against another.

Knocking a resident to the floor: misconduct but not unsuitable to work with vulnerable adults. At a care home, it was alleged by one care assistant that, during the night another (senior) care worker slapped a service user against a wall and then pushed her in the back forcing her to the floor.

The resident had been heading for the smoker's lounge, although claimed to be going to the toilet. The senior care worker stated that the resident had struck out at her and she had raised her hands to block the blow. In so doing, however, she had hit the resident on the shoulder, who then fell to the floor. She was 'mortified' at what had happened. She apologised and checked on the resident through the night. She did not however report it. When it came to light, she did nothing to defend her job, she knew she was going to be sacked – but did not feel she could have done anything differently.

The Tribunal was impressed by her evidence and her approach. Her failure to report the incident amounted to misconduct. However, it noted that prior to her disciplinary hearing she had been given no opportunity to explain her actions and she had herself, 'on all accounts been the victim of an assault…and been offered no support by her employers.' The Tribunal concluded that, notwithstanding the misconduct, she was not unsuitable to work with vulnerable adults or children. The care assistant's appeal succeeded (*Dixon v Secretary of State for Health* [2005] 621 PVA).

The evidence might alternatively be overwhelming, involving the death of a service user and abuse of others:

Sleeping on duty, taunting, flicking water, distressing residents. A 40-year-old carer worked at a care home for adults with learning disabilities. One night she slept and during this time one of the residents trapped his head between the headboard and bed rails. He suffered brain damage and subsequently died. The carer subsequently attempted to persuade another member of staff (young and inexperienced) to change a detail in the records, saying that she had turned the man 16 times during the night rather than just six. This would have given the impression that she had been providing care rather than sleeping. The Tribunal noted that this attempt was a 'flagrant piece of improper conduct'. In addition, the Tribunal found that she had flicked water over another resident who particularly disliked water on her body, distressed a second by threatening to wash her clothes even though she had a propensity to become distressed at such laundering, and a third resident by taunting and mimicking her self-harming actions. The Tribunal found misconduct and unsuitability to work with vulnerable adults (and children). She had started as a very good carer but become a poor one with an attitude which was dangerous to service users (*Close v Secretary of State for Health*).

Care workers may react to considerable provocation, but the Tribunal will bear in mind that dealing with challenging behaviour is part of the job:

Reacting to being spat at. A domiciliary support worker had, in his own words, 'lost it' when a man with challenging behaviour struck out and spat at the worker in the shower. The worker first pushed the man's head hard to the side, then subsequently raised his hand in front of the man's face and caught him on the forehead pushing him backwards. The worker was convicted of assault. He submitted to the Tribunal that he had a phobia about spitting and that he would not react in such a way again. The Tribunal was not convinced and concluded that he was unsuitable to work with vulnerable adults (*SP v Secretary of State*).

Manual handling is by no means always a straightforward issue, but the following case illustrates an unacceptable extreme:

Dragging 20-stone resident across the floor by his underpants. A senior carer in a care home had manoeuvred a fallen resident, weighing 20 stone, by holding and pulling his underpants. He denied dragging the man across the floor in this manner (the Tribunal found this allegation unproven). He received a caution from the police for assault. Initially he had lied about what had occurred. Although he had not received all planning manual handling training, he was an experienced care worker, had received manual handling training in Singapore and had a nursing degree from the Phillippines. The incident was misconduct; and he was unfit to work with vulnerable adults because he failed to recognise the high risk he took with the resident, and because he had denied what had actually happened (*Del Mundo v Secretary of State for Health*).

In the following case, a strict and inflexible regime led to a range of unacceptable treatment of service users:

Strict and inflexible regime, leading to lack of tolerance of people with learning disabilities. A care worker was part of a team supporting three service users with learning disabilities, living in a supported living tenancy. Various allegations were made. On one occasion, a service user dropped his comfort stick; another carer picked it up, but the care worker told the latter to put it back on the floor. The man should pick it up himself. On another occasion, he dropped it into the toilet; the carer told him to put his hand into the toilet to retrieve it. The carer referred to another service user as a 'slaughtered pig' when she was menstruating. In addition was a failure to help service users out of bed. There was also falsification of records. All this was misconduct harming, or placing at risk of harm, vulnerable adults. Overall, the carer had operated a strict and inflexible regime, leading to a lack of tolerance. The carer was unsuitable to work with vulnerable adults (*Johnston v Secretary of State for Health*).

The evidence may simply not hold up and a care worker win an appeal, apparently against all the odds:

Unfounded allegations of sexual misconduct. In a small home for four people with learning disabilities, one of the residents made certain signs which were interpreted as an allegation of sexual, anal penetration by a member of staff. The member of staff was a care worker with an unblemished work record of 30 years as a nurse and a carer. He was suspended and never returned to the home. He was then dismissed, lost an appeal against it, lost his appeal before an Employment Tribunal and lost his appeal against that decision – and was then placed on the POVA list.

The Care Standards Tribunal now doubted whether there had been anal penetration; the police surgeon had found no evidence of it. If there had been, the Care Standards Tribunal could not identify why the staff member should have been the perpetrator. Furthermore there was doubt about what the man had been trying to communicate that day; it seemed most likely it was all about a broken lunch box. This case demanded the 'heightened' standard of proof; but even on the lower civil standard, the Tribunal could not be satisfied that there was any misconduct. The reason for the difference between this Tribunal's finding, and that of the Employment Appeal Tribunal, was that employment law demanded only that the employer have reasonable suspicion of misconduct – which is a lower standard of proof than the civil standard of proof involving balance of probability (*NJ v Secretary of State for Health*).

5.1.6.3 Management failings

A background of management failing seems all too often to be raised in Tribunal hearings. But this will not necessarily save the appellant who wishes to come off the POVA list:

Controlled drugs: poor management but misconduct and unsuitability of nurse confirmed. Incorrect administration of a controlled drug by a registered mental health nurse – even when under pressure – constituted misconduct, following a failure to check the drugs chart and the controlled drugs register. Likewise, was the failure to dispose of controlled drugs that a resident had not taken and to record what had happened. This was notwithstanding woefully inadequate training, support and supervision – and that the nurse appeared to have become a scapegoat for poor practice generally in the nursing home. The misconduct was made out, and the Tribunal held as well that he was unsuitable to work with vulnerable adults or children. His appeal failed (*EK v Secretary of State*).

Conversely, management-related failings may be a significant factor in finding in a care worker's favour – as in the following case which essentially was about a care worker, in good faith, crossing the boundary between paid carer and friend:

Care worker crossing the line between paid carer and friend; risk of financial harm; failures of the domiciliary care agency. The appellant was employed as a cleaner for a woman in her own home. She had a good relationship with the woman, who was of low intellect, housebound, partially sighted and had insulin-dependent diabetes. At some point she became carer, still in her employed role. The woman then alleged she had been exploited by the care worker.

Going on holiday, buying and cleaning carpets, doing the gardening, redecorating the house, putting money into a Christmas club – all outside the care plan. The care worker conceded that she had been on holiday twice with the woman (but the woman had paid only for herself), bought a new carpet with the woman's money which was laid in the woman's house by the carer's husband, bought two new arm-chairs and a bed for her, arranged for her husband to do the gardening for £10 an hour, arranged via the social worker for her husband to redecorate the house at a cost of £400, arranged for her husband to clean the carpets monthly (due to incontinence), and took up to £35 a week to put into a Christmas club for the service user (all this money was properly accounted for).

Lack of training, guidance, support, supervision. The Tribunal found that when her role changed from cleaner to carer, the care worker had received no training, guidance, support or supervision. She had never been given a cash book or received guidance on the handling of money. She had a close relation-ship with the woman. She came across as straightforward and uncomplicated. The decoration by the husband was done to a high standard at a commercial rate. The social worker's sanctioning of this arrangement was bad practice. The woman appeared to have had a good time on holiday, had paid only for herself and the motive on the part of the care worker was one of fondness for the woman, rather than a desire to swindle her. The care worker had made a number of withdrawals from the woman's bank account over the years, but these were authorised by the woman and were consistent with the woman's expenditure patterns. There was no element in all of this of dishonesty or financial exploita-tion.

Overstepping the bounds of good practice. The care worker had clearly overstepped the bounds of good practice, but the Tribunal found that the blame for this fell squarely on the agency because of the lack of training, supervision or even basic management. The Tribunal took the woman's allegations seriously, but noted that the woman had a history of making such allegations, that she could be very 'difficult', that there was evidence that she had struck the care worker twice, and that a neighbour who had previously been banned from the house because of her malign influence was not only present when the allegations were made, but was actively prompting the woman.

Misconduct and risk of harm, but suitable to work with vulnerable adults. The Tribunal held that the care worker was guilty of misconduct because, by crossing the dividing line between carer and friend, she had placed the woman at risk of harm of financial exploitation (although no such harm occurred). However, the Tribunal found that she had been 'left to her own devices, received little training, no supervision and no management. She accepts her failings and is willing to be supervised. Above all she presents as a caring person and we have little doubt that provided she is properly trained, managed and supervised she will provide good quality care in the future.'

The Tribunal also noted the virtue of oral hearings. The papers had presented a damning picture; it was only through seeing and hearing witnesses that a different picture emerged (*Mrs P v Secretary of State for Education and Skills*).

In another case, a care worker at a residential home had clearly left residents at risk of harm, but the root of the problem seemed to lie with management, rather than the unsuitability of the care worker:

Care worker topping up her mobile phone leaving residents unattended in the dark at a care home. A care home worker left residents unattended in order to go to a local shop to top up her mobile phone so that she could make an urgent phone call. She had understood that she was not allowed to use the telephones in the care home itself. She had left one resident, bathed and dressed, in the lounge downstairs in the dark. She left the back door propped open. Although no residents came to any actual harm, the Tribunal was in no doubt that they had been put at risk of harm through misconduct. However, the Tribunal noted that the care worker had considerable family difficulties at the time, and believed she was not allowed to use the phones in the home, even though management denied there was any such ban.

Brisk expedition of management, lack of pastoral approach, quiet reticence of care worker, misunderstanding. The Tribunal found that the root of the problem appeared to lie between 'the brisk expedition…and loquacious exuberance' of the managers on the one hand, and the 'quiet reticence' of the care worker on the other. Had management been a 'little more pastoral and pro-active in their staff management', the problem might have been avoided. Indeed, the documentary evidence showed that the care worker had been pursuing her career with 'diligence and enthusiasm' and management at the home had previously been satisfied with her work and personality. The Tribunal was unable to find that the care worker was unsuitable to work with vulnerable adults (*Matswairo v Secretary of State for Health*).

It might be a catalogue of poor professional practice on the part of a manager herself:

Multiple failings in care. A registered mental health nurse, acting as manager in a nursing home, lost her appeal after the Tribunal found proven allegations which included (a) lack of staff supervision, monitoring and training; (b) failure to check staff references; (c) failure to keep service user files up to date with relevant information; (d) failure to provide adequate wound care and pressure sore care; (e) failure to monitor the weight of residents; and (f) failure to provide adequate care and neglecting residents (*JF v Secretary of State*).

5.1.6.4 Medication, nursing care and general care cases

An easy and thoughtful manner might be insufficient to remedy serious lapses in the giving of medication:

Not giving residents their medication. A senior care assistant in a care home had a thoughtful easy manner with service users, a caring concern for them and a practical interest in their well-being. His demeanour and attitude were those of somebody who could easily get on with people of different backgrounds – an important quality. However, none of this saved him from a finding by the Tribunal of unsuitability to work with vulnerable adults, after he failed to check on the medication required for a new resident – and overlooked one area of the care home on his rounds and so not given residents their medication (*Rathbone v Secretary of State*).

Conversely, when a senior care worker failed to sign certain medication sheets immediately and to give medication to a resident who was drowsy, no misconduct was found. The prescribing doctor confirmed that the latter decision was not improper. On the former issue, it was not in all the circumstances misconduct; it had been a difficult and stressful day with residents restless and difficult. No misconduct was established

(*PHH v Secretary of State for Education and Skills*). Likewise, even when a nurse had been struck off the nursing register for a lapse in the care of a diabetic resident, she was not found to be unsuitable to work with vulnerable adults:

Failure to monitor diabetic resident; mitigating factors: isolated incident, updating of skills, remorse, undoubted skills. When a nurse failed to monitor a resident in a care home properly, he lapsed into a hypoglycaemic coma and had to be taken to hospital for treatment. This was clearly misconduct which placed a vulnerable adult at risk of harm. She had been struck off the nursing register by the Nursing and Midwifery Council, but now wished to work as a carer.

Yet the Tribunal did not hold that she was unsuitable to work with vulnerable adults, finding mitigating factors. The incident had occurred four years previous to the hearing, the nurse was remorseful, had never denied her error and had made genuine attempts to update her knowledge; the misconduct was an isolated incident, a one-off event, in a nursing career spanning 14 years; and she clearly had learnt from her mistake and wanted to use her undoubted skills in the caring profession (*LLM v Secretary of State*).

Thus not every lapse will result in a finding of unsuitability:

Sleeping on the job. Sleeping on duty in a residential complex with 20 flats for elderly, vulnerable people, amounted to misconduct but, in all the circumstances, did not mean that vulnerable adults would be at significant risk from her. Furthermore, any such risk as did exist was as much the responsibility of the employer as the care assistant. The care assistant was therefore not unsuitable to work with vulnerable adults. Her appeal succeeded (*Brown v Secretary of State for Health*).

In another case concerning sleeping on duty, the Tribunal likewise found that the two care workers – in a care home of 42 residents, some requiring nursing and some with dementia – concerned were not unsuitable to work with vulnerable adults. The Tribunal rejected allegations that the sleeping was deliberately planned on the night in question. Although it found that there was some falsification of records by the care workers, the evidence showed that it was routine practice in the home to complete fluid and turning charts in advance and to amend them later if necessary, and that the care workers had received little training or guidance. Contrary to the evidence of the manager, who had maintained the training was of an extremely high standard, it turned out that, at the relevant time, all training had been suspended within the company's homes. The care workers also showed genuine remorse and realised the gravity of their misconduct; they would be unlikely ever to do it again (*LU and DH v Secretary of State for Health*).

5.1.6.5 Fairness and transparency in POVA: equality of arms and disclosure

In a number of cases, the Care Standards Tribunal has expressed itself concerned about fairness in the process of POVA listing. It has stated that the principle of 'equality of arms' means that the more powerful party (i.e. the Secretary of State) must make greater efforts to ensure that all the relevant evidence is provided, so that the Tribunal can make a proper decision.

Inadequate investigation of alleged regular absence of care worker from care home. A care worker absented himself one evening for about 15 minutes to fetch some bedding for his sleep shift at the care home in which he worked. Subsequent to this incident, the allegations were exaggerated without sustainable evidence, accusing the care worker not just of one, but of regular, absence. He was dismissed, losing not only that job but also his full time teaching job as well.

However, there had been no adequate investigation in the home into the alleged absences, and likewise the disciplinary procedures were flawed. The Tribunal pointed out that, without both a proper investigation by the employer and advice or observations of POVA officers, there was no 'reasonable cause to believe' that the care worker regularly left service users. Yet this had been the basis of his inclusion on the POVA list. Furthermore, for the appeal, the home was reluctant to submit the shift sheets and had not done so, even though the appellant had requested disclosure. The Tribunal pointed out that such a decision was (a) not for those running the home to make and (b) the Secretary of State (as respondent) should have made every effort to obtain all the records for the relevant period and given the appellant an opportunity to scrutinise them.

The Tribunal found in the care worker's favour (*TM v Secretary of State for Health*).

In a further case, although it upheld overall the Secretary of State's decision to place a nurse on the POVA list, the Tribunal nonetheless found that the Treasury Solicitors, on behalf of the Department of Health, had 'once again ignored the basic principles of disclosure'. The care home in question had failed to conduct an inadequate investigation and to keep records properly. This meant that it had not investigated properly the allegations of abuse levelled against the nurse. The Tribunal noted the correspondence from the Department of Health to the home. This correspondence made clear that information provided by the home had to be sufficient for the Department to take the view that the home reasonably believed the nurse to be guilty of misconduct. The Tribunal failed to understand how the POVA officers could have been satisfied as to the sufficiency of that information, given that the home's investigation was inadequate. Such matters raised issues under article 6 of the European Convention on Human Rights, namely, the right to a fair hearing (*Smith v Secretary of State for Health*).

5.2 BARRING PEOPLE FROM WORKING WITH VULNERABLE ADULTS

From an expected date of October 2009, a new scheme regulating the social and health care work force will replace the current POVA list scheme that has regulated personal care and independent health care. *In summary only*, the new scheme is as follows. It is underpinned by the Safeguarding Vulnerable Groups Act 2006 (SVGA) and associated regulations. Essentially it is about a 'barring list', inclusion on which will prevent a person working with vulnerable adults if that work involves a regulated activity. It also involves a monitoring list. This is the converse to the barring list; unless a person is on the list, and is therefore subject to monitoring, they will be unable to work with vulnerable adults.

The 2006 Act applies to England and Wales and, by extension, to Northern Ireland. It does not apply to Scotland. However, it contains a provision (s.54) to give effect to the corresponding Scottish legislation, the Protection of Vulnerable Groups (Scotland) Act 2007. The latter has an equivalent provision (s.87) to give effect in Scotland to the 2006 Act.

5.2.1 INDEPENDENT BARRING BOARD

An independent barring board (IBB) has a duty to establish an 'adults' barred list' (and a children's also). If a person is included in this adults' barred list, he or she is barred from engaging in a 'regulated activity' with vulnerable adults (ss.2–3). The legislation refers to this IBB; it is going to be known in practice, however, as the Independent Safeguarding Authority (ISA).

5.2.1.1 Vulnerable adult

A vulnerable adult is defined in the 2006 Act as being 18 years or more and:
- being in residential accommodation or sheltered housing
- receiving domiciliary care
- receiving any form of health care
- detained in lawful custody
- under a court supervision order (under part 1 of the Criminal Justice and Court Services Act 2000)
- receiving certain welfare services
- receiving services or participating in activities (relating to age, disability, physical or mental health problems as prescribed, expectant or nursing mothers receiving community care services)
- receiving community care direct payments
- requiring assistance in the conduct of his or her own affairs (under Mental Capacity Act intervention, independent advocacy under s.248 of the NHS Act 2006, or social security appointeeship) (s.59).

The definition of regulated activity is given below (see 5.2.5). The Act does not apply to any activity carried out in the course of a family or personal relationship (s.58).

Regulations prescribe the information to be held on the barred list. This includes, for example, any alternative names and aliases, address, information submitted by the individual in any monitoring application, information relevant to the barring decision, information from relevant registers (e.g. kept by a professional body) or supervisory authorities (regulatory body), relevant police information provided to the ISA, reasons for barring, information (including representations from the individual) relevant to any subsequent appeal or review, outcome of any such appeal or review (SI 2008/16).

5.2.2 PLACING PEOPLE ON THE BARRED LIST

The ISA will place an individual on the barred list in four main ways.

First, if certain prescribed criteria apply to the individual, the Secretary of State must refer the person to the ISA. Inclusion is automatic, without the right to make representations. A consultation document explained that this category of inclusion is in relation to certain types of offence that are regarded as so serious that the individual would in every conceivable circumstance pose a risk of harm to vulnerable adults. Regulations, passed for the purpose of transition (from the POVA list to the new barred list), stipulate that the offences in this category are those sexual offences contained in ss.30–41 of the Sexual

Offences Act 2003, involving people with a mental disorder (SI 2008/1062; DfES 2007, para 35, annex 1).

Second, if certain other prescribed criteria apply, the Secretary of State must likewise refer the person to the ISA. Inclusion is also automatic, but the individual must be allowed to make representations as to why he or she should be removed from the list. If the IBB considers that it is not appropriate to include the individual on the list, then it must remove him or her. A consultation document explained that this category relates to offences which indicate a very probable risk of harm to vulnerable adults but not neces-sarily in every conceivable case. These offences, to be prescribed, are likely to include a wide range, such as murder, kidnapping, false imprisonment, infanticide, rape, a range of sexual offences, ill-treatment or wilful neglect (under the Mental Health Act 1983 or Mental Capacity Act 2005), causing or allowing the death of a vulnerable adult (Domestic Violence, Crime and Victims Act 2004) (DfES 2007, para 35, annex 1).

Third, if it appears to the ISA that the person has engaged in 'relevant conduct' (see below) and it proposes to include the individual on the list, it must give the person the opportunity to make representations as to why he or she should not be included. If the ISA is satisfied that the person has engaged in the relevant conduct, and that it appears to the ISA that it is appropriate to include him or her on the list, then it must do so (SVGA 2006, schedule 3).

Fourth, and last, is the 'risk of harm' test. If it appears to the ISA that a person may harm a vulnerable adult, cause a vulnerable adult to be harmed, put a vulnerable adult at risk of harm, attempt to harm a vulnerable adult, or incite another person to harm a vul-nerable adult – then the ISA must give the person an opportunity to make representations as to why he or she should not be barred. If it appears appropriate to include the person on the barred list, the ISA must do so (SVGA 2006, schedule 3).

5.2.2.1 Inclusion because of relevant conduct
The third category of inclusion, described immediately above, relates to 'relevant conduct'. This is conduct:
- endangering, or likely to endanger, a vulnerable adult
- which, if repeated, would endanger, or be likely to endanger, a vulnerable adult
- involving sexual material relating to children
- (inappropriate) conduct involving sexually explicit images depicting violence against human beings
- (inappropriate) conduct of a sexual nature involving a vulnerable adult (schedule 3).

Endangering a vulnerable adult occurs where the individual harms, causes to be harmed, puts at risk of harm, attempts to harm, or incites somebody else to harm – a vulnerable adult (SVGA 2006, schedule 3).

Such relevant conduct is not described in terms of 'misconduct', as was required by the scheme's predecessor, the POVA list scheme under the Care Standards Act 2000. On its face, this would appear to broaden the grounds for referral. It would seem not to rule out, at least in principle, harm that has arisen, for example, by accident or mischance, even if unaccompanied by misconduct.

5.2.2.2 Transfer from POVA list to barred list

The ISA must transfer a person already on the POVA list under the Care Standards Act 2000 to the adults' barred list under the 2006 Act. It must give any such person an opportunity to make representations as to why he or she should be removed from the barred list, and must consider those representations – unless, under the 2006 Act, the person falls under the category of person to whom no right of representation is extended (i.e. first category of automatic inclusion: see above) (SI 2008/473).

5.2.2.3 Making representations, minimum barred periods, timing of reviews

Regulations set out the procedure for the making of representations when a person is being placed on the barred list. They also set out minimum periods of barring. For example, if a person was already subject to restriction (under the POVA list) and was 18 at the time of the decision, then the period is ten years less the time already on the POVA list before being transferred to the barred list. Where there were no previous restrictions, the minimum period is one year for a person under 18, five years for a person aged between 18 and 25, and ten years for those 25 or over. The regulations also govern how much time must elapse before the person can seek a review. Generally, the period is one year for people under 18, five years for people aged between 18 and 25, and ten years in any other case (SI 2008/474).

5.2.3 REVIEW OF INCLUSION ON THE LIST

A person, with permission from the ISA, may seek a review with the ISA of his or her inclusion on the barred list. However, application may only be made at the end of the minimum barred period and if he or she has made no other such application. The ISA cannot grant permission unless it thinks that the person's circumstances have changed since inclusion on the list or the last application, and that the change is such that permission should be given (SVGA 2006, schedule 3).

5.2.4 APPEAL AGAINST INCLUSION ON THE LIST

Appeals lie to the Care Standards Tribunal against the ISA's decision to include a person on the list or not to remove him or her from the list. Appeals to the Tribunal can only be made on grounds that a mistake has been made on a point of law, or on a finding of fact. However, the decision made by the ISA as to whether it is 'appropriate' to bar a person is a question of neither law nor fact, and so cannot be appealed against to the Tribunal. If the Tribunal finds no mistake of fact or law, then it must confirm the ISA's decision. Appeals can only be made with permission of the Tribunal.

Beyond the Tribunal, an appeal to the Court of Appeal on a point of law may be made, with that Court's permission (s.4).

5.2.5 REGULATED ACTIVITY

Regulated activity, the key focus of the Act, is defined as follows, if it is carried out frequently by the same person and the 'period condition' is satisfied.

The period condition is that on more than two days in any period of 30 days, the person carries out the regulated activity. Alternatively, except in the case of a communication service or driving activities, the period condition is that the person carries out the activity between 2am and 6am and the activity gives the person the opportunity to have face-to-face contact with vulnerable adults. Regulated activity is defined as:

- **(training etc.)** any form of training, teaching or instruction provided wholly or mainly for vulnerable adults
- **(care)** any form of care for or supervision of vulnerable adults
- **(assistance etc.)** any form of assistance, advice or guidance provided wholly or mainly for vulnerable adults
- **(treatment and therapy)** any form of treatment or therapy provided for a vulnerable adult
- **(communication service)** 'moderating a public electronic interactive communication service which is likely to be used wholly or mainly by vulnerable adults' (includes monitoring the content of matter forming any part of the service, and removing or preventing the addition of matter to the service – but does not include people who do not have access to the content of the matter or contact with service users)
- **(driving)** driving a vehicle used only for the conveying vulnerable adults and any person caring for the vulnerable adults (as prescribed)
- **(other)** anything else done for a vulnerable adult in prescribed circumstances (SVGA 2006, s.5 and schedule 4).

Day-to-day supervision or management of any of the above activities is a regulated activity. Inspections by the Healthcare Commission and Commission for Social Care Inspection (or, in the future, by the Care Quality Commission, count as regulated activities (SVGA 2006, s.5 and schedule 4). In a care home, activity is regulated if it is exclusively or mainly for vulnerable adults and:

- is carried out frequently by the same person or the period condition is satisfied
- is carried out by a person while engaging in any form of work (whether or not for payment)
- carried out for or in connection with the establishment
- gives the person the opportunity, in consequence of anything he or she is permitted or required to do, of contact with vulnerable adults (s.5 and schedule 4).

5.2.6 REGULATED ACTIVITY PROVIDERS

A regulated activity provider is defined as a person responsible for the management or control of a regulated activity. Also, if the regulated activity is carried on for the purposes of an organisation, the person is responsible if she or she is not subject to supervision or direction. Likewise a person is a regulated activity provider if he or she makes or author-ises arrangements for somebody else to engage in the activity.

A person is such a provider if he or she carries on a scheme where an individual agrees to provide care or support to an adult in need of it (i.e. adult placement), and where a requirement to register arises under s.11 of the Care Standards Act 2000.

However, a person is not defined as a regulated activity provider if he or she is an individual and the arrangements made are private arrangements. The arrangements are private if the regulated activity is for the person himself or herself; likewise if they are for a vulnerable adult who is a member of the person's family or a friend of the person (SVGA 2006 s.6).

Therefore, the recipient of a community care direct payment is not a regulated activity provider for the purposes of the Act, and obligations – such as carrying out moni-toring checks (see below) – do not apply.

5.2.7 MONITORING

As well as the barred list itself, monitoring is also crucial, because it is an offence for a person to engage in regulated activity with the permission of a regulated activity provider, if he or she not subject to monitoring (s.8). People who are on the barred list cannot be subject to monitoring. Thus, an individual is subject to monitoring if he or she is not barred from engaging in a regulated activity, has made a monitoring application, satisfies prescribed requirements and pays the prescribed fee.

If an individual applies to become subject to monitoring, the Secretary of State has to make appropriate enquiries as to whether there is relevant information about the individ-ual. This concerns criminal record certificates under the Police Act 1997, information a chief officer of police thinks relevant, and any other prescribed information. The Secre-tary of State must provide the individual with disclosable information or notify the indi-vidual that he or she has no disclosable information (s.24).

In terms of other people making a monitoring check about an individual, the Secre-tary of State has an obligation to provide this information about whether the individual is subject to monitoring (or being assessed for such). This obligation is triggered if a request is made by a range of specified bodies or persons (listed in schedule 7 of the Act), who have declared their relevant status and also that the individual (the subject of the checking) has consented. Likewise, such bodies or individuals can apply to be registered, so that they are automatically informed if an individual ceases to be subject to monitoring (SVGA 2006, ss.30-32).

Regulated activity providers must check whether a person is subject to monitoring and/or (it depends) obtain an enhanced criminal record certificate (s.11 and schedule 5). However, a person receiving a community care direct payment from a local authority does not come under the definition of regulated activity provider (s.6). Instead, direct payment recipients may, but are not obliged, to request a monitoring check (ss.30–32 and schedule

7). They will not have a right of access to enhanced criminal record certificate disclosure (as would a regulated activity provider registered with the Criminal Records Bureau (CRB), see 5.2.8.4 below). This is because they will not be registered with the CRB to ask 'exempted' questions under the Rehabilitation of Offenders Act 1974. Nonetheless, direct payment recipients could request an 'umbrella' body registered with the CRB to carry out a check on their behalf. For instance, a local voluntary organisation or the local authority itself may be registered with the CRB as an umbrella body.

Regulations may be made obliging local authorities to tell recipients of direct payments that they can request information about whether a person is subject to monitoring (s.30).

5.2.7.1 Monitoring checks not required

Monitoring checks are not required in certain circumstances. These exceptions are in connection with people in lawful custody; recreational, social, sporting or educational activity provided wholly or mainly for vulnerable adults (as prescribed); education or instruction provided wholly or mainly for vulnerable adults; provision of services, by or on behalf of a person providing or managing housing, to vulnerable adults in connection with that housing; prescribed welfare services (including support, assistance, advice or counselling but which are not community care services), and appointeeship under social security regulations.

However, these exceptions to the requirement for monitoring do not include activities carried out by local authorities in connection with community care services, activities carried out by care providers under the Care Standards Act 2000, or activities carried out by the NHS (SVGA 2006, s.16).

5.2.8 OFFENCES

A number of offences apply both to people who are barred and to organisations providing regulated activities.

5.2.8.1 Offence for barred person to engage in regulated activity

It is an offence for a barred person to seek to, to offer to, or actually to engage in regulated activity. The offence carries a maximum sentence of five years in prison. There are two main defences; the person could not reasonably have known that he or she was on the barred list; and the person thought it was necessary to engage in that activity to prevent harm to a vulnerable adult (SVGA 2006, s.7).

It is also an offence for any person to engage in regulated activity if he or she is not subject to 'monitoring' (see below). However, this does not apply where the individual has been engaging in the regulated activity continuously since before this offence became law. This offence is summary only, attracting the maximum of a certain level (level 5: £5000) of fine (SVGA 2006, s.8).

5.2.8.2 Offences of regulated activity provider where a person is barred

It is an offence for a person to allow an individual barred from regulated activity to engage in that activity, if the person knows or has reason to believe the individual is barred – and if the individual engages in the activity. Similarly, if a personnel supplier supplies such an individual to somebody else with a view to the individual engaging in regulated activity from which the individual is barred. The maximum penalty is five years in prison. There are defences, as described immediately above, based on lack of knowledge or necessity to prevent harm (SVGA 2006, s.9).

5.2.8.3 Offence of using person not subject to monitoring

A regulated activity provider commits an offence if he or she permits an individual to engage in regulated activity who is not subject to monitoring, knew or had reason to believe this, and the individual engages in that activity. Personnel suppliers also commit an offence if they supply such a person. The maximum penalty is a level 5 fine (SVGA 2006, s.10).

5.2.8.4 Offence of not checking whether a person is subject to monitoring

Regulated activity providers and personnel suppliers commit an offence if they fail to check whether a person is subject to monitoring. But such checks are not required where the individual has been engaging in the regulated activity continuously since before these offences became law (SVGA 2006, ss.11–12).

Such checking involves the obtaining of an 'appropriate verification' (unless exempted from checking: see 5.2.7.1 above).

Basically, such a verification involves making a check under s.30 with the Secretary of State as to whether a person is subject to monitoring or is undergoing 'assessment', and/or (it depends) obtaining an enhanced criminal record certificate under the Police Act 1997. Also it may involve obtaining written confirmation, from another regulated activity provider who is permitting the person to engage in the activity concerned, that the latter provider has no reason to believe the person is barred or is not subject to monitoring – and that the latter provider is registered to be notified if the person ceases to be subject to monitoring (s.11 and schedule 5).

There is a special exemption in respect of NHS activity, where a person moves around but is under the 'umbrella' of NHS employment (SVGA 2006, ss.10–11).

5.2.9 CONTROLLED ACTIVITY

In addition to regulated activity, the Act defines 'controlled activity' relating to vulnerable adults.

Controlled activity is defined as ancillary, or carried out wholly or in relation, to specified activities. The activity must be carried out frequently by the same person or carried out by the same person on more than two days in any period of 30 days, and it must give the person the opportunity to have any form of contact with a vulnerable adult, or the opportunity to have access to the health or social services records of the vulnerable adult, or the opportunity to have access to other information as may be prescribed. The specified activities, to which activity might be ancillary and thus be 'controlled', are the:

- provision of primary care services
- provision of hospital services
- provision of domiciliary care
- making arrangements with an adult placement scheme
- provision of community care services
- making of direct payments under the Health and Social Care Act 2001
- any other prescribed activity (s.22).

Regulations may set out, for example, who is permitted to engage in controlled activity, and steps to be taken by employers before permitting people to engage in controlled activity. A criminal offence will attach to failure to adhere to such regulations (SVGA 2006, s.23).

5.2.10 PROVIDING INFORMATION TO THE ISA

Regulated activity providers (or a person responsible for controlled activity) have a duty to provide information to the ISA.

The duty is triggered if the provider or person has withdrawn permission for the individual to engage in regulated activity, or would have done so if the individual had not already ceased to engage in that activity. This must have been for the reasons that the provider (a) thinks the person falls into the category of person where placing on the barring list is automatic; or (b) the person has engaged in 'relevant conduct' (see 5.2.2 above).

Alternatively, the reason could be that the 'harm test' is satisfied in relation to the individual. The harm test is that the individual may harm a child or vulnerable adult, cause a child or vulnerable adult to be harmed, put a child or vulnerable adult at risk of harm, attempt to harm a child or vulnerable adult, or incite another to harm a child or vulnerable adult.

The duty to provide information to the ISA is downgraded to a power in respect of those services for which monitoring checks are not required (see 5.2.7.1 above). A comparable duty applies to personnel suppliers (SVGA 2006, ss.35–36).

5.2.11 SHARING OF INFORMATION

A detailed set of provisions govern information disclosure, obliging and permitting various bodies and the ISA to share information. Some of these are as follows.

The ISA can require regulated activity providers, responsible persons for controlled activity, and personnel suppliers to provide the ISA with prescribed information relating to an individual whom it is considering for inclusion in, or removal from, the barred list. It is an offence not to supply the information, without reasonable excuse (SVGA 2006, s.37).

Local authorities have a duty to provide the ISA with prescribed information if two conditions are satisfied. First, that certain criteria apply to the person, or that the person has engaged in relevant conduct or the harm test is satisfied. Second, that the local authority thinks the person is engaged, or may engage in, regulated or controlled activity – and that the ISA may consider it appropriate to include the person on a barred list. The ISA may also require local authorities to provide it with prescribed information, and the local authority must comply with the request (SVGA 2006, ss.39–40).

Various professional bodies (e.g. the General Social Care Council, Health Professional Council, the General Medical Council, the Nursing and Midwifery Council) that keep relevant registers must provide the ISA with prescribed information if they believe that the relevant criteria, relevant conduct or harm test apply to an individual (s.41). The ISA can demand prescribed information from these bodies (s.42). Conversely, the Secretary of State must share information with the keeper of the register if the individual is newly barred or has ceased to be subject to monitoring. The ISA also has a duty to provide certain information to the keepers of these registers (s.43). The keeper of the relevant register can apply to the Secretary of State for certain information relating to barring and monitoring (s.44).

'Supervisory' authorities (a regulatory body such as the Care Quality Commission) must refer an individual to the ISA if certain criteria apply, or the individual has engaged in relevant conduct or the harm test is satisfied (s.45). They must also provide information to the ISA on request and have a power to apply for information from the Secretary State about an individual and whether he or she is barred or subject to monitoring (ss.46–47). The Secretary of State must in turn inform supervisory authorities about an individual subject to barring or who is no longer subject to monitoring (s.49). The ISA must also provide information to supervisory authorities if it thinks it relevant (s.50).

5.2.12 LIABILITY FOR MISTAKES
No claims for damages are possible in respect of an individual being included, or not included, on a barred list, or in respect of the provision of information – unless the provider knew the information was untrue. However, this does not affect the power of the courts to award damages under the Human Rights Act 1998 against a public authority (SVGA 2006, s.57).

5.3 CRIMINAL RECORD CERTIFICATES
Under the Care Standards Act 2000 and associated regulations, care providers must obtain criminal record certificates from the Criminal Records Bureau (CRB) in respect of certain types of worker under the Police Act 1997. In future, providers will be obliged in some circumstances to do this under the Health and Social Care Act 2008.

For example, such certificates must be obtained by care providers under the Domiciliary Care Agencies Regulations 2002 (SI 2002/3214, schedule 2) under the Care Home

Regulations 2001 (SI 2001/3965, schedule 2) and under the Adult Placement Schemes (England) Regulations 2004 (SI 2004/2070, schedule 3).

An application for a standard or enhanced disclosure must be countersigned by a person registered with the CRB (Police Act 1997, s.120 and SI 2006/750). However, it is possible for persons or bodies not so registered to find out such details, if they ask another registered body to countersign an application on their behalf. Another body acting in this way is known as an 'umbrella body' (CRB 2001, para 4).

The overall purpose of the criminal record certificate scheme is to put the potential employer in possession of both conviction and sometimes non-conviction information about the potential employee – to assist the former in deciding whether to employ the latter to work with vulnerable adults.

5.3.1 LEVELS OF DISCLOSURE

The Police Act 1997 provides for three different levels of disclosure. The first is basic disclosure, which contains details of convictions held in central police records that are not 'spent' under the Rehabilitation of Offenders Act 1974 (s.112). However, the CRB does not, at time of writing, issue such disclosures.

The second is standard disclosure, containing details of spent and unspent convictions, but also cautions, reprimands and warnings recorded centrally by the police. The disclosure will also indicate whether the person is on the POVA list and thus unsuitable to work with vulnerable adults (s.113A). Certain convictions do not become spent under the provisions of the 1974 Act, for example, in relation to the provision of care services to vulnerable adults, representation or advocacy services for vulnerable adults (approved by the Secretary of State or under statute), health services (SI 1975/1023, schedule 1, paras 12–13).

The third level is enhanced disclosure, which contains the same information as a standard disclosure, but it can also contain additional 'soft', non-conviction information held in local police records, which a chief police officer considers may be relevant. The legislation states that the Secretary of State must request the chief police officer to provide any information relevant as to the person's suitability that the chief police officer thinks (a) ought to be included in the certificate; or (b) ought to be provided but not included in the certificate in the interests of the prevention or detection of crime (s.113B). If an application is made for an enhanced criminal record certificate and accompanied by an 'adult's suitability statement' (i.e. that the person is going to work in a care position with vulnerable adults), a check must also be made against the POVA list (s.113D).

5.3.2 ENHANCED DISCLOSURE: VULNERABLE ADULTS

In respect of community care services for adults, enhanced disclosure applies to workers who occupy a position involving regular care for, training, supervising or being in sole charge of people aged 18 or over – and enables the person to have regular contact in the course of his or her duties with a vulnerable adult. Under the legislation (Police Act 1997, s.115; SI 2002/446):

- A vulnerable adult is defined as a person receiving certain (care) services, because of a certain condition resulting in disability.
- The relevant services are listed as accommodation and nursing or personal care in a care home; personal care or nursing or support to live independently in a person's own home; any services provided by an independent hospital, independent clinic, independent medical agency or NHS body; social care services; services provided in an establishment catering for people with learning difficulties.
- The conditions necessitating the provision of such services are listed as (a) learning or physical disability; (b) physical or mental illness, chronic or otherwise, including drugs or alcohol addiction; (c) reduction in physical or mental capacity.
- Disability is described as:
  - dependency on others in the performance of (or assistance in performance of) basic physical functions
  - severe impairment in ability to communicate with others
  - impairment in a person's ability to protect himself or herself from assault, abuse or neglect.

Enhanced certificates are required, concerning vulnerable adults, for the purposes of considering a worker's suitability in relation to caring for, training, supervising, being in sole charge of a vulnerable adult; to providing care services for vulnerable adults, or representation of; or to advocacy services for such adults, approved by the Secretary of State or under statute – all where the person, in the course of normal duties, has access to vulnerable adults receiving the services (SI 2002/233). Despite a system applying potentially to very large numbers of workers (many millions), it has been reported that tens of thousands of migrants are working with vulnerable people in care homes, without undergoing full criminal record checks. This is because foreign criminal records cannot be accessed reliably or at all. It is estimated that some 240,000 migrants work in the care sector overall (Ford 2008).

Notwithstanding this clear statutory authority for disclosure of information, the question has arisen in the courts as to what extent a presumption of disclosure now applies to the police when providing information – and how this relates to the common law of confidentiality and human rights. In fact the courts have held that the duty under s.115 of the Police Act 1997 has effectively displaced the common law presumption of non-disclosure:

Enhanced criminal record certificate and soft information. An enhanced criminal record certificate was issued under s.115 of the Police Act 1997 concerning an Afro-Caribbean social worker with no convictions. Certain 'soft' information was included, provided by the relevant local police force. This stated that it had been alleged that in December 2001 the social worker indecently exposed himself to a female petrol station attendant. It was alleged that he repeated the offence in May 2002. He was arrested and interviewed; he stated that he did not think he had committed the offence but he was suffering from stress and anxiety at the time. At that time he was employed by a child care company and was charged with two counts of indecent exposure. However, the alleged victim failed to identify the suspect during a covert identification parade. The case was subsequently discontinued.

In the High Court, the chief constable's decision to provide this information in the certificate was found to be unlawful, essentially on the grounds that the balance, in favour of disclosure, had been wrongly struck.

The High Court decision was subsequently overturned in the Court of Appeal. In particular the latter found that the common law principle of confidentiality, though generally entailing a presumption of non-disclosure, did not apply to the present case. The statutory framework created by the Police Act 1997 meant that the position was more positively in favour of disclosure – which had to be made unless there was a good reason for not doing so. Furthermore, the judge had also been wrong in stating that the police should have informed the man before disclosure and have given him an opportunity to make representations. This would place too heavy a burden on the police. As the information was being made available in accordance with the law, there was no breach of article 8 (right to respect for privacy) of the European Convention on Human Rights (*R(X) v Chief Constable of West Midlands Police*).

Following this case, the courts have continued to adhere to a firm line:

Inclusion in certificate of information not relating to a criminal offence: headmistress of special school. The headmistress of a special school for children with disabilities had been prosecuted for manslaughter. This was after a child wandered out and was killed by a passing lorry. He had got out through fire doors (which the Fire Service had said could not have locks on them) and then through the school gates which had been left open by a contractor, contrary to a notice at the gates. It seemed also that the senior member of staff in charge of the child had left him for some minutes without informing any other member of staff.

The judge in the case had withdrawn the manslaughter case from the jury, stating that on the evidence there was no chance of a conviction that she had been grossly negligent (required for manslaughter). However, he had left open the possibility that she might have been ordinarily, rather than grossly, negligent in civil law.

Subsequently, information about the whole episode was included in an enhanced criminal record certificate. The woman now challenged this in a judicial review case, arguing that it should not have been included because, at most, it related to a possible civil wrong, not to a criminal offence. The judge in the present case stated that the question was whether this information 'might be relevant' to a prospective employer in considering her suitability for a position involving work with children. He concluded that there could only be one answer, and that the decision to disclose the information was not irrational (*R(G) v Chief Constable of Staffordshire*).

The Court of Appeal has confirmed in a further case that the 'common law presumption against disclosure of relevant information has been turned on its head.' In addition, it confirmed that relevant information in relation to an enhanced certificate can cover past conduct which, even if proved, would neither constitute a criminal offence nor even reveal a risk that a criminal offence would be committed in the future (*R(L) v Commissioner of Police for the Metropolis*). A further case adhered to the same firm line, despite the admitted weaknesses in the allegations of sexual abuse:

Doubtful allegations of sexual abuse based on facilitated communication included in criminal record certificate. The case involved the deputy principal of a college for young autistic adults. Following reorganisation at work, his employment had been transferred to a national charity, and he was required to obtain a criminal record certificate. It contained details, supplied on behalf of the Assistant Chief Constable, of three allegations made against him of sexual abuse of three autistic young adults on a trip to Wales. No criminal charges were ever brought.

On being threatened with a legal challenge against the certificate, the police had revised the information, still referring to the allegations but containing more detail and noting that they had all been made by 'facilitated communication'. (This is a process by which the facilitator supports the hand or arm of somebody with impaired communication ability, while the person uses a keyboard or typing device. The courts have in the past referred to the dangers of relying on evidence obtained in this way: Re D).

The court noted various weaknesses in the allegations, including in one case the failure to confirm the allegations by using a second 'clean' facilitator, in another the withdrawal at one point of the allegations and failure to make an allegation when an independent facilitator was used – and the upholding, by the police and the Police Complaints Authority, of some of the complaints made by the person about the police investigation. However, the court held that the question for the Chief Constable had been whether the information 'might be relevant', and whether the allegations might be true. Although strong doubt was cast on the allegations, they were not negated, and were not 'so devoid of substance so as to make it unreasonable to conclude that they might be true'. The court therefore found in favour of the Chief Constable, although it noted how damaging all this could be to the person (R(Pinnington) v Chief Constable of Thames Valley).

However, all this presupposes of course that the police are still holding the information and thus have it to divulge. In the 'Soham' case, involving the murder of two girls by Ian Huntley, it transpired that the police had failed to keep the details of various complaints that had been made about him over the years in relation to alleged sexual offences. This was partly because of an incoherent policy on weeding, reviewing and deleting records and because of concerns about the Data Protection Act. As it turned out, the Bichard enquiry exonerated the Act itself; the loss of intelligence was due to failings in the record-keeping systems of the police (Bichard 2004, pp.86, 127).

Conversely, the police were reported in 2007 as still holding information relating to the theft of a packet of meat worth 99 pence in 1984 by a 16-year-old. Likewise, a 19-year-old woman in Stafford had wanted to become a carer. However, a reprimand she had received as a 12-year-old for minor assault was still coming up on criminal record checks. The office of the Information Commissioner commented on such cases that some of the incidents dated back 30 years, were non-custodial offences (some had not even led to convictions) and that there was no justification for such blanket retention. It ordered that the information be destroyed (Ford 2007; ICO 2007). The lesson from these cases is that retention and use of information needs to be balanced and proportionate to the seriousness and risks involved.

Inclusion on the POVA list precludes a person working with vulnerable adults, but this is not the effect of information disclosed in connection with a criminal record certificate. For instance, in the following case, the registered nurse would have a 'formidable hurdle' to overcome given the content of the criminal record certificate, but this did not mean she should not be given the chance to do so:

Enhanced criminal record certificate detailing criminal charges being brought against a nurse. A registered nurse wanted to appeal to the Care Standards Tribunal against a decision by Welsh Ministers not to register her as a manager of a care home. She was on police bail at the time, having been charged with wilful neglect. This was for allegedly failing to ensure that junior staff knew what was required of them, following the death of a resident with senile dementia. A decision had been made not to register her, partly (there were other reasons) with reference to the contents of an enhanced criminal record certificate, which outlined a police investigation into a number of deaths. By the time the court considered the issue, the position had moved from a police investigation to actual criminal charges. However, even then, the court stated that she was still entitled to have her case considered by the Tribunal, even though she would have a formidable hurdle to overcome (*Welsh Ministers v Care Standards Tribunal*).

Nonetheless, although employers should have a policy on employing ex-offenders (Chartered Institute of Personnel and Development), and some will have this, others may in practice simply rule people out. Thus, in one case, three weeks after having received a police caution for assaulting a vulnerable patient, a 69-year-old patient with dementia, a care worker was employed in another nursing home. His new employer explained that it was fully aware of his history and had carried out the necessary criminal record and POVA checks. It regarded him as a hard working and respected employee (*This is Cornwall* 2008). That said, it can all turn out badly. In one case, a carer with a drugs problem had been convicted previously of stealing his father's cheque book. The care agency with which he had now started work carried out a criminal record check but decided to employ him; within six weeks of starting his new job as a home carer he had stolen money from clients in their own homes, was prosecuted and admitted four charges of burglary. The employer said after the case that it would in future 'blacklist' carers known to have a criminal record (Hudson 2006).

In the legal case about disclosure of the allegations of sexual abuse made against a deputy principal of a college for young autistic adults (see immediately above), the court upheld the decision of the police to supply details of the allegations in a criminal record certificate. As a consequence of disclosure, the man had been instantly dismissed because his employer had a blanket policy of insisting on a 'clean certificate'. The court was troubled by this, because the law imposed a relatively low threshold for disclosure and employers needed to understand this; a properly formed decision by the employer would take account of other information or explanation provided by the employee, additional to what appeared in the certificate. But a blanket policy did not allow for this to happen. The court suggested that the person might therefore have a reasonable prospect of contesting his dismissal before an employment tribunal (*R(Pinnington) v Chief Constable of Thames Valley*).

5.4 LEGISLATION, STANDARDS AND REGULATORS TO PROTECT PEOPLE

Under the Care Standards Act 2000, regulations and national minimum standards govern the regulation, registration and inspection of care providers. The legislation, together with the regulations and standards, is due to be replaced by a new registration regime under the Health and Social Care Act 2008. Such registration and inspection should, in principle, play a central role in protecting and safeguarding vulnerable adults.

5.4.1 REGULATORY BODIES

The registration and inspection bodies covering England comprise the Commission for Social Care Inspection (CSCI), and the Commission for Healthcare Audit and Inspection (known as the Healthcare Commission), set up under the Health and Social Care (Community Health and Standards) Act 2003. Such regulatory legislation, and the bodies charged with enforcing it, are meant to play a key role in protecting and safeguarding vulnerable adults.

These bodies replaced the National Care Standards Commission and Commission for Health Improvement in April 2004. By 2007, though, central government had published plans to merge both with the Mental Health Act Commission, with one health and social care regulatory body resulting (DH 2006, p.65). Created by the Health and Social Care Act 2008, the Care Quality Commission is due to take over in April 2009.

Under the 2003 Act, the Healthcare Commission has had registration and inspection responsibilities for independent hospitals, independent clinics and independent medical agencies – but not the NHS (s.5A). However, it does investigate the latter. The CSCI has had responsibility for care homes, domiciliary care agencies, children's homes, residential family centres, nurse agencies, fostering agencies, voluntary adoption agencies, adoption support agencies, and adult placement schemes. This has included services of this type provided by local authorities or NHS bodies (s.5).

The CSCI keeps a register of care providers, and has the power to grant, refuse and cancel registration (Care Standards Act 2000, ss.11–16) and to inspect care providers (s.31). It has the power to enter and inspect premises, to inspect and to take copies of documents, and to interview people working there (Health and Social Care (Community Health and Standards) Act 2003, ss.88–89). Its inspections may be unannounced and result in threats to close down homes – for instance, if a culture demeaning to residents is uncovered (*BBC News* 2007). Likewise, when suspicions arose concerning the poisoning of one or more residents, the CSCI ordered a care home's emergency closure (*Community Care* 2007). Appeals against CSCI's decisions go to the Care Standards Tribunal.

CSCI can also prosecute for various offences. In 2006–7, it issued 2787 requirements notices, 584 statutory notices, five urgent cancellations and six prosecutions. One of the latter involved a person previously prosecuted for operating an unregistered domiciliary care service, who was now running another unregistered care service. He was convicted and sentenced to 18 months probation and 250 hours community service (CSCI 2007b, p.25). Another example involved the successful prosecution of a domestic cleaning company, trading as Tender Loving Care, which also offered personal care to people in their own homes without being registered to do so under the 2000 Act (CSCI 2005).

Urgent cancellation of registration – and therefore closure – was sought and obtained in relation to a care home in Northamptonshire, following a 'no-star rating' and failure by the home to respond adequately to enforcement notices. Management of medication, low staff levels and poor overall management were particular concerns (*Community Care* 2008a. But the home then won an appeal to the Care Standards Tribunal: BBC News 2008e).

Note. In summary, the Health and Social Care Act 2008 provides for a change to the system of regulation. A Care Quality Commission is created with functions of registration, review, investigation in relation to health and social care, and functions under the Mental Health Act 1983. Health care is defined widely, as is social care (s.2). The new Act will cover both the NHS and local authorities, aw well as independent providers of health and social care.

Anybody carrying on a regulated activity, that is the provision of health and social care, must be registered. Such provision includes the supply of staff, the provision of transport or accommodation for people requiring care, and the provision of advice in respect of care (s.8). Health care includes all forms of health care provided for people, whether relating to physical or mental health, and also includes procedures that are similar to forms of medical or surgical care but are not provided in connection with a medical condition. Social care includes all forms of personal care and other practical assistance provided for individuals who by reason of age, illness, disability, pregnancy, childbirth, dependence on alcohol or drugs, or any other similar circumstances, are in need of such care or other assistance (s.9).

It is an offence for a service provider not to be registered for a regulated activity (s.10). Registration can be granted unconditionally or with conditions attached. Registration must be granted if the Commission is satisfied that the requirements have been met of regulations made under s.20 by the Secretary of State (s.12). Managers must also apply for registration as prescribed (s.13).

The Commission can cancel registration on a number of specified grounds; it can also suspend registration (ss.17 and 18). The Act provides for regulations to be made in relation to the quality of services provided, health, safety, welfare, fitness of persons to carry on a regulated activity, management, training, premises, records, financial information and accounts, information about charges for services, requirements for review of the quality of services and for reports, handling of complaints and disputes. Regulations may also be made about preventing health care associated infections (r.20). The Secretary of State may issue a code of practice about compliance with regulations (s.21); and the Commission must issue compliance guidance in respect of the regulations (s.23). The Commission must take account of both the code of practice and the guidance in reaching decisions, and both would be admissible in civil and criminal proceedings; non-compliance would not be decisive in liability (s.25).

The Commission can give statutory warning notices (s.29). It can seek an order from a justice of the peace for urgent cancellation – if there is a serious risk to a person's life, health or well-being (s.30). There is also an urgent procedure for variation or suspension of registration (s.31). Appeals lie to the Care Standards Tribunal (s.32).

It is an offence for providers to fail to comply, without reasonable excuse, with conditions set by the Commission (s.33). It is an offence to carry on regulated activity following suspension or cancellation of registration (s.34). Regulations may specify that it is an offence to contravene them (s.35). It is an offence to give a false description of a concern or of premises, likewise to make false statements in applications for registration (ss.36–37).

The Act gives the Secretary of State power to publish statements of standards relating to health care (s.45). The Commission must carry out periodic reviews of NHS bodies and local authorities. It can conduct special reviews and investigations (s.46). It must recommend special measures to the Secretary of State in the case of failing local authorities (s.50). The Commission has powers of entry and inspection and power to require information, documents and records it considers are necessary or expedient for any of its regulatory functions (ss.60–64).

The Act places restrictions on the disclosure of personal information which the Commission has been obtained, but then provides an extensive list of permitted disclosures (ss.76–80).

5.4.1.1 Effectiveness of regulators

Central government has made a great play of regulation, and continues to chop and change the legislation.

However, as pointed out above, local authorities, for example, sometimes seem to enjoy a false sense of security when they contract out services to registered care providers (see 3.3.2). They sometimes appear to assume that it is unnecessary closely to monitor, and respond to complaints about, these care providers, on the basis perhaps that any provider registered with and inspected by a regulator must be satisfactory. This is of course not necessarily the case. The regulator is not a guarantor of adequate services. This is not to criticise the regulator, but merely to observe that both commissioning body (local authority or NHS body) and regulator have key functions in ensuring reasonable standards of care.

For example, physical abuse at a care home in Hull had gone effectively undetected for a period of three years; eventually some care workers were sent to prison and health and safety prosecutions were brought as well (Mark 2005). Yet during this period, the home was registered and must have been inspected on a number of occasions. Likewise, a care home might pass an inspection, even when at the very same time a woman was dying of horrendous pressure sores through neglect and gross negligence (*BBC News* 2003). In similar vein, it might be a newspaper investigation that prompts a regulator into more drastic action, as in the following case:

Neglect in care home exposed by newspaper: regulator's intervention. After a newspaper undercover report revealed evidence of abuse and neglect in a care home run by Southern Cross, the CSCI inspected the home and found 'inadequate' standards shortly afterward. However, the home had been inspected on a number of previous occasions and received 'poor' inspection reports, which included details about complaints concerning the mistreatment of residents. Yet it seemed that the newspaper's investigations were required to bring things to a head and for CSCI now to issue statutory notices.

Incontinence pads not changed, flies, carers who could not communicate with residents etc. The reporter wrote about residents waiting for hours before incontinence pad were changed; flies were crawling inside one pad when it was removed; manual handling techniques employed persistently in a way that could harm residents; care assistants unable to communicate with residents because of poor English; residents pulled across beds instead of slide sheets being used; stone cold food; inadequate numbers of staff to help people eat and drink; poor staff hygiene with carers not washing their hands, changing gloves or aprons between handling each resident; unavailability of clean clothes; shortages of sheets and towels; broken washing machine.

The manager had called a meeting about turning the care home into a five-star hotel; one of the staff had commented to the reporter that while management talked of posh Italian wallpaper and flat screen televisions, there were no 'bloody sheets' (Newell 2007).

In the following case, an inspection reported that all was well – shortly before suspicions arose about murder:

Favourable inspection just prior to care home owners being arrested on suspicion of murder. In June 2006, a care home was inspected and judged to provide a comfortable and homely atmosphere, with staff who were kind and caring. The following New Year's day, a 97-year-old resident died, and the husband and wife managers were arrested shortly afterwards, before being released on bail.

The CSCI investigated in relation to failure to notify the authorities and to complete paperwork relating to seven deaths over a two-year period. The CSCI subsequently ordered the closure of the home in March 2007. By the summer of 2007, the police had exhumed the bodies of three residents whose deaths were suspicious. In December, the husband and wife were arrested on suspicion of murdering five residents (de Bruxelles 2007).

Sometimes regulatory bodies admit failures. One local authority (at the time responsible for inspection of care homes) paid £1 million in compensation to adults with learning disabilities. In an out of court settlement, it conceded that it had failed properly to inspect the home and to prevent the abuse (*Solicitors' Journal* 2003). Likewise, another local authority admitted some years ago that it should have checked a care home where three mentally ill people were found living in squalor, and where two staff were found guilty of wilful neglect under s.127 of the Mental Health Act 1983 (*Community Care* 1998). And CSCI seemed, just, to admit to the BBC that it did not get things quite right in the following circumstances:

Resident dying of bed sores in care home. A care home in Cheshire had given rise to persistent concerns. Eventually, one of the residents there became malnourished and dehydrated and his pressure sores, which had started on his foot, became worse. He was taken to hospital where his foot had to be amputated and his body was found to be covered in bed sores. The one on the bottom of his spine was found to be eight inches by eight inches, the worst the doctors had ever seen. He died later that week. Previous to this, the CSCI had conducted a series of inspections; inspectors were worried at the number of deaths, broken bones and the time it took to transfer residents to hospital. Yet, while this particular resident was still at this home, five weeks before his death, CSCI's latest report referred to 'a noticeable improvement in the plans of care devised for residents. These addressed health care and personal care needs in a more meaningful and individual manner.' In addition, to all this, a carer at the home was subsequently convicted of ill treating a resident with dementia by twisting a plastic bag over his head, making as if to suffocate him (File on Four 2007).

Of course, the regulator may get it wrong the other way, exaggerating problems and the risk to residents and wrongly putting a care home out of business. However, in just such a case, the Court of Appeal held that, despite the negligence involved, the regulator should not be liable – because it was not in the public interest that it should owe such a duty of care to the care provider (*Jain v Trent SHA*). On the other hand, when the regulator failed to vary its rigid inspection routines in relation to a home known to have significant problems, the ombudsman found maladministration. The failure had contributed to a service user discharging himself and being found dead shortly afterward of a heroin overdose (*North Somerset Council* 1999).

The Care Standards Tribunal, too, found fault with CSCI, when the latter's over-reaction to adult protection concerns included inaccuracies of fact and an apparently excessive determination to try to close down a care home. The consequence was that three local authorities, effectively at CSCI's bidding, abruptly removed all their residents from the home, against the will of some, and in any event without adequate consultation with those residents or their relatives. The Tribunal noted that it was not permissible to try to remove people against their will, certainly not without the local authorities having determined for themselves a significant level of risk. In this case they had not done so. The Tribunal also took the view that it had probably not been in the best interests of the residents to have been removed (*Onyerindu v Commission for Social Care Inspection*).

A second issue which increasingly calls into question the future role of regulation is the current policy of self-directed care (see 3.3.5). The push to implement community care direct payments and individual budgets opens the way for people to use allocated sums of money much more flexibly than is possible when local authorities directly provide (regulated) services. However, that flexibility includes the freedom to purchase unregulated care from, for example, personal assistants.

5.4.2 CARE STANDARDS: REGULATIONS

Under the Care Standards Act 2000, various regulations have been passed to spell out registration requirements for the different types of provider. Both directly and indirectly, they bear on the protection and safeguarding of adults. These include regulations passed in respect of care homes and of domiciliary care services. Regulations relating to adult placements were reissued in August 2004, so that the regulatory effect and burden would fall on adult placement schemes, rather than individual providers; for example, families (SI 2004/2070). In due course, these regulations will be replaced by new ones made under the Health and Social Care Act 2008.

The regulations made under the 2000 Act for care homes (SI 2001/3965, rr.13, 16) and domiciliary care agencies (SI 2002/3214, r.14) make explicit reference to the prevention of harm or abuse and to the handling of money. The care homes regulations also state that the care home (registered person) must inform the CSCI of the death of any service users, of any serious injury, of any serious illness at a care home not providing nursing, any event in the care home adversely affecting the well-being or safety of any service users, any theft, burglary or accident in the care home, any allegation of misconduct (SI 2001/3965, r.37). Indeed a failure to inform the regulatory body of such an adverse event – disappearance of £900 belonging to a resident and the serious fall of a resident – contributed to a decision to cancel the registration of a care home provider. The decision of CSCI was upheld both by the Care Standards Tribunal and the High Court

(*Bamgbala v CSCI*). More generally, these regulations spell out a number of requirements relating to the fitness of the manager and to standards, staffing and facilities.

A number of cases concerning the application of the regulations have come before the courts – or before the Care Standards Tribunal – when a care home has contested a decision of the Commission for Social Care Inspection. Some are directly relevant to safeguarding adults. For example, the following legal case – involving past physical abuse of care home residents – confirmed that the burden lies on the manager of a care home in showing his or her fitness to manage, not on the registration authority in showing unfitness:

Fitness to manage: physical abuse of residents. A Care Standards Tribunal (CST) had in effect given the appellant the benefit of the doubt concerning his background. The fitness question concerned past misconduct involving physical abuse of residents, in particular hitting a resident on the penis with a pen to stop him masturbating, wheeling a resident into the dining room with a waste-paper bin on her head, forcibly administering medication to a resident, and kicking a resident on her buttocks. The CST had overturned (what was then) the National Care Standards Commission's decision that he was not fit to be registered. However, in turn the High Court overturned the CST's decision, on the grounds that it had not explicitly addressed the question of whether he was fit in terms of integrity and good character. The Court of Appeal upheld the decision, confirming that the burden lay on the applicant to show his or her fitness, rather than on the registration authority to show unfitness (*Jones v National Care Standards Commission*).

In a Care Standards Tribunal case, the Tribunal confirmed that an enrolled nurse – an owner and manager of a care home – was unfit on the basis of death by scalding, smell, and separating people from their spectacles in an undignified manner:

Unfitness of manager: death of resident by scalding. Absence of thermostatic mixing valves contributed to the death of a resident, at 3.30 am, in a bath full of scalding water. There had been no adequate risk assessment. Dangerously hot radiators also posed a risk to residents, whilst there were badly stained and odorous parts of the home. As the Tribunal pointed out, 'when dealing with elderly people who often suffer from incontinence, odour control is a priority to maintain dignity.' Another criticism was that residents had been taken to the bathroom and then led back minus their spectacles. Three sets were lined up in the bathroom; the CSCI inspector noted that this went to the heart of the dignity of residents (*Hillier v CSCI*).

When a manager of a care home had misled the regulatory body about past convictions received over a period of 20 years – almost exclusively for dishonesty – the Tribunal was unsympathetic. Even though the last conviction was almost 20 years old, and he appeared to have made changes in his life, he could not be described as a man of integrity and good character. He was not fit to be registered as manager of a care home (*Simpson v NCSC*). Yet the regulatory body should not jump to conclusions, even when the alleged misconduct involved threatening a patient:

Regulatory body jumping to conclusions about unfitness of care home manager for alleged threatening of a service user. When deciding that it would not register a person as manager of a care home, it relied on the fact that he had been dismissed for gross misconduct for threatening a patient. Subsequently an unfair dismissal case was settled in his favour. In his application to be registered he said he had 'won' the case. The National Care Standards Commission, the then regulator, had taken the view (a) that he would not have been dismissed for gross misconduct unless there was substance to the allegation; and (b) that he had misled the Commission by claiming victory in the case. The Tribunal disagreed with this approach. First, it did not share the Commission's confidence in all employers. Second, the word 'won' might have been unfortunate but not to the extent of undermining his integrity. The appeal against the Commission succeeded (*Wilkinson v National Care Standards Commission*).

In respect of domiciliary care, the need for care providers to have effective procedures and safeguards concerning money was highlighted in a local ombudsman investigation:

Lack of financial monitoring. The local authority arranged for a private care provider to provide care for an elderly man who had suffered a series of strokes. The man's son complained about the standard of care; the council accepted this. However, the ombudsman also found maladministration due to a 'complete breakdown' in financial monitoring; withdrawals of the man's money from the social services department office safe were not always recorded and receipts were frequently unclear. The family, when visiting, noticed that there was little evidence in the house of the shopping that the carer supposedly did; there were also items costed that were never apparent in the flat (*Sheffield CC 2001*).

The Care Standards Act 2000 has not applied to the NHS in terms of imposing registration and inspection conditions. However, clearly similar standards are required, as the following example concerning loss of jewellery illustrates:

Loss of jewellery in hospital. A resident of a care home was admitted to hospital, but the admission document was not fully completed; the section on patient's valuables was left blank. When she was admitted to a particular ward later that day, only her spectacles were recorded as valuables. She lapsed into a coma and died a month later; during this time her close friend realised that she was not wearing her wedding and engagement rings. The evidence was compelling that she had been wearing these on admission to hospital; the health service ombudsman found that the lack of record-keeping on admission had contributed to the failure to protect the woman's valuables (*Preston Acute Hospitals NHS Trust 2001*).

5.4.2.1 National minimum standards

In addition to the regulations, the Department of Health has published national minimum standards, which the CSCI must take account of when deciding whether a care provider is complying with the Care Standards Act 2000 and relevant regulations.

For instance, under the standards for people in care homes, standard 18 relates to abuse, from which the registered person must protect residents. Various aspects are referred to, including policy and practice concerning residents' money and financial affairs (DH 2003).

Under the standards for domiciliary care agencies, there is likewise a standard (14) on abuse and a separate one (13) on the safe handling of service users' money and property. This includes reference to matters such as bills, shopping, pension collection, acceptance of gifts, making use of the service user's telephone, borrowing money etc. (DH 2003a).

5.5 PROFESSIONAL BODIES

Another route to the protection of vulnerable adults lies in professional regulatory bodies, such as the General Medical Council, the Nursing and Midwifery Council, the Health Professions Council, and the General Social Care Council. These councils have the power, for example, to suspend or strike off professionals from the relevant register.

5.5.1 GENERAL SOCIAL CARE COUNCIL

The General Social Care Council (GSCC) is responsible for maintaining a register of qualified social workers, as well as social care workers more generally (Care Standards Act 2000, Part 4). Currently, however, it covers only the former. Applicants must provide evidence as to their good character (including fitness to practise), good conduct, physical and mental fitness, competence, relevant qualifications and entitlement to work (i.e. is a national of a European Economic Area state or is not, but is entitled to work under any other enforceable Community right).

It is an offence for a social worker to use the title of 'social worker' if he or she is not on the register. The Council may remove or suspend people from the register on grounds of misconduct (Care Standards Act 2000, Part 4; the *General Social Care Council (Registration) Rules 2003*, and the *General Social Care Council (Conduct) Rules 2003*, published by the General Social Care Council).

A number of professional conduct hearings have in effect been about safeguarding and protecting vulnerable adults. For instance, a social worker who had committed a tax offence outside work had a two-year warning placed on the registration entry by the Council (*Community Care* 2007a). Another social worker who perpetrated benefit fraud totalling £29,000 was struck off (*Community Care* 2007b), as was a social worker convicted of possessing indecent photographs of children and maintaining a grossly offensive website (*Community Care* 2007c). And a social worker was admonished for failing to put the keys and money of a service user into the council's safe. Instead she retained the keys in her handbag and put a container of coins in a filing cabinet. By failing to secure the items and record appropriately, the person's property was put at unnecessary risk, and the social worker had breached fundamental principles of social work practice. The admonishment would remain on her entry on the register for six months (GSCS 2007).

In 2008, it was reported that 40 per cent of conduct hearings involved social workers forming unsuitable relationships with service users or their relatives (*Community Care* 2008). The Council imposed an interim suspension order on a social worker who engaged in sexual intercourse with a service user suffering from depression. His appeal to the Care Standards Tribunal against the order failed (*Bradford v General Social Care Council*). Another social worker began a personal relationship with a particularly vulnerable service user and eventually married her. His work with her gave him privileged contact with her and a detailed knowledge of her personal circumstances and history.

This had created a significant imbalance of power between them. He was removed from the register (GSCC 2008).

A care manager was also barred from practice, having formed a personal relationship with an extremely vulnerable woman and abused his position of power and trust. He was judged to lack insight into the inappropriateness of his conduct; he lacked remorse and had not apologised (GSCC 2008a). In the following case, the penalty imposed for an inappropriate relationship was suspension rather than removal from the register:

Social worker's relationship with client. A woman was suspended for two years from working as a social worker, having formed an inappropriate relationship with a man for whom she was the allocated social worker. She took advantage of a professional relationship, continued to act as the person's social worker, wrote a pre-sentencing report for the Crown Court despite the obvious conflict of interest, and visited him in prison in a non-professional capacity without telling her employer. The committee noted that the relationship had been consensual and accepted evidence that she was a good, or even excellent, practitioner. The issue was more one of protecting the reputation of the profession than the safety of the public. Suspension reflected the gravity of the misconduct, whilst taking account of mitigating factors. The social worker had shown insight into the danger of crossing professional boundaries, but had maintained it was possible to separate personal and professional life. This meant her insight was insufficient (GSCC 2008b).

In one of the cases concerning a sexual relationship with a woman with mental health problems (manic depression), the social worker appealed successfully to the Care Standards Tribunal against the General Social Care Council's refusal to register him as a social worker:

Social worker of good character despite inappropriate relationship. He was not referred to the POVA list at the time and the police took the view that relationship was consensual. He had worked in a health service environment and, on the basis of guidelines from the Council for Healthcare Regulatory Excellence guidelines, he had not viewed the woman as a patient/client because she was not in the direct care of him or his employer. However, she was a user of local mental health services. He recognised that as a social worker, different considerations applied – and that he had followed the wrong guidelines. The Tribunal took into account that he had received no social work supervision. Unlike the General Social Care Council, the Tribunal found him to be of good character, albeit that he had foolishly crossed boundaries and had an inappropriate relationship. He had an exemplary work record. He showed remorse and willingness to attend relevant training. The Tribunal recommended registration as a social worker with certain conditions attached (*DSH v GSCC*).

5.5.2 OTHER PROFESSIONAL BODIES

Other professional bodies deal with cases of abuse in disciplinary hearings, which may result in the professional being suspended, struck off, subject to conditions or receiving a caution. These include the General Medical Council, Health Professions Council, and Nursing and Midwifery Council (NMC). The latter, for instance, has reported that abuse of older people accounts for an increasing number of its misconduct hearings (*Nursing Times* 2005). A number of other examples heard by the Professional Conduct Committee of the NMC are as follows.

5.5.2.1 Striking off from register of nurses

A nurse put a patient's glass eye in a ward sister's drink, painted a smiley face on a patient's fist-sized hernia, and falsified patient records with a magic pen. She was struck off by the NMC (Ward 2006). Following conviction in the Crown Court on six counts of theft, five of false accounting and 13 of obtaining property by deception, a nurse was sentenced to 18 months in prison. The Council struck her off from the register, given the gross abuse of trust of the vulnerable people from whom she had dishonestly obtained property (NMC 2008: 712h2138E).

Another nurse, working in a nursing home, was struck off following a number of allegations including leaving a patient with learning disabilities lying in his own vomit, dragging a patient by his collar, slamming a door in his face, stamping on his foot and calling him a thieving bastard (*South Manchester Reporter* 2004). Sometimes, obviously abusive conduct is part of systematic failings in care which, in terms of adult protection, will put vulnerable people at risk of harm:

Multiple failings in care. The registered manager of a care home was struck off on a whole host of grounds. These included the finding of a resident sitting in a darkened room with a mattress on the floor and faecal matter on the bedding, and a number of residents with their mattress on the floor. However, wider failings, too many to list, included missing toilet seats, showers not working, dirty fridges, malodorous rooms, incontinence pads in waste bins in toilets, call bells missing, fluid intake charts not completed, pressure sore wound assessment and management not recorded etc. (NMC 2008: 75U6681E).

Striking off from the register followed findings that a nurse, amongst other things, had said to a patient, 'if you were a dog you would have been put down, instead I'll smack your arse' (NMC 2008: 83A0008E). Likewise, a nurse was struck off for, amongst other things, rough handling of patients, which represented a failure to treat the patients with dignity and respect (NMC 2008: 83Y0105W). Striking off befell a nurse in respect of various failures including assaulting a resident (for which she had been convicted in court), rough handling of a resident, slapping the resident's hand, and telling the resident that he was a 'naughty boy' (NMC 2008: 02H12440).

A nurse working with people with learning disabilities forced a resident out of a chair, inappropriately requested he remove his crockery without assistance (this was not part of his routine, it put him at physical risk, added to his mental and emotional distress, and was not part of his formal or informal care plan), saw him fall but failed to provide or allow appropriate assistance to be given, and failed to report the fall. In respect of the latter, he was in a state of shock and disarray; the nurse went on hoovering around him. The nurse was struck off (NMC 2007: 79K0365E). Striking off followed for a nurse who had spoken inappropriately to a patient by telling him to shut up, and had roughly handled him by pinning his arm to the bed and putting his hand around his neck – this was 'wholly unnecessary physical restraint' (NMC 2007: 87H01616E).

A nurse was struck off for developing an inappropriate relationship with a patient, who was vulnerable and required care at a time of major crisis in her life; this represented a total abuse of his professional status (NMC 2007: 89H0066H).

Without engagement or explanation by the nurse, or mitigation put forward, a nurse was struck off having spoken to a patient inappropriately, and slapped the patient on the arm (NMC 2007: 72A0213S). And a nurse was struck off for, amongst other things, slapping a resident, verbal abuse to residents ('get your fucking legs off the lift', 'you can't fucking hear anyway', 'talk to the hand because the face ain't listening'), and rough handling of a resident after failing to warn the resident that she was about to move her (NMC 2007: 8711737E).

5.5.2.2 Caution on register of nurses

Sometimes a caution will be placed against a nurse's entry in the register held by the Nursing and Midwifery Council. For instance, a nurse in a care home was cautioned, having taken hold of a resident's hand, put his arm up his back, marched him to his room and pushed him on to the bed. The Council was concerned at this treatment of a vulnerable elderly resident but took into account that it was not done maliciously, that it was a one-off incident, and that there were no other concerns about the nurse's practice (NMC 2007: L71Y1288E).

A nurse who witnessed a care assistant roughly handling a resident failed to stop it, failed to report it, and advised another colleague not to report it. A caution was placed against the nurse's entry in the register. She had a good history, it was an isolated incident, she admitted and regretted it, and had provided good testimonials (NMC 2007: 01G2069O). A caution followed also when a nurse slapped a patient's leg, pulled and yanked it. The nurse nearly suffered removal from the register, because physical abuse of an elderly and demented patient was a very serious matter. But she had a 36-year unblemished work record, it was an isolated incident, she had impressive references and testimonials. A caution was the proportionate response (NMC 2007: 68IO223N).

CHAPTER 6

Mental capacity

KEY POINTS

Almost by definition, a person who is deemed to lack capacity to make significant decisions about aspects of their life becomes potentially a vulnerable adult – for obvious reasons. For example, they may be unable to decide what medical treatment to have, where to live, with whom to have contact, how to manage their money and property, when to wash, what to eat, what to wear, what to do each day – and so on.

The Mental Capacity Act 2005 takes a two-fold approach. On the one hand it seeks to empower people, on the other to protect them. It empowers people by enshrining the principles that incapacity should not be assumed, that people should be assisted to make decisions for themselves, that unwise decisions do not necessarily mean incapacity and that even with incapacity, people should still be involved in decisions as far as possible. All this protects people from having fundamental rights to make decisions being taken inappropriately away from them. In another way, protection comes in the form of actions and decisions taken by other people in the person's best interests, when he or she clearly lacks the capacity to take a particular decision.

This dual function of the Act can sometimes result in a tension when it comes to protecting and safeguarding vulnerable adults, particularly when an adult with capacity to make certain decisions is making those decisions in such a way as to render himself or herself vulnerable to significant harm.

It is beyond the scope of this book to set out the Mental Capacity Act 2005 in detail. Instead it highlights key points and provides practical examples of how the Act is particularly relevant to adult protection and safeguarding adults. However, one helpful way of understanding the 'substituted decision-making' set out by the Act, in relation to the care and treatment of a person lacking capacity, is to consider it in terms of a hierarchy. First, and outweighing the others when it comes to a refusal of medical treatment, are advance decisions (sometimes known as living wills). Second, come the powers exercised by the donee of a lasting power of attorney (given to the donee when the donor still had capacity). Third, the Court of Protection may make orders in relation to care and treatment. Fourth, the Court may appoint a deputy to make ongoing decisions. Lastly, s.5 of the 2005 Act provides protection for those providing care or treatment less formally – but this does not extend to overriding an advance decision, or a decision made by a person with lasting power of attorney or by a deputy (Bowen 2007, p.172).

6.1 BACKGROUND AND SUMMARY OF MENTAL CAPACITY ACT 2005
6.1.1 BACKGROUND

Most of the Mental Capacity Act 2005 came into force in October 2007. Prior to the passing of this Act, the position as regards decision-making capacity was as follows.

As far as finance-type matters were concerned, a person as donor could make an enduring power of attorney, authorising the attorney (typically a family member) to take finance, business and property decisions on behalf of the donor, in case of the donor losing capacity to manage such affairs. This was under the Enduring Powers of Attorney Act 1985. In the absence of such a power of attorney, the Court of Protection could intervene in such matters under the Mental Health Act 1983, making orders or appointing a receiver for ongoing management of a person's affairs. If the only finance to be dealt with was in the form of social security benefits, then an appointee could be appointed by the Benefits Agency. The law remains the same in this latter respect.

If health or welfare decisions had to be made, the law did not allow anybody directly to consent or make decisions on behalf of the person lacking capacity. However, it did allow 'necessity' and 'best interests' interventions, which could range from deciding about what somebody should eat, what clothes they should wear and when they should get washed – to major medical interventions or decisions about where somebody should live. Where significant issues were in question, resort had to be made to the Family Division of the High Court in case of uncertainty, of dispute or of some very serious interventions. The court would exercise its 'inherent jurisdiction' by making a declaration or order as to what should happen. Sometimes the court was called on to decide whether a person himself or herself had capacity to decide the issue in question. Through this legal case law, the court developed a set of rules about decision-making capacity. Many of these rules have found their way into the Mental Capacity Act 2005, and so past case law remains highly relevant to the new Act.

6.1.2 SUMMARY OF MENTAL CAPACITY ACT

In summary, the 2007 Act sets out a number of key principles that run throughout the Act and which should govern decisions and interventions in relation to people lacking capacity. These include the principle that capacity should be assumed unless otherwise shown, and that unwise decisions do not necessarily mean that a person lacks capacity. The Act defines lack of capacity, and states that interventions have to be in people's 'best interests', and should be the least restrictive consonant with those best interests.

It provides legal protection for people who provide care and treatment for a person lacking capacity, so long as they have done so reasonably and in good faith. At the same time the Act prohibits excessive restraint of a person. It contains separate rules about going beyond restraint and instead depriving a person, lacking capacity, of his or her liberty.

A major change introduced by the Act is to replace enduring powers of attorney with lasting powers of attorney. This means that a donor, with capacity, can create such a power authorising the attorney to take not only financial decisions but also health and welfare decisions for the donor, when the latter loses capacity to take those decisions. Parallel with this change in the law, the Act creates a new Court of Protection which can intervene not only in financial, but also in health and welfare, matters. This contrasts with the previous position, in which the Court of Protection (under the Mental Health Act 1983) was limited to interventions relating to finance, business and property only.

The Act clarifies the law about advance decisions or 'living wills' as they are sometimes called. They involve a person with capacity, stipulating in advance their refusal of specified medical treatment, in case at the relevant time he or she lacks the capacity to do so directly.

A statutory independent mental capacity advocacy (IMCA) service is created. This means that in certain circumstances related to the provision of care home and hospital accommodation, or of serious medical treatment, local authorities and NHS bodies have an obligation to instruct an advocate before a decision is made. There is also a power to instruct such an advocate where an adult protection issue has arisen.

The Act also creates a new offence of wilful neglect or ill-treatment of a person lacking capacity.

6.2 CORE PRINCIPLES

Certain core principles are applied throughout the Act. These will directly impact on how decisions about welfare, health and finance are made in relation to a person who lacks, or may lack, capacity. The application of these principles will sometimes be fundamental as to whether or how safeguarding and protective interventions are made under the Mental Capacity Act.

6.2.1 ASSUMPTION OF CAPACITY

First, a person is assumed to have capacity to take a decision unless it is established otherwise (Mental Capacity Act 2005, s.1). The effect of this principle is that whoever is seeking to show lack of capacity has to work all the harder in doing so. In case of doubt, one would therefore lean to capacity rather than incapacity.

The principle in common law has also been that, once capacity has been shown to have been lost, there is a presumption of continuance of that loss. However, the Court of Appeal rejected this approach in the case, for example, of head injury, from which there might be recovery. One reason for taking this approach is because of the drastic consequences of being judged to lack capacity: a person is deprived of important civil rights (*Masterman-Lister v Brutton*). In another case, in which a man with learning disabilities clearly lacked the capacity to consent to marriage, the court noted that the possibility of future improvement in his capacity had to be borne in mind (*X City Council v MB*).

6.2.2 ALL PRACTICABLE STEPS TO HELP PERSON TAKE DECISION

Second, all practicable steps should be taken to help a person take the decision (s.1). So this second principle, too, is of the empowering type.

Such practicable steps could be various. The Code of Practice refers to the importance of relevant information, avoidance of excessive detail, outlining risks and benefits, explanation of the effects of the decision, balanced presentation and consideration of obtaining specialist advice. In terms of communication, 'all possible and appropriate means of communication should be tried'. This may include finding out the best means of communication, using simple language, pictures, objects, illustrations, picture boards, hearing interpreter, mechanical or electronic communication aids, interpreting behaviour which is indicative of feelings, speaking at the right volume and speed with appropriate sentence structure and vocabulary, breaking down information into smaller bits, allowing the person time to understand each bit of information, repeating information, getting help from people the person trusts, awareness of cultural, ethical or religious factors, using a professional language interpreter, using an advocate.

Location might be decisive, for instance, a quiet one free of background noise or other distractions, and one where privacy and dignity is respected; maybe taking a person to the relevant location (such as a hospital) may assist the person to understand what is in issue and to make the decision. Likewise timing may be decisive; a person may be more alert in the morning, less alert immediately after taking drowsiness-inducing medication, become tired or confused if asked to decide too much in one go. Simply delaying the decision may help, so that more steps can be taken to assist the person take the decision. Support from other people may be of benefit; the presence of a relative or a friend may (or may not be) reassuring and reduce anxiety (Lord Chancellor 2007, paras 3.9–3.15).

6.2.3 UNWISE DECISION DOES NOT NECESSARILY INDICATE LACK OF CAPACITY

Third, the fact that a person with a disorder or disability of mind takes what is considered to be an unwise decision does not necessarily mean that he or she lacks capacity (s.1).

This is a key principle, which will frequently arise when local authorities and others consider how to safeguard and protect vulnerable adults. First it recognises the fact that everybody makes unwise decisions. Second, however, it does mean that protecting a vulnerable adult might not be possible (at least under the 2005 Act), even if he or she is at risk of harm or exploitation. As the courts put it: 'It is not the task of the courts to prevent those who have the mental capacity to make rational decisions from making decisions which others may regard as rash or irresponsible.' After all, many people 'make rash and irresponsible decisions, but are of full capacity' (*Masterman-Lister v Brutton*).

The question is not whether the person is making a rational decision but whether he or she has the capacity to make a rational decision (*Lindsay v Wood*). Nonetheless, this does not mean that vulnerability to exploitation is not relevant to the question of capacity. The courts have stated that outcomes can often 'cast a flood of light on capacity', and are likely to be important, though not conclusive, indicators (*Masterman-Lister v Brutton*).

In the following case, the local authority probably viewed such legal issues as an impediment in their attempt to protect a person whom they clearly regarded as highly vulnerable. It wanted to stop her marrying; the court pointed out that the issue was not to do with the wisdom of the marriage:

Marriage between a woman with learning disabilities and a convicted sex offender. A 23-year-old woman person with learning disabilities wished to marry a 37-year-old man with a substantial history of sexually violent crimes; the court was called on to consider whether or not she had capacity to marry. It made the following point: 'The question of whether E has capacity to marry is quite distinct from the question of whether E is wise to marry; either wise to marry at all, or wise to marry X rather than Y, or wise to marry S. In relation to her marriage the only question for the court is whether E has capacity to marry. The court has no jurisdiction to consider whether it is in E's best interests to marry or to marry S. It is not concerned with the wisdom of her marriage in general or her marriage to S in particular' (*Sheffield CC v E*).

The consequence is also that up to a point at least, the risk of – or vulnerability to – making a mistake or being exploited will not in itself indicate a lack of capacity. For instance, in the case immediately below, the judge stated that on the evidence the person was not 'sufficiently vulnerable to the risk of unwise decisions, bad advice or self-interested and manipulative persons to justify the inroads upon his personal freedoms' – were he now to be declared incapable of managing his property and affairs (*Masterman-Lister v Brutton*: High Court stage). Yet this was not to say he was not still vulnerable in some degree to exploitation:

Dysexecutive syndrome and distinction between lack of capacity and vulnerability: brain injury. A challenge was made as to whether or not a person who had suffered a head injury – when a milk float hit his motor cycle – had been capable of managing his property and affairs (for the purpose of Part 7 of the Mental Health Act 1983) when he had previously made a settlement in respect of his personal injury. The court's decision now would affect the validity of that personal injury settlement.

The dysexecutive syndrome that the man suffered from as a consequence of the accident resulted in changes such as obsessionality, immaturity, rigidity of thinking, eccentricity and emotional outbursts. This impaired his ability to organise his life and to plan. However, his pre-accident level of intelligence was largely unchanged. This meant that his relationships with other people and with the problems of life did not always quite 'mesh'. There were conflicting medical views as to his capacity to conduct litigation.

The court made a distinction between wisdom in transactions and understanding; the former was not relevant to capacity. He had perhaps been overly generous to girlfriends, to the Vegan Society and to anti-hunt protestors, caused trouble to some builders, broken a cooker valve and lost the replacement, and overstocked his fridge. But the judge concluded that the evidence of the last 20 years (since the accident) showed that the man was by and large perfectly capable of looking after himself. Indeed there was various evidence of highly responsible actions, such as advising friends on how to maximise social security benefits or avoid sexual harassment at work, alerting the police to the possible exposure of three young girls to sexual abuse at a naturist swimming pool, and writing impressive letters of advice to his nephew who was away at boarding school.

When greater problems arose, he recognised the need to seek assistance. The mental disorders identified in the medical reports were capable of leading to a finding of incapacity, if present to a sufficiently severe degree – but they were not of that degree in this case.

The Court of Appeal agreed, pointing out that the judge rightly distinguished between capacity and outcomes, and between everyday matters and the management of more serious problems. In reaching his decision the judge had considered all the relevant evidence, both medical and lay. He had also considered the man's diaries and letters. Matters such as losing a pressure cooker valve and overstocking the freezer may have been symptomatic of memory loss, but they were mishaps that could occur to those without the claimant's disabilities (*Masterman-Lister v Brutton*).

The following case proceeded on similar lines:

Ability to manage financial affairs: brain injury. The claimant suffered brain damage in 1976 through leaning out of a train window and hitting his head on a railway bridge. At the time, he was awarded damages of £77,000 plus interest; his father and his solicitor undertook to the court to hold the damages on trust for him. At the time it was undecided whether he had 'capacity' to manage his affairs and whether or not he was a 'patient' for the purpose of Court of Protection intervention.

Twenty-six years later, he was now married, with a young son, and wished to emigrate from England to India with his family. He sought access to the trust assets to buy a property and live on the remainder. The medical evidence revealed that he suffered a degree of mental disorder as defined in the Mental Health Act 1983. He had lasting brain damage that had reduced his intellectual capacity.

However, he recognised his own limitations and that he would need to seek advice from his solicitor in handling so large a sum of money (now £192,000). On the evidence, there was therefore 'no question' of him being a patient under the Mental Health Act 1983 such as to trigger Court of Protection intervention (*Tait v Wedgwood*).

The Financial Ombudsman has had to deal with unwise financial transactions. In the first case, the unwise transaction was associated with lack of capacity to enter into it. The second case, however, turned out differently, the man with learning disabilities and autism being held to have had capacity to enter into a loan agreement.

Credit card and loan to person with mental disorder: not liable to repayment. A man with a mental disorder, and observed by several shops in the morning to be unwell and not behaving normally, was given a loan and credit card by the local branch of a 'firm' that same morning, together with a large amount of cash on credit. The shops had refused to do business with him. Later that day, someone took advantage of his confused condition and stole the cash. The father complained to the Financial Ombudsman who judged not only that the man lacked capacity at the time, but that the firm should have known this by paying as much attention to his manner and appearance as the other shops had done. The Ombudsman told the firm that the man was not bound by the loan and credit agreements and was not liable for the debt (FON 2005).

Loan to person with learning disabilities: liable to repayment. When a man with learning disabilities and autism was liable for repayment of a loan from a firm, his mother complained to the Financial Ombudsman that her son had been taken advantage of, because he could not have understood the nature of the loan or his legal obligation. The Ombudsman found otherwise, pointing out that an assumption of lack of capacity should not be made, and that on the evidence the man's learning difficulties did not prevent him from understanding how ordinary banking products worked, and from understanding the particular transaction. Furthermore, he had been employed in a steady job for many years, during which time he had been a customer of the firm and managed his finances without difficulty (FON 2005a).

6.2.4 TENSION BETWEEN EMPOWERING AND PROTECTING PEOPLE
The consequence of the first three core principles, which effectively empower people to the extent that they should not too readily be deemed to lack capacity, means that protection of a vulnerable adult may not be possible under the Act.

With such a lacuna in mind, the Scottish Parliament has taken the view that additional protective legislative measures were required, in order to protect just such vulnerable adults even where they do not lack capacity to decide the issue in question. Thus, it passed the Adult Support and Protection (Scotland) Act 2007, in addition to Scottish incapacity legislation in the form of the Adults with Incapacity (Scotland) Act 2000. The English courts have more recently considered whether they might use their 'inherent jurisdiction' to intervene in cases where a person possesses capacity to take a particular decision, but is nonetheless so vulnerable as to require protection (see below 6.19).

6.2.5 INTERVENTIONS MUST BE IN A PERSON'S BEST INTERESTS
Fourth, acts done or decisions made for people lacking capacity must be in their best interests (s.1). Best interests are defined in section 4 of the Act (see below).

6.2.6 LEAST RESTRICTIVE INTERVENTION

Before an act is done for a person lacking capacity, regard must be had to whether the purpose of the act can be as effectively achieved in a way that is less restrictive of the person's rights and freedom of action (s.1). Intervention in the case of a person lacking capacity is a major intrusion because, by definition, it is effected without the person's consent. Therefore the Act makes clear that it should be no more restrictive than necessary. This is the fifth core principle.

Restrictive interventions may be various in nature and give rise to adult protection concerns. Restraint is one obvious example, and the Act elaborates on the rules about restraint concerning its being a proportionate response to the risk of harm (s.6).

Assuming, for instance, that the patients concerned lacked capacity in respect of their daily care, then the restraint of patients on commodes in the North Lakelands (CHI 2000), the tying of a person into his wheelchair 16 hours a day in Cornwall (HC and CSCI 2006), and the unnecessary use of a restrictive arm splint in Sutton and Merton (HC 2007c) – would all potentially offend against this principle.

However, there are other interventions which could equally fall foul of this principle. For instance, the Healthcare Commission found a universal teapot – ready milked and sugared – being used at mealtimes for people with learning disabilities (HC 2007c). On the assumption, for illustrative purposes, that those around the table lacked capacity to choose, this could be characterised as an over-restrictive way of acting in those persons' best interests.

On the other hand, it is not necessarily about minimising risk at all costs. As the court put it in one case involving a highly vulnerable woman, 'what good is it making someone safer if it merely makes them miserable?' This was in a case where allowing the continuation of a sexual relationship (to which she could consent) with her longstanding boyfriend, would be a clear benefit to her – but also carry a number of risks in relation to her mental health and to other matters on which she lacked the capacity to decide (*Local Authority X v MM*).

6.3 LACK OF CAPACITY

The Act states that 'a person lacks capacity in relation to a matter if at the material time he is unable to make a decision for himself in relation to the matter because of an impairment of, or a disturbance in the functioning of, the mind or brain' (s.2). The test is therefore twofold, concerning (a) whether there is a disturbance in the functioning of mind or brain affecting a particular decision at a particular time; and (b) whether there is an inability to take a decision.

6.3.1 DISTURBANCE IN THE FUNCTIONING OF THE MIND OR BRAIN

The first part of the test relates to an impairment or disturbance in the functioning of the mind or brain. This may be permanent or temporary. The Code of Practice states that examples of impairment or disturbance in the functioning of the mind or brain might include:

- conditions associated with some types of mental illness
- dementia
- significant learning disabilities
- brain damage
- physical or mental conditions causing confusion, drowsiness or loss of consciousness
- delirium
- concussion following head injury
- symptoms of alcohol or drug abuse (Lord Chancellor 2007, para 4.12).

The impairment or disturbance relates to a particular decision at a particular time (s.2). Thus, capacity is not all or nothing; it is both issue and time specific.

The 'issue specific' nature of decision-making may well be relevant in situations potentially linked to safeguarding concerns. For instance, in one case, the court held that a person had the capacity to make an enduring power of attorney in respect of the management of her affairs – if she understood the nature and effect of the power – even if at the same time she lacked the capacity to manage those affairs (*Re K*). Such a situation might at first glance raise safeguarding concerns – but in this case the court held there was nothing untoward. A comparable distinction, but in respect of time, between making a will and signing it, was drawn in the following court case:

Validity of a will. A woman was terminally ill. She made her final will in March, two days before she died. The medical evidence suggested that on that day she lacked the testamentary capacity (i.e. the capacity to make a will). However, the will had been prepared in accordance with instructions she had given in December when she did have undisputed testamentary capacity. In March, she was able to understand that the document she was signing had been in accordance with those instructions. The will was therefore valid (*Clancy v Clancy*).

Nonetheless, in case of marriage, the question is not whether the person has the capacity to marry one person rather than another, but rather whether he or she has the capacity to marry at all. Thus, with safeguarding concerns in mind, the local authority may wish to protect a woman with learning disabilities from marriage with a convicted sex offender; but it would be the wrong approach to make the test of capacity partner specific, as it were (*Sheffield CC v E*). In the following case, the court had to consider instead the question of time and whether there had been a lucid interval, in relation to what otherwise were suspicious circumstances:

Making of will and lucid interval. An 84-year-old woman lived with her sister. On 8 April she was admitted to hospital, suffering from various matters including uncontrolled diabetes and dehydration. Her medical notes indicated she had been increasingly confused a few days before this admission. A care plan was set up by social services and she was discharged home on 26 April. A friend whom she had known for 20 years then suggested that she make a will, making the friend sole executrix and beneficiary. The will was drawn up by the friend's brother-in-law who was a solicitor and to whom the friend communicated the woman's instructions. The draft will was returned to the friend who made arrangements for its execution when the sister was out of the house, on the afternoon of 13 May. That morning, a GP specialising in geriatric medicine had visited and found the woman confused; towards the end of the day, a neighbour had visited and found the same. However, the friend maintained at the time of the will's execution that the woman had not been confused.

The judge stated that the burden of showing testamentary capacity lay on the friend – since she had procured the execution of the will and was beneficiary. He concluded that the woman's confusion was the product of her diabetes and drug regime – and, on all the evidence, it was not credible that she had had a period of lucidity on the day in question in between the earlier and later periods of confusion on that same day (*Richards v Allan*).

Similarly, in the following case, the question of whether apparently rapacious carers could keep their allegedly ill-gotten gains from a vulnerable widow, hinged in part on the latter's capacity at the particular time when she had made a gift of her farmhouse home:

Gift of farmhouse and three cars to carers. An elderly couple live in a converted farmhouse just outside a village. The husband died and the woman received help and care on a private basis from two carers in the form of mother and daughter from the local village.

In 1996, she was introduced by the mother to a solicitor who had been suspended by the Law Society. He prepared a statement which the woman signed, saying she wished to change solicitors. She never met the new solicitor, although did meet the assistant solicitor twice. Otherwise her 'instructions' were conveyed to the solicitor either by the suspended solicitor or by the mother.

In February 1996, the woman met the assistant solicitor and agreed to transfer her home, a farmhouse, worth nearly £300,000, for £50 and on terms that she would occupy it for the rest of her life and that the carers would provide care for her. She subsequently made a number of lifetime gifts to the mother-carer in order to enable the carer's family to buy three cars; in addition, regular withdrawals of £2000 to £3000 a month were made, with the mother-carer as co-signatory, for some months before the woman's death. The amounts were significantly larger than the woman had previously withdrawn.

The woman was found dead, aged 77 years, in April 1997, with her clothing tangled in the stairlift. Great Ormond Street Hospital was one of the residuary beneficiaries of her will. The hospital subsequently brought a case to challenge the validity of the transactions that the woman had entered into, on grounds of her mental incapacity at the time to enter into them, of undue influence or of unconscionable bargain.

The court decided that the transactions should be set aside, since a wealth of evidence showed that she had been suffering from senile dementia at the time as a consequence of Alzheimer's disease.

Evidence had been taken from many witnesses who had seen the woman in life at the relevant time, and two of whom had examined her brain in death. These included three general practitioners, a hospital senior house officer, a pathologist and another hospital consultant who had examined histological slides of the woman's brain, a chiropodist, friends, neighbours, a social worker, a retired Methodist minister, a solicitors' clerk and a borough council emergency contact service supervisor (*Special Trustees for Great Ormond Street Hospital v Rushin*).

Nonetheless, the fact that capacity is issue specific can complicate matters, when a local authority is seeking to safeguard and protect an adult. In the following case, the understandable anxiety of the local authority to protect a highly vulnerable woman led it to an unbalanced decision which the courts objected to.

Woman lacking capacity to make most major decisions, but with capacity to consent to sexual relations. A woman suffered from schizophrenia, characterised by prominent visual, auditory and tactile somatic hallucinations, made worse by stress. She had a moderate learning disability and had poor cognitive functioning. She had significantly impaired or non-existent verbal recall, and was functionally illiterate. She lacked the capacity to litigate, decide where and with whom to live, to determine whom she should have contact with, to manage her own financial arrangements and to marry. But, legally, she had the capacity to consent to sexual relations.

Longstanding personal relationship. For 15 years, she had conducted a personal, sexual relationship with a man who himself had a psychopathic personality disorder and misused alcohol. He led an unstable and nomadic life; he had been violent towards the woman, and was alleged to have used her benefit money to buy alcohol. He had previously encouraged her to follow him which, according to the local authority, led to a deterioration in her mental health. However, equally, it was clear that the relationship was all-important to the woman and that she derived considerable benefit from it in terms of positive emotional feelings. Also, she was more than capable of expressing her wishes and feelings 'as her oral evidence and the manner in which she gave it so vividly demonstrated.'

Care plan effectively terminating personal relationship. The local authority now sought to implement a care plan, which would involve living in a particular supported accommodation unit. The plan included a condition that she could see him once month for two hours, supervised and at a place chosen by the local authority.

Human rights, balance, risk, public authority intervention, issue specificity. First, the court held that this was unacceptable; it was inconsistent with a proper respect for both the woman and man's family and private life under article 8 of the European Convention.

Second, a balance was required which was not about avoiding all risk but about sensible risk appraisal. What good was it 'making someone safer if it merely makes them miserable?'

Third, public authorities should not rush into separating vulnerable adults from their relatives, partners friends or carers – unless the State is going to provide a better quality of care than that which they have been hitherto receiving.

Fourth, the issue specific approach did create some questions about logic. One such was how a person could be said to lack capacity to decide with whom to have contact, but nevertheless have capacity to consent to contact with a potential sexual partner – since 'contact, however fleeting, is, in the nature of things, a necessary perquisite to sexual intercourse.' However, this was resolved by explaining that a person may consent to sexual relations without having the capacity necessary to decide more complex questions about long-term relationships. Thus she might have understood the implications of sexual intercourse with the man, but have been unable to 'appreciate and evaluate all the possible implications and risks for her of staying in contact with him.'

Conclusion. Overall the court had no objections to the local authority's care plan, given the need to protect the woman. However, it needed to modify it in terms of contact with the man. This should be more frequent, at least weekly, for at least four hours and unsupervised – with any risks arising from this being, in the court's view, manageable and acceptable (*Local Authority X v MM*).

Similarly, but involving instead specificity of time, another case centred on the capacity of a woman with a schizo-affective disorder. The matters to be decided included her capacity to marry (she had already had a number of husbands), to decide where to live, to decide about contact with her mother and sisters, and to consent to sexual relations. In respect of the last matter, the evidence had already established that at times she had capacity, at other times not. The capacity was fluctuating. This, in turn, gave rise to a concern within the local authority about how it could protect her from harmful sexual activity at times when she did have capacity (*Ealing LBC v KS*).

6.3.2 INABILITY TO TAKE A DECISION

The second part of the test is what has been labelled the functional approach, as opposed to a status or outcome approach, to capacity (Law Commission 1995, para 3.3). The status approach would be based on a person's medical diagnosis or condition, the outcome approach on the consequences of a person's decision. Both have made way for the functional approach. It will be sometimes be relevant where attempts are being made to protect a vulnerable adult who is making an extremely unwise decision but who will be judged to have the capacity to make it. Section 3 of the 2005 Act states that:

- a person is unable to take a decision if he or she is unable to understand the relevant information, or to retain it, or to use or weigh it as part of the decision-making process, or to communicate it
- however, the person is not to be regarded as unable to take the decisions if he or she can understand an explanation in a way appropriate to his or her circumstances (eg using simple language, visual aids or any other means)
- if the person can retain the information relevant to the decision for a short time only, this does not necessarily mean the person cannot make decisions
- information relevant to a decision includes information about the reasonably foreseeable consequences of deciding one way or another, or of failing to make the decision (s.3).

The following example was a landmark case, illustrating the courts' rejection of the status and outcome, in favour of the functional, approach. The outcome of the person's decision was that he might well die; the status issue was that he was a mental health patient in a special hospital. However, neither fact meant that he necessarily lacked the requisite decision-making capacity, which overrode the doctors' wish to protect him:

Amputation of gangrenous leg. A patient detained in a special secure hospital suffered from chronic paranoid schizophrenia. He was found to be suffering from an ulcerated, gangrenous foot and transferred to a general hospital, where the surgeon recommended amputation. The patient refused but agreed to conservative treatment; and sought an injunction to stop amputation unless he consented in writing. The court held that his schizophrenia did not mean that he could not understand the nature, purpose and effects of the treatment. He understood the relevant information, believed it and arrived at a clear choice. The court granted the injunction (Re C (Adult: refusal of treatment)).

This case illustrates the potential tension between empowering a person to take their own decisions, and the wishes of others to protect the person. Similarly:

Risk of septicaemia. The courts held that a prisoner had the capacity to refuse medical treatment, which accordingly could not be given. It was required because he was at risk of death from septicaemia, after he had cut open his right leg and kept it open by forcing foreign objects into it (Re W (Adult: refusal of treatment)).

However, another court case, also concerning a detained mental health patient, had a different result:

Mental health patient unable to weigh up information on medical treatment. An elderly woman, detained under s.3 of the Mental Health Act 1983, refused to accept medical treatment because she regarded it as part of a plot against her. The hospital sought the court's declaration that it was in the woman's best interests to have a general anaesthetic and CT scan, in order to investigate a suspected renal carcinoma. They gave the hospital permission to carry out the procedures, since the woman was clearly unable to believe the relevant information and weigh up the benefits; she appeared to have no insight into her condition (*Doncaster & Bassetlaw Hospitals NHS Trust v C*).

Similarly, a mentally ill patient who did not believe he was mentally ill was, because of this, unable to use and weigh in the balance the relevant information and thus lacked capacity to consent to treatment for that mental disorder (*R(B) v Dr SS*). The psychopathology suffered by a person about body image and bodily integrity distorted the patient's thinking such that he could not weigh up the arguments for and against drug treatment (*R(B) v Dr Haddock*). And when a woman was refusing treatment for an apparently cancerous ovarian cyst, the court found that her delusional beliefs about her condition meant she lacked the capacity to make a relevant decision (*Trust A v H (An Adult Patient)*). However, in line with this functional approach, the fact that a person has learning disabilities and severe behavioural disturbance will not necessarily mean that she lacks capacity to take a decision about vital medical intervention:

Not treating renal failure. A 25-year-old woman had learning disabilities and severe behavioural problems. Suffering from renal failure, she nevertheless resisted attempts to administer dialysis treatment. The court held that on the evidence she had capacity to make this decision; and that the dialysis could not be provided compulsorily against her will as treatment for mental disorder under the Mental Health Act 1983. Therefore provision of the treatment without her consent would amount to both a criminal assault and a civil wrong (*JT (Adult: refusal of medical treatment)*).

Similarly, age, medication or dementia will not necessarily be legally decisive as to incapacity:

Cocktail of drugs. A 79-year-old woman made a will in hospital five days before she died, leaving her entire estate to her brother. Her son contested the will, mainly on the grounds that the cocktail of drugs his mother was receiving must have meant that she lacked testamentary capacity. However, the court accepted that it was not a foregone conclusion that the drugs would have had this effect; and that evidence from medical witnesses suggested that she had had her wits about her (*Barrett v Kasprzyk*).

But, in line with the issue specific nature of decision-making capacity, delusions in themselves will not necessarily render a will invalid. In an older 19th century case, the testator had been in the county lunatic asylum. He had delusions that he was pursued and molested by a certain man and by devils or evil spirits. The jury nonetheless found that he had the capacity to make his will (*Banks v Goodfellow*).

The courts have sometimes referred to a 'golden rule', to the effect that if a solicitor is drawing up a will for an aged or seriously ill person, it should be witnessed or approved by a medical practitioner (*Kenward v Adams*).

Making of will by a woman with mild to moderate dementia. A woman made a new will in 1994, which changed the terms of her previous will made in 1987; beneficiaries under the 1987 will were displaced by the 1994 will and were aggrieved. At the time she made the second will, the woman suffered at least mild to moderate Alzheimer-type dementia. However, the court found that, on the balance of probabilities, she understood the claims of the former beneficiaries, and was capable of understanding without further explanation, and knew and approved, the contents of the will (*Hoff v Atherton*).

The functional approach to capacity dovetails with the principle in s.1 of the Mental Capacity Act 2005, that unwise decisions do not necessarily indicate a lack of capacity (see above).

6.3.3 EXISTING COMMON LAW TESTS OF CAPACITY

Tests of capacity for some particular transactions have developed their own rules. It is expected that the courts will consider these rules in the light of the general test of capacity in the 2005 Act. However, these particular rules remain applicable and a number are particularly relevant to safeguarding and adult protection issues – such as capacity to make a will, make a gift, consent to medical treatment, get married, and engage in sexual activity.

How the courts will consider these rules in light of the 2005 Act has been subject to some scrutiny. The Code of Practice states that the judges will adopt the 2005 Act test 'if they think it is appropriate' (para 4.33). The courts have stated that this does not mean judges can simply disregard the 2005 Act test but that in cases, other than in the Court of Protection – for example, cases about capacity to make wills, gifts, to litigate, to marry – the court can 'adopt the new definition if it is appropriate – appropriate, that is, having regard to the existing principles of the common law' (*Local Authority X v MM*). In the case of capacity to litigate, however, the relevant civil procedure rules have adopted the definition of capacity contained in the 2005 Act – thus, the latter does directly apply, outside of the Court of Protection, to the question of capacity to litigate (*Saulle v Novet*).

6.3.3.1 Wills: test of capacity

For wills, the test relates to an understanding of the nature of the act, the extent of the property, an appreciation of the claims of others, there being no disorder of mind poisoning the affections, and no 'insane delusions' influencing the disposal.

Test of capacity for wills. 'It is essential…that a testator shall understand the nature of the act and its effects; shall understand the extent of the property of which he is disposing; shall be able to comprehend and appreciate the claims to which he ought to give effect; and, with a view to the latter object, that no disorder of mind shall poison his affections, pervert his sense of right, or prevent the exercise of his natural faculties – that no insane delusion shall influence his will in disposing of his property and bring about a disposal of it which, if the mind had been sound, would not have been made' (*Banks v Goodfellow*).

Thus, when a highly educated pharmaceutical tycoon cut his son out of his will, and instead left ten million pounds to the Conservative Party, the will was held to be invalid on grounds of lack of testamentary capacity. This was because his natural affection for his son had been poisoned or distorted by delusions about an international conspiracy of dark forces ranged against him, in which his family members were implicated (*Kostic v Chaplin*).

6.3.3.2 Gifts: test of capacity

In respect of gifts, the degree of understanding required is relative to the transaction; a gift trivial in nature requires less understanding than, for example, at the other extreme, disposal of the person's only valuable asset. This latter would require as high a degree of understanding as required for a will:

Test of capacity for gifts. 'The degree or extent of understanding required in respect of any instrument is relative to the particular transaction which it is to effect... Thus, at one extreme, if the subject-matter and value of a gift are trivial in relation to the donor's other assets, a low degree of understanding will suffice. But, at the other, if its effect is to dispose of the donor's only asset of value and thus, for practical purposes, to pre-empt the devolution of his estate under the...will...then the degree of understanding required is as high as that required for a will, and the donor must understand the claims of all potential donees and the extent of the property to be disposed of' (*Re Beaney (Deceased)*).

6.3.3.3 Marriage and sexual relations: test of capacity

Marriage and sexual relations may be key issues in respect of protection of a vulnerable adult. In the case of marriage, the test has been characterised thus:

Marriage. 'There are thus, in essence, two aspects to the inquiry whether someone has the capacity to marry. (1) Does he or she understand the nature of the marriage contract? (2) Does he or she understand the duties and responsibilities that normally attach to marriage? The duties and responsibilities that normally attach to marriage are as follows: marriage, whether civil or religious, is a contract, formally entered into. It confers on the parties the status of husband and wife, the essence of the contract being an agreement between a man and a woman to live together, and to love one another as husband and wife, to the exclusion of all others. It creates a relationship of mutual and reciprocal obligations, typically involving the sharing of a common home and a common domestic life and the right to enjoy each other's society, comfort and assistance' (*Sheffield CC v E*).

Setting the test of capacity for marriage too high could operate as an 'unfair, unnecessary and indeed discriminatory bar against the mentally disabled'. Furthermore, the test is whether the person understands the nature of marriage in general; it is not a test that is specific to a particular prospective spouse (*Sheffield CC v E*). The test for sexual relations has been held to be as follows and is a much narrower and simpler test than for marriage:

Sexual relations. 'Does the person have sufficient knowledge and understanding of the nature and character – the sexual nature and character – of the act of sexual intercourse, and of the reasonably foreseeable consequences of sexual intercourse, to have the capacity to choose whether or not to engage in it, the capacity to decide whether to give or withhold consent to sexual intercourse (and, where relevant, to communicate their choice...)?' (*X City Council v MB*).

In the same case, a sexual relationship was held generally to be implicit in any marriage. Thus, a person who lacked the capacity to consent to sexual relations would necessarily lack the capacity to marry; but the converse would not necessarily be true. It was unsuccessfully argued in one case that understanding the 'reasonably foreseeable consequences' of sexual activity should be interpreted broadly in ascertaining capacity; this would have allowed the local authority to protect a vulnerable adult on grounds of incapacity:

Reasonably foreseeable consequences of sexual activity. The local authority wished to protect a woman with schizo-affective disorder. Some of the time she clearly lacked capacity to consent to sexual relations; at other times she had capacity. However, the local authority wished to protect her under mental capacity law at all times, and so argued in effect for a higher threshold for capacity to consent (thus rendering legally incapacitated for more or all of the time).

It maintained that understanding the 'reasonably foreseeable consequences' could include matters such as (a) the risk in deterioration in her mental state should she become pregnant or a romantic relationship collapse, (b) the social and emotional consequences of having sexual intercourse (whether or not it leads to pregnancy), (c) her beliefs about whether she would be allowed to keep any baby born to her, (d) her belief that any man who had sexual intercourse would marry her, and (e) her belief that she would only be happy when married and a mother.

The court stated that the local authority had blurred the line between capacity and best interests and that the law had 'not yet come to the stage, and I hope never will, that it will seek to intervene to prevent acts on the part of the citizen which it does not consider to be that citizen's best interests which are nevertheless lawful acts and which the citizen has the capacity to agree to'. The court was not prepared to consider and judge minutely the realism of the woman's beliefs. The local authority relied on the false beliefs of the woman to demonstrate incapacity; the court pointed out that 'sadly many young women in society who do not suffer from the particular afflictions of [the woman] similarly persuade themselves as to the attitude and intentions of their man towards them' (*Ealing LBC v KS*).

The test of marriage and sexual relations might not set a high threshold, but the courts have adhered to it, even when cultural issues have arisen in relation to other countries which do not set such a threshold. For instance, in one particular case, a man with learning disabilities – who lacked the capacity to understand the nature of marriage – was married, in a Muslim ceremony conducted on the telephone, to a woman in Bangladesh. The intention of the parents was clearly that the matrimonial home was to be in England. Accepting in this particular case that the marriage was indeed contracted in Bangladesh, and that it was valid in that country, the Court of Appeal was emphatic that it would not be valid in England. The court was very clear that the man had to be protected from abuse permitted or encouraged by his parents:

Abusive and injurious marriage. The expert evidence suggested that 'the marriage which his parents have arranged for him is potentially highly injurious. He has not the capacity to understand the introduction of NK into his life and that introduction would be likely to destroy his equilibrium or destabilize his emotional state… Were IC's parents to permit or encourage sexual intercourse… NK would be guilty of the crime of rape under the provisions of the Sexual Offences Act 2003. Physical intimacy which stops short of penetrative sex would constitute the crime of indecent assault… Their engineering of the telephonic marriage is potentially if not actually abusive of IC. It is the duty of the court to protect IC from that potential abuse. The refusal of recognition of the marriage is an essential foundation of that protection' (*KC v City of Westminster Social and Community Services Department*).

Note. A marriage generally is voidable if 'either party to the marriage did not validly consent to it, whether in consequence of duress, mistake, unsoundness of mind or otherwise' (Matrimonial Causes Act 1973, s.12c).

Government guidance points out that there is no specific criminal offence of forcing someone to marry, but nonetheless offences could be committed – such as threatening behaviour, assault, kidnap, abduction, imprisonment or murder, whilst sexual intercourse without consent would be rape. The Crown Prosecution

Service defines domestic violence as 'any criminal offence arising out of physical, sexual, psychological, emotional or financial abuse by one person against a current or former partner in a close relationship, or against a current or former family member' (Home Office 2004, p.3).

The Forced Marriage (Civil Protection) Act 2007 amended the Family Law Act 1996, so as to provide for forced marriage protection orders, with the possibility of attached powers of arrest where use of threat of violence is an issue. A marriage is forced if a person is forced into it without giving free and full consent. Force is defined to include coercion by threats or other psychological means (Family Law Act 1996, ss.63A–63S). These changes are expected to come into force in late 2008.

6.3.3.4 Litigation: test of capacity

The test of capacity to litigate has been characterised as follows:

Capacity to litigate. 'The mental abilities required include the ability to recognise a problem, obtain and receive, understand and retain relevant information, including advice; the ability to weigh the information (including that derived from advice) in the balance in reaching a decision, and the ability to communicate that decision' (*Masterman-Lister v Brutton & Co*, Court of Appeal).

6.3.3.5 Medical treatment, where to live and with whom to have contact: test of capacity

The courts have held that the test of capacity to consent to medical treatment is as follows:

Capacity to consent to medical treatment. 'A person lacks capacity if some impairment or disturbance of mental functioning renders the person unable to make a decision whether to consent to or to refuse treatment. That inability to make a decision will occur when: (a) the patient is unable to comprehend and retain the information which is material to the decision, especially as to the likely consequences of having or not having the treatment in question; (b) the patient is unable to use the information and weigh it in the balance as part of the process of arriving at the decision' (*Re MB: caesarean section*).

The courts have held that this same test applies to the question of capacity relating to where a person should reside and to the decision as to whom he or she should have contact with (*Local Authority X v MM*).

6.3.4 ASCERTAINING INABILITY TO TAKE A DECISION

Ultimately the question of capacity is a legal one not a medical one. Indeed, the Act and Code of Practice envisage that all manner of person may be taking this decision. The onus of taking reasonable steps to make this decision lies on the person – who may be a professional, but who may alternatively be a family member, for example – proposing to act in somebody else's best interests.

The Code of Practice states that the person who assesses capacity will usually be the person directly concerned with the decision that has to be made. This means, for 'most day-to-day' decisions, the immediate carer. For acts of care or treatment, the assessor must, under s.5 of the Act, have a reasonable belief that the person lacks capacity. More complex decisions are likely to need more formal assessments, but the final decision is to be made by the person intending to make the intervention in terms of care or treatment. Of course professionals such as doctors or solicitors will have to assess capacity in relation to proposed medical treatment or legal transactions respectively.

The Code goes on to state that carers, including family carers, do not have to be expert assessors, but must be able to explain the reasonable steps they have taken to ascertain the lack of capacity. Thus reasonable steps will depend on individual circumstances and the urgency of the decision; professionals would normally be expected to undertake a fuller assessment than family members without formal qualifications. However, a professional opinion may be required when a complex or major decision has to be made. This might be from a general practitioner or, for example and depending on the condition or disorder, consultant psychiatrist, psychologist or speech and language therapist (Lord Chancellor 2007, paras 4.38–4.51). In a case involving a woman with fluctuating capacity to consent to sexual relations, the court emphasised that neither it nor the local authority could prevent her having such relations at times when she had capacity. However, it agreed with the local authority that her carers should be given a clear list of indicators of possible loss of capacity to consent to sexual intercourse or other sexual contacts (*Ealing LBC v KS*).

There is thus no rule that the evidence about capacity can only be medical; but in case of doubt, medical doctors may be substantially relied upon, including by the courts. The lack of medical evidence in the following case, which 'bristled with suspicion', told against the son who was the main beneficiary of a new will:

Failure to obtain medical evidence. A woman had a stroke, lacked the ability to communicate, was deteriorating and had suffered a fall. She made a new will under pressure from her family. The will was drafted by one of her sons, the main beneficiary of the new will. He was advised by solicitors that an expert medical opinion be obtained concerning his mother's capacity. He ignored this advice. The judges found the circumstances bristled with suspicion; in which case the son had to prove that his mother had testamentary capacity. He came nowhere near this; the will was set aside because of grave suspicion not only about her knowledge and approval of the contents, but also about her capacity (*Vaughan v Vaughan*).

In coming to the conclusion in one case that a person, arguably vulnerable to financial exploitation, did not lack capacity to manage his financial affairs, the court took particular account of the person's diary entries made over a period of many years. The medical experts giving evidence in the case had not reached a consensus, and so the judge had to look particularly hard at non-medical evidence (*Masterman-Lister v Brutton*).

In Scotland (governed by different capacity legislation but to roughly the same effect), the Mental Welfare Commission reported on a failure to protect a 67-year old woman from a series of serious sexual assaults over a prolonged period of time. She had been in the care of the local authority since she was eight years old. It underlined the limitations of relying only on medical views as to capacity. Contributing to this failure was the judgement that she lacked competence as a witness in any criminal proceedings. This judgement had been made by psychiatrists and psychologists; but the Commission thought that the 'assessment of an individual's capacity to be a reliable witness is far too complex an issue to undertake without the involvement of those who are closely involved in his/her ongoing care'. Furthermore there was no clear evidence that the professionals involved had considered how support might have been given to help the woman act as a witness (MWCS 2008, p.2).

In another case, involving serious financial abuse by carers from a neighbouring village, the evidence to the court was from many quarters:

Evidence about a woman's capacity. In a case concerning exploitation by carers of an elderly woman (now dead, found strangled by her clothing on a stairlift), and whether the transfer of her home to the carers should be set aside, the court heard evidence from a whole range of people including three general practitioners, a hospital senior house officer, a pathologist and another hospital consultant who had examined histological slides of the woman's brain, a chiropodist, friends, neighbours, a social worker, a retired Methodist minister, a solicitors' clerk, and a borough council emergency contact service supervisor (*Special Trustees for Great Ormond Street Hospital v Rushin*).

Likewise the following decision in a case about a disputed will was not based solely on the medical evidence:

Evidence to establish capacity. In a dispute about the validity of a will, the court concluded that the woman who made it (the testatrix) lacked testamentary capacity. This was in the light of the medical evidence that cast doubt on such capacity both before and after the signing of the will, a solicitor's assessment that lucidity was present only in intervals at the relevant time, her wandering off – and her inability to understand that her husband had died and her failure to recognise close members of her family (*Brown v Mott*).

In another, well-publicised case – which involved suggestions of impropriety – an elderly woman had become close friends with a Chinese family which ran a select Chinese restaurant in Witham, Essex. She died, aged 89 years old, leaving property worth £10 million to the family. Her nieces and nephews disputed the will claiming that when it was made their aunt had lacked capacity. Not only did the medical evidence conflict, but none of the doctors, 'however eminent', had actually seen the woman; they were basing their evidence on inferences – which ultimately it was for the court, and not expert witnesses, to make. She had made the will in 1994 and by December 1993 had mild dementia. However, the judge concluded, weighing up various factors including non-medical evidence, that she had capacity at the relevant time (*Blackman v Kim Sing Man*).

6.3.4.1 Refusal of assessment of capacity

Some people might refuse or object to an assessment of mental capacity. The Code of Practice states that nobody 'can be forced to undergo an assessment of capacity. If someone refuses to open the door to their home, it cannot be forced.' It points out that that if there were serious concerns about a person's mental health, it may be possible to obtain a warrant and force entry under s.135 of the Mental Health Act 1983. However, the Code underlines that 'simply refusing an assessment of capacity is in no way sufficient grounds for an assessment' under the 1983 Act (Lord Chancellor 2007, para 4.59).

6.4 BEST INTERESTS

In protecting and safeguarding an adult who lacks capacity to take a particular decision, the person intervening must decide and act in the person's best interests. In summary, the rules about this are:

- **(best interests)** any act done or decision taken, for or on behalf of a person lacking capacity, must be in that person's best interests
- **(avoiding unjustified assumptions)** in determining best interests, the person making the determination must not make it merely on the basis of the person's age or appearance or a condition or aspect of behaviour, which might lead others to make unjustified assumptions about what might be in his best interests
- **(considerations)** best interests involve the decision-maker in:
    - ◦ **(regaining of capacity)** considering whether it is likely that the person will at some time have capacity and, if so, when that is likely to be
    - ◦ **(participation of person)** permitting and encouraging the person to participate as fully as possible in the decision and any decision affecting him
    - ◦ **(not desiring to bring about death)** where life-sustaining treatment is in issue, the decision-maker must not be motivated by a desire to bring about the person's death
    - ◦ **(past and present wishes etc.)** considering, if reasonably ascertainable, the person's past and present wishes and feelings (and, in particular, any relevant written statement made by the person when he or she had capacity), beliefs and values, other factors
    - ◦ **(consulting others)** taking into account, where consultation is appropriate and practicable, the views of anyone named person by the person, any person caring for the person or interested in the person's welfare, any donee of a lasting power of attorney, any Court of Protection appointed deputy.
- **(reasonable belief)** this section of the Act is complied with if the person doing the act or making the decision reasonably believes that the act or decision is in the best of the interests of the person concerned (MCA 2005, s.4).

The person making the decision or intervention ultimately has to decide about the best interests, after applying the above test. There is no indication in the Act as to which, if any, of these factors should take precedence in the reaching of a best interests decision. The Code of Practice states that, for example, that a person's wishes and feelings, values and beliefs 'will not necessarily be the deciding factor in working out their best interests.' Yet the Code notes the legal requirement to pay special attention to any written statements the person may have made before losing capacity (Lord Chancellor 2007, paras 5.38–5.42). The courts have stated in this respect, that the 'further capacity is reduced, the lighter autonomy weighs' (*Re C (Adult: refusal of treatment)*). So, conversely,

The nearer to capacity, the greater weight on wishes in determining best interests. 'The nearer to the borderline the particular adult, even if she falls on the wrong side of the line, the more weight must in principle be attached to her wishes and feelings, because the greater distress, the humiliation and indeed it may even be the anger she is likely to feel the better she is able to appreciate that others are taking on her behalf decisions which vitally affect her – matters, it may be, as here [a personal, sexual relationship], of an intensely private and personal nature' (*Local Authority X v MM*).

Although it is the decision-maker who has to decide about best interests, nonetheless those best interests are not confined to issues within the expertise of that decision-maker. For instance, a decision about a medical intervention would encompass not just medical but also emotional and all other welfare issues. Furthermore, deciding about a person's best interests is not just about identifying a range of acceptable options, but instead is about identifying the 'best', a superlative term. This does not therefore equate with the common law duty of care owed by professionals, which is at least to adopt a reasonable course of action, but not necessarily the best (*SL v SL*).

The courts have also made clear that the best interests in issue are those of the person lacking capacity – even if, for example, the decision in question affects the life or death of a close family member (*Re Y (Adult Patient) (Transplant: Bone Marrow)*).

6.4.1 BEST INTERESTS: DRAWING UP THE BALANCE SHEET

Over a number of years, the courts have been increasingly called on to make important welfare decisions about best interests, often involving potential or actual safeguarding issues – for example, about whether a woman with learning disabilities should be sterilised for non-therapeutic reasons (*SL v SL*), where people with learning disabilities should live (*Newham LBC v BS*), whether they have capacity to marry or have sexual relations (*Sheffield CC v E*), or whether elderly people with dementia should remain at home, cared for by a spouse, or be admitted to hospital or care home (*B Borough Council v Mrs S*). The decisions are not always easy, as the court attempts to draw up a balance sheet, weighing up the pros and cons of a particular course of action. The courts have made clear that they should be wary of embarking upon social engineering and should not lightly interfere with family life, for fear the intervention itself may become abusive. In sum:

Quality of public care must be better than what a person is being rescued from: the State must be careful not to expose a person to the risk of abusive treatment. In one case, the court stated 'At the end of the day, the simple point, surely, is this: the quality of public care must be at least as good as that from which the child or vulnerable adult has been rescued. Indeed that sets the requirement too low. If the State is to justify removing children from their parents or vulnerable adults from their relatives, partners, friends or carers it can only be on the basis that the State is going to provide a better quality of care than that which they have hitherto been receiving ....

The fact is that in this type of case the court is exercising an essentially protective jurisdiction. The court should intervene only where there is a need to protect a vulnerable adult from abuse or the real possibility of abuse ... The jurisdiction is to be invoked if, but only if, there is a demonstrated need to protect a vulnerable adult. And the court must be careful to ensure that in rescuing a vulnerable adult from one type of abuse it does not expose her to the risk of treatment at the hands of the State which, however well intentioned, can itself end up being abusive of her dignity, her happiness and indeed of her human rights.

That said, the law must always be astute to protect the weak and helpless, not least in circumstances where, as often happens in such cases, the very people they need to be protected from are their own relatives, partners or friends' (*Local Authority X v MM*).

Sometimes, the court may have to pronounce on best interests as a result of a dispute between wholly private parties, rather than a public body being involved:

Removal of man to Norway. A dispute arose between the family of a man who had become unable to express his preference following a severe stroke, and the woman with whom he had set up home – as to where he was to be cared for and by whom. The court accepted that the issue as to where the patient's best interests lay was a matter it could deal with.

The family had tried to remove the man from a hospital in England and to take him back to Norway; the woman had obtained an interim injunction preventing this. The family claimed that in the absence of a legal relationship between the man and woman, the court had no jurisdiction to grant such relief. The Court of Appeal now found, in the light of the evidence relating to the relationship between the man and woman, that the court anyway did have jurisdiction; but that, also, the woman could have demonstrated a legal right had it been necessary for her to do so (which it was not) (*Re S: hospital patient*).

The courts will wish to ensure that, as section 4 of the Act states, assumptions about a person's best interests are not made on the basis of a person's condition:

Hospital treatment of person with severe learning disability. An 18-year-old had the capacity of a five- to six-year-old child – with severe learning disability, autism and epilepsy. He was admitted to hospital for acute renal failure; haemodialysis was required. A dispute arose between the hospital and mother as to whether or in what circumstances a kidney transplant would ever be suitable for him and whether there was a possibility of a different form of haemodialysis by use of AV fistula.

The court found that the medical and nursing team's approach had been coloured by past experience with the man and the difficulties of verbal communication. However, other evidence in the case showed that steps could be taken to enable him to cope with certain treatment and that the possibility of an AV fistula should not be ruled out. Neither should kidney transplantation be ruled out on non-medical grounds.

The court made the point that it was crucial that he was not given less satisfactory treatment than a person who understood the risks, pain and discomfort of major surgery. 'To act in any other way would be contrary to the rights of a mentally incapacitated patient both under our domestic law and under the European Convention' (*An Hospital NHS Trust v S*).

The decisions may be by no means easy, as the judges struggle to draw up a balance sheet, weighing up the pros and cons of a particular course of action – as in the following case which the local authority had pursued along adult protection lines:

Removal of adult daughter from father. The case concerned a young woman, 33 years old, of Afro-Caribbean background. She had a moderate to severe learning disability, atypical autism and epilepsy. She did not have the capacity to decide where she should live and who should provide care for her. In 1995, her mother died. Since then, her father (now 66 years old) had been her sole carer assisted by support workers, mostly privately arranged.

Adult protection procedures. Following an incident in which the father allegedly struck his daughter, the local authority instituted adult protection procedures. A court application was made; exercising the inherent jurisdiction, the court made a number of interim declarations, making it lawful for the authority to place the woman in residential care, to prevent removal by the father and to limit contact.

Local authority's case. The local authority then sought confirmation of the interim declaration; the father opposed the local authority. The authority's case was that there was a real risk of further physical abuse; that the father's age and health meant he would find it more difficult to manage as time went on; that his volatile temperament and inability to work cooperatively with social services would probably compromise his ability to care (there was a long history of disputes with the local authority). Also alluded to were his failure in the past to recognise the importance of his daughter's siblings in her life and to put her needs above his own, and his alleged drinking habits.

The father's case. The father's case was that many of the local authority's allegations were old and unfounded and many related to the stressful time when his wife died from cancer. At the time the local authority had not acted on any of these concerns. Furthermore, some of his complaints about the local authority's conduct had been upheld. An incident going back to 1991, related by a support worker, when he allegedly threatened to beat his daughter with a belt, the judge discounted for lack of evidence on the file. A 1992 incident, reported by a nurse, that he had hit his daughter four times with his fist about the head and face, the judge also discounted on the evidence. The older allegations of drinking to excess, the judge also discounted, insofar as they came from his two other children, since they were so hostile to their father. A more recent allegation was also found to be unreliable; the judge took account of the fact that the witness, as a Muslim, did not drink alcohol; and a senior local authority community worker pointed out that the father's explanation was that he relieved pain in his neck and shoulder by rubbing them with Bay Rum, a preparation which can be used for medicinal purposes.

Appraisal of father's ability to care. The judge found the father to be a proud man, verging on authoritarian toward his family, a regular member of his local Pentecostal Church. He cared for his daughter and felt it his strong duty to do so. However, he was not an easy person to deal with for the local authority; but the latter had not treated him as sympathetically as it might have. He loved his daughter. He had cared for her with the assistance of carers; he had provided adequately for her needs. He was 66. He had diabetes and arthritis; there was no contingency plan if he should fall ill. He had a fractured relationship with his other two children, which meant they could not come to the house to visit their sister.

Declaration in favour of the local authority. When the judge drew up a final balance sheet he recognised the father's sense of duty and love for his daughter. However, he was 66 years old, had diabetes and arthritis and would find it increasingly difficult to cope. Furthermore, professional evidence pointed out the advantage of the proposed alternative accommodation in terms of meeting the daughter's needs. The balance sheet therefore pointed to the daughter living in the accommodation proposed by the local authority; this would be in her best interests (*Newham LBC v BS*).

Likewise, the following two cases involved people with learning disabilities and parents who wished their adult child to remain living with them, as against the local authority's belief that their children's best interests would be served elsewhere:

Determining where an adult is to live. A 19-year-old man had a chromosomal abnormality which resulted in him having the developmental level of a two-year-old; he also had physical disabilities. He had always been cared for by his father. He had previously been placed on the child protection register, following concerns about him not being bathed properly and kept out of school. (The father blamed the local authority for the bathing issue, arguing that it refused to pay for a walk-in shower.)

Whilst still under 18, he had been physically injured by his father when the latter had lost his temper and placed in respite care. Now he was 18 years old, the local authority had brought the proceedings to determine where he should live. It argued that he should not live with his father because of the risk of physical and emotional abuse; that the father could not work cooperatively with the authority; that he should live in a specialist nursing home; and that he should have supervised contact with his father away from the father's home.

The court had to draw up a balance sheet weighing up potential benefits and disadvantages of the options. It had also to recognise the importance of family life under article 8 of the European Convention. Furthermore, other things being equal, the parent in such a situation will normally be the appropriate person to care for the child, rather than a public authority, however well intentioned.

Nevertheless, in this case, the result of the balance sheet exercise pointed in favour of the local authority. Although the father was motivated by love and concern, he had buckled under the strain; had failed to accept responsibility for the incident in which he had injured his son; and there was a long history of disputes between him and the council due to his unreasonable demands (*Re S (Adult patient)*).

In another case involving a woman with learning disabilities, the local authority wanted her to remain living at a residential unit where she enjoyed substantial social activities and opportunities. Her parents wanted her to live at home with them; otherwise they threatened to sever contact altogether. The judge accepted that it was in her best interests for a shared care scheme to operate, but this was not at present possible because of the uncompromising stance of the parents. The parents currently lacked the ability to bring the best out of their daughter. Thus her best interests would be served by full-time placement at the unit, but attempts should continue to be made to implement a shared care arrangement, if the parents relented from their present position (*A Local Authority v E*).

The decision may not necessarily be about removal of the adult with learning disabilities whose capacity and best interests are in question. For instance, in child protection proceedings, involving care and placement orders, the court set out what should happen if questions arose about the mental capacity of the parents to give instructions in the proceedings. It referred to the Public Law Outline Guide to Case Management in Public Law Proceedings, and stated that the parent should be referred to the local authority's adult learning disability team (or its equivalent) for help and advice. This would be with a view to preparation for the proceedings, the appointment of a litigation friend and involvement of the Official Solicitor. It was important that judgements about the parent's capacity were not made by the local authority's child protection team (*RP v Nottingham City Council*).

6.4.2 MOTIVATION TO BRING ABOUT DEATH

The Code of Practice explains that in case of deciding about best interests and life-sustaining treatment, the decision-maker must not be motivated to bring about the death of the person. However, if treatment is futile, overly burdensome or there is no prospect of recovery, a decision may sometimes be made that further life-sustaining treatment is not in the person's best interests. However, this would not be the same as being motivated to bring about the person's death, even if this is from a sense of compassion. By the same token, this rule cannot be interpreted to mean that doctors are obliged to provide life-sustaining treatment where this is not in the person's best interests (Lord Chancellor 2007, paras 5.31–5.33).

6.5 DEPRIVATION OF LIBERTY

The question about deprivation of liberty of people lacking the capacity to consent has been pronounced for over ten years, since a major legal case in the mid-1990s. Following an extended legal saga, the government amended the Mental Capacity Act 2005, so as to put in place safeguards. Such safeguards are very much a safeguarding matter; clearly depriving a person of liberty, when he or she lacks the capacity to decide, is a drastic intervention with the potential to go wrong.

6.5.1 BACKGROUND TO DEPRIVATION OF LIBERTY AND THE LAW

In the mid-1990s, the English courts held that in the case of a mentally incapable, but compliant, person, it was not necessary that he or she be formally sectioned under the 1983 Act – in order to effect a deprivation of liberty. The common law of best interests and necessity sufficed, making lawful what would otherwise be unlawful. The courts decided this, though, with some unease because of the absence of formal safeguards:

Removal to hospital. A 48-year-old man had been autistic since birth. He was unable to speak and required 24-hour care, and unable to go outside alone. He had no ability to communicate consent or dissent to treatment or to express preferences as to where he should live. He was frequently agitated, had no sense of danger and had a history of self-harm. From the age of 13, for over 30 years, he was resident at a hospital. He was then discharged on a trial basis into the community, going to live with paid carers.

One day he was attending a day centre and became agitated and was banging his head against a wall, and hitting his head with his fists. The day centre got in touch with a local doctor who came and administered a sedative; the social worker with overall responsibility for him was contacted and recommended that he be taken by ambulance to accident and emergency. There, after further agitation, a psychiatrist assessed that he needed inpatient treatment. However, it was decided that he could be admitted informally, rather than making use of s.2 or s.3 of the 1983 Act, because he appeared to be fully compliant and did not resist admission. He subsequently remained in hospital for several months on this informal basis, before eventually being formally detained (after the Court of Appeal had ruled his informal detention to be unlawful) and then discharged a few weeks later.

The House of Lords, overruling the Court of Appeal, held that it was permissible to admit informally to hospital (s.131 of the Mental Health Act 1983) patients who lacked the capacity to consent but who did not positively object. The court stated that the removal, care and treatment of the person had been in his best interests and was justified by the common law doctrine of necessity, which was not excluded by the provisions of the 1983 Act. Nevertheless, one of the law lords pointed out that this conclusion was not wholly satisfactory, since it meant that the formal safeguards contained in the Mental Health Act did not apply to this particular class of vulnerable informal patient. In addition, although the majority of the court ruled that he had not in fact been detained, the minority pointed out that to suggest the man had been free to leave was a "fairy tale" (*R v Bournewood Community and Mental Health NHS Trust, ex p L*).

The case was then taken to the European Court of Human Rights, which found that he had been deprived of his liberty in breach of article 5 of the European Convention on Human Rights, because of the lack of legal safeguards – that is, the deprivation had not been in accordance with an adequate procedure prescribed by law, since the common law doctrine of necessity lacked fair and proper procedures (*HL v United Kingdom*).

In the light of the judgment of the European Court, the Department of Health issued guidance in December 2004 stating that it would bring forward proposals for appropriate procedural safeguards. However, until these were in place, the guidance made clear that to provide care or treatment (whether in hospital or other residential settings) for a mentally incapacitated patient, amounting to a deprivation of liberty, was unlawful unless the person was detained under the Mental Health Act 1983. It suggested, amongst other things, that:

- the NHS and local authorities should ensure they have systems in place to assess whether a person is being deprived of his or her liberty
- wherever possible to avoid situations in which professionals take 'full and effective control' of a person's care and liberty
- decisions should be taken in a structured way
- there should be effective, documented care planning
- there should be consideration of alternatives to hospital admission or residential care, and that any restrictions placed on the person are kept to the minimum necessary in all the circumstances
- both assessment of capacity and care plan should be kept under review, and an independent element to this may well be helpful
- if it is concluded that there is no way of providing appropriate care without a deprivation of liberty occurring, then consideration should be given to use of the formal powers of detention under the 1983 Act.

However, the guidance also included a note of caution, pointing out that not all patients, subject to restrictions amounting to deprivation of liberty, can be detained lawfully under the 1983 Act. For instance, their mental disorder might not warrant detention in hospital. In addition, there were dangers in using the Act simply to be on the 'safe side'; formal detention might be perceived as a stigma. Further, significant increased use of the 1983 Act would place considerable pressure on local authority approved social workers, second opinion appointed doctors (SOADs) and on the operation of Mental Health Review Tribunals (DH 2004a).

Between the European Court ruling in *HL v UK* and the coming into force of the 'authorisation' legal rules (see below), the courts made clear that – in this interim period – a court with a built-in reviews order represents the necessary safeguard to prevent human rights being breached (*City of Sunderland v PS. Also: JE v DE and Surrey County Council*). Such an order could authorise proportionate restrain where necessary – for example, in the context of an order providing for the assessment in hospital of a person with severe, complex and uncontrolled epilepsy (*A Primary Care Trust v P*).

6.5.2 DEPRIVATION OF LIBERTY: PERMITTED UNDER THE MENTAL CAPACITY ACT 2005

The Mental Capacity Act 2005 does not authorise any person to deprive any other person of his or her liberty – subject to certain exceptions, in which case the Act applies specific safeguards. These safeguards are contained in the Mental Health Act 2007, which amends the 2005 Act; at the time of writing they are not in force but are expected to be so by April 2009. The Act states that its deprivation of liberty provisions – that is, safeguards – apply if a person lacking capacity to decide is 'detained in circumstances which amount to a deprivation of liberty' (schedule A1, paras 1(2) and 15).

Deprivation of liberty is defined in the MCA 2005 with reference to article 5 of the European Convention on Human Rights and applies whether the deprivation is publicly or privately funded (s.64). The European Court itself has struggled with the concept, and has outlined it as follows. The difference between deprivation of, and restriction of, liberty is one of degree or intensity, not one of nature or substance. Relevant issues include type, duration, effects and manner of implementation (*Ashingdane v UK*). Compliance by a person in giving up himself or herself for detention is not determinative (i.e. there could still be a deprivation of liberty: *HL v UK*). Indicators of deprivation of liberty might include, as the European Court found in *HL v UK*:

- professionals having complete, effective, continuous and strict control and supervision over a person's care, movements, assessment, residence, treatment, contacts
- attempts to leave informal detention would have resulted in compulsory detention (under the Mental Health Act 1983)
- whether a ward is locked or lockable is relevant but not determinative of the issue.

In a subsequent case, the High Court identified three relevant propositions to whether deprivation of liberty has occurred, so as to breach human rights:

- an objective element of a person's confinement in a restricted space for a not negligible length of time
- a subjective element, in that the person has not validly consented
- the deprivation must be imputable to the State (*JE v DE and Surrey CC*).

With such factors in mind, the court found a deprivation of liberty in the *JE v DE* case, when the local authority sought to protect a man it felt would be at serious risk were he to return home – but had not gone through the legal procedural safeguard of getting a court order:

Refusal to let a person go home: deprivation of liberty? A man had a major stroke aged 76 years old. This left him blind with significant memory impairment. He suffered from dementia, although could express wishes and feelings with some force. The evidence suggested strongly that he lacked capacity. On a particular day, his wife, who had intermittent mental health problems of her own, felt she could no longer cope. She placed him in a chair on the pavement. He was dressed in pyjama bottoms, shirt and slippers. She then informed the police who notified the local authority.

The local authority subsequently placed in him a nursing home. While there, significant restrictions were put in place. He was not allowed to visit his wife at home, not even at Christmas. His wife was not to remove him. The local authority said on a number of occasions that it would call the police if his wife tried to take him home. During this period of over a year, the man repeatedly asked to go home; repeatedly he was told he could not.

In its evidence to the court, the local authority stated that had he tried to go home, it would not have prevented him – but the court pointed out that this had never been communicated to the man or his wife. The court also dismissed the authority's claim that, first, his wishes largely flowed from his wife's urgings. Second, that it had no objection to him living elsewhere – just not with his wife. Third, that the police would not in fact have had any power to prevent him leaving. This last, the judge dismissed as 'legal sophistry', pointing out that a person can be deprived of his or her liberty 'by the misuse or misrepresentation of even non-existent authority as by locked doors and physical barriers.' The deprivation of liberty had been contrary to article 5 of the European Convention (*JE v DE and Surrey CC*).

However, in another case, the judge concluded that a man who had been placed in a care home may have had his liberty restricted but he had not been deprived of it. Restriction, as opposed to deprivation, of liberty does not amount to a breach of article 5 of the European Convention. Some of the relevant factors the court took into account were that (a) the care home was an 'ordinary care home where only ordinary restrictions of liberty applied; (b) the family was able to visit on a largely unrestricted basis and could take him on outings; (c) the man was personally compliant and expressed himself happy; (d) there was no occasion on which he was objectively deprived of his liberty' (*LLBC v TG*).

Prior to the amended Mental Capacity Act coming into force, the courts identified in the following case that the safeguard needed in case of deprivation of liberty was for the local authority to seek a court order – as it was in fact doing:

Preventing daughter discharging mother from hospital: court order. The daughter of a woman lacking capacity and in physical ill health wished to discharge her mother from hospital into her own care – rather than back to the residential unit her mother had been living in previously. The local authority was greatly concerned about the welfare of the mother, but was concerned about depriving the mother of her liberty if it took steps to prevent her leaving or being removed from the unit. The court made an order stating that it was 'lawful being in the [mother's] best interests for the local authority by its employees or agents to use reasonable and proportionate measures to prevent [the mother] from leaving the unit.' This could involve 'perimeter security' and, in an extreme situation, the use of reasonable force to prevent removal, the force being applied to the daughter rather than the mother (*City of Sunderland v PS*).

6.5.3 AUTHORISATION OF DEPRIVATION OF LIBERTY: RULES

The amended Mental Capacity Act 2005 (MCA) sets out a complex system of safeguards, to ensure that a person is not arbitrarily deprived of his or her liberty in a hospital or care home. The safeguards are due to come into force in April 2009. They are detailed and by no means straightforward; the following is a summary only and not exhaustive. In addition, a code of practice, supplementary to the main code for the Mental Capacity Act, has been published (Ministry of Justice 2008).

6.5.3.1 Deprivation of liberty only in specific circumstances

The Act does not allow deprivation of liberty except in certain circumstances. These are when (a) giving effect to a relevant court order (concerning personal welfare) under s.16 of the MCA; (b) it is authorised in accordance with specific safeguards in schedule A1 of the MCA; or (c) the deprivation is connected with life-sustaining treatment or a vital act whilst a decision is sought from the court. A vital act is doing anything which the person doing it reasonably believes to be necessary to prevent a serious deterioration in the person's condition (ss.4A–4B).

However, if a person is ineligible (see below) to be deprived of liberty, the court may not include in a welfare order, made under the MCA, any provision authorising such a deprivation (s.16A).

The safeguards contained in schedule A1 of the Act apply if a person is detained in a hospital or care home in circumstances which amount to a deprivation of a person's liberty (schedule A1, paras 1, 6).

6.5.3.2 Qualifying requirements

For a person to be deprived of his or her liberty by way of authorisation under the safe-guards in schedule A1 of the MCA, he or she must meet what are called 'qualifying requirements'. These relate to age, mental health, mental capacity, best interests, eligibility and 'no refusals'. These requirements are as follows:

- **(age)** the person must be 18 or over
- **(mental health)** the person is suffering from a mental disorder as defined in the Mental Health Act 1983, but disregarding any exclusions in this definition for people with learning disabilities (in the 1983 Act, the disability must be associated with abnormally aggressive or seriously irresponsible conduct. The assessment must be carried out by a s.12 (under the 1983 Act) doctor or by a doctor with special experience in the diagnosis and treatment of mental disorder
- **(mental capacity)** the person must lack capacity to decide whether to be accommodated in the relevant hospital or care home for the purpose of given the relevant care or treatment
- **(best interests)** the person is, or is to be, a detained resident, it is in their best interests to be a detained resident, the detention is in order to prevent harm to the person, the detention is a proportionate response to the risk of harm (seriousness and likelihood
- **(eligibility)** the person will meet this requirement, unless not eligible to be deprived of liberty, because of overlap with the Mental Health Act 1983 (see immediately below)
- **(no refusals)** the person will meet this requirement unless they have made a valid advance decision, which is applicable to some or all of the relevant treatment. There is also a refusal if the deprivation of liberty in a care home or hospital, for the purpose of receiving some or all of the relevant care or treatment, would be in conflict with a valid decision of a donee or deputy under the Mental Capacity Act (schedule A1, paras 12- 20).

The 'eligibility' requirement deals with the interface between the Mental Capacity Act 2005 and the Mental Health Act 1983. A person does not meet the eligibility requirement for deprivation of liberty if, under the 1983 Act, he or she is subject to detention under the Mental Health Act (under ss.2, 3, 4, 17, 35, 36, 38, 44, 45A, 47, 48, 51). Likewise if the person is on leave of absence from detention (s.37), subject to guardianship (s.7), subject to supervised community treatment (s.17A) or subject to conditional discharge –and is subject to a measure that would be inconsistent with the authorisation.

If a person is on leave of absence, supervised community treatment or subject to conditional discharge, then authorisation cannot be given if it is about detaining a person in hospital for treatment of mental disorder. The person would instead be recalled to hospital under the 1983 Act.

In the case of guardianship, ineligibility will also arise (apart from the deprivation not being in accordance with a requirement under the guardianship order) if (a) the deprivation would authorise the person becoming a mental patient in terms of being given medical treatment for mental disorder, and (b) the person objects to being given some or all of the mental health treatment – and no valid consent has been given by a donee or deputy.

Lastly, authorisation cannot be given if the person is within the scope of the 1983 Act (i.e. would meet the criteria for detention under s.2 or s.3) and objects to being a mental health patient (i.e. admission to hospital for treatment) or being given some or all of the treatment. However, a person's objections do not make him or her ineligible if the donee of a lasting power of attorney or a deputy has made a valid decision to consent to the detention in hospital and treatment – on his or her behalf. In determining whether the person objects, his or her behaviour, wishes, feelings, views, beliefs and values must be had regard to. Past circumstances are only to be had regard to insofar as it is still appropriate to do so (MCA 2005, schedule 1A).

6.5.3.3 Supervisory bodies and managing authorities

If these qualifying requirements are met, deprivation of liberty may follow if the 'supervisory body' (NHS primary care trust or local authority) has given a standard authorisation. A 'managing authority' will request that the supervisory body grant an authorisation.

In the case of a hospital, the PCT will be identified as supervisory body if it is commissioning the relevant care or treatment, or if it is the PCT for the area in which the hospital is situated. In the case of a care home, the local authority will be identified as supervisory body according to where the relevant person is ordinarily resident. If the person is not ordinarily resident within a local authority, then it is the local authority for the area in which the care home is situated.

A managing authority, in respect of a hospital, is the NHS body with responsibility for the administration of the hospital – for example, a primary care trust, NHS trust, or NHS foundation trust. In the case of an independent hospital, the managing authority is the person registered under Part 2 of the Care Standards Act 2000. Managing authority in respect of a care home means the person registered under the Care Standards Act 2000 (MCA 2005, schedule A1 paras 175–182).

6.5.3.4 Request for standard authorisation

A supervisory body cannot give a standard authorisation unless requested by the managing authority of the relevant hospital or care home, or asked by a third party. A managing authority must request a standard authorisation if it appears to it that the person is already being detained or likely to be so within the next 28 days:

- is not yet accommodated in the relevant hospital or care home but is likely to be a detained resident within the next 28 days and meet the qualifying requirements; or
- is already accommodated in the relevant hospital or care home, is likely to be detained within the next 28 days and is likely to meet the qualifying requirements; or
- is already a detained resident and meets the qualifying requirements or is likely to in the next 28 days. Likewise, a request must be made if an authorisation already exists but there is to be change in the place of detention.

A request to the supervisory body is not necessary if a court order authorises detention of the person. But if a Court of Protection order authorising deprivation of liberty is about to expire, then a request must be made by the managing authority before the expiry (schedule A1, paras 21–27).

6.5.3.5 Carrying out of assessments for standard authorisation

The supervisory body must ensure that assessments are carried out in relation to all the qualifying requirements (schedule A1, para 33).

The Act sets out in detail what the best interests assessor must do. This includes consulting the relevant managing authority, and having regard to (a) the mental health assessor's conclusions; (b) any relevant needs assessment; and (c) any relevant care plan. He or she must also state the maximum authorisation period (which can be no more than one year) (schedule A1, paras 38–45).

However, if there are existing (no older than 12 months) assessments which meet all the requirements, and there is no reason to doubt their accuracy, then the supervisory body does not have to ensure that new assessments are carried out. In deciding the question of continuing accuracy in respect of best interests assessment, information provided by the person's personal representative (or IMCA specially appointed for the purpose) must be taken into account (schedule A1, para 49).

6.5.3.6 Assessors for standard authorisations and reviews

It is for the supervisory body to select a person to carry out an assessment in connection with a request for a standard authorisation or a review. Regulations carry details about the suitability and eligibility of people to carry out assessments. The same person must not be selected to carry out both the mental health and best interests assessments (schedule A1, paras 126–136).

Regulations state that supervisory bodies have to be satisfied about the skills and experience of assessors. Mental health assessors must be approved under s.12 of the Mental Health Act 1983 or be a registered medical practitioner, with (to the satisfaction of the supervisory body) special experience in the diagnosis and treatment of mental disorder.

Best interests assessments can be carried out by approved mental health professionals (under s.114 of the Mental Health Act 1983), registered social workers, first level nurses in mental health or learning disabilities, occupational therapists, chartered psychologists.

Mental capacity assessments can be carried out by anybody eligible to carry out a mental health or best interests assessment. The supervisory body cannot appoint certain people as assessors, for example, those with a financial interest in the care of the person (any close relative of somebody with such a financial interest), close relatives of the person. There are further restrictions on who can be best interests assessors; they may not be involved with the care of the person, or employed in the care home or hospital where the detention takes place (SI 2008/1858).

6.5.3.7 Assessments: time and information

Regulations also set out timeframes; assessments must be completed within 21 days of the supervisory body receiving a request for a standard authorisation. If the managing authority has given an urgent authorisation (see 6.5.3.11), and a standard authorisation is now sought, the assessments must be completed during the period of the urgent authorisation.

Requests for a standard authorisation must contain the information set out in the regulations. If a question arises about the ordinary residence of the person, and thus about responsibility for authorisation, the local authority body receiving the request should act as supervisory body until the question is resolved – unless the other authority agrees to do this (SI 2008/1858).

6.5.3.8 Giving standard authorisation

If all the assessments are positive and written copies are in the hands of the supervisory body, it must give a standard authorisation.

Such authorisation must be in writing, stating the name of the relevant person, the name of the hospital or care home, the period of the authorisation, the purpose, any conditions, the reason why each qualifying requirement is met. A copy must be given to the relevant person's personal representative (or IMCA), the managing authority, the person themselves, and every interested person consulted by the best interests assessor. Likewise, if an authorisation is not granted (schedule A1, paras 50–58).

6.5.3.9 Effect of standard authorisation

If an authorisation is granted, a number of rules then come into play concerning:

- the managing authority ensuring the person understands (if practicable) his other right to make a court application, to request a review or to have an IMCA appointed
- the supervisory body keeping a written record
- restrictions on variation of the authorisation

- the seeking of a new standard authorisation
- coming into force and cessation of a standard authorisation (schedule A1, paras 59–65).

6.5.3.10 Unauthorised deprivation of liberty

Where it appears that a person is being deprived of their liberty without authorisation as set out in s.4A of the Act, an 'eligible person' (anybody other than the relevant managing authority and with an interest in the person's welfare) may request that the supervisory body decide whether there is an unauthorised deprivation of liberty. A number of conditions attach to such a request. The supervisory body has to appoint somebody to assess, unless the request appears vexatious or frivolous, or the issue has previously been decided and there has been no change of circumstance (schedule A1, paras 67–69).

6.5.3.11 Urgent authorisation

In addition to standard authorisations are 'urgent authorisations'. These may be given by a managing authority (hospital or care home) if the need is so urgent that there is no time to request, or at least to obtain, a standard authorisation. The maximum period of an urgent authorisation is seven days.

A number of rules apply (the authorisation must be in writing, certain details must be included, certain people must be notified). Extension of an urgent authorisation – up to a further seven days – can be requested of the supervisory body by the managing authority. The supervisory body may grant this extension if it appears that the management authority has requested a standard authorisation, there are exceptional reasons why no decision has yet been reached, and it is essential for the existing detention to continue (schedule A1, para 84).

6.5.3.12 Suspension and reactivation of standard authorisation

If a person ceases to meet a qualifying requirement, provision is made for a standard authorisation to be suspended – and to be reactivated if the person becomes eligible once again within 28 days (schedule A1, paras 91–97).

6.5.3.13 Reviewing a standard authorisation

Review of a standard authorisation may be made at any time by the supervisory body. However, it must conduct a review if requested by the person themselves, their representative, or the managing authority of the relevant hospital or care home. These can ask for a review at any time. Managing authorities are under a duty to make such a request, if any of the qualifying requirements appear to be reviewable (age, mental health, mental capacity, best interests, no refusals).

Qualifying requirements are reviewable on the ground that the person no longer meets any one of them. This might be because the actual reason as to why the person meets the requirement is not the reason stated in the standard authorisation – or because there has been a change in the person's case, and it would be appropriate to vary the conditions to which the authorisation is subject (schedule A1, paras 101–107).

6.5.3.14 Relevant person's representative and IMCAs

First, the supervisory body must appoint a person to be the 'relevant person's representative' as soon as practicable after a standard authorisation is given – if it appears that the representative would maintain contact with, represent and support the person. The functions of any such representative do not affect the authority of any donee, deputy or powers of the court (schedule A1, paras 137–141). The functions of the representative are to maintain contact with, represent and support the person lacking capacity. They are additional to, and do not affect, the appointment and functions of a donee of a lasting power of attorney or – and do not affect the powers of the court (para 140).

Second, if a person becomes subject to the authorisation provisions, and the managing authority is satisfied that there is nobody (other than a person engaged in providing care or treatment for the person in a professional capacity or for remuneration) appropriate to consult about the person's best interests – then it must notify the supervisory authority. The latter must then instruct an independent mental capacity advocate (IMCA). A person becomes 'subject' to the authorisation provisions if an urgent authorisation is given, or a request for standard authorisation is made (MCA 2005, ss.39A–39B).

Third, if an authorisation is in force, and the appointment of a representative ends, or the managing authority is satisfied that there is nobody – other than a person engaged in providing care or treatment for the person in a professional capacity or for remuneration – appropriate to consult about the person's best interests, it must notify the supervisory body. The latter must then instruct an independent mental capacity advocate (IMCA) to represent the person. This appointment ends when a new representative is appointed (MCA 2005, s.39C). Lastly, an IMCA must be appointed if an authorisation of deprivation of liberty is in force under schedule A1, there is an appointed representative, that representative is not being paid and the following applies. First, the person lacking capacity or the representative requests an advocate, or, second, the supervisory body has reason to believe (a) that without the help of an advocate, the person and the representative would be unable to exercise their right to apply to court or right of review, or (b) that the person and the representative have failed, or are unlikely to exercise such rights, when it would have been (or would be) reasonable to exercise them (MCA 2005, s.39D).

Regulations prescribe eligibility conditions and procedure for the appointment of a representative. For example, the representative must be 18 years or over, be able to keep in contact with the person, be willing, not be financially interested in the managing authority (or not be related to somebody who is so financially interested), not be linked through work to the managing authority etc.

If the person is judged by the best interests assessor to have the capacity, the person can select a family member, friend or carer as his or her representative. In case of lack of capacity, a donee or deputy with relevant powers can select. If the person or the donee or the deputy, do not want to select somebody, then the best interests assessor can do so –

but this is subject to the objection of the person, donee or deputy. Failing all this, the supervisory body may select a representative to perform the role in a professional capacity, with satisfactory skills and experience, who is not a family member friend or carer, and who is not employed to work in the managing authority or supervisory body.

Procedural matters are also covered in the draft regulations, including a number of grounds for termination (SI 2008/1315).

6.5.3.15 Monitoring of the safeguards

The Act allows for regulations to be made giving a monitoring body the power to report generally on the operation of these rules, to visit hospitals and care homes, to visit and interview people accommodated in hospitals and care homes, and to require the production of, and to inspect, records (schedule A1, para 162). In future, it is expected that this monitoring body will take the form of the Care Quality Commission.

6.6 ACTS IN CONNECTION WITH CARE OR TREATMENT

Section 5 of the Act provides a general defence for people providing care or treatment for a person lacking capacity. This might be an important safeguard if, for example, in a safeguarding context, somebody had to act in haste to protect a person, and did so reasonably – but hindsight revealed an error about either the person's capacity or best interests. It states that:

- a person is protected from liability if he or she does an act in connection with care or treatment, and
- he or she took reasonable steps to establish that the person lacked capacity in respect of the matter in question, and reasonably believed that the person lacked that capacity and that it was in his or own best interests that the act be done
- however, this does not exclude civil liability for loss or damage, or criminal liability, arising from negligence in doing the act. However, s.5 of the 2005 Act does not provide protection to the extent of overriding an advance decision, or a decision made by a person with lasting power of attorney or by a deputy appointed by the Court of Protection.

The Code of Practice points out that simply because somebody has come to an incorrect conclusion about a person's capacity or best interests does not mean that he or she will not be protected from liability. But they must 'be able to show that it was reasonable for them to think that the person lacked capacity and that they were acting in the person's best interests at the time they made their decision or took action' (Lord Chancellor 2007, para 5.59). As a consultant psychiatrist has put it, decisions regarding mental capacity and best interests should be carefully documented, not least because there may be in many cases no 'right answer' – and good documentation will go a long way in protecting both patient and doctor (Hotopf 2005).

The protection from liability is in respect of both civil and criminal liability that could otherwise arise from doing things for or to a person without their consent. For instance, as the Code of Practice points out, a carer dressing a person without the latter's consent could theoretically be prosecuted for assault. A neighbour entering and cleaning the house of a person lacking capacity to give permission could be trespassing on the person's property (Lord Chancellor 2007, para 6.2).

The Code gives a non-exhaustive list of the sort of actions that are covered by way of care under s.5. These include help with washing, dressing, personal hygiene, eating, drinking, communication, mobility – and with a person's taking part in education, social or leisure activities. Also included are going to a person's house to see if they are alright, doing the shopping with the person's money, arranging household services, providing home help services, undertaking actions related to community care services (e.g. day care, care home accommodation, nursing care) and helping a person move home.

Health care and treatment might include diagnostic examinations and tests, medical or dental treatment, medication, taking a person to hospital for assessment or treatment, nursing care, other procedures or therapies (e.g. physiotherapy or chiropody), emergency care (Lord Chancellor 2007, para 6.5).

6.7 LIMITATIONS ON RESTRAINT AND ON SECTION 5

The Act permits restraint of a person lacking capacity, but only if certain conditions are met. Section 6 states that:

- **(prevention of harm)** to restrain a person and be protected under s.5, the person (the restrainer) must reasonably believe it is necessary to prevent harm to the person lacking capacity
- **(proportionality)** the response must be proportionate in relation to the likelihood of the person suffering harm and the seriousness of that harm
- **(deprivation of liberty)** however, this section does not apply if the intervention is more than just restraint and the person is being deprived of their liberty (to be repealed, probably in late 2008)
- **(definition)** restraint involves use or threats to use force to secure the doing of an act which the person resists – or restriction of liberty of the person's movement whether or not the person resists
- **(conflict with attorney's or deputy's decision)** section 5 does not authorise an act which conflicts with a decision made, by a donee of a lasting power of attorney or a court-appointed deputy (within the scope of the donee's or deputy's authority). But this does not stop a person providing life-sustaining treatment, or doing any act which he or she believes necessary to prevent a serious deterioration in the person's condition – while a decision about any relevant issue is sought from the court.

The Code of Practice points out that the common law also imposes a duty of care on health care and social care staff to take appropriate and necessary action to restrain or remove a person – with challenging behaviour or who is in the acute stages of illness – who may cause harm to themselves or other people (Lord Chancellor 2007, para 6.43).

Past cases, when the court applied the common law along similar lines, involved just such a weighing up of factors and justification for the proposed restraint. For instance, it might be lawful to impose treatment and overcome resistance by sedation and reasonable use of restraint if the treatment (a total hysterectomy) was in the patient's best interests. Nonetheless a careful balancing of benefit and disadvantage had to take place, and care need to be taken that the patient's human right (under article 3 of the European Convention on Human Rights) was not thereby infringed (*Trust A v H (An Adult Patient)*).

Similarly, the court accepted that the administering of a general anaesthetic, in order to carry out a CT scan on an uncooperative patient lacking capacity, was permissible and would be compliant with human rights – given the doctor's evidence that the nurses were trained in safe restraint techniques and that this usually led to uneventful anaesthesia (*Doncaster & Bassetlaw Hospitals NHS Trust v C*).

6.8 PAYMENT FOR NECESSARY GOODS AND SERVICES

Section 7 deals with the question of a person entering into a contract for goods or services, even though he or she lacks the capacity to do so. It states that:
- if necessary goods or services are supplied to a person lacking capacity to contract for them, the person must nevertheless pay a reasonable price for them
- necessary means suitable to a person's condition in life and to his or her actual requirements at the time when goods or services are supplied.

The Code of Practice explains that in general, a contract entered into by a person lacking capacity cannot be enforced if the other person knows, or should have known, about the lack of capacity. The Act modifies this rule by stating that such a contract is enforceable if the goods or services contracted for are 'necessary' (Lord Chancellor 2007, para 6.57).

6.9 EXPENDITURE: PLEDGE OF PERSON'S EXPENDITURE

In relation to section 5 (care or treatment), it is lawful for the carer to pledge the person's (who lacks capacity) credit for the purpose of expenditure or to use money in the person's possession. The carer can reimburse himself or herself from money in the person's possession or be otherwise indemnified by the second person (MCA 2005, s.8). The Code of Practice explains that the carer could use cash that the person lacking capacity may have, or use his or her own money with a view to being paid back by the person lacking capacity (Lord Chancellor 2007, para 6.61).

6.10 LASTING POWER OF ATTORNEY

A donee of a lasting power of attorney is able to take various decisions for a person (the donor) lacking capacity. These decisions can include a range of finance and welfare matters. Some attorneys will abuse their power and this may give rise to safeguarding and protection concerns.

A number of conditions must be fulfilled for such a power to valid. In addition, the power can be revoked by the Court of Protection on a number of grounds, including the situation where the power is being misused. Sections 9–14 of the Act deal with lasting power of attorney:

- **(capacity and age of donor)** a person, the donor, is able to create a 'lasting power of attorney', whilst he or she retains the capacity to do so, and must be at least 18 years old
- **(scope of power)** such a lasting power can give the attorney authorisation to deal with property and financial affairs, as well as personal welfare matters (including health care decisions) – when the donor no longer has capacity
- **(prescribed form)** the power must be contained in an instrument of a certain form and must be registered with the Public Guardian, otherwise it is not effective
- **(principles of Act apply)** a lasting power of attorney is subject to the provisions of the Act, in particular the principles in s.1 of the Act, as well as any conditions or restrictions specified in the instrument (s.9)
- **(age of donee)** a donee must be at least 18 years old
- **(attorneys acting jointly or severally)** attorneys may be appointed to act jointly, jointly and severally – or jointly in respect of matters, and jointly and severally in respect of others (s.10)
- **(restraint)** the use of the power to restrain the donor is restricted to where it is necessary and proportionate (to the likelihood of the person suffering harm), and the person lacks capacity or the attorney reasonably believe that the person lacks capacity in relation to the matter
- **(welfare powers useable only on loss of capacity)** the personal welfare powers cannot be used unless the donor lacks capacity or the attorney reasonably believes that the donor lacks capacity
- **(relation to advance decisions)** the personal welfare power is subject to any advance decisions on treatment made by the donor – and does not cover decisions about life-sustaining treatment, unless this has been expressly included by the donor in the lasting power of attorney
- **(health care treatment)** the personal welfare power can be specified so as to include consent, or refusal of consent, to health care treatment (s.11)
- **(restrictions on gifts)** there are restrictions on gifts, other than on customary gifts or charities to whom the donor might have made gifts, insofar as the value of any such gift is reasonable in respect of the donor's estate
- **(prescribed information)** the document must include prescribed information
- **(donor signature)** the donor must sign a statement that they have read the information and want the power to apply when they have lost capacity
- **(named people to be informed)** the document must name people who should be informed when an application is made to register the power
- **(attorneys' signature)** the attorneys must sign to say they have read the information and understand their duties, including the duty to act in the person's best interests

- **(certification by third party of donor's understanding)** the document must include a certificate completed by an independent third party to the effect that in their view, the donor understands the power being created, no undue pressure of fraud has been used, and there is nothing to stop the power being created (schedule 1)
- **(identity of certifying third party)** the independent third party (not a family member) can be someone who has known the donor personally for two years, or a person chosen by the donor on account of their professional skills and expertise, and whom the donor reasonably considers to be competent to certify the relevant matters (SI 2007/1253)
- **(Public Guardian and registration)** the Public Guardian charges registration fees (SI 20072051)
- **(separate forms and fees for welfare and finance)** there are separate forms for a welfare power and a finance power (SI 2007/1253, and the fee of £150 payable for each (SI 2007/2051).

In summary, a person aged 18 years or over, with capacity to do so, can make what is called a lasting power of attorney. This authorises the attorney to deal with property and financial affairs and (or) welfare matters when the donor loses capacity to take such decisions. Welfare decisions can include matters such as health care, place of residence, contact etc. More than one attorney can be appointed. There is a choice of appointing the attorneys to act jointly, or jointly or severally. Acting jointly is clearly a safeguard but could be more cumbersome. There are restrictions on gifts that can be made; otherwise, application must be made to the Court of Protection.

The Code of Practice spells out that attorneys must follow the principles of the Act, make decisions in the donor's best interests, have regard to the Code and remain within the authority contained in the power of attorney. In addition, as agent of the person lacking capacity, the attorney has a common law duty of care to apply reasonable standards of care and skill, a fiduciary duty (including principles such a trust, good faith, honesty, not taking advantage of the position and acting so as to benefit the donor, not themselves), should not delegate their authority, has a duty of confidentiality, a duty to comply with Court of Protection directions, a duty not to give up the role without notifying the donor and the Office of the Public Guardian, a duty to keep accounts, a duty to keep the donor's money and property separate from their own (Lord Chancellor 2007, paras 7.52–7.68).

6.10.1 ABUSE OF POWERS OF ATTORNEY

Enduring powers of attorney were the legal predecessors of lasting powers of attorney, up to October 2007 (see below). It has been recognised that a proportion of enduring powers of attorney have in the past been abused, perhaps some 10 to 15 per cent. The extent of abuse ranges from the making of unauthorised gifts at one extreme to criminal fraud on the other. For instance, one fraud involved about £2 million, siphoned from a spinster over 90 years old, living in a care home, with no known relatives – and involving an attorney who had not registered the power and was proprietor of the care home (Cretney and Lush 2001, p.133).

Abuse of enduring power of attorney. A spinster in her eighties suffered two strokes and three serious falls. She lost her hearing and ability to write. She entered a nursing home in 1996. Her niece, who was the donee of an enduring power of attorney, operated the power and in March 1997 sold shares worth over £23,000; the next year she sold more shares worth over £72,000. Both sums were placed in her bank account; some of the money was lent to her husband's companies. The courts found that she had abused the power of attorney (*Jennings and Lewis v Cairns*).

In the following case the son, with an enduring power of attorney for his mother, was in clear breach of his fiduciary duty:

Son with enduring power of attorney in clear breach of fiduciary duty toward mother. When the son of an elderly woman had an enduring power of attorney, he used her assets to place a new house in his name, but not his mother's, bought a sports car and power boat, moved large sums of money into a company account owned by his wife, and sold shares and paid the proceeds into another account to be drawn on by his wife. The mother was left with no assets, nothing to pass on to her grandchildren, nothing to use to provide for her own needs at the end of her life. She obtained no benefits from the transfers. The court noted that the law imposed 'rigorous and inflexible duties on fiduciaries who enter into transactions with the person to whom the duty is owed' – i.e. where the mother's assets were flowing directly into the son's possession. This meant justifying the transaction and proving affirmatively that the transaction was fair, and entered into on the basis of proper and independent advice. The son, and his wife, were in clear breach of their fiduciary duty (*Hodson v Hodson*).

On the other hand, it may not be straightforward to identify breach of fiduciary duty:

Making gifts without the Court of Protection's authorisation. The donor of an enduring power of attorney was a 90-year old woman living in a nursing home. There were three siblings between whom there had been a history of hostility. The eldest had been granted the power.

The making of £20,000 of gifts by the donee from the donor's estate, even-handedly to herself and siblings, for estate planning purposes, did not necessarily make the attorney unsuitable - even though she should have sought the Court of Protection's authorisation (because the attorney's power to make gifts was extremely limited). However, at worst, she 'ought to have known the law if she was to take on the responsibility of such an important fiduciary position'. But what had occurred did not portray a picture of greed. Furthermore, the other siblings, who had now brought the case to displace the third sibling, had not complained at the time. It was also possible that, at the time the gifts were made, only shortly after the power had been executed, the donee was acting under the instructions of the donor – since the latter might have had capacity to direct that the gifts were made.

In addition, the fact of hostility between the three children did not automatically make the donee unsuitable. In this case it did not. In other circumstances, it might have done so – for instance, if the donor's estate had been complex and required strategic decision-making requiring consultation and work with the other siblings (*Re a power given by Mrs. W a donor*).

In the following two cases, dishonesty was abundantly clear. In the first, a 60-year old woman had an enduring power of attorney on behalf of her former husband's uncle. When his mental health deteriorated, he entered a care home and she then managed his finances. She made cash withdrawals for herself from his building society account, making out cheques to pay off her own overdraft and to buy Christmas presents. He had wanted her to buy a car and authorised £5000 for this, but she bought one for £4400 and kept the rest. With the money she stole, she funded family holidays as well as her gambling habit. In total she was charged, and pleaded guilty to, theft of £17,500. She was sentenced to nine months' imprisonment, as the judge put it, having taken advantage of an elderly and vulnerable victim. The irony, which she was not aware of at the time, was that much of the money she had stolen was from her own inheritance, detailed in the man's will (*Wiltshire Gazette and Herald* 2005).

In the second, a local authority social worker had been advised to make an application for a Court of Protection order for a 79-year old client. Instead, she obtained enduring power of attorney for herself and proceeded to steal nearly £65,000:

Social worker failing to seek Court of Protection order for client, instead obtaining enduring power of attorney for herself and attempting to steal tens of thousands of pounds. A local authority social worker was convicted of theft, after receiving a referral in respect of a 79-year old woman with no known relatives. She had dementia, £25,000 in cash and owned her own home. The social worker helped the woman go into a care home. A consultant psychiatrist recommended that a Court of Protection order be sought because of the woman's lack of capacity to manage her affairs. The social worker took no steps to do this. Instead she started to steal money and obtained an enduring power of attorney, even though the woman lacked the capacity to make it. The power was not registered with the Court of Protection.

She then started to make cash withdrawals. She withdrew £8180 from cash machines, followed by other withdrawals at about £250 per week. She eventually sold the woman's house for some £87,000. She then began to write cheques out to herself, including one for £42,000. A further banker's draft for £5000 was made payable to Age Concern – but the social worker's husband was the regional manager of that charity.

Another local authority officer was asked to reassess the woman, now in the care home. This social worker became suspicious when she found out that the social worker was still visiting. It transpired that the social worker had asked the care home to remove the woman's name from the records; and the woman's social services file was missing.

She was sentenced to three and a half years in prison, having stolen nearly £65,000. The judge referred to the deliberate plan to take advantage of an old lady who could not look after herself – referring to it as deliberate, cynical, and a gross breach of trust. The social worker knew perfectly well that the victim would not be able to do anything about it. He described it as the most serious breach of trust by a social worker that he had come across in twenty years on the bench. For sentence, the judge took a starting point of five years. After considering the mitigation (guilty plea, good references, high standard of behaviour in prison, low risk of re-offending), he arrived at three and a half years, which was upheld on appeal (*R v Hardwick*).

6.10.2 LASTING POWER OF ATTORNEY: FINANCE, HEALTH AND WELFARE

The Act allows a donor of a lasting power of attorney to specify not just finance, business and property issues, but also health or welfare matters. However, the power does not have to cover all these things. The donor can specify. It is not all or nothing. Equally, the donor might appoint one attorney to deal with finance, and another to deal with welfare. Up to five attorneys may be appointed. Joint attorneys must always act together; joint and several attorneys can act either together or independently. The donor could even specify that some matters could be dealt with severally, but others jointly.

The distinction between finance and welfare issues will usually be clear enough. There will nevertheless be a grey area, in which a decision concerning property or finance will overlap with welfare matters. For instance, a decision about whether to enter a care home is strictly speaking a welfare decision; but deciding how much to spend on the care placement is a financial one.

Lasting powers of attorney can be registered with the Office of the Public Guardian at any time and cannot be used until registered. A finance, property and business power can be used by the attorney before the donor loses capacity; but a welfare power can be used only when the donor lacks the capacity to take a relevant welfare decision (MCA 2005, ss. 9, 11).

6.10.3 REVOCATION OF LASTING POWER OF ATTORNEY

Lasting powers of attorney may be subject to revocation in a number of situations. One of these is where the donor, at any time he or she has capacity, decides on revocation (s.13).

Section 22 of the Act sets out the power of the Court of Protection to intervene and determine whether the requirements for creation of a lasting power of attorney have been met, whether the power has been revoked, whether fraud or undue pressure was exercised, whether the donee is behaving inconsistently with the authority given by the power or not behaving in the donor's best interests. The court has the power to prevent registration of the power (s.22).

6.10.4 EXISTING ENDURING POWERS OF ATTORNEY

From October 2007, no new enduring powers of attorney could be made. Any made before that date remain valid, whether or not the donor has yet lost capacity and the power has been registered with the Court of Protection (Mental Capacity Act 2005, schedule 4).

Unlike lasting powers of attorney, enduring powers can only cover finance, business and property – and not health or welfare matters. This limitation sometimes leads to misunderstanding on the part of the attorney, who believes he or she is authorised under the power to make health or welfare decisions. In the past, professionals too have likewise been unclear. For example, the local ombudsman found that social workers not involving attorneys in matters with which really they should be involved, such as the management of personal finances, because they were 'very woolly' about what such the enduring power entailed (*Nottinghamshire CC 2002*).

6.11 COURT OF PROTECTION

Sections 15 to 20 outline the function of the new Court of Protection. The Court is likely to play a crucial role in cases relevant to protecting and safeguarding vulnerable adults. Some of the key points are as follows:

- **(declarations about capacity and interventions)** it has the power to make declarations about whether or not a person has capacity, and about lawfulness of any act done or proposed to be done in relation to the person (s.15)

- **(making orders, appointing deputies)** it can make a decision (by making an order) or alternatively, appoint a deputy, whose powers may extend to personal welfare, as well as to property and affairs

- **(orders preferred to deputies)** a decision of the court is to be preferred to the appointment of a deputy. The powers conferred on a deputy should be as limited in scope and duration as is reasonably practicable

- **(court subject to principles of Act)** the powers of the court are subject to the provisions of the Act, in particular the principles in s.1 and the test of best interests in s.4 (s.16)

- **(scope of welfare decisions)** personal welfare decisions could include in particular where the incapacitated person is to live, with whom he or she should have contact, consent or refusal to health care treatment (s.17)

- **(age of deputy, joint or several)** a deputy must be at least 18 years old. Two more deputies may be appointed to act jointly or severally (s.19)

- **(restraint)** if a deputy restrains the person, such intervention must be within the scope of the deputy's authority, necessary and proportionate, and the person lack capacity or the deputy reasonably believe that the person lacks capacity in relation to the matter)

- **(property, wills)** a deputy cannot be given power to settle any of the person's property, to execute the person's will or to exercise any power vested in the person (e.g. trusteeship)

- **(life sustaining treatment)** a deputy cannot refuse consent to life-sustaining treatment

- **(limit to authority)** a deputy cannot make a decision inconsistent with the scope of his or her authority or with a decision made by the donee of a lasting power of attorney

- **(contact and health care)** a deputy cannot be given powers to prohibit a named person from having contact with the person lacking capacity, nor to direct a person responsible for the person's health care to allow somebody else to take over the responsibility (s.20)

- **(fees)** where deputies are appointed, there are both appointment fees and supervision fees (specified at three levels) charged by the Public Guardian. There are exemptions in relation to receipt of benefits and also reduction and remission and fees in exceptional circumstances involving undue hardship (SI 2007/2051)

- **(deprivation of liberty)** in relation to standard authorisations concerning deprivation of liberty, the court can determine questions relating to whether the person meets the qualifying requirements, the period the authorisation is to be in force, the purpose of the authorisation, the conditions attached to the authorisation. It can vary or terminate the authorisation or direct that the supervisory body do so (s.21A).

Receiverships (dealing only with property, business, finance) previously put in place by the former Court of Protection under Part 7 of the Mental Health Act 1983 remain valid but are treated as equivalent deputyship (Mental Capacity Act 2005, schedule 5).

In the absence of a more suitable person, the Court of Protection might indicate that it would be appropriate and desirable for a local authority (for example, in the form of the director of social services) to be appointed deputy. Were the local authority to refuse, a challenge to that refusal would need to be by means of a judicial review decision in order to scrutinise the rationality or lawfulness of that refusal (*R(M) v Birmingham CC*).

6.11.1 COURT OF PROTECTION: INVOLVEMENT

Court of Protection involvement is intended to be a last resort for welfare issues. For instance, the Code of Practice states that in a dispute about best interests (about welfare matters), a decision-maker could be challenged through use of an advocate, getting a second opinion, holding a case conference, mediation, or use of a complaints procedure. Only then, the Code states, should application be made to the Court (Lord Chancellor 2007, para 5.68).

However, the Code states that application to the Court about personal welfare, including health, interventions, may be necessary in case of particularly difficult decisions, disagreements that cannot otherwise be resolved, or situations where ongoing decisions may need to be made. The courts have in the past stated that certain serious medical interventions should always go to court, including decisions about artificial nutrition and hydration for patients in a persistent vegetative state (*Airedale NHS Trust v Bland*), bone marrow donation (*Re Y (Mental incapacity: bone marrow transplant)*), and non-therapeutic sterilisation (*SL v SL*).

For finance and property, a Court order will usually be necessary unless the only income involved is from state benefits or an enduring or lasting power of attorney exists. The Code of Practice states that the court may make a particular finance decision, for example, to terminate a tenancy or to make or amend a will. However, it may appoint a deputy for ongoing management of such affairs (a) for dealing with cash assets over a specified amount; (b) for selling a person's property; or (c) where the person has a level of income or capital that the court thinks a deputy needs to manage (Lord Chancellor 2007, paras 8.27–8.35).

A dispute may be not only about a serious welfare matter, but also be heated. The following case, albeit involving a child, indicates how significant disagreement and conflict can arise about a person's best interests, and that application to the court should have been made earlier:

Hospital treatment dispute between family and doctors. A boy, 12 years old, severely physically and mentally disabled, was admitted to hospital in July. He became critically ill and was put on a
ventilator. During treatment, his mother was informed by hospital staff that her son was dying and that
further intensive care would be inappropriate. Nevertheless, he improved and returned home on 2
September. He was readmitted six days later. Doctors discussed the possible use of morphine with his
mother, to alleviate distress. The mother was opposed to this, wanting instead resuscitation and
intubation in case of deterioration. At the time one of the doctors noted that in case of total disagreement a court order might be required.

Threat to arrest mother. A few weeks later, on 20 October, his condition deteriorated. The doctors
thought he was dying, and recommended diamorphine for distress. The mother did not agree and
opposed use of the diamorphine, on the grounds that it would reduce his chances of recovery. A
meeting was held between the mother and the doctors, with a police presence. The mother wanted
to take her son home; the police officer advised that if she attempted to do so, she would be arrested.

A dispute subsequently broke out involving other family members, who attempted to prevent
doctors from entering the hospital room. Hospital security staff were called; they threatened to
exclude the family members by force. A 'do not resuscitate' order was put on the patient's notes,
without consultation with the mother.

Physical fight on ward. The next day the boy's condition had deteriorated; the family demanded cessation of diamorphine. The doctor would only accede to this if the family agreed not to attempt to
resuscitate him. The family tried to revive him and a fight broke out between the family members and
the doctors. During the fight, the mother successfully resuscitated her son. Police were summoned,
several of whom were injured. All but one of the other patients on the ward had to be evacuated. The
son's condition improved and he went home on 21 October.

Breach of human rights. The European Court of Human Rights held that the boy's article 8 rights
had been breached; namely his right to respect for his private life and in particular physical integrity.
This was because although the doctors could not have predicted the level of confrontation and hostility that had arisen, nevertheless the NHS trust should have made a High Court application at an
earlier stage since serious disagreement with the mother was clearly foreseeable. Even at a late stage,
the court felt that such an application could have been made; if there was time to secure the presence
of the police at a meeting, there should have been time to make a court application at short notice.
Therefore the decision of the 'authorities' to override the mother's objection was a breach of article
8 of the European Convention (*Glass v UK*).

The court may be dealing with, for example, issues concerning medical treatment, where
a person with learning disabilities should live, marriage of a person with learning disabilities, where older people should live and be cared for etc. Prior to October 2007, the High
Court was dealing with just such matters by exercising its inherent jurisdiction. Many of
the principles it applied are now embodied in Mental Capacity Act 2005; so these cases
are directly relevant to the working of the Act.

The court may be called on to confirm a lack of capacity and make an order – as in one
case about preventing a woman's parents (motivated by strong cultural and religious
influences) from entering into a contract of marriage for her, and forbidding them to take
her abroad (to Pakistan) without permission from the court (*M v B*). Alternatively, it may
decide not to make an order. In another case concerning a possible marriage in Pakistan
for a man with learning disabilities who clearly lacked capacity to marry, the court
refrained from such an order on the grounds that his parents were honourable people and

the court would accept their undertakings not to contract a marriage or take him to Pakistan without application to the court (*X City Council v MB*).

In a further case, the court granted an order to prevent the wife of a person with dementia from interfering with his transfer from a nursing home to hospital. It also sought to prevent her visiting hospital without the prior written agreement of the local authority and even then, only in the presence of a local authority employee. The court granted the order sought. She had previously been caring for him at home; he was 90 years old, lacked capacity, had difficult and challenging behaviour, together with extensive care needs including incontinence and lack of mobility (*B Borough Council v Mrs S*).

In that case, the court stressed that 'without notice' applications should not be the norm – since they did not allow the other side to be heard before an order was granted. It noted with regret how frequently without notice applications were made on the basis of 'largely unparticularised assertions', without any third party material to support them. The court appreciated that in 'many instances there is a very real urgency and there will not be third party evidence of allegations of abusive behaviour that are readily available but in others there will be.' The points made in this case were endorsed in a subsequent case, in which a local authority sought and gained a without notice order on the basis of largely false allegations:

Order removing man from daughter on basis of false allegations by local authority. This involved another without notice application, with the real authority seeking an order to transfer a 78-year-old man with dementia out of the care of his daughter and grand-daughter into a care home. He lacked capacity to decide for himself. A first court hearing had resulted in a without notice order to have him removed. A second court hearing challenged the making of that without notice application, in the first hearing, by the local authority. Virtually all the local authority's assertions, on which it had relied to obtain the without notice order, were shown subsequently to be false (*LLBC v TG*).

6.11.2 COURT OF PROTECTION: APPLICATION TO

Permission is not needed to make an application to the Court by a person lacking, or alleged to lack, capacity, by a person with a parental responsibility for a person under 18 years old, by a donor or donee of a lasting power of attorney, by a court-appointed deputy, or by a person named in an existing court order (with which the application is concerned). Otherwise permission is required (s.50). Applications to the Court are governed by detailed rules (SI 2007/1744).

Fees are charged, but there are exemptions in relation to receipt of benefits and also reduction and remission of fees in exceptional circumstances involving undue hardship (SI 2007/1745).

6.12 ADVANCE DECISIONS

Sections 24–26 set out the rules about advance decisions or 'living wills' as they have commonly been known. These are about people's refusal of medical treatment in advance of loss of capacity. A knowledge of the rules may be crucial both in raising or allaying –

depending on the circumstances – suspicions about what is happening to a vulnerable adult. The crucial point is that if all rules are complied with and conditions met, then an advance decision is legally binding.

- **(age and capacity to specify refusal of medical treatment)** a person aged 18 or over, with the capacity to do so, may specify the circumstances in which at a future date, if he or she lacks capacity, specified treatment is *not* to be given
- **(withdrawal)** the person may withdraw or alter an advance decision
- a withdrawal need not be in writing
- **(alteration)** an alteration need not be in writing, unless it relates to life-sustaining treatment s.24)
- **(treatment)** treatment is defined to include a 'diagnostic or other procedure' (s.64)
- **(invalidity)** the advance decision is not valid if the person has withdrawn it, subsequently conferred authority for the making of such a decision through a lasting power of attorney, or done anything inconsistent with the advance decision
- **(non-applicability)** the advance decision is not applicable to the particular treatment in issue if at the time the person has capacity to refuse or to consent to the treatment, or if the treatment in question is not specified in the advance decision, or if the circumstances specified in the advance statement have not arisen, or if there are reasonable grounds for believing that circumstances now exist that the person did not anticipate at the time of the advance decision, but which would have affected that decision had they been anticipated
- **(life-sustaining treatment: must be in writing)** the advance decision is not applicable to life-sustaining treatment unless the decision is verified by the person that it is to apply to that treatment even if life is at risk – and is in writing, signed by the person or by somebody else in the presence of, and by the direction, of the person, the signature is made or acknowledged by the person in the presence of a witness, and the witness signs it or acknowledges his/her signature in the person's presence (s.25)
- **(effect of valid and applicable decision)** otherwise an advance decision that is both valid and applicable to the treatment in question has effect as if the person had made it (and had the capacity to do so) at the time when the question arises about whether to carry out the treatment
- **(liability)** a person does not incur liability for providing treatment unless he or she know there was a valid and applicable advance decision
- **(Court of Protection)** the Court of Protection can make a declaration about the existence, validity or applicability of an advance decision
- **(interim treatment)** nothing in an apparent advance decision prevents the provision of life-sustaining treatment of prevention of serious deterioration in the person's condition, while a decision is sought from the Court (s.26).

Under the Act, an advance decision about life-sustaining treatment must be in writing, but not necessarily written by the person making the decision. For instance, somebody else can sign at the direction of the person making the decision, and in the presence of a witness. In the following case the person making the decision could not have written and signed anything, but somebody else could have signed in the presence of a witness:

Advance statement by means of slight eyelash movement. A man with motor neurone disease had slight eyelash movement as his only means of communication to express his wishes. By this means, he stated that when he lost this last means of communication, he wished the artificial ventilation to cease. The court stated that such a valid advance indication would be effective and that doctors would not be entitled to act inconsistently with it – so long as he did not subsequently indicate that his wishes had changed (*Re AK (medical treatment: consent)*).

The person must have the requisite capacity at the time of making the statement. For instance, a person with borderline personality disorder, who self-harmed by cutting herself and by blood-letting, made such a statement refusing blood transfusions. She believed her blood was evil and contaminated the blood that was being transfused. The evidence showed that she lacked capacity at the time of making the statement; it was therefore not legally effective (*An NHS Trust v Ms T*).

Advance decisions concern refusal of medical treatment only. Any other advance statement – for example, about medical treatment desired, or about location of care – would have to be taken account of in the best interests test applied under s.4 of the Act, but would not be legally binding. The following case, heard before the Mental Capacity Act 2005 was in force, well illustrates the two questions of whether an advance decision is both valid and applicable:

Religious beliefs and validity of advance decision in the light of mother's wish for her daughter to go without treatment and father's opposed wish. A 24-year-old woman had been born to Muslim parents. Her parents separated. Her mother became a Jehovah's Witness, as did her daughter. When she was 22 years old she made an advance decision, which expressly stated an absolute refusal to have a blood transfusion. She suffered from aortic valve disease. Two years later she was taken seriously ill and was rushed to hospital. She was unconscious. Her mother and other relatives were adamant that the advance directive should be observed. The situation became critical over the next couple of weeks.

The matter was referred to the High Court. The father made a statement including the following points. First, for the past few months, his daughter had been betrothed to a Turkish Muslim man on condition she would revert back to being a Muslim. Second, following a promise to her fiancé, she had during this time not attended any Jehovah's Witness meetings, which she used to attend twice weekly. Third, prior to her collapse, she had admitted herself to hospital for two days, did not mention the advance directive and had said to her aunt and brother that she did not want to die. Fourth, she had announced to the family two months previously that she would not allow anything to get in the way of marrying her fiancé, and that she would follow his Muslim faith.

The judge set out certain principles. First, the burden of proof lies on those who seek to establish the existence, validity and applicability of an advance directive, because if there is doubt, that doubt should be resolved in favour of life. The proof needs to be clear and convincing, no more than the civil standard (balance of probability), but nonetheless stronger and more cogent in relation to the gravity of the issue.

He went on to point out that it is 'fundamental that an advance directive is, of its very essence and nature, inherently revocable.' Furthermore, such revocation need not be in writing because, clearly, a 'patient who has changed his mind is not to be condemned to death because pen and ink are not readily to hand.'

Ultimately, in this case, the judge found compelling the evidence of the father that his daughter had rejected her faith in the Jehovah's Witness religion, on which the advance directive was entirely founded. The directive was no longer valid. Even if he was wrong about this, the father's evidence – at the very lowest – threw 'considerable doubt' on the validity and of the directive. And such doubt had to be resolved in favour of preservation of his daughter's life (*HE v A Hospital NHS Trust*).

Nothing in the Act changes the law relating to murder, manslaughter or assisted suicide (s.62). Thus, assisted suicide remains unlawful, even in the light of human rights legislation (*Pretty v United Kingdom*).

An advance decision could refuse the artificial nutrition and hydration but not basic care: 'An advance decision cannot refuse actions that are needed to keep a person comfortable (sometimes called basic or essential care). Examples include warmth, shelter, actions to keep a person clean and the offer of food and water by mouth. Section 5 of the Act allows health care professionals to carry out these actions in the best interests of a person who lacks capacity to consent… An advance decision can refuse artificial nutrition and hydration.' (Lord Chancellor 2007, para 9.28)

In addition, artificial nutrition and hydration (ANH) will be clinically indicated, unless a clinical decision has been taken that the life in question should come to an end. However, such a decision could not lawfully be taken if a competent patient expresses a wish to remain alive: a doctor who deliberately interrupts 'life-prolonging treatment in the face of a competent patient's expressed wish to be kept alive, with the intention of thereby terminating the patient's life, would leave the doctor with no answer to a charge of murder.' Nonetheless, a competent patient could refuse to receive life-prolonging treatment, including ANH. Where a person lacks capacity, and a best interests decision needs to be taken about ANH, the decision will depend 'on the particular circumstances' (*Burke v General Medical Council*).

Thus, what clinicians cannot do is decide positively to administer treatment to shorten life. For instance, a GP was accused of murder, not for easing suffering, but deliberately intending to kill his patients (who were seriously but not terminally ill) with massive dose of morphine. He was accused of having decided that their time to die had come. He was acquitted for lack of evidence (Wainwright 2005; *BBC News* 2005).

6.12.1 OLDER ADVANCE DECISIONS

If an advance decision concerning life-sustaining treatment was made before the coming into force of the MCA (1 October 2007), it may still be valid and applicable in certain circumstances. These are that:

- a person providing health care to the individual reasonably believes that such an advance decision had been made before 1 October 2007 and that since 1 October the individual has lacked the capacity (a) to verify by a statement that the advance decision is to apply to the treatment in question even if life is at risk; and (b) to carry out the requirement that the advance decision be signed and witnessed

- the advance decision is in writing
- the person did not withdraw the decision when he or she still had capacity to do so, and has not done anything else clearly inconsistent with the advance decision
- the person lacks the capacity to decide about the treatment in question at the material time
- the treatment in question is specified in the advance decision
- the circumstances specified in the advance decision are present
- there are no reasonable grounds for believing circumstances exist which the individual did not anticipate at the time of the advance decision and which would have affected that decision (SI 2007/1898).

The requirements that then do not have to be met are (a) the verifying statement that the decision is to apply to treatment even if life is at risk; and (b) the signing and witnessing of the decision.

6.13 DECISIONS EXCLUDED FROM THE MENTAL CAPACITY ACT

Sections 27 and 29 sets out a range of decisions that are not permitted under the Act, where the person themselves lacks capacity to take the decision. These exclusions include consent to marriage or civil partnership, consent to sexual relations, consent to divorce based on two years' separation, consent to a dissolution order in relation to civil partnership based on two years' separation, consent to child being placed for adoption, consent to making of an adoption order, discharging parental responsibilities in matters unrelated to child's property, giving consent under Human Fertilisation and Embryology Act 1990 (s.27). Voting is also excluded (s.29).

The courts have pointed out that, in relation to such questions and capacity, best interests are simply irrelevant. If the person has capacity to take such a decision, then best interests have no part to play because the person can do as he or she likes. If there is lack of capacity, then likewise best interests are irrelevant, because the person cannot take the decision anyway. In a case about whether a young woman had the capacity to marry, the court noted that there was significant confusion underlying an important part of the case. The local authority was asking the court to decide whether it was in the woman's best interests to marry. But, the court had 'no business – in fact…no jurisdiction – to embark upon a determination of that question' (*Sheffield CC v E*).

6.14 MENTAL HEALTH ACT

In principle, the Mental Capacity Act 2005 does not interfere with rules under the Mental Health Act 1983. This principle is not without a degree of complexity.

Generally, under s.28 of the 2005 Act, the Mental Capacity Act 2005 (MCA) does not authorise the giving of treatment for mental disorder if it is treatment regulated by part 4 of the Mental Health Act 1983.

The MCA Code of Practice states that the MHA may have to be used if a person cannot be given care or treatment without a deprivation of liberty, treatment cannot be given under the MCA because of an advance decision, restraint may be required that is not allowed under the MCA, compulsory treatment is required (and the person may regain capacity to consent or to refuse consent), the person has the capacity to refuse a vital part of the treatment and has done so, or there is some other reason why the person might not get the treatment and they or somebody else will suffer harm.

However, compulsory treatment under the MHA cannot in any event be given unless the patient's mental disorder justifies detention in hospital. It also cannot be used if the treatment required is only for physical illness or disability.

The MCA will apply to people subject to the MHA as it applies to anybody else with four exceptions: (a) if a person is detained under the MHA, decision-makers cannot normally rely on the MCA to give treatment for mental disorder; (b) if a detained person can be treated for mental disorder without their consent under the MHA, then health care staff can override an advance decision refusing that treatment; (c) if a person is subject to guardianship under the MHA, the guardian has an exclusive right to take certain decisions including where the person is to reside; (d) health care staff cannot (under the MHA or MCA), in any circumstances, give psychosurgery or surgical implantation of hormones to reduce sex drive to a person who lacks the capacity to consent to such treatment (Lord Chancellor 2007, pp.225–6).

This guidance has to be read in the light of the changes to the Mental Capacity Act, due in late 2008, which will enable the authorisation of deprivation of liberty in some circumstances (see section 6.5 above). Also the position will be affected by other changes under the 2005 Act and the Mental Health Act 1983, as amended by the Mental Health Act 2007, which will probably be in force by late 2008.

As amended, s.28 of the Mental Capacity Act will be as follows. The general prohibition will remain, to the effect that nothing in the 2005 Act authorises anyone to give, or consent to, a patient's medical treatment for mental disorder – if the treatment is regulated by Part 4 of the Mental Health Act 1983. Section 5 of the Act (legal defence for care or treatment given under the Mental Capacity Act: see above) does not apply to treatment of supervised community treatment patients (under Part 4A of the 1983 Act) who have not been recalled to hospital. However, there is authority to give the treatment to such a patient if the person has capacity to consent to it, or a donee or deputy or the Court of Protection authorises it. In addition a number of other conditions have to be met (other than in the case of immediately necessary treatment) (Mental Capacity Act 2005, s.28; Mental Health Act 1983, as amended, ss.64A–64G). It is beyond the scope of this book to set out the detail.

6.15 INDEPENDENT MENTAL CAPACITY ADVOCATES (IMCAS)

The Act provides for independent mental capacity advocates (IMCAs) to be appointed. In particular, in addition to various duties, there is a power for NHS bodies or local authorities to appoint such an advocate where adult protection issues have arisen. In such circumstances, an IMCA could play a key role.

6.15.1 ROLE OF IMCA

Generally, section 35 places a duty on the Department of Health to make arrangements for independent mental capacity advocates. Local authorities are responsible for contracting locally with appropriate organisations. Such an advocate has the power to:

- interview the person whom he or she has been instructed to represent
- at all reasonable times examine and take copies of a health record, a local authority social services record, or a record of registered care provider – which holder of the record considers may be relevant to the advocate's investigation.

The advocate's core functions are to provide support, obtain and evaluate relevant information, ascertain what the person's wishes, feelings, beliefs and values might be (if the person had capacity), ascertain alternative courses of action, and obtain a further medical opinion where treatment is proposed (if the advocate thinks this should be obtained) (s.36). The advocate must prepare a report for the authorised person who instructed him or her. The advocate subsequently has the same rights to challenge the decision as if he or she were any other person engaged in caring for the person or interested in his or her welfare (s.36 and SI 2006/1832).

6.15.2 DUTY TO APPOINT IMCA: ACCOMMODATION OR SERIOUS MEDICAL TREATMENT

Appointment of an IMCA may be a duty or power. First, a duty arises (a) if the person lacking capacity is unbefriended – that is, if the local authority or NHS body is satisfied that there is no other person (other than one providing care or treatment in professional capacity or for remuneration) whom it would be appropriate to consult about the person's best interests; and (b) if serious medical treatment or placement in a hospital or care home is in question. In the case of a hospital the placement must be likely to last longer than four weeks, in a care home longer than eight weeks.

The Code of Practice makes clear that just because a 'family disagrees with the decision-maker's proposed action, this is not grounds for concluding that there is nobody whose views are relevant to the decision' (Lord Chancellor 2007, para 10.79). There is also no duty to appoint an advocate if there is another person, nominated by the person lacking capacity, to be consulted on matters to which the duty relates; if there is a donee of a lasting power of attorney authorised to make decisions on those welfare matters; or if there is a court-appointed deputy with the power to make decisions in relation to those welfare matters (s.40).

Serious medical treatment involves providing, withdrawing or withholding treatment in the following circumstances:

- in the case of a single treatment, there is a fine balance between benefit, and burden and risk, to the patient
- where there is a choice of treatments, a decision as to which one to use is finely balanced; or
- what is proposed would be likely to involve serious consequences for the patient (SI 2006/1832).

The duty to appoint an IMCA falls either on the NHS body in the case of serious medical treatment, or hospital or care home placement – or on the local authority in case of a care home placement.

There are in addition special IMCA provisions relating to authorisations to deprive a person of his or her liberty under schedule A1 of the MCA 2005. Basically, if a person does not have a personal representative but is subject to the deprivation of liberty principles, or the supervisory body believes that the person and the representative are not exercising relevant rights, then it must appoint an IMCA (ss.39A–39E: due in force in April 2009).

In case of urgency, the rules are relaxed, and the IMCA should be subsequently appointed, in the case of provision of accommodation (ss.37–39).

6.15.3 POWER TO INSTRUCT ADVOCATE IN CASE OF ABUSE OR NEGLECT
A power (rather than a duty) arises to appoint an IMCA in two circumstances. First if adult protection measures are being or are going to be taken – whether or not there are family or friends appropriate to consult (see immediately below). Second, if the hospital or care home accommodation is being reviewed, where the person has been in the accommodation for at least 12 weeks continuously (ss.36–39 and SI 2006/2883).

The power in relation to adult protection arises if the NHS body or local authority proposes to take, or has taken protective measures, for a person lacking capacity (a) following receipt of allegation of abuse or neglect (by another person); or (b) in accordance with arrangements made under adult protection guidance issued under s.7 Local Authority Social Services Act 1970. This is referring to the *No secrets* guidance issued in 2000 (DH 2000). Protective measures are defined to include measures to minimise risk of abuse or neglect.

The power is not dependent on the absence of another person, other than one providing care or treatment in a professional capacity or for remuneration, whom it would be appropriate to consult about the person's best interests (SI 2006/2883). Although the protection of vulnerable adults features increasingly prominently in the work of local authorities, there is nonetheless concern that financial restrictions may limit use of this power to appoint an IMCA (Gorczynska and Thompson 2007).

6.16 OFFENCE OF ILL-TREATMENT OR WILFUL NEGLECT

Section 44 creates an offence of ill-treatment or wilful neglect by any person who has the care of another person who lacks, or who the first person reasonably believed to lack, capacity – or by any deputy or person with lasting power of attorney (s.44). This is dealt with below (see section 8.6.2).

6.17 OFFICE OF THE PUBLIC GUARDIAN

A new Public Guardian is created, supported by the Office of the Public Guardian (MCA 2005. s.57). The functions of the Public Guardian are to protect people lacking capacity and include (a) setting up and managing separate registers of lasting powers of attorney, of enduring powers of attorney, of court order appointed deputies; (b) supervising deputies; (c) sending Court of Protection visitors to visit people who may lack capacity and also those who formal powers to act on their behalf; (d) receiving reports from attorneys acting under lasting powers of attorney and from deputies; (e) providing reports to the Court of Protection; and (f) dealing with complaints about the way in which attorneys or deputies carry out their duties (Lord Chancellor 2007, para 14.8).

6.18 APPOINTEES

The law relating to appointeeship remains outside of the Mental Capacity Act 2005. Where a person is receiving social security benefits, but is 'for the time being unable to act', then an appointee may be appointed to manage the benefits, assuming that no deputy with the relevant power has been appointed by the Court of Protection (SI 1987/1968)

It is a matter of somebody applying to be appointee to the Benefits Agency. If there is no-one willing and able to take on the role, a local authority for example can take it on, with named officers signing the paperwork etc. If a care home manager or owner becomes an appointee, it is the policy of the Benefits Agency to inform the registration body, as a safeguard against any possible financial abuse (Bateman 2001).

6.19 INHERENT JURISDICTION OF THE HIGH COURT

The 2005 Act means that many decisions previously taken by the Family Division of the High Court under common law, the inherent jurisdiction, will now be made by the Court of Protection. However, some issues may arise that fall outside the 2005 Act and so may call still for the exercise of the inherent jurisdiction.

For instance, the High Court has held that it can exercise the jurisdiction in respect of a competent adult whose capacity to consent to marriage is overborne by fear, duress or threat, such that she is deprived of the capacity to make relevant decisions (Re SK). Subsequently, the courts stated that the inherent jurisdiction is not confined only to cases involving lack of mental capacity or to cases where, although not lacking capacity, the adult is unable to communicate his or her decision. In addition, it could extend to a vulnerable adult who 'even if not incapacitated by mental disorder or mental illness, is, or is reasonably believed to be, either (i) under constraint, or (ii) subject to coercion or undue influence or (iii) for some other reason deprived of the capacity to make the relevant decision, or disabled from making a free choice, or incapacitated or disabled from giving or expressing real or genuine consent' (*Re SA*). Thus, in the same case, the court granted the order sought to protect the woman:

Protecting a person with the capacity to understand marriage. A woman was profoundly deaf. She had no speech and no oral communication. She had profound bilateral sensory neural loss, and significant visual loss in one eye. She communicated in British Sign Language, which was based in English. Her ability to communicate with her parents was very limited because their first language was Punjabi. She had limited capacity to lip read English. She could not understand, lip read or sign in either Punjabi or Urdu. Neither of her parents could communicate with her using British Sign Language.

She had been assessed as having a rudimentary but clear and accurate understanding of the concept of marriage, the implications of a marriage contract, of a sexual relationship and its implications. However, the assessing doctor, a chartered forensic psychologist, was concerned that she might marry a person who could not communicate with her, especially outside the UK where she might be surrounded also by people with whom she could not communicate.

She had made it clear that although she wished to travel to Pakistan for an arranged marriage, she did not want to live there and wished to return to her home town. If this were not possible, she would rather not marry. However, she did not understand that any such husband might be prevented from returning with her by the immigration authorities. It had now come to the local authority's attention that a trip to Pakistan might be imminent.

It was argued that the court should intervene, prohibiting her parents from threatening, intimidating, harassing her, using violence, preventing her communicating alone with her solicitor, applying for travel documents for her, removing her from England and Wales without express written consent (translated and explained in BSL) and duly notarised. They would also be prohibited from making arrangements for her to be married unless they had her express written consent (as above), notarised consent of the bridegroom, allowed her to return to her home town within four months of the marriage ceremony, allowed her to reside in her home town, allowed a visit by a worker from the British High Commission in Islamabad four months after the ceremony to interview alone as to whether she wished to return to England and Wales. A power of arrest was also sought, to be attached to any order made.

The court granted the order sought. In summary, the court stated that the person was a 'vulnerable adult who there is every reason to believe may, by reason of her disabilities, and even in the absence of any undue influence or misinformation, be disabled from making a free choice and incapacitated or disabled from forming or expressing a real and genuine consent' (*Re SA*).

The Court of Appeal is clear that the inherent jurisdiction survives, albeit reinforced by the Mental Capacity Act 2005 (*KC v City of Westminster SCSD*).

It has been argued, unsuccessfully, that the inherent jurisdiction might be exercisable by the High Court not just in relation to incapacity to take a decision (when the case falls outside the Mental Capacity Act) - but also in relation to protection of a vulnerable adult from harm, even when the person has the capacity to take the decision in question, but the decision would lead to harm. This was in a case involving the fluctuating capacity of a mentally disordered woman to consent to sexual relations. The local authority could use the Mental Capacity Act 2005 to protect her when she lacked capacity; but it argued also that the court should exercise its inherent jurisdiction to make a protective order to apply at those times when she had capacity. The court rejected this. It referred back to the *Re SA* case (see above), concluding that 'there are instances where a person cannot in truth consent although not incapacitated within the meaning of the 2005 Act'. But that case was talking of 'persons who are deemed not to have capacity in the true sense, and not of persons where a paternalistic authority considers the acts unwise'. The courts could not intervene in the latter circumstance (*Ealing LBC v KS*).

6.20 ACT'S APPLICATION TO CHILDREN AND YOUNG PEOPLE

The Act does not apply to people under 16 years old, unless the Court of Protection is making a decision about a child's (without capacity) property, where the child is likely still to lack capacity at age 18 (Mental Capacity Act 2005, s.18). In addition, the offence of ill-treatment or wilful neglect of a person who lacks capacity can also apply to people under 16.

The Act does apply to people aged 16 or 17 years but (a) only people aged 18 or over can make a lasting power of attorney (s.9); (b) only people aged 18 or over can make advance decisions (s.24); and (c) the Court of Protection can only make a statutory will for a person aged 18 or over (s.18).

Legal proceedings in respect of 16- or 17-year-olds who lack capacity to make the relevant decisions may be heard either by the Court of Protection or the family courts. Proceedings can be transferred between the two (s.21 and SI 2007/1899).

The deprivation of liberty safeguards in relation to standard or urgent authorisations, due to come into force in April 2009, do not apply to people under 18 years old. The rules concerning the detention and treatment of children, particularly 16- and 17-year-olds, are somewhat complex as a result of these amendments to the Mental Capacity Act 2005 and amendments to the Mental Health Act 1983 (both sets of amendments being introduced by the Mental Health Act 2007).

CHAPTER 7

National Assistance Act, environmental health, Mental Health Act and other interventions

KEY POINTS

In addition to interventions under the Mental Capacity Act, a number of other legal avenues exist which may be relevant to cases of abuse or neglect. In case of a person living neglected and in squalor, the National Assistance Act 1948 or environmental health legislation might be relevant. The Mental Health Act 1983 may afford an intervention. For instance, guardianship allows a local authority to protect a person by determining where he or she should live; and there has been a number of legal cases in which the courts have traced the line between this intervention and use of the mental capacity law.

In addition, in case of abuse including violence or threatened violence, court orders in relation to harassment under the Protection from Harassment Act 1997 may be relevant. In the case of a person closely associated with the vulnerable adult, a non-molestation or occupation order might be available under the Family Law Act 1996. Alternatively an anti-social behaviour order might be relevant. All these orders could play a part in safeguarding a vulnerable adult from abuse. Sometimes, however, such orders are sought not just to protect such an adult, but also against such an adult on account of his or her own behaviour.

Legislation about 'whistle-blowing' is arguably of great importance in the protection of people from abuse and neglect, where it stems from within an organisation or institution. In principle, the Public Interest Disclosure Act 1998, which amended the Employment Rights Act 1996, protects employees when they speak out about matters of concern, including a criminal offence or health and safety matter.

7.1 NATIONAL ASSISTANCE ACT 1948, S.47: REMOVAL OF PEOPLE FROM OWN HOME

Under s.47 of the National Assistance Act 1948, local authorities (district councils or borough councils) can by magistrate's order remove to institutional care people who:

- are suffering from grave chronic disease or, being aged, infirm or physically incapacitated, are living in insanitary conditions
- are unable to devote to themselves, and are not receiving from other persons, proper care and attention.

A medical officer of health (i.e. community physician) must certify to the authority that removal is necessary either in his or her own best interests, or for prevention of injury to the health of, or serious nuisance to, other people.

The authority can apply to a magistrates' court for an order that may authorise the person's detention for up to three months; although this may be extended by court order. Seven days' notice is required to be given to the person before a court can consider the application. The period of notice can be dispensed with under powers in the National Assistance (Amendment) Act 1951, if it is certified both by the medical officer of health and another registered medical practitioner that in their opinion it is necessary in the interests of the person that he or she be removed without delay.

However, the person does not have to be mentally incapacitated or mentally disordered for s.47 to operate. Thus, there exists a view that s.47 of the 1948 Act is contrary in principle to the Human Rights Act 1998. This would be on the basis that neglect alone is not a ground on which people may be deprived of their liberty under a.5 of the European Convention on Human Rights. The article refers to people of unsound mind, alcoholics, drug addicts or vagrants – but not to people who neglect themselves or are neglected, who have the mental capacity to decide where and how they want to live (and so are not of unsound mind), and who are not otherwise diagnosed as mentally disordered.

For instance, medical opinion is reportedly divided about intervention in the case of people who suffer from so-called Diogenes syndrome, which is characterised by extreme self-neglect, domestic squalor, social withdrawal and apathy and tendency to hoard rubbish. They often refuse assistance and have many physical problems including nutritional deficiencies, but may be content and survive without external support. Many might not be suffering from mental disorder, but have rejected normal standards of behaviour (Persaud 2003, pp.304–6).

Whether s.47 would be held by the courts to be contrary to human rights – at least in some circumstances – is not clear, given the case of *HM v Switzerland*, heard before the European Court of Human Rights (the United Kingdom courts must take account of, though not necessarily follow, the European Court's judgments).

Removing a person from her own home. Under the Swiss Civil Code, a person can be deprived of liberty on grounds of mental weakness or neglect. A woman in her eighties was living at home, was fairly infirm and had leg sores, and was nearly blind but capable of making decisions for herself. She was receiving a home help service from a voluntary organisation. This service was withdrawn because of difficulties in the home – the son opening the door skimpily dressed and only after a delay, rubbish around the house impeding the home help workers, unheated rooms, chaos in the woman's bedroom, etc. The family did not respond to a request to ameliorate these conditions.

The local authority ordered that the woman be removed, against her will, for an unlimited period to a nursing home on the ground of serious neglect. She was not placed in the locked ward of the nursing home; she had freedom of movement and had social contacts with the outside world. The woman complained, arguing that she was able to wash and dress herself, that her son (also an invalid) could cook for her and that she did not want him left alone. The local authority disputed this. Both the Appeals Commission and Federal Court upheld the local authority's action.

She was removed on grounds both of neglect and 'vagrancy' (an article 5 term) and unsoundness of mind. Yet she had never been examined by a medical expert in respect of the latter issue, although one of the members of the Appeals Commission was a medical expert.

The European Court held that article 5 was not engaged because she had not been deprived of her liberty. This conclusion was based on the fact that she had been placed in the home in her own interests in order to provide her with the necessary medical care, as well as satisfactory living conditions and hygiene (*HM v Switzerland*).

Nevertheless, one of the judges strongly dissented in *HM v Switzerland*. He believed that article 5 had been breached on various grounds. Most important, and decisive for this dissenting judge, was the fact that the finding by the Appeals Commission that she effectively lacked capacity had been challenged by the woman and never confirmed by a medical expert; whilst the Federal Court had declined to examine the issue on the grounds that serious neglect would anyway justify removal. It would seem, in any case, that this decision has been sidelined by the European Court as suspect (see the analysis in *JE v DE and Surrey County Council*).

7.2 PROTECTION OF PROPERTY: NATIONAL ASSISTANCE ACT 1948, S.48

A duty to protect a person's property arises for a local authority if:

* a person is admitted to hospital, admitted to residential accommodation under s.21 of the 1948 Act, or removed under s.47 of the 1948 Act
* it appears to the local social services authority that there is danger of loss of, or damage to, any of the person's movable property by reason of his or her temporary or permanent inability to protect or deal with the property
* no other suitable arrangements have been or are being made.

If these conditions are satisfied, then the local authority must take reasonable steps to prevent or mitigate the loss or damage. The authority has the power, at all reasonable times, to enter the person's place of residence and to deal with any movable property in a reasonable way to prevent or mitigate loss or damage. The local authority can recover reasonable expenses either from the person concerned or anybody else liable to maintain him or her (National Assistance Act 1948, s.48). Examples of reasonable steps might include, for example, securing the premises, informing the police about an empty property, taking an inventory, turning off utilities, disposing of perishable food, and arranging for pets to be cared for (Jones 2004, para D1–088).

7.3 ENVIRONMENTAL HEALTH INTERVENTIONS

In the context of safeguarding adults, gaining entry into domestic premises (via an appropriate legal channel) in cases of neglect is not necessarily easy, if the person is not opening his or her door. However, local authority environmental health departments do have various statutory powers to enter premises.

7.3.1 ENVIRONMENTAL PROTECTION ACT 1990

Under the Environmental Protection Act 1990 (EPA), local authority powers of entry apply in respect of statutory nuisances. On the production of the requisite authority, an authorised person can enter premises at any reasonable time to ascertain whether a statutory nuisance exists, or to take action or execute work authorised under part 3 of the 1990 Act. In the case of residential property, then 24 hours' notice is required, unless it is an emergency such as danger to life or health (EPA 1990, schedule 3).

Statutory nuisance is defined as including premises that are in a state prejudicial to health or nuisance, smoke, fumes or gases emitted from premises so as to be prejudicial to health or a nuisance, any accumulation or deposit prejudicial to health or a nuisance, any animal kept in such a place or manner as to be prejudicial to health or a nuisance, and noise emitted from premises so as to be prejudicial to health or a nuisance (EPA 1990, s.79).

A local authority has a duty to serve an abatement notice if a statutory nuisance exists (EPA 1990, s.80). If the notice is not complied with, the local authority may itself abate the nuisance and recover expenses reasonably incurred (s.81).

7.3.2 PUBLIC HEALTH ACT 1936

Under the Public Health Act 1936, local authority powers of entry apply in respect of certain public health issues referred to in the Act (s.287). These include filthy, unwhole-some, verminous premises (s.83); verminous person or clothing (including removal of person) (s.85); cleaning or destroying filthy or verminous articles (s.84). Also there is a power to require vacation of premises during fumigation (Public Health Act 1961, s.36). The usefulness of such powers, but also the need to exercise them carefully, was demonstrated in the following local ombudsman case:

Cleaning of premises under the Public Health Act 1936. A man was in poor health with limited ability to care for himself. His home became dirty and cluttered to the point where it required thorough cleaning in order to prevent a health and safety risk to himself and his care workers. His sister got in touch with the local social services authority; it then liaised with the environmental health department. Under s.83 of the Public Health Act 1936 the latter proposed to clean the flat, and explained to the sister that it would do the work and recover the cost from her brother. However, the council sent a very much larger bill (over £1100) than the cost (£300) the sister claimed originally to have been advised by the local authority.

The ombudsman concluded that the council had not been clear enough in its explanation; the bill had also been wrongly calculated. It included VAT in error; and an inflated amount for environmental health officer time had been included. He recommended that the bill be corrected and then reduced by £300, that the sister receive £200 in recognition of her time and trouble, that the council review the wording of its letters about such work and charges for it, and that it check that all bills for such work carried out since January 2003 had been correctly calculated (*Ealing LBC 2004*).

7.4 POLICE POWERS OF ENTRY

A police constable may enter premises in order, amongst other things, to recapture any person whatever who is unlawfully at large and whom he is pursuing – or to save life or limb or prevent serious damage to property (Police and Criminal Evidence Act 1984, s.17).

7.5 GAS AND ELECTRICITY OPERATORS

There are powers of entry associated with utility companies: for instance, gas operators have such powers under the Gas Act 1986 (schedule 2B, paras 20–28) and Rights of Entry (Gas and Electricity Boards) Act 1954.

7.6 MENTAL HEALTH ACT INTERVENTIONS

Where mental disorder is an issue, adult protection and safeguarding may be served by certain interventions under the Mental Health Act 1983. Interventions may break or prevent a cycle of abuse or neglect, but can only be exercised if the relevant statutory grounds are made out. Complusory interventions are a measure of last resort. It is beyond the scope of this book to consider the 1983 Act in any detail. However, guardianship is considered in a little more detail, because it has arisen in a number of legal cases concerning adult protection and mental capacity.

7.6.1 MENTAL HEALTH ACT 1983: INTERVENTIONS AND MENTAL DISORDER

Mental disorder has in the past been defined in s.1 of the Mental Health Act 1983:

- **Mental disorder** is defined as mental illness, arrested or incomplete development of mind, psychopathic disorder and any other disorder or disability of mind and 'mentally disordered' shall be construed accordingly.
- **Severe mental impairment** means a state of arrested or incomplete development of mind, which includes severe impairment of intelligence and social functioning and is associated with abnormally aggressive or seriously irresponsible conduct on the part of the person concerned.
- **Mental impairment** means a state of arrested or incomplete development of mind (not amounting to severe mental impairment) which includes significant impairment of intelligence and social functioning and is associated with abnormally aggressive or seriously irresponsible conduct on the part of the person concerned.
- **Psychopathic disorder** means a persistent disorder or disability of mind (whether or not including significant impairment of intelligence) which results in abnormally aggressive or seriously irresponsible conduct on the part of the person concerned.

The Mental Health Act 2007 amends this definition simply to mental disorder being any disorder or disability of mind. However, learning disability remains excluded unless it is associated with abnormally aggressive or seriously irresponsible conduct (although this condition is not imposed for detention under s.2: see below). Under the changes, learning disability is defined as a state of arrested or incomplete development of mind which includes significant impairment of intelligence and social functioning. These changes are due to come into force in late 2008.

Under the Act as is stands, approved social workers have various functions; as amended, these functions will be exercisable by 'approved mental health professionals' (Mental Health Act 1983, s.114). These will be social workers, first-level nurses practising in the mental health or learning disability fields, occupational therapists, chartered psychologists – with appropriate training and competencies.

7.6.2 LIMITED DETENTION FOR ASSESSMENT (AND TREATMENT)

Under s.2 of the 1983 Act, an application for admission for assessment is made on two grounds, both of which must be made out:

- The 'patient' is suffering from mental disorder of a nature or degree that warrants his or her detention in a hospital for assessment (or for assessment followed by medical treatment) for at least a limited period (up to 28 days).
- He or she ought to be detained in this way in the interests of his own health or safety or with a view to the protection of other persons.

Thus, the following detention, although clearly designed for the protection of both mother and baby, was held to be unlawful, and illustrates that good intentions and a concern to protect somebody is not enough:

Unlawful detention. A woman in the late stages of pregnancy was suffering from pre-eclampsia; there was a risk to the lives of both herself and the unborn baby. She fully understood the potential risks and clearly rejected medical intervention; she wanted the baby to be born 'naturally'. She was then sectioned (unlawfully as it turned out) under s.2 of the Mental Health Act 1983. It was unlawful because although mental disorder was present (depression), it was not of a type that warranted detention in hospital (*R v Collins, ex p S*).

However, the breadth of s.2 (mental disorder including 'any other disorder or disability of mind') could allow detention of a person with a learning disability even in the absence of abnormally aggressive or seriously irresponsible conduct – compared to s.3 (detention) or s.7 (guardianship), both of which require such conduct. (The amendment to be introduced by the Mental Health Act 2007, which states that for mental disorder to cover learning disability, the latter must be associated with abnormally aggressive or seriously irresponsible conduct, does not apply to s.2.)

7.6.3 LONGER TERM DETENTION FOR TREATMENT

Under s.3 of the 1983 Act, an application for admission for treatment is made on the following grounds, all of which must be made out in each case:

- The patient is suffering from mental illness, severe mental impairment, psychopathic disorder or mental impairment and his mental disorder is of a nature or degree which makes it appropriate for him or her to receive medical treatment in a hospital (the Mental Health Act 2007 amends this so as simply to substitute mental disorder).
- In the case of psychopathic disorder or mental impairment, the treatment is likely to alleviate or prevent a deterioration of his condition (the 2007 Act removes this, instead stating that for all mental disorder, appropriate medical treatment must be available).
- It is necessary for the health or safety of the patient or for the protection of other people that he should receive such treatment – and that it cannot be provided unless he is detained.

As amended by the Mental Health Act 2007, the 1983 Act will allow patients detained under s.3 to be subject to supervised community treatment orders (CTOs) when discharged – and remain subject to recall. The requirement will be that the person is suffering from mental disorder and that appropriate treatment be available. If the person has a learning disability, it will not be considered a mental disorder under s.3 unless it is associated with abnormally aggressive or seriously irresponsible conduct.

7.6.4 ENTRY AND INSPECTION OF PREMISES

Under s.115 of the Mental Health Act 1983, an approved social worker may enter and inspect premises (not a hospital) in the area of that authority, if he or she has reasonable cause to believe that a mentally disordered person is living there and is not 'under proper care'.

This power to enter and inspect applies at all reasonable times after the social worker has produced, if asked to do so, some duly authenticated document showing that he or she is such a professional. Although s.115 does not allow for force to be used, obstruction could constitute an offence under s.129 of the 1983 Act. This provision is due to be amended in late 2008 by the Mental Health Act 2007, providing for an approved mental health professional rather than approved social worker.

7.6.5 WARRANT FOR SEARCH AND REMOVAL

Under s.135 of the Mental Health Act 1983, a justice of the peace may issue a warrant authorising a constable to enter premises, using force if necessary, in order, if it is thought fit, to remove a person to a place of safety. This would be with a view to making an application under the Mental Health Act 1983 or other arrangements for care and treatment.

Such a warrant may be issued if it appears to the justice of the peace, from information received on oath by an approved social worker (from late 2008, an approved mental health professional), that there is reasonable cause to suspect that a person believed to be suffering from mental disorder (a) has been, or is being, ill-treated, neglected or not kept under proper control; or (b) is unable to care for himself or herself and is living alone.

7.6.6 REMOVAL OF A MENTALLY DISORDERED PERSON FROM A PUBLIC PLACE

Under s.136 of the Mental Act 1983, a constable may remove to a place of safety a person appearing to be suffering from mental disorder from a place to which the public have access. The constable may do this if (a) the person appears to be in immediate need of care and control; (b) the constable thinks it necessary in the interests of the person or other people. The person may then be detained for up to 72 hours in the place of safety, so that he or she can be examined by a medical practitioner and interviewed by an approved social worker (from late 2008, approved mental health professional), and so that necessary arrangements for treatment or care can be made.

7.6.7 GUARDIANSHIP

Guardianship is a potentially useful tool in adult protection since it can be used to specify where somebody should live. Under s.7 of the Mental Health Act 1983, a guardianship order can be made for a patient aged 16 years or over on the following grounds:

- that he or she is suffering from mental disorder in terms of mental illness, severe mental impairment, mental impairment or psychopathic disorder (the 2007 Act changes this simply to suffering from mental disorder)
- that the mental disorder is of a nature of degree that warrants his or her reception into guardianship
- that this is necessary in the interests of the welfare of the patient – or for the protection of other persons that the patient be so received.

Under s.8 of the Act, the guardian (either the local social services authority or other person) has the power:

- to require the patient to reside at a place specified by the authority or person named as guardian
- to require the patient to attend at specified places and times for medical treatment, occupation, education or training
- to require access to the patient to be given, at any place where the patient is residing, to any registered medical practitioner, approved social worker or other specified person.

The Mental Health Act 2007 (schedule 3, para 3) also amends s.18 of the 1983 Act, so that not only can a person subject to guardianship be fetched back (as at present) but also taken and conveyed to the required place of residence in the first place. Prior to this amendment, there was no explicit power in the Act to convey the person to the place of residence, but there has been a power to return him or her, if he or she has absconded (Mental Health Act 1983, s.18). However, in practice, persistent non-cooperation generally might render guardianship ineffective.

The courts have held previously that there is an implied duty under s.7 of the 1983 Act to act generally for the person's welfare in ways not explicitly referred to in s.8 (*R v Kent CC, ex p Marston*). More recently, they have held that if, in addition to place of residence (which is explicitly covered by s.8 of the Act), the issue of contact with other people arose, then s.8 would not be authority for dealing with it. There would be a statutory lacuna, and a declaration from the courts would be required if the person lacked the capacity to decide himself or herself (*Lewis v Gibson*). Since October 2007, the avenue would be the Mental Capacity Act 2005 and the Court of Protection if necessary, in case of lack of capacity.

7.6.7.1 Guardianship unavailable: question of abnormally aggressive or seriously irresponsible conduct

For many people with learning disabilities, for whom guardianship might be desirable, it is simply not available. This is because in the past, the definitions in the Act of impairment and severe mental impairment, which would apply to people with learning disabilities, include the requirement that the impairment be associated with abnormally aggressive or seriously irresponsible conduct. Under the amending Mental Health Act 2007, this rule effectively remains (see 7.6.1 above).

This requirement is likely to exclude many people with learning disabilities from guardianship, since the courts have taken a restrictive approach to the term serious irresponsibility (*Re F (Adult Patient)*). Thus neither a young person's wish to go home against a background of possible sexual exploitation (*Re F (A Child)*), nor a person's lack of road sense (*Newham LBC v BS*), constituted seriously irresponsible conduct. On the other hand, historical conduct and the potential for aggressive or irresponsible behaviour to recur will be relevant and may mean that, even if there has been amelioration in a person's condition, the conditions for guardianship will be made out (*Lewis v Gibson*).

The courts have been increasingly asked to intervene in order to declare or order where the best interests of people with learning disabilities lie. The issue of guardianship has arisen on a number of occasions as an alternative to relying on mental capacity law. For instance:

Protecting a young woman with learning disabilities. A young woman, 18 years old, was in the care of the local authority. She had a level of intellectual functioning of a child aged five to eight years old. The local authority wished to control contact with her family and require her to live in local authority accommodation. The daughter had expressed a wish to return to her family. The local authority was concerned, because its view of the home situation was one of chronic neglect, lack of minimum standards of hygiene and cleanliness in the home, serious lack of adequate parenting, and worrying exposure to those engaged in sexual exploitation and possible sexual abuse (seven other younger children are now in the care of the local authority). The mother opposed the local authority, arguing that it had no legal power to supervise and restrict contact, and was breaching human rights.

The court had already ruled, when the woman was 17 years old, that guardianship under the Mental Health Act was not appropriate. This was because there was no abnormally aggressive or seriously irresponsible conduct; the local authority had argued the latter simply because the daughter wanted to return home to her mother. Yet the court could not characterise the wish of a child in care to return home as seriously irresponsible (*Re F (A Child)*).

On the assumption that the daughter lacked the capacity to decide the issue for herself, the court held that it had the inherent jurisdiction to make a declaration as to the daughter's best interests in the terms sought by the local authority. In addition, article 8 of the European Convention of Human Rights would not be breached, since it contained not a right to family life, but a right to respect for family life. This meant an entitlement (within limits) to what was benign and positive in family life (*Re F (Adult Patient)*).

The rules have not always been understood:

Inappropriate pursuit of guardianship. A complaint was made to the local ombudsman, following a protracted dispute between the local authority and the family of a man with learning disabilities, about where he should live. The ombudsman criticised the local authority's persistent attempts to pursue guardianship. This was despite medical opinion each time that the conditions for guardianship were not met, in particular the absence of abnormally aggressive or seriously irresponsible conduct (*Bury MBC 2000*).

7.6.8 INFORMAL MENTAL HEALTH PATIENTS

There is nothing in the 1983 Act to prevent a person who needs treatment for mental disorder from being admitted to hospital without formal detention, or from remaining in hospital informally following any formal detention (Mental Health Act 1983, s.131). However, safeguards, under the Mental Capacity Act 2005, will apply in the case of informal patients who lack the capacity to make the decision about their care and treatment themselves (see 6.5).

7.7 HARASSMENT

The Protection from Harassment Act 1997 creates both civil and criminal remedies. In summary, it states that a person must not pursue a course of conduct (a) which amounts to harassment of another; and (b) which he or she knows, or ought to know, amounts to harassment of the other (s.1). Harassment is not defined in the Act, and is capable of being interpreted widely depending on the particular circumstances.

The Act creates a criminal offence of harassment (s.2) and, more specifically, of putting a person in fear of violence on at least two occasions (s.4). It also creates a civil right to claim damages (s.3) and gives the courts the power to issue restraining orders in respect of a criminal offence, or a restraining injunction in respect of civil proceedings – breach of which itself is an offence with a maximum sentence of five years in prison (ss.3, 5).

There is no need for the persons involved to be 'associated' as is the case of a non-molestation order under the Family Law Act 1996 (see below). However, there has to be a course of conduct – one act is not enough. Harassment can include alarming a person or causing distress (s.7). The courts have however held that irritations, annoyances and even upset are commonplace in everyday life. So, to become harassment – to go from the regrettable to the unacceptable – there has to be misconduct of an order that would sustain criminal liability under s.2 even if the case is about civil liability (*Majrowski v Guy's and St Thomas' NHS Trust*). It needs to be oppressive and unacceptable (*Conn v Sunderland CC*). However, the conduct has only to be proved to the civil standard in civil proceedings – even though a breach of an injunction could result in imprisonment (*Hipgrave v Jones*).

7.8 NON-MOLESTATION ORDERS

Under the Family Law Act 1996, the court can issue civil non-molestation orders, breach of which is a criminal offence. Molestation is not limited to violence or threats of violence. The word is not defined in the Act; it need not involve violence and could include pestering, annoying, inconvenience, harassing. In relation to the adults concerned, there must be an association that in effect is a domestic connection. For a relevant association to apply, the adults must:
- be, or have been, married
- be, or have been, civil partners

- be cohabitants or former cohabitants, live or have lived in the same household (other than through one of them being the other's employee, tenant, lodger or boarder); this includes same sex co-habitants
- be people who have had an intimate personal relationship of significant duration who have not cohabited
- be relatives
- have agreed to marry (whether or not the agreement has since been terminated)
- in relation to a child, be the parents or have parental responsibility, be party to the same set of family proceedings (s.62).

The court has a discretion to make an order, and must have regard to all the circumstances including the health, safety and well-being of the applicant, the other party and any relevant child (s.42). In the past, the court had the power to attach a power of arrest to an order. From July 2007, breach of an order without reasonable excuse is automatically a criminal offence, with up to five years in prison (s.42A).

Non-molestation orders might sometimes be relevant in the context of safeguarding and protecting vulnerable adults. For instance, a non-molestation order, with a power of arrest, could be granted against a son from going within 100 metres of his mother's home, where there had been a history of violence and threats of violence against his mother (*Hutty v Hutty*). However, in the following court case, the order was being sought against an adult who might himself have been classed as a vulnerable adult – namely a man whose mental condition meant that he had become abnormally jealous of his wife, violent and abusive toward her, and had been detained under the Mental Health Act 1983.

Capacity to understand non-molestation order. An 82-year-old man lived with a 62-year-old woman in the same house. They divorced, although both continued to live in the matrimonial home. The woman had brought in a lodger with whom she ended up sharing her bedroom. The woman sought a non-molestation order on the grounds that her former husband had behaved improperly toward her. A social worker gave evidence that the man did not meet the criteria for residential care and that she had never found him to be aggressive. The man was having difficulty remembering things, as he was suffering from the early stages of dementia. The court held that, on the evidence, this was a borderline case; that the judge in the original case was entitled to have made the non-molestation order; but that now the evidence suggested that the man's mental capacity was such that the order could not be continued. This was on the basis of a previous case (*Wookey v Wookey*), in which it had been held that such an order should not be made against a person who was incapable of understanding its nature (*Harris v Harris*).

Similarly the courts have held that a non-molestation order could not be made against a person, previously detained under the Mental Health Act 1983, whose abuse toward her husband was a symptom of her mental condition and was such that she could not control it. Furthermore, although her verbal and physical aggression toward her husband put a strain on him, it did not significantly affect his health. A care regime, now in place, would ensure she was properly looked after and her husband relieved of the burden of care. In addition, the harm caused to the wife in making the order, would be significantly greater than the harm to the husband if the order was not made (*Banks v Banks*).

In another case a man was sentenced to nine months in prison, after breaching non-molestation and exclusion orders made under the Family Act 1996. They were aimed at preventing him from entering or attempting to enter the home of the mother of his child – and excluded him from two particular areas. However, the sentencing judge had been informed neither of the man's disabilities and vulnerabilities, nor even that the Official Solicitor was on that account involved. In addition, as it turned out, the woman no longer lived in the relevant area at the relevant time, so the orders were now irrelevant and unsustainable in any case. The nine-month sentence was overturned, and substituted by a shorter sentence which would allow the immediate release of the man from custody (*Pluck v Pluck*).

So the vulnerability can clearly cut both ways and may require local authority social services intervention:

Repeated breaches of non-molestation orders by vulnerable man: need for social services involvement. A 33-year-old man with a vulnerable personality, low intelligence and learning difficulties falling short of disability, had been prohibited from using or threatening violence against his mother, or returning to her house, where he had lived up to age of 28. In fact a series of such orders had been made, of which there had been 20 recorded breaches. He had now been sent to prison for 21 months for another breach which involved him going home, though not engaging in or threatening violence.

The Court of Appeal found the sentence to be excessive and reduced it to 12 months, meaning he would due for release within two weeks of the court hearing. It was a 'most unfortunate case'. It called out for 'pro-active steps to be taken by...social services'. The man had great difficulty living independently and had never had permanent accommodation outside his mother's house. The court was 'of the very strong opinion that a plan must be formulated by [the man's] advisers in conjunction with...social services... Otherwise there is a very strong likelihood that he will be in breach again' (*Gull v Gull*).

In the following case, the court referred to the implications of care in the community, namely, that vulnerable people needed support from social services, housing and the NHS, and that such support might be more effective than a judicial remedy in the form of injunctions. Implicitly, the court seemed to be suggesting that such support had not been forthcoming:

Support in the community may be more effective than injunction. An injunction was issued against a man with severe disabilities. He had Usher's syndrome, was deaf, dumb and had tunnel vision; his IQ was, however, average. He had separated from his wife. An injunction with a power of arrest had been made prohibiting him from going to the former matrimonial home. He breached it on numerous occasions. It appeared that he had the capacity to give instructions to solicitors and could understand the difference between right and wrong but did not have full capacity to understand the relevance of court proceedings and the implications of them. The judge decided that the man did have sufficient understanding in relation to the injunction, refused to discharge the injunction, but did not think he should go to prison.

The man appealed that the injunction should be discharged on the basis of his lack of understanding; it was argued that it was not so much a matter of him not retaining and understanding information, as the fact that his disabilities meant he might not receive the information in the first place. The Court of Appeal also acknowledged the issue specific nature of capacity generally, but that this would be unsatisfactory in the particular context. A degree of understanding might be sufficient for the issuing of the injunction. The court was not prepared to overturn the judge's original findings that the injunction should continue.

However, the court noted that more people with disabilities or mental health problems were living in the community, and that the courts had to balance the need to protect victims of violence or harassment against the difficulties of restraining offenders. The court faced the invidious choice between the compulsive behaviour of a most unfortunate individual and the safety and well-being of his family. Living in the community rather than an institution, he needed considerable support and protection in the community. Without such measures his family remained at risk of harm, but they were measures which lay outside the powers of the court. Social services, housing and mental health had an important part to play (*Page v Page*).

7.9 OCCUPATION ORDERS

Under the Family Law Act 1996 (s.33 and following), the courts have a discretion, and sometimes a duty, to issue occupation orders. The precise rules vary, depending on the entitlement to occupy the dwelling of the applicant or of the respondent respectively. There needs to be an association or domestic connection between the applicant and the respondent (see 7.8 above). The court can include a penal notice in the order and attach a power of arrest to the order (Family Law 1996, s.47).

In summary, an the order could allow the applicant – or forbid the respondent, the other person – to occupy the home or part of it, require the respondent to leave the home and not to return, prevent application of the applicant, require the party in occupation to take reasonable care of the home, regulate the use of furniture and chattels in the home, require either applicant or respondent to pay the mortgage.

7.9.1 APPLICANT WITH ENTITLEMENT TO OCCUPY DWELLING

If the applicant is entitled to occupy the dwelling house, then the order can cover a number of matters that could be relevant to safeguarding vulnerable adults. These are (a) entitlement to remain in occupation; (b) requiring the respondent to permit the applicant to enter and remain in the dwelling house or part of it; (c) regulating the occupation of the dwelling house by both parties; (d) prohibiting or suspending or restricting the right of the respondent to occupy the dwelling (if he or she is otherwise entitled to do so); (e) if the respondent has matrimonial home rights, the restriction or termination of those rights; (f) requiring the respondent to leave the dwelling or part of it; and (g) excluding the respondent from the specific area within which the dwelling lies.

The court has to have regard to the respective housing needs and resources of the parties and of any relevant child, financial resources of the parties, the likely effect of any order or of any court decision not to exercise its powers on the health, safety, and well-being of the parties and of any relevant child, and the conduct of parties to each other and otherwise.

The court's power turns into a duty if the applicant or any relevant child is likely to suffer significant harm. However, the order still need not be made if the respondent or relevant child is also likely to suffer significant harm if the order is made – and that harm would be as great as, or greater than, the harm attributable to the conduct of the respondent and likely to be suffered by the applicant or child, if the order is not made (Family Law Act 1996, s.33).

7.9.2 OTHER CATEGORIES OF APPLICANT FOR AN OCCUPATION ORDER

The court also has a power to make many, but not all of, the occupation orders listed at 7.9.1, in relation to other categories of applicant. These are namely (a) former spouse or civil partner with no right to occupy the dwelling; (b) one cohabitant or former cohabitant with no existing right to occupy; (c) neither spouse or civil partner entitled to occupy; and (d) neither cohabitant or former cohabitant entitled to occupy (ss.35–38).

7.10 ANTI-SOCIAL BEHAVIOUR

Anti-social behaviour orders may serve, amongst other things, to protect a vulnerable adult.

At the same time, sometimes those classed as vulnerable adults may themselves be associated with anti-social behaviour. For example, the serious case review into the murder of a man with learning disabilities in Cornwall, noted that he had been viewed by several agencies 'not primarily as a vulnerable adult to be protected from abuse and neglect but in terms of his own anti-social behaviour.' This complicated matters (Cornwall County Council 2008, para 6). Similarly, a series of cases heard under the Disability Discrimination Act 1995 have centred on the attempts of landlords to evict tenants with a mental disorder, on grounds of anti-social behaviour leading to breach of a tenancy condition (e.g. *Manchester CC v Romano*).

7.10.1 ANTI-SOCIAL BEHAVIOUR ORDERS

Anti-social behaviour injunctions or orders (ASBOs) can be made against those engaging in anti-social behaviour; such measures can protect vulnerable adults, or sometimes may be taken against them.

7.10.1.1 Housing Act 1996: landlord injunctions

In the Housing Act 1996, s.153A, under which landlords can seek anti-social behaviour injunctions, anti-social conduct is defined as conduct capable of causing nuisance or annoyance to 'some person' (the other person does not necessarily have to be identified). The court to which an application is made is either the county court or High Court.

A relevant landlord may apply to the court for an anti-social behaviour injunction against a person who is engaging or threatening to engage in 'housing-related conduct' capable of causing a nuisance or annoyance to (a) a person with a right to live in accommodation owned or managed by the landlord; (b) a person engaged in lawful activity in or in the vicinity of the that accommodation; or (c) a person employed in connected with the landlord's management functions (s.153A).

Injunctions are also available in respect of a person using or threatening to use the landlord's accommodation unlawfully (s.153B). The court can attach a power of arrest to an injunction, if the conduct involves the use or threat of violence, or there is a significant risk of harm to the person the injunction is aimed at protecting (ss.153C–153D). The injunction can, for example, prohibit the subject of it from entering premises or a particular area – and have the effect of excluding that person from their normal place of residence.

A relevant landlord is a local authority, registered social landlord or housing action trust (s.153E).

7.10.1.2 Crime and Disorder Act: anti-social behaviour orders

Under the Crime and Disorder Act 1998, an anti-social behaviour order is available on application by a relevant authority. This means a local authority, the police (including British Transport police), a social landlord, a housing action trust. It can be in respect of, the person's acting in an anti-social manner, which means 'in a manner that caused or was likely to cause harassment, alarm or distress to one or more persons not of the same household.' The order must be necessary to protect relevant persons from further anti-social acts. It can be given against anybody aged ten years or over. If the person breaches the order without reasonable excuse, the maximum sentence is five years' imprisonment (s.1). The court can also make individual support, interim or intervention (in relation to misuse of controlled drugs) orders (ss.1A–1G).

Although ASBO proceedings are civil in nature, the standard of proof to be applied in proving the anti-social behaviour complained of is the criminal standard (*R(McCann) v Manchester Crown Court*).

7.10.1.3 Anti-Social Behaviour Act 2003: closure orders, premises and drugs

Under s.1 of the Anti-Social Behaviour Act 2003, closure orders may be sought in relation to premises being used in connection with the unlawful use, production or supply of a Class A controlled drug – where the use of the premises is associated with the occurrence of disorder or serious nuisance to members of the public. A closure notice must be served by a constable. An application must then be made to a magistrates' court for the closure order which can last up to three months, but can be extended for up to six months in total (ss.1–11).

7.11 CRIME AND DISORDER STRATEGIES

Under the Crime and Disorder Act 1998 (ss.5–7), 'responsible authorities' have certain obligations. They are the local authority (county or unitary) and the following bodies (any part of whose area comes within that of the local authority): chief officer of police, police authority, NHS primary care trust, and fire authority. These authorities must formulate and implement a strategy for the reduction of crime and disorder and for combating the misuse of drugs, alcohol and other substances in the area. In addition, each authority must have due regard to the effect of the exercise of its functions on – and to the need to prevent – these matters (s.17).

7.12 MULTI-AGENCY PUBLIC PROTECTION ARRANGEMENTS (MAPPA)

Under the Criminal Justice Act 2003, a duty is placed on 'responsible authorities' (chief of police, probation board and the Prison Service) to establish arrangements for assessing and managing risks in relation to certain offenders. The duty applies to certain specified categories of violent and sex offender, as well to other people who have committed offences and who a responsible authority considers pose a risk of serious harm to the public.

In addition, other specified organisations must cooperate insofar as such cooperation would be compatible with the exercise of their functions under any other legislation. These organisations include local authorities with social services responsibilities, primary care trusts, other NHS trusts, strategic health authorities, Jobcentres Plus, local youth offending teams, registered social landlords that accommodate MAPPA offenders, local housing authorities, local education authorities, electronic monitoring providers (LASSL (2004)3). Such cooperation 'may' include the exchange of information (Criminal Justice Act 2003, ss.325–327).

Extensive guidance has been published by the National Probation Service (NPS 54/2004). It covers a number of points, including the three categories of offender (registered sex offenders, violent and other sex offenders, other offenders), risk assessment, risk management, and the duty to cooperate.

Department of Health guidance explains that there is a three-level structure of case referral of people presenting a serious risk of harm. The first level involves a single agency only, normally the Probation Service. The second will involve more than one agency because, even if the risk is high, management may not be complex. The third, dealing with a few critical cases, will trigger meetings of the Multi-Agency Public Protection Panel (MAPPP) meetings – in the case of the highest risks or highly problematic risk management issues (LASSL(2004)3).

The question of information exchange has given rise, unsurprisingly, to legal dispute about confidentiality and human rights. In the following case the courts held that a presumption against disclosure still obtained (see 10.3):

Disclosure of information to manager of sheltered accommodation. A 64-year-old had killed his wife. Six years later he was due to be released on licence on the recommendation of the Parole Board. Conditions were not set. A medical report prepared for the Crown Prosecution Service at the time of the trial stated that the offence occurred at a time when the relationship between A and his wife was strained, in part, as a consequence of his health problems. The report concluded that the offence occurred in the specific context of the relationship and was unlikely to be repeated.

The man wished to purchase and live in a flat in a sheltered accommodation complex. Under Multi-Agency Public Protection Panel Procedures (then under the Criminal Justice and Court Services Act 2000, ss.67–68), the National Probation Service carried out a risk assessment and disclosed the man's background to the manager of the accommodation. The court held that the risk assessment had been conducted carefully, but had approached the question of disclosure from the wrong starting point, namely a presumption of disclosure rather than one of disclosure. Furthermore the risk assessment had not addressed the man's rights, nor explicitly balanced the need for disclosure with the potential harm to the man (*R(A) v National Probation Service*).

This case was decided under previous legislation (Criminal Justice and Court Services Act 2000) before the relevant provisions were superseded in the 2003 Act, and before the express duty of cooperation, carrying with it a power (but not a duty) to exchange information, was added. Furthermore, the court noted that the housing provider to whom disclosure was to be made was not a public body and not a 'partner agency'. The court noted that the MAPPA guidance from the Home Office stated that only exceptionally should disclosure of information be made to a third party outside the MAPPA agencies (NPS 54/2004, para 93).

However, the 2003 Act sets out a list of agencies which have a duty to cooperate (see above). It states that the duty of cooperation, including information sharing, must be 'compatible with the exercise by those persons of their functions under any other enactment' s.325). The MAPPA guidance states that each MAPPA agency sharing information must have a statutory or common law power to do so. Clearly, there is such statutory power under s.325 of the 2003 Act; and also for some agencies, including local authorities, the NHS, police, probation under s.115 of the Crime and Disorder Act 1998 (see 10.3). Therefore, it concludes, 'all MAPPA agencies will have the prima facie legal power to exchange information with the Responsible Authority.' However, it notes that information should only be shared if there is a necessity, it is shared safely and securely, and there is accountability for such sharing (NPS 54/2004, paras 85–89).

7.13 PUBLIC INTEREST DISCLOSURE ACT 1998: 'WHISTLE-BLOWING'

If employees have serious concerns about matters at work, they are protected if, in certain circumstances, they 'whistle-blow'. This comes under the Employment Rights Act 1996, as amended by the Public Interest Disclosure Act 1998. In summary, the Act provides for a hierarchy of reasonable actions for the concerned employee to take. These are summarised below.

They may of course be crucial to adult protection and the safeguarding of adults. For instance, the mistreatment and abuse of patients at the North Lakelands NHS Trust was identified after two student nurses raised their concerns (CHI 2000).

7.13.1 PROTECTED AND QUALIFYING DISCLOSURES

For the employee to be protected from detriment perpetrated by the employer in retaliation to the disclosure, there needs to be a 'protected disclosure' (s.43B). A protected disclosure has to be (a) a 'qualifying' disclosure; and (b) to comply with various require-ments relating to whom the disclosure was made.

A qualifying disclosure means the 'disclosure of information which, in the reasonable belief of the worker making the disclosure' is about a criminal offence, breach of a legal obligation, miscarriage of justice, health and safety, damage to the environment – or is about any of these matters being deliberately concealed (s.43B). The protection afforded the person making the qualifying disclosure is on a sliding scale, depending on the identity of the person to whom the disclosure is made.

7.13.2 DISCLOSURE TO THE EMPLOYER

First, protection arises if the disclosure is made to the employer, or to somebody else where the failure relates to the conduct of that other person, or where legal responsibility is held by that other person rather than the employer. Likewise, if the disclosure is made to somebody else, in accordance with the employer's own procedure (s.43C).

7.13.3 DISCLOSURE TO REGULATORY BODY

Second, protection is given to a person who makes a qualifying disclosure (a) in good faith; (b) to a person 'prescribed by the Secretary of State'; and (c) where she or he reason-ably believes that the failure is relevant to the prescribed functions of that person – and that the information and allegation are substantially true (s.43F).

The persons in this category, to whom disclosure might be made, include regulatory bodies such as the Healthcare Commission, Commission for Social Care Inspection or, in future, the Care Quality Commission, General Social Care Council, Health and Safety Executive, local authorities with health and safety enforcement functions, the Informa-tion Commissioner (SI 1999/1549. Public Interest Disclosure (Prescribed Persons) Order 1999).

7.13.4 WIDER DISCLOSURE

Third, there comes wider disclosure beyond the employer or relevant regulatory body – for instance, to the press. Protection arises if a qualifying disclosure is made (a) in good faith; (b) in the reasonable belief that the information disclosed, and any allegation made, are substantially true; (c) the disclosure is not made for personal gain; and (d) in all the cir-cumstances of the case, it is reasonable to make the disclosure.

In addition, the worker must (a) reasonably believe that he or she would be subjected to detriment if the disclosure were made instead either to the employer or in accordance with s.43 F (e.g. to the relevant regulatory body); or (b) that, if there is no relevant (regula-tory) body under s.43F, evidence about the failure will be concealed if disclosure is made to the employer; or (c) the worker had previously made a disclosure of substantially the same information to the employer or to a regulatory body (s.43G). In the following Employment Tribunal case, wider disclosure in the form of a satirical letter to the press by a ward manager of the crisis in the hospital, and the miserable treatment of older patients, was protected under the Act:

A published letter to Tony Blair: hospital waiting times, bed shortages, older patients put into inappropriate wards. A satirical letter to the press was written by a highly qualified hospital ward manager. There were acute bed shortages; it was published in a publication called *The Journal*. It was in the form of a letter to Tony Blair, the Prime Minister at the time – Christmas time, in fact. It referred to poor, sickly old patients, a shortage of beds, trolleys, waiting time statistics, and 'shoving' elderly patients into an old shed with a crib and baby, which turned out to be the obstetric and gynaecology ward. The staff there would not know how to care for elderly people, but the patients wouldn't complain because they were deaf or demented. They might soon be moved in any case to the laundry instead, where with a bit of luck they might catch pneumonia, die and create a few more vacant beds.

It came within the third category of wider disclosure. The manager was disciplined and issued with a final written warning that he had acted in an unprofessional and totally unacceptable manner. The Employment Tribunal reached the conclusion that it was a protected disclosure; he had a reasonable belief that it was substantially true; it was not made for personal gain, and he had previously made a disclosure of substantially the same information to his employer. He was not aware of any other route by which he could raise the matter. The Tribunal found in the ward manager's favour (*Kay v Northumbria Healthcare NHS Trust*).

Certainly the protection may be retrospective insofar as workers who raise their concerns may have to resort to an Employment Tribunal in order to gain compensation for being sacked. For instance, when six employees spoke to the press about failures in a children's home, they were sacked – but subsequently were compensated by the council in advance of an Employment Tribunal. The settlement was reportedly in the region of £1 million (*Community Care* 2007d).

Whistle-blowers may indeed risk immediate retaliation by their employer when they speak out, whether or not they have adhered to the rules under the Act. For instance, a community psychiatric nurse spoke to the press over restructuring of mental health services in Manchester and the arguably serious implications for users of services. She was sacked for gross misconduct. On one view, it was reported that the trust had behaved highly unreasonably. In effect it had objected to her having been interviewed about the transfer of NHS care, her having told people she had been suspended but was innocent, and her having allowed the press to print misleading statements. The NHS mental health trust involved was rated 173 out of 175 in the country (Steel 2007).

In another case, when a nurse alerted the police to the standard of care in a care home, an adult protection investigation was launched. The Commission for Social Care Inspection visited the home and produced a confidential report. The nurse used the Freedom of Information Act 2000 to bring about its publication. It noted, amongst other things, faeces on beds in empty rooms, unkempt residents, broken showers and toilets, pressure sores covered in faeces and emaciation – and the fact that the inspectors were shocked. The nurse was reported by the home to the Nursing and Midwifery Council for aggression toward a resident, but the hearing went in his favour (*Nursing Standard 2005*).

CHAPTER 8

Physical and sexual harm and abuse

KEY POINTS

Some physical and sexual harm and abuse may constitute a criminal offence, including assault and battery, manslaughter, murder, sexual offences etc. A number of these offences are summarised below and illustrated with examples concerning vulnerable adults.

In addition, there is an offence of wilful neglect or ill-treatment which is contained in both the Mental Health Act 1983 and the Mental Capacity Act 2005. And, under the Domestic Violence, Crime and Victims Act 2004, there is an offence of causing the death of a vulnerable adult, either by causing it directly or failing to take reasonable steps to prevent it.

Health and safety at work legislation has on occasion been used to prosecute in the case of abuse, where management failings effectively allowed the abuse to go unchecked. And vulnerable adults may have civil remedies in the courts in relation to abuse or neglect, for example by bringing negligence or trespass to the person cases.

Lastly, restraint remains a contentious issue, in particular when it is permitted legally and when it becomes abuse.

8.1 OFFENCES AGAINST THE PERSON

There are various criminal offences against the person which may be committed in circumstances related to adult protection.

8.1.1 ASSAULT

Common assault occurs when a person intentionally or recklessly causes somebody else to apprehend or anticipate any immediate and unlawful violence or touching (*R v Savage and Parmenter*). Battery occurs when a person intentionally or recklessly applies unlawful force to somebody else – that is, intentional touching of another person without the consent of that person and without lawful excuse. It need not necessarily be hostile, rude or aggressive (*Faulkner v Talbot*). These are (probably) still to be regarded as common law offences, although sentences are governed by s.39 of the Criminal Justice Act 1988, with a maximum six months' imprisonment. Battery is usually accompanied by assault, and the latter term is generally used in cases of battery. (With police intervention in domestic violence in mind, s.10 of the Domestic Victims, Crime and Violence Act 2004 made common assault an arrestable offence. In fact before s.10 ever came into force, it was superseded by ss.110 and 111 of the Serious and Organised Crime and Police Act 2005 – which created a power of arrest without warrant for offences generally: see Hester *et al.* (2008) for discussion).

For instance, when a care assistant bent back the thumbs of residents as part of the way she handled them, she was found guilty of six offences of assault (*Mwaura v Secretary of State for Health*). A nurse at a care home was jailed for 15 months on various charges, including assault, for stuffing a deodorant can into the mouth of a 95-year-old man to stop him shouting (Davidson 2007). A nurse, acting as matron, screamed a tirade of abuse at a mental health patient in a nursing home, before slapping her twice across the face. The assault was witnessed by an inspector from the local NHS primary care trust. The nurse was sent to prison for three months for common assault (*Bury Times* 2006). The deputy manager of a care home was jailed for three months for assault because of the manual method of massage which she used to relieve constipation of a resident. She and other staff had all been on a training course which had taught that this method was 'outlawed'. The resident, with dementia, had struggled and was clearly in pain; when staff members had asked the deputy manager to call a doctor, she had refused, saying it would look bad for the home (*South Wales Guardian* 2004).

Two care workers were sentenced for assault, on evidence that they had punched, slapped and mishandled residents, whom they had been described as treating like animals on a cattle farm. The home had previously been heavily criticised by the Commission for Social Care Inspection for employing staff who had not been properly checked (*Community Care* 2007e). A care worker at a care home in Portsmouth was sent to prison for assaulting residents. She had thrown a cup of tea at a woman in her eighties who wouldn't get up from her chair; she had claimed to be following the example of a more senior colleague who used casual violence to get the residents to comply with a strict routine (*File on Four* 2007).

There does, however, have to be evidence of intention or recklessness for the offence to be committed. Thus, when three carers were accused of assault, by pouring talcum power into the mouth of an 87-year-old care home resident, they were acquitted. Whilst the district judge noted that the care had been below standard, and two of the carers admitted using unnecessary force when washing and handling the woman, nonetheless he could not be sure beyond reasonable doubt of intention or recklessness (Dayani 2004).

8.1.1.1 Other offences going beyond common assault

There are more serious offences. Assault occasioning bodily harm under s.47 of the Offences Against the Person Act 1861 carries a maximum of five years' imprisonment. This offence is distinguished from common assault by the degree of injury resulting. For instance, common assault might typically concern grazes, scratches, abrasions, minor bruising, swellings, reddening of the skin, superficial cuts, or a black eye. Whereas actual bodily arm could include loss or breaking of a tooth or teeth, temporary loss of sensory functions including consciousness, extensive or multiple bruising, displaced or broken nose, minor fractures, minor but not superficial cuts, psychiatric injury beyond fear, distress or panic.

Unlawful wounding or infliction of grievous bodily harm comes under s.20 of the Offences Against the Person Act 1861, carrying a maximum of five years' imprisonment. Wounding would cover more serious cuts or lacerations, as opposed to more minor ones. Grievous bodily harm is serious bodily harm including, for example, injury resulting in permanent disability or permanent loss of sensory function, more than minor, permanent, visible disfigurement, broken bones, compound fractures, substantial loss of blood, injuries resulting in lengthy treatment or incapacity, psychiatric injury.

Section 18 of the Act contains a similar offence but there must also be intent to cause wounding or grievous bodily harm (CPS/1).

8.2 FALSE IMPRISONMENT

False imprisonment is a common law offence involving the unlawful and intentional or reckless detention of a person:

False imprisonment and death in a shed of vulnerable adult at the hands of those who has befriended him. A vulnerable and epileptic man died, after being kept in a shed for a period of four months by three people who had befriended him. He was found dead with extensive bruising and burn marks. The prosecution could not prove that death was not due to his epilepsy; the three defendants were jailed for some ten years each for assault, causing actual bodily harm and false imprisonment (de Bruxelles 2007a). However, a subsequent coroner's hearing concluded that he had been unlawfully killed, almost certainly due to a loss of blood (*Metro Newspaper* 2008).

The act must be unlawful. So, for instance, when a man lacking capacity was taken to hospital in his best interests, and kept there for care and treatment, the courts held that 'necessity' justified what would otherwise have been unlawful in terms of the civil tort of false imprisonment (*R v Bournewood Community and Mental Health NHS Trust, ex p L*). The European Court of Human Rights subsequently held that this breached the man's human rights (*HL v UK*: see 6.5.1).

8.3 MANSLAUGHTER AND MURDER AND ASSISTED SUICIDE

Manslaughter divides into involuntary and voluntary manslaughter. Both may arise in the context of vulnerable adults.

Involuntary manslaughter arises in three circumstances, (a) gross negligence; (b) an unlawful act; or (c) recklessness (*R v Lidar*). On the other hand, a charge of murder is reduced to voluntary manslaughter in three instances: diminished responsibility, provocation or acting in pursuance of a suicide pact (Homicide Act 1957, ss.2,3).

8.3.1 MANSLAUGHTER THROUGH GROSS NEGLIGENCE

Gross negligence resulting in a person's death may constitute the basis of a criminal charge of involuntary manslaughter. For example, when two medical doctors failed to realise the gravity of a patient's condition (toxic shock syndrome), with the consequence that he failed to get the requirement treatment and died, they were convicted of manslaughter by reason of gross negligence (*R v Misra*). Likewise, an anaesthetist was convicted in connection with the death of a patient (*R v Adomako*). This contrasts with ordinary negligence, which may precipitate a civil legal case, but not a criminal one. The following is an example of a 1977 case of neglect, death and manslaughter charges. The vulnerable adults concerned included both victim and perpetrators:

Informal carers guilty of manslaughter through gross negligence: vulnerable adults both victim and perpetrators. A partially deaf and almost blind man of low intelligence lived with a woman described as his mistress and as ineffectual and inadequate – together with the man's mentally impaired son. The man's sister came to live in the house as a lodger, in one room without ventilation, toilet or washing facilities save for a polythene bucket.

The sister was morbidly anxious not to put on weight, denied herself proper meals, and spent days at a time in the room. After three years, she had become helplessly infirm. The mistress, who took the sister food, tried to wash the sister with the help of a neighbour, who advised her to contact social services. Also, the licensee of a pub frequented by the mistress and the man advised her to get a doctor. The sister refused to give the name of her doctor whom the man and mistress had attempted to locate. The man tried to get his own doctor to attend unsuccessfully. Neither the man nor the mistress made any further efforts to obtain professional assistance, not even mentioning anything to the social worker who visited the son.

Three weeks after the attempt to wash the sister, she died of toxaemia, spreading because of infected bedsores, immobilisation and lack of food. Had she received medical attention during that three weeks, she would probably have survived.

The Court of Appeal upheld the conviction (although reduced the sentence) and described gross negligence in the following way: 'The duty which a defendant has undertaken is a duty of caring for the health and welfare of the infirm person. What the prosecution have to prove is a breach of that duty in such circumstances that the jury feel convinced that the defendant's conduct can properly be described as reckless, that is to say a reckless disregard of danger to the health and welfare of the infirm person. Mere inadvertence is not enough. The defendant must be proved to have been indifferent to an obvious risk of injury to health, or actually to have foreseen the risk but to have determined nevertheless to run it' (*R v Stone*).

Family members were likewise convicted of gross negligence manslaughter when the mother and half-sister of a 16-year old girl failed to call an ambulance after she had taken an overdose of heroin. Both knew the symptoms of an overdose, having experienced such themselves. They were jailed for two and four years respectively (*The Times* 2008).

Pressure sores have accounted for the conviction for manslaughter of a nursing services manager of a care home and her deputy. Septicaemia had resulted from sores the size of a fist, which had penetrated to the bone and gave off an overpowering smell of rotting flesh. The woman died in July 1999, having been resident since March. The home had passed a regulatory inspection in May of that same year. The jury rejected the defendants' claim that it was the system that was to blame (*BBC News* 2003).

In the following case, the Court of Appeal was reluctant to consider manslaughter in the context of personal care, when it refused to overturn a decision of the Crown Prosecution Service. The latter had decided not to prosecute anybody for manslaughter, following the death by drowning of a disabled person in a local authority care home. The court pointed out that, even if there had been ordinary common law negligence, this was not the same as criminal negligence, involving recklessness:

Death by drowning in a care home: no prosecution for manslaughter. A man with profound mental and physical disabilities, resident in a local authority care home, died by drowning in five inches of water. The police and Health and Safety Executive both concluded that there was inadequate evidence to prosecute. The Director of Public Prosecutions (DPP) concluded the same.

In the case of one of the care staff, it never crossed her mind that the man might be unsafe in the bath during the four to five minutes that he was left alone, since he had always kept his head out of the water in the past.

From an organisational point of view, there was a care plan, but it did not deal with the matter of bathing. The DPP had concluded that a formal policy on leaving a severely disabled person was not required because it was common sense. Furthermore, some risks were managed, some training was provided and staff members were appropriately experienced. The DPP decided that it would be difficult to find a guilty 'directing mind' at organisational level, and that there was an absence of conduct so 'bad' as to be described as gross negligence.

The court held that even if there had been ordinary common law negligence, criminality or badness still had to be established for a manslaughter case. The presence or absence of subjective recklessness was a relevant issue and the DPP had applied the right legal test (*Rowley v DPP*).

Nonetheless, when a patient detained under the Mental Health Act committed suicide, it was argued that a failure to take reasonable steps to prevent the risk of suicide constituted a breach of article 2 of the European Convention (a civil, rather than a criminal, offence). The NHS trust argued that in order to contemplate a breach of article 2, gross negligence (which would be sufficient to sustain a manslaughter charge) rather than ordinary negligence (which underpins a civil case for damages) was required. The court held that it was not necessary to show gross negligence in order to argue a breach of article 2 (*Savage v South Essex Partnership NHS Foundation Trust*).

Things of course may not be as they seem. A nursing home matron was accused of manslaughter of a resident, by force-feeding him with rhubarb and custard so that he choked to death. She was also charged with assaulting other residents. She was acquitted of all charges; she had denied feeding the man on the day of death, and a pathologist said food could enter the airway after death. The jury was also told that staff had fabricated the allegations because the matron had strict standards (*BBC News* 2005a).

8.3.2 MANSLAUGHTER: VIOLENCE BUT DEATH NOT INTENDED

Involuntary manslaughter can arise also in the case of an unlawful act. This must be an act, as opposed to an omission, which a reasonable person would realise would subject the victim to some risk of physical harm, albeit not serious harm – whether or not the perpetrator realised this (CPS/2).

Physical abuse of man with learning disabilities by teenagers before death in river. A man with learning disabilities was subjected to a campaign of physical abuse in his home, by a group of teenagers. Having previously shaved clumps of hair from his head, daubed make-up on his face, urinated in his drinks, smoked cannabis in his flat, scrawled graffiti on his walls and poured bleach on him, they then beat him and threw him into the River Mersey where he died. They were jailed for life for manslaughter. He had learning disabilities and was a heavy drinker, and had the capacity to make his own decisions but his vulnerability meant that he 'couldn't say no to the people who came to his door' (Carter 2007).

8.3.3 MANSLAUGHTER THROUGH DIMINISHED RESPONSIBILITY

The charge of murder may in some circumstances be reduced to voluntary manslaughter because of diminished responsibility. This is where the person was suffering from such abnormality of mind – whether arising from a condition of arrested or retarded development of mind or any inherent causes or induced by disease or injury – so as substantially to have impaired his or her mental responsibility for his or acts omissions in doing or being a party to the killing (Homicide Act 1957, s.2).

One such case involved a 72-year-old man who started a relationship with a woman on a low security, mixed sex, mental health ward in a care home. He had a history of assaults on women. He stabbed the woman to death, after he had failed to receive a three-weekly injection of anti-psychotic drugs. He was jailed for life (Brody 2006). It was similarly manslaughter through diminished responsibility when an 82-year-old care home resident bludgeoned a fellow resident to death with an iron:

Care home killing: diminished responsibility through undetected psychopathic illness. An 82-year-old woman, charged with murder, was convicted of manslaughter on grounds of diminished responsibility. Using an ornamental iron, she had bludgeoned to death a 93-year-old fellow resident in a care home in Newcastle-upon-Tyne. She told police she had not hit the woman enough. She suffered from a psychopathic illness, having previously spent 14 years in secure hospitals, and been convicted ten years earlier of grievous bodily harm for attacking a 72-year-old woman with a chair. Her medical records and criminal history had not been passed on to the care home (Norfolk 2005).

A very different type of case, though resulting in a similar verdict, also reached the courts, involving family carers who had reached breaking point through stress. They had then killed in desperation and with diminished responsibility – as in the following case of a mother of a 36-year-old man with Down's syndrome:

Mother killing disabled son, unbearable pressure, diminished responsibility, role of social services. A mother killed her 36-year-old son who had Down's syndrome. She gave him 14 sleeping pills and suffocated him with a plastic bag. She then swallowed some pills herself and attempted to kill herself with a kitchen knife.

The judge acknowledged the exceptional nature of the case and the unbearable pressure she had been under for more than 30 years. She had pleaded for help from the local authority (social services) and from her GP. Her eldest son gave evidence that her devotion to her disabled son had been saintly. Her son had flourished in early life before developing autism in his twenties and harming himself; he blinded himself in one eye. He had been enrolled in a day centre but was excluded for disruptive behaviour. He did better when he was assisted by a social integration team, but this was disbanded for lack of funds.

Most recently, social services had not provided a care manager, although it acknowledged the urgency of her situation. Social services stated that it had offered services but the mother had refused them. She was convicted of manslaughter on the grounds of diminished responsibility and given a suspended two-year prison term (Laville 2005).

Questions about social services involvement also arose in a case where a mother was convicted of manslaughter by reason of diminished responsibility, after drugging and suffocating her two adult sons, both of whom had cerebral palsy. She was suffering from depression, as well as a degenerative neurological condition. The judge criticised social services and called on them to conduct an inquiry (Kelso 2000).

And when a father suffocated his mentally ill daughter, he was convicted of manslaughter due to diminished responsibility and given a two-year suspended jail sentence. She had repeatedly tried to kill herself, suffered from severe personality disorder and deep depression, and was an alcoholic. She had been asked to leave a specialist NHS unit the day before. The daughter had leaned toward her father for him to cover her head with a plastic bag; when that failed, he suffocated her with a pillow (Smith 2001).

A similar verdict was reached in the case of man who helped his wife kill herself; she was suffering from the degenerative effect of multiple sclerosis. She had previously attempted to kill herself on a number of occasions. He suffocated her after she had taken an overdose of pills (Fletcher 2008).

Further along the spectrum, such killings may amount to murder, rather than manslaughter through diminished responsibility. When a man killed his wife of 33 years (who suffered from an irritable bowel condition), after she had persuaded him to help her die, he was convicted of murder. He had bought her nearly 100 paracetamol tablets, roses and two farewell cards. He placed a plastic bag over her head and smothered her with a pillow (Batchelor 2007).

8.3.4 CORPORATE MANSLAUGHTER

The question may arise as to whether 'corporate' manslaughter charges should be brought against an organisation for a systemic failure which leads to death. The question may arise in the context of safeguarding vulnerable adults.

For instance, in July 2006, the Healthcare Commission published a report into nearly 40 deaths at Stoke Mandeville Hospital – and the serious illness of many more – from the bacterium *Clostridium difficile*. The Commission found that the trust board had compromised the safety of patients, by putting performance and finance targets – set by central government – ahead of infection control and the safety of patients. Despite having received good advice from its infection control team, senior management and the board ignored it (HC 2006). At the time of publication, there was speculation about whether corporate manslaughter charges might be brought. However, no such prosecution followed; although the trust's chief executive, the chair of the board and the chief nursing officer did all resign (Carvel 2006).

Some 15 months later, the Healthcare Commission published another report of an investigation into hospitals in Kent. *Clostridium difficile* was at the heart of 90 deaths, a significant contribution being the appalling hygiene conditions and poor standards of care. Again there was talk of the trust having deliberately prioritised finance and performance targets ahead of patient care (HC 2007a). And again it was reported that Kent police would consider whether to bring corporate manslaughter charges against either the NHS trust or the chief executive personally (Rose 2007a).

It seemed nonetheless unlikely that such charges would ever be brought, either corporately (see below) or against any individuals, in such cases given (a) the difficulty in pinning down responsibility for the severe lapse in care and infection control standards; (b) possible problems of showing that death was caused by such lapse of standards in any particular case (it might be argued the person was likely to die anyway); and (c) the extreme political sensitivity of what took place, because of the close link between the systematic and gross lapses in standards of care, and the financial and performance targets set by central government. In due course, therefore, the Kent police and the Health and Safety Executive announced in August 2008 that no criminal charges would be brought. The police stated there was no evidence of grossly negligent actions, and the Health and Safety Executive stated that there was insufficient information to link the actions of any individual with the spread of infection – or to show that any senior manager was personally responsible for any direct failure that led to infection (Moore 2008).

Nonetheless, there is an instructive comparison to be made between the deliberate shortcuts take with infection control in these hospitals, and that taken with the maintenance of an air conditioning system in Barrow-in-Furness. In the latter case, too, infection followed in the form of Legionnaire's disease, and the council officer responsible was prosecuted, though not convicted, of manslaughter. However, the prosecution lay against the architect as an individual, rather than against the council corporately. Instead she was convicted under s.7 of the Health and Safety at Work Act 1974 (duty of employees) and fined £15,000 (Hogg 2006).

In fact, at the time of writing, the only legal action apparently in the offing in respect of what happened in Kent, concerns the chief executive who departed shortly before publication of the Health Commission's report. She was reported in April 2008 as launching a High Court action to increase her pay-off from the reported £75,000 to some £250,000 (HSJ 2008). Unsurprisingly, the chief executive was subject to considerable vilification in the press, especially when it was revealed that she had been chief executive in the past at hospitals with a poor record on hygiene (Rayner and Smith 2007). In some ways, such vilification misses the point. As the Healthcare Commission has pointed out (HC 2006; HC 2007a), the events at both Stoke Mandeville and in Kent stemmed from characteristics of the system. In other words, it is arguable that such chief executives are the inevitable product of a system which puts targets and finance ahead of fundamental patient welfare.

8.3.4.1 Corporate manslaughter legislation

The Corporate Manslaughter and Corporate Homicide Act was passed in 2007. It makes clear that an organisation such as an NHS trust or local authority, amongst many others, commits the offence of corporate manslaughter in certain circumstances. This is where it owes a duty of care in negligence which has been grossly breached – substantially as a result of how its activities are managed or organised by senior management. Senior management means people who played a significant role in decisions, or in the actual managing or organising of the whole or a substantial part those activities. A breach of the duty of care is gross if it falls far below what can be reasonably be expected of the organisation in the circumstances (ss.1–2). At present, the duty of care to patients detained under the Mental Health Act 1983 remains unimplemented under the 2007 Act.

The Act makes clear that this will not include decisions as to matters of public policy, and in particular the allocation of public resources or the weighing of competing public interests (s.3).

In case of failure to comply with health and safety legislation, the jury must consider how serious that failure was and how much of a risk of death it posed. They may also (a) consider the extent to which, on the evidence, there were attitudes, policies, systems or accepted practices that were likely to have encouraged any such failure; and (b) have regard to any health and safety guidance that relates to the alleged breach (s.8).

Conviction of the organisation carries an offence of an unlimited fine. Remedial orders can be made, forcing the organisation to remedy the problems leading to the breach. In addition, publicity orders can also be made, forcing the organisation to publish the details of the conviction (ss.9–10).

8.4 MURDER

Murder consists of a person of sound mind unlawfully killing a human being with intent to kill or cause grievous bodily harm (CPS/2). The following examples make clear the relevance to vulnerable adults. For instance, in the following case a vulnerable adult was murdered, despite a measure of social services involvement:

Man with learning disabilities befriended by gang and then murdered. A man with severe learning disabilities was befriended by a 'gang'. He thought they were his best friends. For a year, they exploited and cheated him, taking control of his money, his flat and his life, dragging him around his bedsit on a dog's lead. They then tortured him into confessing falsely that he was a paedophile, sentenced him to death, forced him to swallow 70 painkilling tablets, marched him to the top of a viaduct, forced him over, and stamped on his hands as he hung on. He fell 30 metres and died. Three of the gang were convicted of murder, another of manslaughter. During the period in question, social services had been visiting him but stopped before his death, apparently in response to his wishes (Morris 2007).

Two teenagers, both trained boxers, and an older man, were involved in a bet made at a bus stop about whether they could knock out a man with learning disabilities. They then repeatedly hit him, chased him across two housing estates, continuing to attack him by punching, stamping, kicking and head-butting. After the murder they posed for pictures. All three were convicted of murder (*BBC News* 2008).

A vulnerable, timid adult was taken to a remote hillside, where he was strangled, hit with a brick, kicked and stamped on, before being set on fire, by two cousins who wrongly believed he was a paedophile. They were given life sentences; the planning, mental and physical suffering of a vulnerable man and the attempt to conceal the body were aggravating features (*BBC News* 2007a).

A man with learning disabilities was humiliated, tortured and then thrown into a river to drown by four of his neighbours who suspected he was a paedophile (Vinter 2007). Another man with learning disabilities, also wrongly believed by his killers to be a paedophile, was gagged, bound, tortured, stabbed and disembowelled. His two killers were, on appeal, sentenced to 28 years and 22 years in prison (*BBC News* 2006).

In contrast, the murder charge may relate to a senior health care professional, such as a hospital matron, described as eccentric, bossy, popular and well respected. Charged with poisoning three patients, although suspected of having murdered many more, she committed suicide before trial (Jenkins 2005). Another nurse drugged an 84-year-old care home resident, who suffered from senile dementia, by giving her an overdose of a sedative (heminevrin). The judge stated that she had committed murder largely because she didn't want the trouble of caring for the woman, who needed up to half an hour's care and attention from staff every two hours (*BBC News* 2001).

In March 2008, a staff nurse was convicted of murdering four elderly patients and attempting to murder a fifth, by means of administering insulin to induce hypoglycaemic coma and death. The judge stated that he was an essentially lazy man who believed that the elderly required too much care. All the victims were frail elderly women admitted to the orthopaedic ward following hip fractures (Jenkins 2008).

8.4.1 ATTEMPTED MURDER

Under s.1 of the Criminal Attempts Act 1981, attempted murder is when a person does an act that is more than merely preparatory to murder, with an intention to kill.

For instance, a few days after her father had been diagnosed with inoperable stomach cancer, a woman simply decided, unbidden, to kill him by trying to smother him with a pillow. He tried to push her away, called for help and her daughter rushed into the room and managed to pull her mother away. She was charged with attempted murder, given a suspended sentence and sentenced to 150 hours community work (Wood 2008). In another case, an 84-year-old man was convicted of attempted murder of his wife following threatened withdrawal of care by social services:

Manual handling dispute about care of woman with Alzheimer's disease leads to attempted murder by husband. An elderly couple were due to celebrate their diamond wedding anniversary in two weeks' time. The wife had Alzheimer's disease; she was doubly incontinent and immobile, receiving visits from two carers three times a day, seven days a week. The council then allegedly told the husband that unless they accepted a hoist, the carers would be withdrawn. On one particular day, the carers refused to lift the wife manually, leaving him unable to feed or clean her. The husband became distraught and anxious and tried to kill both himself and his wife by attaching a hose to the exhaust of his car and leading it into the couple's bedroom. A neighbour saved them. He had left a typed note, referring to the social worker and owner of the private care company as two of the most 'evil people' he had encountered in recent years. His wife was placed in a care home where she died a month later from an unrelated infection.

The husband confessed to attempted murder and was put on a year's probation by the judge. The latter condemned the decision of the Crown Prosecution Service to bring the case at all (*R v Bouldstridge*).

8.5 ASSISTED SUICIDE

Under the Suicide Act 1961, it remains an offence to assist a person to commit suicide, in terms of aiding, abetting, counselling or procuring the suicide (s.2). It has been established that this law is not contrary to human rights. When a woman suffering with motor neurone disease wanted an assurance that her husband would not be prosecuted if he assisted her to commit suicide, she brought a human-rights based legal challenge. The challenge failed in both the English courts and at the European Court of Human Rights (*Pretty v United Kingdom*). Nonetheless, the courts are sometimes minded to impose light sentences, as in the following case when a husband aided and abetted his ill and disabled wife's suicide:

Aiding and abetting suicide of wife with multiple sclerosis. A husband was found guilty of aiding and abetting his wife's suicide, but was sentenced to nine months in prison, suspended for a year – and to unpaid work of 50 hours. His wife, suffering from multiple sclerosis, had already attempted suicide twice. When he came home from work, he found a note stating that she had taken 175 valium tablets. She had a plastic bag over her head. He chose to tighten the string around the bag, rather than see his wife fail in her suicide attempt. She blamed him for the failure of her previous attempts. The judge noted that he was entirely of good character and no risk to the community (Cumming 2006).

During 2008, the courts gave leave for a judicial review on the law concerning assisted suicide to be brought by a woman suffering from primary progressive multiple sclerosis. She was concerned, when her condition deteriorated further, that if her husband helped her to travel to Switzerland for an assisted death, he would be prosecuted. (The Home Office reports that in 13 per cent of 'mercy killing' cases and in 15 per cent of assisted suicide cases, criminal charges are dropped on the advice of the Director of Public Prosecutions or never initiated: Scorer 2008).

8.6 ILL-TREATMENT OR WILFUL NEGLECT

Both the Mental Health Act 1983 and the Mental Capacity Act 2005 contain offences concerned with the ill-treatment or wilful neglect of people with mental disorder or mental incapacity respectively.

8.6.1 ILL-TREATMENT OR WILFUL NEGLECT: MENTAL DISORDER

It is an offence for employees or managers of a hospital, independent hospital or care home to ill-treat or wilfully neglect a person receiving treatment for mental disorder as an inpatient in that hospital or home; likewise, ill-treatment or wilful neglect, on the premises of which the hospital or home forms a part, of a patient receiving such treatment as an outpatient.

It is also an offence for any individual to ill-treat or to wilfully neglect a mentally dis-ordered patient who is subject to his or her guardianship under the 1983 Act or otherwise in his or her custody or care (Mental Health Act 1983, s.127). The courts have held that ill-treatment and wilful neglect are not the same and need to be charged separately. Ill-treatment must (a) be deliberate conduct which could be described as such, irrespective of whether it damages or threatens to damage the health of the victim, and (b) involve a guilty mind (*mens rea*), namely an appreciation by the perpetrator either that he or she was inexcusably ill-treating a patient or was reckless as to whether he or she was acting in that way. Wilful neglect is a failure to act when a moral duty demands it, whereas ill-treatment is a deliberate course of action. (This was decided in a case involving the owner of a resi-dential home and allegations of assault and ill-treatment. The wider backdrop to the charges was described at trial by former members of staff. The owner referred to the older residents as 'babies', the home smelt of urine, there were insufficient staff, the food was inadequate, wet mattresses were never dried out, there were insufficient linen and blankets, residents' clothing was regarded as communal, residents were washed with a common flannel and soap etc.: *R v Newington*).

However, the section is arguably weakened by the fact that no proceedings can be brought under it for an offence unless the Director of Public Prosecution brings, or at least gives consent to, such proceedings.

Criticism was levelled previously at limits to the sentencing powers available, a maximum of two years in prison (although subsequent legislative amendment increased this to five years from October 2007). For example, the judge in the 'Longcare' case, a care home in Buckingham, where adults with learning disabilities were systematically abused, did so. One manager, sentenced to 30 months in prison, had ordered a woman to eat meals outside as a punishment, pulled another down the stairs by her hair, and deprived two other residents of toiletries in order to save money (*Disability Now* 2003).

In the following case, a carer was convicted under this section in a badly run residen-tial care home, where there was loose supervision, generally irregular care and a lack of discipline and routine:

Pulling hair (ill-treatment) and excessive isolation (wilful neglect). The carer was convicted of ill-treatment for pulling the hair and nipping the nose of a resident aged 37, with a developmental age of two years, suffering from epilepsy and severe learning disabilities. In addition, she was convicted of wilful neglect for leaving another male resident in a sensory room by himself for too long; he was 54 years old but with a developmental age of 12 months. He was severely physically and mentally disabled, suffered from meningitis, was epileptic, communicated by grunting only, and was paralysed to some extent in all four limbs. She was sentenced to three months' imprisonment (*R v Lennon*).

In another, 2007 case, a carer in a nursing home was convicted under s.127 for placing a bag over the head of an 88-year-old resident as he struggled to breathe. He told his horri-fied colleague not to worry, saying 'no bruise, no proof'. The convicted carer had almost completed his studies to become a doctor in his native Lithuania. He would be sentenced after an application for his deportation (*R v Poderis*). Likewise, when residents of a care home were incited racially to abuse each other and also to kick each other, the convictions of three carers and the manager of the care home followed – for wilful neglect and ill-treatment (Gadelrab 2006). In another case there was a catalogue of ill-treatment and wilful neglect involving two managers and a nurse:

Sedatives, rough handling, verbal abuse, bullying, kicking footballs at residents (ill-treatment); not getting patient with broken ribs to hospital (neglect). Two managers of a South Wales nursing home, and another nurse, were convicted under s.127, one for wilful neglect, the other two for ill-treatment. The ill-treatment included the administering of sedatives to keep patients quiet, rough handling, neglecting requests to be taken to the toilet, verbal abuse, and bullying. The ill-treatment perpetrated by the nurse, not just at this nursing home but another – for which he had already been sentenced to 12 months in prison – included kicking footballs at residents, giving heavy doses of medication to residents so he could sleep undisturbed on his shift, throwing a 75-year-old man across a room, and leaving an elderly woman naked and exposed to the elements near open windows and doors. The wilful neglect included not taking a resident, who had suffered two broken ribs, to hospital for two days (*BBC News* 2001a; *BBC News* 2003a).

The nurse, who had been sentenced to 12 months' imprisonment for ill-treatment and referred to in the case immediately above, appealed on the basis that the judge had gone wrong procedurally on one group of the allegations.

Appeal against catalogue of ill-treatment allegations. The allegations concerned a resident with Alzheimer's disease and dementia. These were (a) forcible administration of medication (so that the resident had to take the medication in order to breathe), (b) forcible administration of sedatives, (c) manhandling and ejecting a resident from the staff room, (d) flicking the resident's nose causing red marks, (e) throwing the resident across the lounge (causing him to fall into a footstool and then holding him down by the throat causing him to choke and his face to go purple), and (f) regularly abusing the resident verbally. The Court of Appeal did reduce the sentence to nine months on the basis of procedural error, but the carer would still have to serve twelve. This was because he had been anyway sentenced to twelve months on another count, namely meeting the resident in the hallway, putting him in a double arm lock and pulling him to the floor (*R v Spedding*).

Another care worker at the same home admitted ill-treatment and was sentenced to 150 hours' community service for slapping a resident (*Independent* 2002).

In another case, a four-month suspended sentence for ill-treatment was given to a hospital nurse who had kicked one patient, slapped another and dragged a third by his neck. She was subsequently struck off the nursing register (*The Times* 2002). And when three mentally ill people were found living in squalor, a former mental health nurse and his wife admitted three counts of wilful neglect and were sentenced to 200 hours of community service (*Community Care* 1998). Ill-treatment may be sustained over a considerable period of time.

Three-year regime of physical abuse of residents with severe learning disabilities. In a Yorkshire care home, a regime of physical abuse had persisted for some three years. The eight victims with physical and learning disabilities had mental ages of less than two years old, and could not speak for themselves. They suffered bullying, kicking, slapping, nipping, hair-tugging and other assaults. One resident was kicked five times in the groin by a female carer wearing high heeled shoes; another had his face rubbed in urine as though he were a puppy; another resident was force-fed; another had incontinence pads changed roughly. One prevalent view was that these residents with learning disabilities did not feel pain in the normal way.

Of 33 charges, 23 were proven. Seven carers were sentenced to a total of 66 months in prison mainly on grounds of ill-treatment and wilful neglect variously; one who had shown genuine remorse and shame to ten months, another (mother of three children and five months pregnant) to 12 months, a third to 12 months, his sister (who was pregnant) to 12 months, a fifth (a supermarket worker with a previous conviction for wilful neglect of a child, but who had accepted her misbehaviour) to eight months, a sixth to nine months and a seventh to three months. Of the seven, six were women (Wood 2005).

Cleared of 15 charges of ill-treatment, a care home manager was convicted on the last charge, concerning the taking of blood from the arm of a resident in her late eighties. He took the blood in a rough and inappropriate manner, such that the needle went right through the patient's arm, leaving her with bruises (*Cheshire Guardian* 2004).

In a residential home near Oxford, relatives were encouraged to ring ahead of visiting, so that care workers could hide the stench of urine with air freshener and scrape faeces off the curtains. Upstairs, an 89-year old man was lying with suppurating pressure sores, which had rotted his flesh down to the bones. He was in too much pain to move and too much confusion to cry out. The owner attempted to clean the wounds by hacking at the skin around the sores with office scissors and ripping out pieces of rotting flesh – wearing gloves with which moments before he had scooped faeces from the sheets. The man was referred to by staff as the 'body in the attic'. The owner was charged with ill-treatment and wilful neglect and convicted; he served twelve weeks of a nine month prison sentence (Hill 2001).

Another care home owner, originally charged with manslaughter, was convicted instead of wilful neglect. The resident concerned had mental health problems, as well as Alzheimer's disease and Parkinson's disease. He had been awarded the Sword of Honour during his career in the armed forces. He died from septicaemia and pneumonia, and had been found previously by his family lying in soiled clothing, sweating and unconscious. He was severely dehydrated at times and during a period of ten days he lost two stone. The home was also in breach of many of the regulations applying to care homes. The judge stated that 'those who wilfully neglect, with serious consequences, should expect to go to prison. This is the message that should go out'. She was sentenced to six months' imprisonment. She had been arrested after the coroner had informed the police, so concerned was he about the man's appearance (Narain 2008).

An 84-year old woman died within five weeks of entering a nursing home. A nurse working there pleaded guilty to wilful neglect for not administering the correct medication (*BBC News* 2008d). Eight other care workers at the home were cleared of charges relating to fractures to her collar bone and a rib, to bruising, and to a ligature mark around one of her forearms. These injuries could have been innocent, according to expert evidence (*BBC News* 2008e).

8.6.2 PEOPLE LACKING CAPACITY: OFFENCE OF ILL-TREATMENT OR NEGLECT

The Mental Capacity Act 2005 creates an offence of ill-treatment or wilful neglect by any person who has the care of another person who lacks, or who the first person reasonably believed to lack, capacity – or by any deputy or person with lasting power of attorney under the 2005 Act, or any person with enduring power of attorney as created under previous legislation. The maximum sentence is five years in prison (s.44).

The Code of Practice on the 2005 Act states that the offences are separate. Ill-treatment involves deliberation or recklessness and it does not matter whether the behaviour was likely to cause, or actually caused, harm or damage to the victim's health. The meaning of wilful neglect varies with circumstances but would usually mean that a person had deliberately failed to do something he or she knew was a duty (Lord Chancellor 2007, p.252; and see *R v Newington*, as referred to at 8.6.1 above).

The first apparent conviction under this section involved a care home manager locking three people with learning disabilities in a car for three hours:

Care home manager locking vulnerable people in car. A care home manager and an employee went to a betting shop and amusement arcade. For three hours during the visit, they locked three vulnerable people in a car on a hot and muggy day. The three had severe learning disabilities, autism and epilepsy. They were rescued when passers-by spotted them in distress and trying to get out. The police freed them and found them dehydrated and very hot. The judge in the Crown Court sentenced the manager and employee to 300 hours and 250 hours of community service respectively for wilful neglect. They were in serious breach of their responsibilities, and the three men must have suffered very considerable stress and discomfort in the unventilated vehicle. They had been on the 'cusp' of going to prison, but were previously model citizens. Both were sacked by their employer (*Daily Mail* 2008).

8.7 OFFENCE OF CAUSING DEATH OF VULNERABLE ADULT

The Domestic Violence, Crime and Victims Act 2004 contains an offence of causing or allowing the death of a vulnerable adult. In outline, it applies when:

- a vulnerable adult dies as a result of an unlawful act
- the person who committed the act was a member of the same household and had frequent contact with the victim
- the victim was at significant risk of serious physical harm by an unlawful act by such a member of the household
- the person either directly caused the victim's death – or was or ought to have been aware of the risk, failed to take reasonable steps to protect the victim, and the act occurred in circumstances that the person foresaw or should have foreseen.

For the offence to be made out, the prosecution does not have to prove whether the person actually did the act or instead failed to protect the victim. The maximum sentence is 14 years' imprisonment. The purpose of the offence is to overcome the problem of showing which of two perpetrators committed the act when, for example, each is blaming the other and the evidence is otherwise inconclusive.

A person could be classed as a member of the same household even if he or she does not live there but visits so often and for such periods of time that it would be reasonable to regard him or her as such a member.

A vulnerable adult means a person aged 16 or over whose ability to protect himself or herself from violence, abuse or neglect is significantly impaired through physical or mental disability or illness, through old age or otherwise (s.5).

For instance, in 2001, a 78-year-old woman went to live with relatives. Five weeks and 49 injuries later, she died. All the relatives denied responsibility for the injuries, the cause of her death could not be established, and so no charges were laid. It is thought that cases such as this could be caught by the offence under the 2004 Act (Hamilton 2005). In 2008, the first reported conviction under the Act was as follows:

Wife systematically beaten and abused by husband for months: four family members also convicted for doing nothing. A 19-year-old woman was systematically beaten and abused by her husband for three months. When she died, she had 15 broken ribs and bruising over 85 per cent of her body. Her husband was convicted of murder; however, his mother, two sisters, and brother-in-law were all found guilty of allowing the death of a vulnerable adult. The Crown Prosecution Service commented that the family had chosen to do nothing and that if 'families or other people with a duty to look after those who need protection deliberately choose not to do so, their neglect will not be ignored by the law enforcement agencies, and prosecution will follow' (Jenkins 2008a).

8.8 ENDANGERING LIFE BY WILFUL NEGLIGENCE

When elderly residents in a care home in Clacton were forced to drink vast amounts of liquids by the owner, who was obsessed with avoiding dehydration in residents, two of them died. It was reported that the owner was given a suspended 15-month prison sentence under a common law offence not used for 200 years: endangering human life or health by wilful negligence (Horsnell 2001).

8.9 CORONERS' FINDINGS

Working under the Coroners Act 1988, coroners may sometimes shed light on matters relevant to adult protection.

For instance, a 93-year-old man died, malnourished with multiple bed sores on arms, back, hips, buttocks, groin, legs and feet – and was stuck in the foetal position unable to uncurl. A 54-year-old woman had been living with him, and had told police that she loved him and looked after him. The coroner found that the man's death had occurred, 'aggravated by neglect' – and that he would be writing to a number of agencies (*Westmoreland Gazette* 2001).

Appearances may be deceiving. After 11 patients suffering from dementia died, allegations were made that they had been starved by nursing staff on Rowsley Ward in a Derby hospital. In fact, an inquest concluded that they had died from natural causes –

although there had been an absence of official protocols, and patients were deprived of food and fluid if there was thought to be a risk of choking (*Nursing Standard* 2005a).

The following case involved the deaths of residents at a care home in Birmingham in connection with allegations about anti-psychotic drugs, inadequate antibiotic treatment for pneumonia, and the restrictive effect of bucket chairs. The court found the coroner's decision not to hold an inquest to be unlawful:

Deaths in care home and holding of inquest. Expert evidence suggested that the death of a care home resident 2002 had been caused or contributed to by excessive doses of an anti-psychotic drug, coupled with the restrictive effect of a bucket chair and a possible failure to give adequate antibiotic treatment for pneumonia. The bucket chair was a low slung seat from which elderly, and maybe restless, residents would have difficulty getting up unless assisted.

This gave reasonable cause to suspect that the death was unnatural under s.8 of the Coroners Act 1988. However, the coroner failed to hold an inquest; a successful judicial review case was brought challenging this decision. The death had taken place in the Maypole Nursing Home in Birmingham, operated by two general practitioners. Most of the residents were funded by social services and the NHS. A number of residents had died. The National Care Standards Commission had taken steps to close the home compulsorily, although the owner closed it voluntarily. The strategic health authority also investigated and disciplinary action was taken by the General Medical Council against the two general practitioners, who were suspended (*Bicknell v HM Coroner for Birmingham/Solihull*).

8.10 SEXUAL OFFENCES

The Sexual Offences Act 2003 reformed the law on sexual offences. In relation to adult protection, there are, in addition to the basic offences (rape, sexual assault, etc.), a number of offences specifically related to mental disorder.

The general offences could of course be charged in the case of mental disorder, where the person is unable to consent. They include rape which consists of (a) intentional penetration of vagina, anus or mouth of the victim with the penis; (b) lack of consent; and (c) the perpetrator does not reasonably believe that the victim consents (s.1).

Assault by penetration consists of (a) intentional penetration of the vagina or anus of with a part of the perpetrator's body or with anything else; (b) the penetration being sexual; (c) lack of consent; and (d) the perpetrator does not reasonably believe that the victim consents (s.2).

Sexual assault consists of (a) intentional touching of another person; (b) the touching being sexual; (c) lack of consent; and (d) the perpetrator does not reasonably believe that the victim consents (s.3). In Scotland the equivalent offence is indecent assault – for example, a nurse in a care home was sent to prison after being convicted of handling the naked breast of an 86-year-old woman with dementia (Davidson 2007).

Causing sexual activity without consent consists of (a) intentional causing of another person to engage in an activity; (b) the activity being sexual; (c) lack of consent; and (d) the perpetrator does not reasonably believe that the victim consents (s.4).

In addition are a number of offences specifically related to mental disorder. Mental disorder bears the same meaning as in s.1 of the Mental Health Act 1983.

8.10.1 SEXUAL OFFENCES, MENTAL DISORDER, AND INABILITY TO REFUSE

Sections 30–33 of the 2003 Act contain certain offences that rely on the victim being unable, because of his or her mental disorder or for a reason related to it, to refuse the sexual activity.

The offences are (a) sexual activity with a mentally disordered person (s.30); (b) causing or inciting a person with a mental disorder to engage in sexual activity (s.31); (c) engaging in sexual activity in the presence of a person with a mental disorder for the purpose of sexual gratification of the perpetrator; and (d) causing a person with a mental disorder to watch a sexual act for the purpose of sexual gratification of perpetrator (ss.30–33).

For the purposes of ss.30 and 31, the sexual activity constituting an offence is defined as touching (a) involving penetration of the victim's anus or vagina with a part of the perpetrator's body or anything else; (b) penetration of the victim's mouth with the perpetrator's penis, penetration of the perpetrator's anus or vagina with a part of the victim's body, penetration of the perpetrator's mouth with the victim's penis.

The inability to refuse must be because either (a) the victim 'lacks the capacity to choose whether to agree to the touching (whether because he lacks sufficient understanding of the nature or reasonably foreseeable consequences of what is being done, or for any other reason) or (b) is unable to communicate such a choice'.

This set of offences also relies on the perpetrator knowing, or reasonably being expected to know, of the mental disorder – and that because of it, or a reason related to it, the person is likely to be unable to refuse (ss.30–33). Thus, on this last point, a conviction was obtained and upheld in the following case:

Inability to communicate choice. The victim lived in a public house with her parents. She was 27 years old (but had a much lower developmental age) and had cerebral palsy. A 73-year-old man, of previous good character, allegedly touched her over her clothing in the area of her vagina, whilst exposing himself and placing her hand on his soft penis. The defence accepted that the woman suffered from a mental disorder, but argued that she did not lack the capacity to agree to the touching. The magistrates' court had accepted that she understood the nature of sexual relations but did not have the capacity to understand that she could refuse. The High Court took this reasoning to mean that, whilst she might have understood about sexual activity, she was unable to communicate her choice (*Hulme v Director of Public Prosecutions*).

It has also been pointed out that the reference to the mental disorder, or a 'reason related to it', widens the ambit of these offences. For instance, it might encompass the situation in which the effects of the medication taken for the mental disorder render the person unable to refuse (Card 2006, p.342). Nevertheless, there is a limit to the application of these sections of the Act and, as the following Court of Appeal case shows, it is by no means straightforward. The court made a number of points about s.30 of the Act. The incapacity had to concern an inability to *agree* to sexual activity not just an inability to *refuse*. And even if the woman's fright was irrational and linked to the mental disorder, it did not necessarily follow that she lacked capacity to agree. Further, any such irrational fright, which meant the woman felt unable to communicate her choice, did not come under the second leg of s.30 (inability to communicate choice).

Irrational fear, mental disorder and capacity to choose to agree to sexual activity. A woman lived in a supervised hostel. She had a schizo-affective disorder and an emotionally unstable personality disorder. These disorders could result in impulsive and aggressive behaviour, agitation, delusion, hallucination, depression, and mania. She met a man who offered to help her and she went with him to the house of another man. She was given crack cocaine there and engaged in sexual activity with both men. The men were prosecuted and convicted under s.30 of the 2003 Act. They appealed.

The Court of Appeal held as follows. First, the court contrasted ability to refuse with ability to agree to sexual activity. It was not enough for the woman to be unable to refuse the sexual advances because of an irrational fear arising out of the mental disorder. The Act referred to an inability to choose to refuse to agree to sexual touching. Second, the effect of a mental disorder must be severe before it would have the effect that a person was unable to choose to agree to sexual activity. Third, if the woman consented to sexual activity against her inclination because she was frightened, even if her fear was irrational and caused by her mental disorder, it did not follow that she lacked capacity to choose whether to agree.

Fourth, it did not follow necessarily from any irrational fear, that the woman would not have been capable of choosing whether or not to agree sexual activity, in circumstances which did not give rise to that fear (this was relevant because lack of capacity could not be person or situation specific). Fifth, an irrational fear that meant the woman felt unable to communicate her choice would not come under the second leg of s.30 (ability to communicate). This second leg of s.30 was designed to address those whose mental disorders impaired their ability to communicate. There was no evidence that the woman was unable to communicate any choice she had made.

Nonetheless, if the evidence showed that her mental disorder had left her so distressed or confused that she was not capable of making a coherent decision to agree to sexual activity, whoever might make the request, the jury could conclude that she lacked capacity.

The convictions were quashed and a retrial ordered, because the judge had given mistaken directions to the jury (R v C).

Having made this judgement, a subsequent application was made by the Crown. The Court of Appeal responded by certifying three point of law as questions of general public importance. First, whether the Court of Appeal had, in its original decision, been correct to state that capacity to consent to or to refuse sexual activity was issue specific but could not be person or situation specific. Second, whether the court had been correct to state that an irrational fear related to a mental disorder, so preventing the exercise of choice, could not be equated with lack of capacity to choose. Third, whether, the court had been correct to hold that inability to communicate a choice under s.30 of the Act could only apply to physical inability to communicate (and not, for example, to such inability brought about by fear) (R v C). So there is clearly uncertainty.

More straightforwardly, a 22-year old carer was convicted of sexual activity with a mentally disordered 77-year old woman in a nursing home. This occurred during the night; the woman needed emergency surgery after losing a litre of blood in the attack (*BBC News* 2008c). Likewise the following case:

Sexual activity between mentally disordered woman and next-door neighbour. A 20-year old woman with Down's Syndrome and severe impairment of intelligence lived with her parents. She had gone uninvited to a neighbour's house, where sexual activity took place. The neighbour subsequently took advantage of moments when they were alone to engage in further sexual activity – in the snooker room of the social club (where the woman helped out) or in a lay-by when he took her for a drive. There were four instances of digital, and two of oral, penetration. The offender had no previous convictions, and the judge referred to him as a man of 'spectacularly good character'. He was convicted under s.30 of the Sexual Offences Act 2003 and sentenced to four years in prison. The Court of Appeal found this too lenient and substituted five and a half years; it would have been seven years, but this was reduced because of the unsatisfactory sentencing process to which the man has been subjected earlier in the case (*R v Charles*).

A nurse was convicted under s.30 of the 2003 Act, having engaged in sexual activity with an elderly woman at a nursing home; he was caught by a female colleague who found him in a toilet with the woman, with one hand down the front of the woman's trousers and performing a sex act on himself (Hills 2008). For example, he was placed on the sex offenders register under s.80 and schedule 3 of the Act, as would anybody else convicted under s.30. Such registration means that the offender becomes subject to notification requirements (a duty to register with the police) under the Act. Depending on the offence, the requirement is either absolute (irrespective of sentence) or conditional (dependent on sentence). The offences related to mental disorder under ss.30–37 are absolute; those involving care workers and mentally disordered people are conditional on sentence.

Under previous sexual offences legislation (the now superseded Sexual Offences Act 1956), a psychiatrist was convicted of rape and indecent assault of vulnerable women. Such was the abuse of trust that a sentence of eight years was too lenient; on appeal this was increased to ten years (*R v Allison*).

8.10.2 SEXUAL OFFENCES, MENTAL DISORDER, NO RELIANCE ON INABILITY TO REFUSE

A further number of offences do not require an inability to refuse on the part of the mentally disordered person. In other words, these offences would be more easily made out, insofar as consent issues are not decisive. However, they do still require the perpetrator to know, or reasonably to be expected to know, that the victim has a mental disorder.

These offences all concern inducement, threat or deception to (a) procure sexual activity with a person with a mental disorder; (b) cause a person with a mental disorder to engage in sexual activity by inducement, threat or deception; (c) engage in sexual activity in the presence, procured by inducement, threat or deception, of a person with a mental disorder; or (d) cause a person with a mental disorder to watch a sexual act by inducement, threat or deception (ss.34–37).

8.10.3 SEXUAL OFFENCES, MENTAL DISORDER AND CARE WORKERS

A third set of offences applies in the context of care workers and mentally disordered people. The offences do not rely on the inability of the victim to refuse; in effect they do not rely on the issue of whether there was consent. The perpetrator must have known or reasonably be expected to have known that the victim had a mental disorder. However, if it is proved that the victim has a mental disorder, then it is assumed that the care worker knew or should reasonably have known this, unless sufficient evidence is led to question such an assumption.

The offences apply to a care worker (a) engaging in sexual activity with a person with a mental disorder; (b) causing or inciting sexual activity; (c) engaging in sexual activity in the presence of a person with a mental disorder; or (d) causing a person with a mental disorder to watch a sexual act (ss.38–41).

A care worker is defined as somebody having functions in the course of his or her employment that brings, or is likely to bring, him or her into regular face-to-face contact with the mentally disordered person in various circumstances. These include (a) in a care home; or (b) in the context of the provision of services by the NHS or an independent medical agency or in an independent hospital or clinic. Alternative to either of these is where, whether or not employed to do so, the perpetrator provides care, assistance or services to the victim in connection with the victim's mental disorder – and so has, or is likely to have, regular face-to-face contact with the victim (s.42).

The care worker offences do not apply where (a) the mentally disordered person is 16 years old or more, and is lawfully married to the care worker; or (b) a sexual relationship existed between the mentally disordered person and the other person immediately before the latter became involved in the care of the mentally disordered person (ss.43–44). The definition of care worker is wide enough for these exceptions to cover, for instance, one partner or spouse now providing care at home – for the other who has become mentally disordered during the relationship.

Conviction of approved social worker for sexual activity with a consenting, but mentally disordered, client. A senior social care practitioner, who was an approved social worker, had sexual intercourse on three occasions with a service user and he was convicted under s.38 of the Act. At the time, the woman concerned was suffering from a mental disorder in the form of depression. Following the last occasion, she confessed to her husband and they subsequently informed the social worker's manager. The police were then involved. She had consented to the sexual activity. He was sentenced to 17 months' imprisonment. He was also removed from the register of social workers (*Bradford v General Social Care Council*).

8.10.4 SEXUAL OFFENCES AND PSYCHOLOGICAL CONDITION

Conviction for a sexual offence requires 'mens rea', the guilty mind. For example, when a man was convicted of rape and indecent assault on his estranged wife, a successful appeal was made. This was on the basis that the evidence of a consultant forensic psychiatrist showed that he suffered from Asperger's syndrome which would affect his ability adequately to determine somebody else's intentions and desires or to understand their wishes. This was relevant to the question of mens rea, to the jury's view of the honesty of his evidence about what he believed to have been the situation – and to why he had behaved so oddly during the trial. A re-trial was ordered (*R v TS*).

8.11 PHYSICAL HARM AND HEALTH AND SAFETY AT WORK LEGISLATION

In some circumstances, health and safety at work legislation may be employed to prosecute in the context of adult protection.

For instance, in the following case, s.3 of the Health and Safety at Work Act 1974 (duty of employer toward non-employees) was used to prosecute both the company, and individual managers, of a care home for failing to investigate and prevent a sustained regime of physical abuse:

Health and safety obligations in relation to abuse at care home. People with physical and learning disabilities living in a care home in Hull had been subject to a regime of sustained abuse for three years. This included humiliation, rough behaviour, force-feeding, shouting, slapping, hair pulling, swearing and dragging residents across the floor. Most of the residents had a mental age of under two years. Seven carers were sent to prison under s.127 of the Mental Health Act 1983, for ill-treatment and neglect.

In addition, however, under the Health and Safety at Work Act 1974, the company was prosecuted and fined £100,000 together with £25,000 costs. It pleaded guilty to failing to take appropriate action to investigate and prevent the ill-treatment of vulnerable adults. Five senior managers were prosecuted as well for failing to protect residents from this ill-treatment; they had failed to act on reports of abuse. They were fined sums ranging from £4000 down to £360 (Mark 2005).

Thus, neglect or omission may provoke a prosecution under s.3 of the 1974 Act. For instance, a local authority pleaded guilty in relation to the death in a care home of a 23-year old man, who was quadriplegic and suffered from cerebral palsy. He was asphyxiated as a result of the failure to make sure the bed rails were maintained in effective working order and good repair – and to ensure staff were properly trained in fitting, maintaining and using the bed rails (24dash.com 2007). Likewise, another council was prosecuted under s.3, and fined £115,000 following the death of their severely disabled son in a bubble bath in a care home (*Bolton Evening News* 2004). This followed the failure of the family, in a judicial review case, to challenge the Crown Prosecution Services's failure to bring a gross negligence manslaughter case (*Rowley v Director of Public Prosecutions*).

A couple who ran a private residential home were not only convicted of ill-treatment and wilful neglect (under s.127 of the Mental Health Act 1983) but also of breach of the Health and Safety Work Act 1974 (*BBC News* 2004b). The judge found they had abused their position of trust and created a regime that centred on oppressive conduct and oppressive punishment; residents were repeatedly bullied, underfed (one man lost four stone) and given inappropriate medicines (*Norwich Evening News* 2006).

8.12 HARM AND CIVIL TORTS

In the context of adult protection, civil torts (i.e. wrongs) may be committed and give rise to civil actions for damages. Two such torts are trespass to the person and false imprisonment. Negligence is another.

Trespass to the person is the civil law equivalent of assault and battery in criminal law (see 8.1.1). In the following case, concerning an NHS trust's failure to withdraw a medical intervention on the request of the patient, the court concluded that the trust had acted unlawfully in terms of the tort of trespass to the person:

Unlawful failure to withdraw ventilator and trespass to the person. A former social worker suffered a haemorrhage in the spinal column of the neck. At the time she executed a living will. This stated that if a time came when she could not give instructions, but was suffering from a life-threatening condition, permanent mental impairment or permanent unconsciousness, then she wished for treatment to be withdrawn. She subsequently suffered another major bleed and became tetraplegic, following which she had to use a ventilator in order to breathe. She asked for the ventilator to be switched off in March 2001. She could not do it herself. A year later, at the time of the court's judgment, it had still not been turned off.

Considering the evidence, the court started with the presumption of capacity; it considered that this had been displaced between April and August 2001. However, on the evidence the court concluded that she had in fact had capacity from August 2001 onward. The court criticised the NHS trust's consistent failure for not attempting to resolve the dilemma urgently. The woman had been treated unlawfully by the trust (i.e. trespass to the person), for which a small award of damages should be made.

The court drew a distinction between the duties of the team of doctors and nurses and that of the trust as a whole; it was unfair that the burden of decision and responsibility had remained in the hands of the former – when it was the trust's responsibility to act (Re B *(adult: refusal of treatment)*).

Likewise in the following case, a caesarean section, carried out against a woman's will, constituted unlawful trespass to the person. It had been carried out in good faith, but was inconsistent with the law:

Unlawful caesarean section and trespass to the person. A woman in the late stages of pregnancy was suffering from pre-eclampsia; there was a risk to the lives of both herself and the unborn baby. She fully understood the potential risks and clearly rejected medical intervention; she wanted the baby to be born 'naturally'. After she had been detained in hospital unlawfully under the Mental Health Act 1983, the hospital then purported to act in her best interests from necessity – on the ground that she lacked mental capacity – by performing a caesarean section. It did so, having obtained an emergency declaration from the High Court, on the basis of inadequate and misleading information being given to the judge.

The woman subsequently brought a legal case against the approved social worker and the hospital. On the evidence, she had possessed capacity to decide about the operation, although she had ceased to offer resistance at the time, when told that the caesarean would go ahead anyway (following the court's emergency declaration). The court now pointed out that this had not been consent but submission; thus the caesarean section, together with the associated medical procedures, constituted unlawful trespass to the person (R v Collins, ex p S).

In an ostensibly similar case, the outcome was different. A 40-week pregnant woman was refusing to have a caesarean section, required because the baby was in the breech position. The court held that to perform the operation would be in her best interests. This was because she was rendered temporarily incapable of making the decision by her all-pervasive fear of needles, which dominated everything and overrode the consent she had given in principle to the operation (*Re MB (caesarian section)*).

8.12.1 NEGLIGENCE (AND NEGLECT)

Civil negligence cases can be brought for physical (and sometimes psychological) harm caused by carelessness. The standard components which have to be shown are the existence of a duty of care, breach of that duty, and causation in the sense that the breach caused the harm complained of.

For instance, negligence cases may be relevant in the context of adult protection, as in the following case involving neglect of an elderly man in hospital:

Dehydration and ill-nourishment in hospital causing death. Following the neglect and death of a man in hospital, a negligence case was settled out of court for some £15,000. A former metal worker, he had been admitted for a broken leg, but within a few days became ill. He became dehydrated and ill-nourished, eventually dying of renal failure, septicaemia and a chest infection. Fluids and nutrition had not been administered and his poor state of health was only identified when he had been discharged to a rehabilitation unit. He was immediately readmitted to hospital intensive care but died (*BBC News* 2004). Despite instructions from doctors to do so, staff had failed to provide a saline drip for 12 days. The hospital stated that it could have done things better, but was under-funded (Wright and Carson 2002).

Another case involved an elderly man with senile dementia who went into a care home. Within two months he was in a distressing state, heavily sedated, thin and bony, being shouted at to sit down and often sopping wet. He was admitted to hospital as an emergency, with a huge sore at the base of his spine which had rotted the skin to the bone. The family brought a negligence case against the care home and accepted an out-of-court settlement of £45,000 (Pannone 2006).

When NHS trusts have taken shortcuts with infection control, and people have suffered or died as a consequence, a negligence case might be possible. For instance, the Healthcare Commission reports on outbreaks of *Clostridium difficile* (see 4.2.3) would suggest breach of the duty of care of the hospitals towards their patients. Where this breach could be shown to have at least substantially contributed to harm and even death, then negligence cases may be possible. For instance, an actress and model was compensated with £5 million for negligence on the part of a hospital which led to her contracting the MRSA infection (Sanderson 2008).

In sexual abuse cases involving children, the courts have held that it is possible to bring a civil case in tort against the employer of the abuser, on the basis of vicarious liability of the employer for the acts of the employee (*Lister v Hesley Hall*). There is no reason why this principle might not apply in the context of adults. For instance, when three carers were acquitted of assault (feeding talcum power to an elderly woman), nonetheless two other courses of action followed. First, the local authority terminated its contract with the agency that employed the carers. Second, the woman then brought a civil case against the agency. It was settled out of court, the agency admitting negligence and agreeing to pay over £10,000 in compensation (Dayani 2004; Carvel 2006a).

One local authority (at the time responsible for inspection of care homes) paid £1 million in compensation to adults with learning disabilities. In an out of court settlement, it conceded that it had failed properly to inspect the home and to prevent the abuse (*Solicitors' Journal* 2003).

Negligence need not always be about physical harm; it can sometimes relate to psychological or financial harm. In the following case, an elderly gentleman in Eastbourne, with uncertain understanding and partial memory, had fallen into the hands of a confidence trickster who first cleared out his savings account, then put him up to raising a mortgage on his house, which money was then also taken. However, the court held a solicitor liable for loss of the mortgage money for blatant breach of his duty of care in facilitating the mortgage, even though the money had been appropriated by an unknown third party, for whom the solicitor was of course not responsible:

Confidence trick on elderly gentleman facilitated by negligent solicitor. An elderly gentleman had fallen into the hands of an unknown confidence trickster. The latter first of all took all the man's savings via his bank account. Then a mortgage application was drafted, which the man was persuaded to sign. The court found that if his solicitor had done his job he would immediately have realised that the man did not want the mortgage, did not need it, and could not afford it (inevitably he defaulted on the first interest repayment, with the predictable outcome that the mortgage lenders sought repossession of the house). The solicitor would have realised that the mortgage application was to benefit somebody else. Nonetheless, the solicitor went ahead and arranged a £55,000 mortgage against the house worth £70,000.

The solicitor was held to have breached his duty of care by arranging the mortgage transaction. Had the solicitor exercised his duty of care, it would have been patently obvious that 'as soon as the money was advanced it would have been out the other door again'. The specific breach of duty here was the solicitor's failure to check (with the man) the mortgage proposal agreement, which the lenders had sent back by fax to the solicitor precisely in order that it should be checked. Had the solicitor done this, it would have become apparent that the man could not afford the mortgage. The lenders had been supplied with untrue information relating to affordability and the man's wish to purchase a second house; this would have come to light had the solicitor taken care. The solicitor also owed a duty to the lender by ensuring that the man understood the obligation he was incurring, and the resources he would need to repay the capital and income.

The judge described the facts of this case as quite exceptional, and held that the solicitor was liable for the mortgage capital and interest repayments – even though it was the confidence trickster, an unknown third party, which has ultimately walked off with the money (*Finsbury Park Mortgage Funding v Burrows*).

8.12.2 LOCAL AUTHORITIES AND THE NHS PROTECTED FROM LIABILITY IN NEGLIGENCE

The courts have nevertheless a track record of trying to protect local authorities and the NHS from certain types of negligence case, by holding that the local authority or NHS body did not have a duty of care in the first place. This means that even if there is ostensible carelessness, it is irrelevant because there is effectively no duty of care to breach.

The courts have sometimes taken this approach particularly when the alleged failure is closely connected with what the court perceives to be the public body's statutory duties, or where policy and resource issues are in play. The issue has arisen as to whether it is fair, just or reasonable to impose a duty of care in child protection (*X v Bedfordshire CC;*

Barrett v Enfield LBC; JD v East Berkshire NHS Trust), education (*Phelps v Hillingdon LBC*), aftercare under s.117 of the Mental Health Act 1983 (*Clunis v Camden and Islington HA; K v Central and North West London Mental Health NHS Trust*), regulation of care providers (*Jain v Trent SHA*) and protection of witnesses by the police (*Chief Constable of Hertfordshire v Van Colle*).

The courts have struggled to state exactly what the law is and to maintain a consistent line. All of which makes potentially significant the following case, involving a local authority's failure to safeguard and protect two highly vulnerable adults with learning disabilities from being tortured by a third party. (At the time of writing, the case is subject to an appeal by the local authority). The local authority had argued that it simply owed no duty of care in negligence (whether or not it had acted carelessly) and that any challenge should be by way of judicial review (to review the lawfulness of its actions) rather than negligence (concerning the payment of damages).

Torture of couple with learning disabilities over a weekend; local authority failure to act; negligence. The two claimants, represented by the Official Solicitor, had learning disabilities. They lived together in a flat, together with the woman's two children, one of whom also had learning disabilities. The family was able to live as a unit in the community, but functioned at a low level in some respects. It was vulnerable. Two parts of the local authority's social services department had been involved with the family before the relevant weekend.

Background to weekend. 'For a period of time prior to the relevant weekend the claimants had been befriended and then taken advantage of by a number of youths. It is not known exactly when this began to happen, but the evidence suggests that it probably did so at or about the end of the summer of 2000. As time went by some of these youths would use the claimants' flat as a place at which to live, take drugs, engage in sexual activity, leave stolen goods, and generally misbehave. X was assaulted quite seriously in a MacDonald's restaurant on 11th October 2000 by one of the youths, who believed that X had "grassed" on him in relation to some stolen goods found by the police at [the claimants' flat] on the previous day'.

The weekend. 'During the relevant weekend the claimants were effectively imprisoned in their own home, and repeatedly assaulted and abused, often in the presence of the two children. Both claimants later made statements to the police, describing their ordeals. What follows is intended only as a brief summary. X said that at one stage the youths confined him and Y to their bedroom, and made them perform sexual acts. They threw many of X's and Y's possessions over the balcony. They forced pepper and fluid into X's eyes. They locked him in the bathroom for a time, in the dark. They made him drink urine, eat dog biscuits, dog faeces and the faeces of one of the youths, threatening him that he would be stabbed if he did not. They made him put a vibrator up his bottom, and then lick it. They sprayed kitchen cleaner in his mouth, face and hair. They slashed him repeatedly all over his body with a knife or knives. Y's statement was to similar effect, adding that she too was made to put the vibrator in her mouth. The children too were abused, assaulted and locked in their bedroom from time to time. Even the family dog was abused. It is unnecessary to go into further detail, or into the physical and psychological injuries suffered by the Claimants as a result'.

Local authority's failure to act and duty of care. The judge considered in detail both the local authority's responses to the deteriorating situation leading up to the weekend and the relevant case law. He acknowledged the past reluctance of the courts to impose a duty of care where there has been a negligent failure in the exercise of a statutory function by a public body. Nonetheless, he concluded that before the weekend in question, the council's emergency procedure for moving the couple from their flat should have been triggered. The fact that this did not occur resulted from a lack of cooperation and communication between the social services and housing departments, a failure to appreciate the gravity and urgency of the situation indicated by the evidence, and a failure to give the case the priority it warranted. In all the circumstances, it was fair, just and reasonable to impose a duty of care (*X, Y v Hounslow LBC*).

8.13 PHYSICAL (AND OTHER) RESTRAINT

The physical restraint of adults, as well as of children, remains a substantial issue. On the one hand, total prohibition on restraint might sometimes result in harm to both the service user and other people. Equally, improper restraint runs the risk of resulting in, for example, injury to the restrained or the restrainer, breach of human rights, the criminal offence of assault and battery, and the civil tort of trespass to the person.

In response to such concerns, the Department of Health issued guidance in 2002 on physically restrictive interventions for people with learning disabilities or autism in health, education and social care settings (DH 2002). In summary, the guidance emphasises that interventions are legally permissible in certain circumstances (e.g. self-harm or injury to others) – and that any interventions should be the least restrictive necessary. They should be planned as far as possible, result from multi-disciplinary assessment and be part of a wider therapeutic strategy detailed in individual care plans. Prevention should be the primary aim, in order to avoid the use of restraint if possible. There should be clear organisational policies and adequate training (DH 2002).

The Mental Capacity Act 2005 specifically deals with restraint, permitting it but only where it is to prevent harm to the person and it is employed proportionately (s.6). The Code of Practice points out, more generally, that the common law also imposes a duty of care on health care and social care staff to take appropriate and necessary action to restrain or remove a person – with challenging behaviour or who is in the acute stages of illness – who may cause harm to themselves or other people (Lord Chancellor 2007, para 6.43). The Mental Health Act 1983 Code of Practice also contains guidance on restraint (DH 1999, paras 19.1–19.14).

Care standard regulations, governing the provision of care by registered providers of both care homes and domiciliary services, states that no service user must be subject to physical restraint of any kind, unless it is the only practicable means of securing the welfare of him or her or of any other service user and there are exceptional circumstances. Any such restraint must be recorded (SI 2001/3965, r.13; SI 2002/3214, r.14).

On any view, the effect of all these legal and guidance provisions is that safeguards are required. In the following case, the health service ombudsman found they were absent, where policy, planning, training and an individual care plan were all lacking:

No policy or care plan for restraint. An elderly man in hospital had chronic obstructive airways disease, peripheral vascular disease, and had suffered a stroke that left him with right-sided weakness. Previously, whilst at home, he had displayed signs of irritability and frustration, and verbal and physical aggression toward his wife. He was admitted to hospital for respite care for social reasons, since he could not cope whilst his wife, his main carer, herself required hospital treatment. He became disturbed during the night, after going to the day room to use his nebuliser. Nursing staff restrained him. When his daughter visited she found that he had an injured arm, carpet burns on his face and a cut on his hand.

The health service ombudsman found that the NHS trust had no policy on control and restraint, and in that respect there was no particular plan for this particular patient. This latter failing was made worse by the fact that there had been a previous incident of restraint a few nights earlier involving the same patient. The ombudsman severely criticised the lack of planning and training which led a disabled, elderly man to be restrained in such a way (*Oldham NHS Trust 1999*).

Despite the Department of Health's guidance on restraint (DH 2002), the dividing line between what constitutes reasonable and unreasonable restraint might be difficult to discern:

Use of armchair with fitted table. During the course of a defamation court case concerning an undercover BBC investigation of practices at a Scottish nursing home, it came to light that a Parker Knoll chair with fitted table was used to restrict the movements of one of the residents. However, the court found that it was acceptable that, for example, at meal times the chair should play a useful part in the care of a resident with dementia. Likewise, because of his disruptiveness and the risk to himself, he was not always in his room at night but installed in his chair in the nurses' sitting room. The judge rejected the allegation that he was in his chair most days for 24 hours (*Baigent v BBC*).

Conversely, the findings of the Commission for Health Improvement, that patients at an NHS mental health hospital had been tied to commodes while they had breakfast or generally for restraint, left no doubt that unacceptable physical restrictions had been employed. Such incidents had been part of a culture that allowed unprofessional, counter-therapeutic and degrading – even cruel – practices to take root (CHI 2000, p.10).

In 2007, the Commission for Social Care Inspection published a report on the use of restraint in the care of older people. It found a range of examples of the use of restraint which were unacceptable and arguably constituted a breach of human rights. These included people fastened into wheelchairs or kept in chairs by means of trays, use of low chairs to stop people getting up, wrapping up people in bed to the point of immobility so they could not remove their incontinence pads, excessive use of bed rails, dragging a person by her hair and tying her to a chair, excessive drug-based sedation, not taking people to the toilet when they want to go, punishing people by leaving them sitting in soiled pads – and so on.

The Commission referred to restraint as including physical intervention, physical restraint, denial of practical or staff resources to manage daily living, environmental restraint, chemical restraint, electronic surveillance, medical restraint, and forced care. It emphasised that restraint had to be justified in each case and might be if:

- consideration is given to the best interests of the individual and others
- there is a serious risk of harm to older people or others
- other methods to control the situation, such as de-escalation, have been tried and found to be unsuitable or have failed
- the least practicable amount of force is used for the shortest time

- it is used according to agreed guidelines, on the basis of a risk assessment and recorded decisions
- it is a last resort (CSCI 2007c).

8.13.1 SECLUSION

As far as seclusion goes, the Department of Health guidance on restraint states that if seclusion is required, other than in emergency, for periods of more than a few minutes or more than once a week, then advice should be sought about statutory powers under the Mental Health Act 1983 or Children Act 1989 (DH 2002).

The Mental Health Act Code of Practice states that seclusion should be a last resort, for the shortest possible time and not be used as a punishment, as part of a treatment programme, because of shortage of staff or where there is a risk of self-harm. It also sets out procedures in terms of length of time, periodic checking and reviewing (DH 2008a, paras 15.43–15.62).

Adherence to the code in respect of such procedures was the subject of consideration by the courts:

Seclusion and the Mental Health Act code of practice. The courts have held that the code should be followed unless there is good reason not to in the case of an individual patient or individual group of patients. However, it should not be departed from as a matter of policy. Otherwise, this could be in breach of article 8 of the European Convention on Human Rights, because the interference with the right to respect for privacy (including physical and psychological integrity) would then not be in accordance with the law. This would be, in turn, because such interference would not have the necessary degree of predictability and transparency required by article 8. The court also accepted that although seclusion did not necessarily breach article 3 of the Convention, nevertheless it would do so if it resulted in inhuman or degrading treatment. Giving weight and status to the code of practice was precisely the sort of step and safeguard required in order to avoid breach of human rights (*Munjaz v Mersey Care NHS Trust*).

CHAPTER 9

Financial abuse

KEY POINTS

Financial abuse of vulnerable adults is perceived to be a serious problem. It may involve a range of people in positions of trust, including close family members, friends, neighbours, both informal and paid carers, nurses, social services staff, solicitors, and the clergy. The organisation, Action on Elder Abuse, believes that financial abuse in families is significant and that 'middle-aged sons and daughters are the people most likely to rob older people of their cash, valuables and even their homes' (Action on Elder Abuse 2007).

In civil law, gifts and wills may be deemed invalid by the courts if the donor or testator was subject to 'undue influence'; likewise such transactions can be set aside if it can be shown that the person lacked capacity at the time of making the gift or will. In criminal law, financial abuse may be tantamount to various offences, including theft, burglary, robbery, fraud, false accounting and forgery. The number of legal cases easily identified and involving financial abuse, both by carers and other professional in positions of trust, might suggest that the problem is more than trivial. It is tempting to conclude from these cases that financial abuse on a smaller or larger scale is regarded by a significant minority as a perquisite (or 'perk') of the job of caring, or handling the financial affairs, of vulnerable older or disabled adults.

As much a cause for concern as it is difficult to deal with both legally and practically, is what has become known as 'cold calling', whereby vulnerable people are tricked or pressurised into parting with sometimes large sums of money in return for little or no work carried out by dishonest or simply bogus tradespersons. In addition, the financial harm to vulnerable adults, in which local authorities are sometimes implicated, has been discussed in Chapter 3.

This chapter outlines some of the relevant law, illustrating it with various examples, to bring home just how vulnerable some people are, and how other people – in a position of trust to a greater or lesser extent – are only too ready to take advantage .

9.1 UNDUE INFLUENCE

Apart from lack of capacity, there is sometimes an alternative ground on which a transaction may be set aside in civil law. This is on the basis of a legal, equitable concept known as undue influence. Generally speaking, undue influence can be summarised as follows. First, the exploited person has capacity, otherwise it is arguable that he or she cannot be unduly influenced (e.g. *Tchilingirian v Ouzounian*). Second, he or she is influenced to enter into a transaction not of his or her own free, informed, will. Third, the undue influence can be either 'express' (in the case of gifts of wills) or 'presumed' (in the case of gifts only).

That this legal doctrine is relevant to safeguarding adults would seem clear. In fact the courts have observed the renewed interest in it, owing to the greater longevity of people now and their concomitant vulnerability to suggestion by family members. The following case concerned a vulnerable 70-year-old man, described as physically and mentally disadvantaged all his life, who lost his house to the undue influence of his sister. The court set out at some length what it regarded as a social trend:

Lifetime gifts and transfers: importance of independent exercise of free will. The instant case is evidence of another social trend. With the increase in home ownership and the rising value of residential property more people have more property to dispose of in their lifetime and on death and more people expect to benefit substantially from inheritance.

People living longer, inheritors waiting longer. As people live longer, the inheritors have to wait longer. There is, however, the unwelcome prospect that the longer the wait, the greater the risk that even a modest estate will be seriously diminished by the high cost of care in the old age or infirmity of the home owner, and by the impact of inheritance tax on death.

Elderly and infirm vulnerable to suggestions. The elderly and infirm in need of full-time residential care are vulnerable to suggestions that they should dispose of the home to which they are unlikely to return. In my view, these social trends are already leading to a renewed interest in the law governing the validity of lifetime dispositions of houses, both in and outside the family circle, by the elderly and the infirm. The transfer of a house is a substantial transaction. A house is the most valuable asset that most people own. If a transfer is made by one person on the dependent side of a relationship of trust and confidence to a person in whom trust has been placed, it must be shown by the trusted party that the disposition was made in the independent exercise of free will after full and informed consideration.

No need for reprehensible conduct for finding of undue influence. The court may grant relief to the transferor, even though the transfer was not made as the result of any specific reprehensible conduct on the part of the trusted transferee (*Pesticcio v Huet*).

9.1.1 EXPRESS UNDUE INFLUENCE

If it is argued to be express, then evidence is required of how exactly the influence was exercised in terms of overt, improper pressure or coercion (*Royal Bank of Scotland v Etridge (no.2)*). For instance, a woman changed her will and left everything to her heavy drinking son, with whom she lived and of whom she was afraid, whilst disinheriting her other son. The court found that the first son had exercised undue influence. It set aside the new will, finding sufficient evidence of express undue influence:

Mother frightened and unduly influenced by her son. The heavy drinking son (T) had every motive for persuading his mother to change the will. He was fearful for his own security in his mother's home, and furious with the other brother and the latter's wife. He had already demonstrated vindictiveness toward them. 'There is also no doubt in my mind that T had the opportunity to use undue influence in persuading his mother to change her will. He had taken his mother back [to her own home from a nursing home] despite medical advice to the contrary; had deterred [his brother and wife] from visiting, even if there was no formal ban; and he had tried to push [his brother] out of the house on the day that the will was executed. She was frail and vulnerable and frightened of T. Did he take that opportunity? In my judgment he did.' There was no other reasonable explanation for the false allegations the mother made against the other son, and for the reasons she gave for changing the will. She was 'simply doing as she was told.' Her discretion and judgement had been overborne. This was undue influence (*Edwards v Edwards*).

The vulnerability of an 85-year-old woman, and the forcefulness of her nephew, meant that the courts found the latter had expressly unduly influenced her into resigning her position as trustee and landlord of a farm. This was after he had threatened court proceedings. Evidence was given that his aunt was distressed and upset, and frightened of both her nephew and court proceedings (*Daniel v Drew*).

An older case characterised express undue influence as having to involve 'some unfair and improper conduct, some coercion from outside, some over-reaching, some form of cheating and, generally though not always, some personal advantage obtained by a donee placed in some close and confidential relation to the donor' (*Alcard v Skinner*).

Nonetheless not all suspicious circumstances, even with evidence of pressure, will lead to a finding of express undue influence:

Changing of a will by person with early onset Alzheimer's Disease: persuasion and influence but not undue influence. An elderly woman suffering early onset Alzheimer's Disease was persuaded by her daughter to change her will largely in favour of the daughter. The daughter had written to her mother about how disappointed she had been over the previous will, and how she had expected her mother would leave the estate to her only surviving child and not split it also with her grandchildren (children of the mother's deceased son). The judge pointed out that, quoting *Governor & Company of the Bank of Scotland v Bennett*, that not all influence is undue influence, not even necessarily strong persuasion or heavy family pressure. Furthermore, the judge found no evidence that the daughter had repeatedly pestered or badgered her mother (*Scammell v Scammell*).

9.1.2 PRESUMED UNDUE INFLUENCE

Alternative to express undue influence is presumed undue influence. The latter relies on a relationship of trust and confidence, and the relationship being abused – resulting in a disadvantageous transaction, or at least a transaction that 'calls for an explanation'. Once these two elements are established, then the 'evidential burden' shifts to the other party to give an innocent explanation for the transaction. If this explanation is not forthcoming or convincing, undue influence will be made out. Importantly it is not necessary to prove that the other party did anything 'wrong'. Relationships of trust and confidence are recognised by the law courts in well-known categories (such as doctor–patient) but also in other relationships (such as carer and cared for person).

This second form of undue influence, presumed, can be relevant in the context of adult protection work and has been broken down in detail by the courts as involving the following:

- **Unfair advantage**. One person takes unfair advantage of another where – as a result of a relationship between them – the first person has gained influence or ascendancy over the second, without any overt acts of persuasion.
- **Trust and confidence assumed**. However, some relationships (e.g. parent and child, guardian and ward, trustee and beneficiary, solicitor and client, medical adviser and patient) will give rise to an irrebuttable presumption that a relationship of trust and confidence existed. The reposing of trust and confidence does not have to be proved.
- **Trust and confidence**. However, such relationships are infinitely various; a key question is whether the one person has posed sufficient trust and confidence in the other.
- **Reliance, dependence, vulnerability**. It is not just a matter of trust and confidence; exploitation of a vulnerable person would be included for example; thus trust and confidence, reliance, dependence, vulnerability, ascendancy, domination or control are all relevant terms.
- **Transaction calling for an explanation**. Undue influence must be proved by the person alleging it; however, a relationship of trust and confidence, coupled with a transaction that 'calls for an explanation', will normally be enough to discharge this burden of proof.
- **Shift of evidential burden**. The evidential burden then shifts to the other person to counter the inference of undue influence, i.e. to rebut the presumption.
- **Degree of disadvantage**. Even within the special class of relationships (assuming trust and confidence), not every gift or transaction will be assumed to have been down to undue influence unless otherwise proved (otherwise Christmas presents, or the payment of reasonable professional fees, would be caught); it should be only where the transaction calls for an explanation. The greater the disadvantage to the vulnerable person, the greater the explanation called for.

- **Independent advice**. The receipt of independent advice is a relevant consideration but will not necessarily show that a decision was free from undue influence (*Royal Bank of Scotland v Etridge (no.2)*).

In the context of safeguarding adults, when financial abuse takes place, the doctrine of undue influence may give interested parties (e.g. the exploited person or another member of the family) a civil remedy. The courts have repeated that it is not necessary to show that anybody has done anything wrong (*Pesticcio v Huet*: transfer of house by vulnerable man to his sister). Furthermore, even if the donor of a gift denies that he or she has been pressurised, for example to transfer land, presumed undue influence may still be made out – since direct pressure for a particular gift is not necessarily required (*Goodchild v Bradbury*).

The relationships giving rise to a relationship of trust and confidence can be various, apart from those that automatically do so. For instance, the relationship of aunt and nephew (*Randall v Randall*), or husband and wife (*Royal Bank of Scotland v Etridge (no.2)*), may do so. Similarly, undue influence cases might involve carers. The following court case illustrates how a live-in companion rapidly exercised such influence over the elderly man she was purporting to assist, to the point of having him 'at her mercy'. It also shows how supposedly independent advice might be suspect:

Depleting an elderly man's estate. An elderly man's wife died in 1958. Shortly after she died, he employed a woman as secretary-companion. In the last five years before he died in 1964, he made gifts to her of nearly £28,000; his estate had been reduced from £40,000 to £9500. His general practitioner's description of him was that he was elderly, weak, a little vacant, courteous, introspective, depressed at times; a gentle old man. His memory was not worse than that of many people of that age. He was not particularly fit and active; he was happy up to a point.

The companion became increasingly entrusted with handling his financial and business affairs. He agreed to sell his house and to move to another house the companion had always wished to reside in. He made a gift of it to her; he was described on 'some government form' that had to be filled in as the 'lodger'. The judge concluded that at this point he was entirely at the mercy of the companion. The solicitor involved in the transaction was purportedly acting for both the man and the companion; he said nothing to the man about the desirability of independent advice. The man therefore did not receive the independent advice that could have supported the argument that he had exercised 'full, free and informed thought' – which in turn could have removed the influence of the companion.

The judge held that there was in fact a relationship of trust and confidence between the man and the companion; and that there was a presumption of undue influence in the case of the gifts. It was for her to rebut this; she had failed to do this, even though there was no direct evidence of pressure being brought to bear by her. Furthermore the onus on the carer was a heavy one, because of the otherwise seemingly objectionable nature of her behaviour (*Re Craig*).

The obtaining of truly independent advice may indicate that undue influence has not been exercised, but this is not decisive. For instance, it might have been inadequate advice:

Poor independent advice from solicitor. In one case, a 70-year-old man, physically and mentally disadvantaged for most of his life, lived at home with his widowed mother. She had made a gift of the house to him. Some 18 years later, he was admitted to hospital falling a serious fall and discharged to a nursing home six months later. Shortly afterwards, having received some inadequate advice from his own solicitor concerning local authority rules about care home fees, he transferred the house to his sister who shortly afterwards sold it. The court made a finding of undue influence. The sister had not obviously done anything wrong, but as a matter of public policy it could be set aside. The advice from his solicitor had been 'not such as a competent adviser would give' if acting solely in the interests of the man. (The solicitor had in fact been initially contacted by the sister.) It had not been so as to free him 'from the impairment of the influence on his free will and to give him the necessary independence of judgment and freedom to make choices' (*Pesticcio v Huet*).

In the case below, involving a situation where an elderly man was taken under the proverbial wing of a neighbour, the court emphasised the significance of the presumption of undue influence and of the carer having to provide an innocent explanation for what had occurred. In the absence of such an explanation, 'public policy' demanded a finding of undue influence, even in the absence of direct evidence of a wrongful act. The reference to the 'care authorities' and the 'care coordinator' might suggest (it is unclear) that the local social services authority was unwittingly involved in assisting the woman to exercise the undue influence:

Taken under the wing of a neighbour. A 72-year-old retired teacher and bachelor was living alone. He had become physically dependent on others because of limited mobility. His neighbour, whom he had met at a supermarket when he was holding onto railings and was in distress, 'took him under her wing'. Following a fall, hospital admission and then discharge, he became more dependent. She 'volunteered to the care authorities' to be responsible for giving him two meals a day. At the suggestion of the care coordinator, he then signed a third-party mandate, authorising her to draw on his current account. After further falls and hospital admission, he said he wanted to make a gift to her of certain investments; these amounted to nearly £300,000, nearly 91 per cent of his liquid assets.

There was a relationship of trust and confidence; the gift was very large. These facts gave rise to a presumption of undue influence. It was for the woman to rebut this. Given that the man had received no advice, independent or otherwise, the presumption was not rebutted, and undue influence was made out. The court also made the point that this would be so even if the woman's conduct had been 'unimpeachable' and there had been nothing 'sinister' in it. This was because the court would interfere not on the ground that any wrongful act had in fact been committed by the donee but on the ground of public policy. Such public policy required that it be established affirmatively that the donor's trust and confidence had not been betrayed or abused (*Hammond v Osborne*).

Undue influence might come in different guises, not necessarily in an obvious caring or family situation:

Undue influence from 'alternative' group. A woman in her sixties became involved with a group of people sharing an interest in art therapy, alternative medicine and spiritual writing. The group purchased a small estate, which they ran partly as a hotel and partly as a cultural centre; they formed a company. The woman first raised a mortgage on her house to loan £34,000 to the group; she subsequently sold her house and gave the proceeds of some £180,000 to the estate as a loan, repayable when the company/estate was dissolved or was sold.

The judge held that the second, larger loan had clearly been procured through undue influence. A relationship of trust and confidence existed; the woman had already allowed her house to be used by the defendants for two years before selling it; she was physically isolated at her house and emotionally reliant and dependent on the defendants. She also believed that one of the defendants had a gift of healing. It was a transaction that called for explanation, since by the sale she alienated her only remaining asset for the foreseeable future if not for ever. Furthermore, she did not receive proper, dispassionate advice from the defendants about the nature of the transaction; and her detachment from her past life and friends meant that the influence of the defendants went unchecked (*Nel v Kean*).

A nurse obtained £300,000 from the life savings of a doctor she was supposedly caring for, having been hired through a private care agency. He was suffering from a 'chronic brain wasting disease', was a bachelor and lived frugally. She had earned £36,000 a year as a live-in nurse. With the money she booked an £8000 cruise, bought a house with a £100,000 loan from the doctor and persuaded him to change his will and sign over his £250,000 flat to her. A prosecution for theft was dropped, but an undue influence case was taken, and she was ordered to repay the money, could not and was bankrupted. Two flats she owned were repossessed, and she faced being evicted from her £350,000 home (Scott 2008).

9.1.3 UNDUE SUSPICION RATHER THAN UNDUE INFLUENCE

Of course not all transactions are suspicious; it might even be the challenge itself that is dubious:

Transfer of house to second wife by terminally ill man: no undue influence. A man transferred his house into the joint names of himself and his second wife as beneficial joint tenants. This followed the death of his first wife, although he had long since known his future second wife. Some months before the transfer, he had been diagnosed with terminal cancer. His children attempted to have the deed of gift set aside on grounds of undue influence. They failed.

The court took account of various factors. He had been married to his second wife for 14 years; and the judge did not accept the children's view that she did not care for him properly when he was ill. He did not personally lose by the transaction (he continued to own half of, and to live in, the house), and the sons had previously upset the father in relation to family company payments. The judge also took the view that these facts 'did not speak for themselves' so as to raise the question of presumed undue influence. This meant that the burden did not fall on the second wife to explain the transaction; it remained with the children to try to show express undue influence; but this could not be shown in this case (*Glanville v Glanville*).

Likewise, generous gifts of provisions in wills might be innocent:

Elderly woman's will in favour of housekeeper. An elderly woman left her sizeable residuary estate to a live-in housekeeper and her husband. The woman's housekeeper had taken up her role in 1979; she and other members of her family lived in the woman's house until the latter's death in January 2000 at the age of 87. The woman was physically frail but had remained mentally alert. The will was dated May 1999. The woman's next of kin argued that either the woman had not known or approved of the contents of the will, or that there had been undue influence.

The court noted that the housekeeper had been present at two important meetings concerning the will; and that she had sometimes prompted the woman in respect of telephone calls about it. Furthermore, the woman was elderly and vulnerable, substantially dependent on the housekeeper; against this background, there could have been scope for the exercise of subtle undue influence.

Nevertheless, the will was consistent with a 'perfectly innocent' explanation, which the judge preferred, when deciding the case in favour of the housekeeper. The woman had been highly intelligent, had possessed the mental capacity to make the will, and had had the full extent of her estate explained to her only weeks before making it. Although elderly and vulnerable, she had remained intelligent, sensitive and independent minded, capable of making her own decisions. She was genuinely fond of the housekeeper and her family (Re: Ethel Mary Good).

Sometimes the suspicion of undue influence might arise not just in respect of friends or relatives but local authority staff. This occurred in the following case, but the local ombudsman declined to find maladministration, pointing out that genuine kindness could provide an explanation:

Making of will to benefit local authority care home assistant. A social services home care assistant was named as beneficiary in the will of a service user for whom she had provided care (£10,000 to her, £10,000 to each of his grandsons, and the rest to his son). When he died she expressed great surprise that she was a beneficiary. The son claimed that she had exercised undue influence; and that the extra jobs she had done for him outside her duties (such as collecting a television and moving a bed downstairs for him) were evidence of her gaining that influence and playing on his father's gullibility.

The council had a policy about refusing gifts or being named as beneficiary in a service user's will. However, the woman and her solicitor pointed out that this provision in the will was unsolicited and that she had been unaware of it – and that to terminate her employment would constitute unfair dismissal. The council's principal solicitor believed that she should not face disciplinary procedures if she kept the bequest. He thought it was common for conscientious workers to be remembered in wills, there was nothing wrong with this, and refusal to give up the bequest was not evidence of undue influence.

The ombudsman stated that it was for the courts to decide about undue influence; it was his job to decide whether the care assistant's actions equated to maladministration. In his view they did not; the evidence suggested neither coercion nor that she had known the contents of the will; and the television collection and bed moving appeared to be acts of genuine kindness (Bexley LBC 1998).

9.1.4 BRINGING AN UNDUE INFLUENCE CASE

From a practical point of view, undue influence cases are usually brought by family members of a person now deceased (or other beneficiaries of a will), the person themselves (*Royal bank of Scotland v Etridge* (no.2: wives alleging undue influence from husbands), or maybe a 'litigation friend' of a still living person (*Goodchild v Bradbury*: a solicitor with an enduring power of attorney of a person now lacking capacity to manage his affairs).

However, other parties may do so. For instance, Great Ormond Street argued both lack of capacity on the part of, or undue influence exercised over, an elderly woman – who had willed her house to the hospital. However, she had made a gift of the house to carers before she died (*Special Trustees of Great Ormond Street Hospital v Ruskin*).

Local authorities are unlikely to bring a case in order to restore the vulnerable adult's wealth to the family. However, as part of their adult protection activities, they may advise vulnerable clients, who they observe are probably being unduly influenced and seriously exploited, to seek independent advice. And, in one case, the local authority actually brought the case itself. But this was when it was owed care home fees by a woman who had given her house on trust to her son, in order to avoid paying. The undue influence argument lay against the son (Woolcock 2002).

9.2 PROPRIETARY ESTOPPEL: RELYING ON ASSURANCES OR PROMISES

Care must be taken not to assume that carers who are left substantial assets have been up to no good. For instance, some cases illustrate how, after years of care provided to a (now) elderly person, informal carers may quite properly be entitled to some recompense. The cases have involved a civil, equitable principle known as proprietary estoppel. The elements of this, roughly, have been that the person (e.g. a carer) making the claim has acted to their own detriment, on the basis of assurances by the other person, by providing services to that other person.

'This will all be yours one day'. A self-employed bricklayer had begun to provide gardening services to an elderly woman. As she became more incapacitated with arthritis and leg ulcers, he would do more and more for her, without payment. This included collecting prescriptions, helping her dress and go to the toilet, making sure she had food and drink, as well as helping in the garden. In the last few months of her life, he did even more. For the last ten years or so, she had stopped paying him. When he queried this, she had said not to worry, to the vague effect that 'this will all be yours one day'.

She died intestate, and the man challenged the extent of his entitlement. On the basis of proprietary estoppel, the court used its discretion – taking account of a number of factors – and held that his equitable interest amounted to £200,000 out of a house and furniture valued at some £435,000 (*Jennings v Rice*).

In another case, a lodger had increasingly provided services and care to an elderly couple who had told him that whatever happened he would have a home for life. Instead, the house passed first to the man's wife and then, on her death, to her nieces. Far from him having exploited the couple in any way, the court held that he had an equitable interest amounting to £35,000 (out of a house valued at £160,000 (*Campbell v Griffin*).

9.3 LACK OF CAPACITY

Gifts or wills can be set aside by the courts if the person (the donor or testator) is shown to have lacked capacity at the time they were made.

For instance, one case involved the transfer of a house to, and also the purchase of cars for, two private carers. The woman, for whom they provided care, had made the transfer of property and money. After the woman died, a case was brought by Great Ormond Street Hospital against the carers, to whom the woman had bequeathed her house in her will. It sought to have the transaction of the house set aside on one of three grounds; (a) lack of capacity; (b) undue influence (if lack of capacity could not be shown); and (c) unconscionable bargain. On the evidence, she was judged to have lacked capacity at the time she transferred the house, and so the transfer was set aside. Had the capacity argument not succeeded, the judge would have still found in favour of the hospital on grounds of undue influence (*Special Trustees of Great Ormond Street Hospital v Rushin*).

There are specific common law tests of capacity applied by the courts to gifts and wills (see 6.3.3); these and capacity issues in general are covered in Chapter 6.

9.4 THEFT

Under s.1 of the Theft Act 1968, a person is guilty of theft if he or she dishonestly appropriates property belonging to somebody else. This must be with the intention of permanently depriving the other person of it.

Such an appropriation is not dishonest if the person believes he or she had a right in law to deprive the other person of it. Alternatively it is not dishonest if he or she believed that the other person would consent, if the other person knew of the appropriation and the circumstances.

In the context of safeguarding adults, the question of theft might arise where, for instance, carers financially exploit vulnerable adults. The significance of the following court case is that theft could be made out on the basis of the jury's overall view of whether there had been dishonesty; and that this would not necessarily depend on the man being shown to have lacked the requisite capacity to make a gift of the money involved:

Financial exploitation of and theft from a vulnerable person. A man of limited intelligence, 53 years old, was assisted and cared for by a 38-year-old woman on a private basis. Over a period from April to November, he made withdrawals almost every day up to the maximum £300 allowed from the building society – to the amount of £60,000 (his saving inherited from his father).

The money ended up in the carer's bank account. The building society employees stated that the carer did most of the talking and would interrupt the man if he tried to talk. A consultant psychiatrist gave evidence that the man's IQ was between 70 to 80 (as opposed to the average of 90 to 110), that he could lead a normal if undemanding life (he had worked in a dairy as a packer for 30 years) – and that he was naive and trusting and had no idea of the value of his assets or the ability to calculate their value. The consultant however accepted that he would be capable of making a gift and understood the concept of ownership – and so would be able to divest himself of money but could probably not take the decision alone.

The carer was convicted of theft in the Crown Court; the case went on appeal to the House of Lords, which refused to interfere with the conviction. The court placed great weight on leaving the matter to the jury to decide about whether there had been dishonesty in all the circumstances. It was not crucial whether the man had the mental capacity to make a gift of the money. This was because the court was not prepared to read into the s.1 of the Theft Act the words 'without the owner's consent'. In other words, consent was not necessarily fatal to the success of a charge of theft (it had been argued that, as a matter of law, it could not be theft if the man did have the capacity to make a gift; and that the Crown Court judge should have directed the jury to that effect) (R v Hinks).

The *Hinks* case effectively overrules a slightly earlier Court of Appeal case, in which a maid, employed by an elderly woman aged 89 years, was prosecuted for allegedly cashing cheques to the value of £37,000 and stealing a brooch and crystal ornament. The appeal against conviction was allowed, on the basis of the failure of the judge's directions to be clear about the relevance of mental capacity. This meant the jury had felt able to make a moral judgement about the maid, instead of deciding whether there was theft (*R v Mazo*).

Nevertheless, the *Hinks* case, which takes precedence because it was a House of Lords case, did not follow the *Mazo* approach. Instead it took the approach followed by the Court of Appeal in another earlier case, which also held that mental capacity to transfer the property by way of a 'gift' was not decisive:

Theft of 99-year-old care home resident's assets. A 99-year-old woman lived in a care home. She was virtually blind. She went to live there in 1991; her daughter died in 1992; at this point the two owners of the home took control of her affairs. A large number of cheques were drawn on her account; they argued that they were gifts. The owners obtained power of attorney and liquidated the woman's gifts and stocks; the proceeds were paid into a bank account held in their names and the woman's. Only one signature was required. A series of payments was subsequently made from that account for the benefit of the owners of the home. They were prosecuted for theft.

They appealed against their conviction, on the grounds that the judge should have directed the jury that there could be no theft if the woman consented to the 'gifts' (and thus had the capacity to give that consent). Furthermore the judge had failed to indicate the level of mental capacity required in order to make the acts of appropriation dishonest.

The appeal failed. The court held that the relevant term in s.1 of the Theft Act 1968 was 'dishonest appropriation'; this did not necessarily mean 'without the consent of the owner' (*R v Kendrick*).

In the following case, friendly neighbours were convicted of criminal offences following a social worker's visit:

Friendly neighbours. When a social worker and police officer visited an elderly woman, they found her to be frail, dirty and unkempt, and the house to be dirty and smelling of urine. She was apparently happy but mentally confused and forgot who her visitors were after five minutes. It became clear subsequently that two friendly neighbours (a married couple) had over a period from 1995 to 2001 obtained sums of money from the woman amounting to £110,000. The couple unsuccessfully challenged the admissibility of evidence relating to the woman's dementia and mental capacity (some of the offences for which they were charged and convicted were also under the Forgery and Counterfeiting Act 1981) (*R v Bowles*).

Theft might be perpetrated by a person in a formal position of trust, for example, a person with an enduring power of attorney:

Abuse of enduring power of attorney amounting to theft. For instance, a 60-year-old woman, niece-in-law of an 86-year-old man, had enduring power of attorney and was executor of his will. She was convicted of theft of £17,500. She had full access to his bank accounts, in order that she might spend money in his best interests. Instead she purchased for herself a car, washing machine, tumble dryer and two holidays. She also gambled money. Of previous good character, she was sentenced to nine months in prison and ordered to repay £17,500 within 28 days (*R v Carter*).

In just such a position of trust in relation to vulnerable people, a financial adviser was convicted of theft, false accounting and forgery. The total amount stolen was some £2 million. His victims included a man with severe learning disabilities, a chronically ill woman and even a member of his own family. He took money he had been given to invest on people's behalf; and also borrowed a client's credit card, before failing to pay back the amount he had 'borrowed' (Jenkins 2006). Health professionals, too, may abuse their position:

Nurse stealing cash card from dying war hero. A nurse (needing to pay her telephone bill) took an 83-year-old, dying patient's cash card from a hospital locker. He had won the Croix de Guerre at the D-Day landings in the Second World War; she was given a suspended three-month jail sentence (*The Times* 2007a).

Theft may arise from gross overcharging for services. For instance, one solicitor (also a coroner) charged 250 per cent more than would have been reasonable from the estates of dead clients. He was found guilty of six counts of theft, amounting to £155,000. Among beneficiaries that lost out were the Royal National Lifeboat Institute, the Salvation Army and a cottage hospital in Thirsk (Norfolk 2003).

Equally, the person may be a private, informal carer, who has befriended and won the trust of the victim. Just such a carer, a 41-year-old woman, was charged with ten counts of theft. One charge concerned the taking of a frail 89-year old woman to the bank and cashing a cheque; the others to withdrawing money from the woman's account using her cash card. The carer pleaded guilty to seven cash withdrawals and was sentenced to 12 months' in prison (*R v Singh*). Neighbours may exploit trust shown in handling money for a vulnerable person, so as to end up committing theft:

Stealing from terminally ill neighbour. A 34-year-old woman stole more than £20,000 from a terminally ill neighbour, who was living in a nursing home. Having been trusted by her neighbour to withdraw small amounts of money with a bank card, she began by taking loans with the woman's knowledge. This then escalated to systematic theft, amounting to over £20,000. She was ordered to repay money to the bank within 28 days and given a suspended 12-month jail sentence (*IC Wales* 2007).

Another neighbour was convicted of conspiracy to steal. She (and her half-sister) had befriended an elderly man with some form of senile dementia or Parkinson's disease. She began to visit him frequently. Soon, his building society balance dropped dramatically and, over a period of three months, £5980 was withdrawn. The building society staff noticed that he always seemed to be accompanied when he came in to make the withdrawals. The money was given to the women and spent on drugs (*R v Stockdale*). Taking vulnerable people to banks or building societies is thus a theme (see the *Hinks* case above):

Controlling and directing an elderly confused man to withdraw money from the building society. An elderly confused man living alone in Birmingham had a number of building society accounts with significant balances. He came under the control or direction of the perpetrator, who would take him to the building society. Acting ostensibly on the man's behalf, and pretending to be his grandson, the perpetrator would ask for a cheque to be made out to the man, and specify the amount and the payee (always one of the perpetrator's associates – one of whom was ordered to pay £27,000 compensation to the victim). He was convicted of theft and sentenced to four years in prison (*R v Kelly*).

A woman befriended an elderly lady living in a care home. Twice she forged lady's signature in letters to the bank, obtaining a total of £11,000. She was sentenced to four months in prison (*R v Clarke*). It may be somebody in a much more formal position, such as a banker. One such stole more than £2 million from elderly and vulnerable bank customers, in order to fund his obsession with exotic birds, including gold macaws at £20,000 a pair and black cockatoos at £20,000 each. He admitted 24 counts of theft and asked for 203 similar offences to be taken into consideration (Barkham 2003; and also *BBC News* 2003b).

It may even be professional social workers employed by a local authority, the lead agency charged with safeguarding and protecting vulnerable adults. In one case, a social worker, instead of seeking a Court of Protection order for a 79-year old client, took out an enduring power of attorney for herself and stole some £65,000 (*R v Hardwick*). Another social worker, in the grip of a loan shark, was convicted of theft, having stolen money from four mental health patients. She worked in a hospital, obtaining money from patients, and pretending to buy things for them – and also stole money from the office lottery scheme. She was sentenced to ten months in prison suspended for two years and ordered to do 150 hours community service (Hunt 2008).

9.4.1 THEFT BY CARERS AND NURSES

Carers and nurses in care homes or supporting people in their own homes may be involved in theft to greater or lesser extent. In a care home on the Isle of Man, a carer pleaded guilty to 15 counts of theft and two of false accounting over a period of three years (*BBC News* 2006a). A 21-year-old care home worker was jailed for eight months after stealing £6400 from the bank accounts of two care home residents, aged 92 years and 71 years. Her duties had included taking the residents out shopping and she had dishonestly used their bank cards to take money for herself (*Craven Herald* 2007). On a larger scale still was the former matron who had extracted large sums of money from highly vulnerable, including dying, residents:

Cynical disregard for terminally ill residents: raiding of bank account by managing director of care home. A former matron, then the managing director of a care home, admitted 24 specimen counts of theft, false accounting and obtaining property by deception, involving a total of £5515. However, the total amount of money that might have had to be paid back was in excess of £100,000 – a court order was already in place at the time of conviction freezing an estimated £138,000 of her assets. She had raided the bank accounts of terminally ill residents when she realised that accounting procedures were not as strict as they should have been. The judge referred to her 'cynical disregard' for the families who had relied on her to look after the physical and financial welfare of the residents. She was sentenced to 18 months in prison (*Bromsgrove Advertiser 2006*).

A nurse was both struck off from the nursing register and sentenced to prison, after she was found guilty of 55 counts of theft. Using the bank cards of a man and woman with learning disabilities, residents at care homes where she worked, she stole some £13,000 over a five-year period. She blamed the thefts on the financial pressures following the break-up of a relationship (*IC Wales* 2007a). A nurse working at a hospital in Leicester stole money from patients while they attended a breast-screening clinic, taking a total of £275 from the handbags of three of them. She was sentenced to 240 hours' community and service and also struck off the nursing register (*BBC News* 2004).

The theft might not directly be from patients, but nonetheless be patient-related. A nurse in Bradford used a hospital credit card to go on a £6000 spending spree – from the £5000 annual budget set aside to improve facilities such as pictures and games for patients. The nurse had also kept a £600 donation from a former patient. She admitted theft and obtaining property by deception, was sentenced to 80 hours' community service and ordered to repay £6276 (*Telegraph and Argus* 2005).

A 49-year-old care worker at a nursing home was sentenced to four months in prison, after stealing more than £7000 from a 71-year-old resident – who, having suffered a paralysing stroke 30 years before, suffered another on learning of the theft. The carer had stolen the money after the resident had given her cash card and PIN number, so the carer could do the shopping for her (Traynor 2008).

A care worker pleaded stress following the break-up of his marriage, after he was convicted of 13 offences of stealing money from a resident with learning disabilities at a care home. The carer had been entrusted with managing the resident's financial affairs and had direct access to his bank account (*Swindon Advertiser* 2001). Another cash card case involved a care home worker stealing a Post Office card from the room of a 91-year-old resident where he had found it together with the PIN number. He admitted using the card fraudulently to take £100 from her account (*Yourcanterbury* 2008). A hospital nurse was convicted of theft after she was caught on a bank security camera using the bank card, which had disappeared the previous day, of an elderly hospital patient in Dundee (*BBC News* 1998). An informal carer befriended and won the trust of an 89-year-old woman, before getting the woman to write her out a cheque and using a cash card to take money from her. She was sentenced to 12 months in prison (Hounslow Council 2007).

A carer had been sacked by a domiciliary care agency, but visited clients nonetheless, pretending she was still working for the agency. She had stolen money from clients' wallets, amounting to several hundred pounds (*Dorset Echo* 2001). Similarly, another home carer was caught on closed circuit television riffling through the wallet of her client, a man with multiple sclerosis whom a team of carers supported in his own home. Suspicions had arisen previously, and police had installed secret cameras. She was sentenced to four months' imprisonment suspended for a year (Alder 2007).

Drug addition might be the driver behind the theft:

Theft from man with learning disabilities driven by drug debts. A carer was entrusted with the money of a man with severe learning disabilities who lived in a sheltered housing complex. The carer had developed a cocaine habit and had to repay £11,000 to drug dealers. He made internet payments from the man's bank account and withdrew money from his account on shopping trips, stealing some £2000. He was sentenced to nine months in prison. The judge said that the carer presented 'the classic tale of an otherwise perfectly decent man' who became enmired in drug use and degradation which had led to his downfall (Cox 2007).

The manageress of a care home for older people was convicted of theft of £12,000. She persuaded residents to sign cheques in her name, telling them the money was to pay for their care. She was sentenced to 15 months in prison, the breach of trust being the aggravating feature (The Argus 2005). An elderly woman in her eighties, with learning disabilities, was incapable of looking after her finances. A carer, employed by a care company, helped her do so by withdrawing up to £3650 on the woman's behalf from the latter's bank account. The carer claimed the woman went on extravagant shopping sprees; however, the woman's new carer noticed that the money withdrawn exceeded by far the total of receipts for the woman (Journal Live 2007). As so many of these cases seem to show, if it is not cheques, it is use of a personal identification number (PIN) for a person's bank or building society account, which is the means of theft and gross breach of trust:

Carer stealing from 76-year old blind woman who treated her 'like a daughter'. For instance, a carer (a mother two children) was treated like a daughter and with absolute trust by a 76-year old blind woman, for whom she provided care twice a week. In order to obtain statements, she had been given the woman's saving account card and PIN – although she had never been asked to withdraw money. The woman regularly paid her late husband's mining pension into the account. In fact, over a 17-month period, about £200 at a time, the carer took over £5000. The thefts came to light when the woman realised she had only £190 left. The carer tried to stop the woman alerting the police. The carer was sentenced to one year's imprisonment (Northern Echo 2004).

The motive may be greed and the wish to live in better style, in whatever form that may take. For example, in one case, a carer befriended a 78-year old woman after working for her as a carer, and stole nearly £4000 using the woman's debit card; most of the money went on slot machines. She was sentenced to one year in prison suspected for 18 months, and ordered to repay some of the money. Her husband had left her and she had four children (*Sunderland Echo* 2007). It might be foreign holidays:

NHS care assistant caught by secret camera in teddy bear. In another, a health care assistant attending a 75-year old leukaemia sufferer stole in order to to go on holiday to Las Vegas. After the family realised that money was going missing they installed a small surveillance camera, at the suggestion of the woman's grand-daughter who was a forensic science graduate. It was placed in the eye of a pink teddy bear in the woman's room and it caught on film the care assistant stealing £60. She was convicted and sentenced to six months in prison. The judge referred to the seriousness of the offence, given the age and terminal illness of the victim. The carer worked for Liverpool NHS primary care trust (Hull 2008).

As has already been seen from some of the above examples, it may be pressing financial matters which are argued in mitigation, explanation or excuse – such as keeping up with mortgage payments and dealing with postnatal depression. So argued a pregnant carer convicted of theft for cashing cheques belonging to an 84-year old woman for whom she cared – and then keeping the money herself. She helped the woman with shopping and household chores. Her contract with the care company prohibited her from becoming involved with clients' finances (Kelly 2008). It might be spending money on a two-year old child that is raised:

Stealing money from 93-year old woman by cashing cheques on the Market Hill. In Sudbury, Suffolk, an Age Concern carer paid – over a period of several weeks – nine visits to the bank on the Market Hill. She cashed cheques – on behalf of the 93-year old woman she provided care for – ostensibly for shopping, but in fact stealing £2575 for herself. The carer said the money was to spend on her two-year old daughter. The judge referred to the 'particularly mean and wicked series of offences' in sentencing her to nine months in prison suspended for 12 months – with 200 hours community work, and a repayment order starting with a lump sum of £500 and then £25 a fortnight (*Suffolk Free Press* 2008; *Sudbury Mercury* 2008).

Similarly, a carer withdrew an 86-year old woman's money for legitimate purposes, but then kept more than £1000 – her husband had lost her job, she had bills to pay and Christmas presents for the children to buy. She was sentenced to two months in prison (*Lancashire Evening Telegraph* 1999). When the husband of a team leader in a residential home left her, she had mounting debts, and eventually had to declare herself bankrupt and go to live with her parents. In order to try to stave this off, she used the cash cards and PIN numbers of residents with Alzheimer's disease, stealing nearly £5000 before she admitted the offences to the police. She was sentenced to 12 months in prison, suspended for two years with 100 hours community service. Her family repaid the victims (*The Echo* 2006). Sometimes the discovered theft seems less explicable, given the carer's background and other circumstances:

Inexplicable thefts by carer. A respected 57-year old carer worked for the council; she had worked as a carer for thirty years. As her defence lawyer put it, there was no explanation since she had no debts and was not addicted to anything. She stole £50 from the victim, for whom she had been caring for six years. There were five separate incidents of theft, until she was caught stealing on the camera the family ha set up. She was sentenced to six months in prison suspended for 18 months, with 200 hours community service. The judge noted that these were serious breaches of trust, made all the more inexplicable because the carer looked after her own infirm mother (Nowaczyk 2008).

It may not only be money. One care home worker was convicted for stealing pain relief tablets of a resident, and substituting artificial sweeteners (*Shropshire Star* 2008). A nurse, addicted to pethidine, was convicted on various charges including theft, relating to controlled drugs. One count involved injecting an anodyne substance into the patient, who needed the pain-killer on an orthopaedic hospital ward, and keeping the pethidine herself (*R v Webster*). A carer targeted an elderly couple, stealing not only £7000 using a bank card (£300 a week withdrawn) but also paintings worth £3000 which she sold on e-Bay. She was sentenced to 18 months in prison. The husband died shortly after; he had trusted her completely, and the family believed the stress contributed to his death (*Hemsley* 2008).

The carer might be providing sustained amounts of care, either through a private arrangement or through direct payments provided by the local authority:

Live-in carer abuses trust to arrange fake burglary in home of elderly couple. For example, a live-in carer obtained a job to help a retired major-general and war veteran care for his wife. Within nine months, the carer had looked up the value of the antiques in the house and staged a fake burglary. Paintings, objets d'art, jewellery, furniture, silverware and many sentimental items were taken. The wife died two months later, and the husband sold the house. The judge referred to the appalling breach of trust by the carer; she was convicted of conspiracy to steal and conspiracy to obtain property by deception (Daily Telegraph 2007).

In another case, a woman with multiple sclerosis employed a carer; there was genuine affection between the two women. However, first of all the woman loaned £7500 to the carer; the carer then stole over £3000, which she was able to do because she had access to the woman's money (through credit cards) for doing the shopping. The carer was convicted of theft and sentenced to nine months' imprisonment (*Oxford Mail* 2006).

9.5 BURGLARY

The offence of burglary comes under s.9 of the Theft Act 1968 and involves (a) a person entering a building as a trespasser with the intention of stealing or inflicting grievous bodily harm or doing unlawful damage; and (b) having entered a building, the person steals or attempts to steal something or inflicts or attempts to inflict grievous bodily harm. Burglars sometimes specifically target vulnerable people:

Burgling the homes of elderly people, particularly the blind, deaf and partially sighted. For instance, one burglar raided 600 homes within 18 months, and travelled hundreds of miles in order to steal £267,000 by deceiving vulnerable elderly people, some in their nineties. He posed as a policeman and targeted in particular blind, deaf and partially sighted people. Sometimes he would persuade people to give him their valuables to take to the police station for safekeeping; at other times he would simply rifle under beds for cash or other valuables. After being caught and admitting burglary by deception, he asked for 587 similar offences to be taken into account. He was jailed for seven years (Bird 2003).

A home help working for a care agency admitted four charges of burglary. For example, he went to the home of one 75-year-old woman to help her with the cleaning and took £75 from a fruit bowl. He was suspended and he resigned following this, but then returned to another client unofficially, again to help with cleaning, but took £120 from her purse and £400 savings in an envelope also went missing (Hudson 2006).

Two brothers called at the home of a 91-year old man, offered to cut his hedge, entered the house, restrained the man, stole his wallet with money, cuttings of funerals (of his wife, older brother and stepson), documentation for his pacemaker and bank cards – 'exactly the sort of offence which is likely to cause extreme distress to an elderly man'. They were convicted of burglary and sentenced to seven and eight years' in prison, given that they had been convicted previously for similar offences of targeting the elderly (*R v Cawley*).

In similar vein, a 22-year old man impersonated a police officer and entered the home of a 93-year old man, whom he proceeded to lock in the kitchen. He then stole £140 in cash. The judge was in no doubt that he was targeting elderly people; when the perpetrator stated that he thought the victim was in his sixties rather than his nineties, the judge noted that he was not convinced that 'had he shown you his birth certificate that you would have immediately backed away rather than thinking that you had a sort target in front of you'. The perpetrator had a father involved in crime as a way of life, had been physically abused as a child, left home to live rough with travellers, and had shown remorse. The judge had sentenced him to five years in prison; this was reduced to three and a half years on appeal (*R v McInerney*).

9.6 ROBBERY

A person is guilty of robbery if he or she steals – and immediately before, or at the time of doing so and in order to do so, he or she uses force on any person or puts or seeks to put any person in fear of being subjected to force (Theft Act 1969, s.8). For example, in the following case, the three perpetrators went to the home of a the victim, whom they knew to be vulnerable:

Robbery at home of man known to be vulnerable and regularly pestered by children for money. Three men went to the home of the victim whom they knew to be vulnerable. He had learning disabilities, and needed help in carrying out basic activities such as washing and shaving. He tended to be pestered by children for money. One of the children to whom he had given money was the stepson of one of the perpetrators. They pushed him into the hallway, demanded money and stole £100, the whole of his savings from benefits. He was punched in the face and suffered fractures to the cheek bone and eye socket. An initial sentence of three years for robbery was increased on appeal to five years, six months (*R v Randall*).

In another case, the perpetrator had been observed earlier that day paying attention to elderly pedestrians near sheltered accommodation. Eventually he forced his way into the home of 79-year old frail man with severe arthritis, who had just returned from a shopping trip. The man was pushed to the floor and had money stolen, before being punched in the face. He was sentenced to four years in prison for robbery, a relatively lenient sentence (*R v Johnson*). The following case involved intensive targeting of vulnerable people, all within the space of a month. In each instance, the woman involved first gained a degree of trust from each of the victims, before robbing or stealing :

Intensive targeting of elderly people through gaining their trust: robbery and theft. The offence of robbery concerned a couple living in a block of flats. The wife was bedridden, the husband suffered from Alzheimer's disease. The perpetrator, a 38-year old woman, had befriended the husband and been invited into the flat. She told the wife that her husband owed £18 to the off-licence where the woman claimed she worked. She also offered to buy a new kettle, because the existing one was leaking. She was given £40 by the wife (who had reached under her pillow for the money), and another £5 for food, and she borrowed the keys. She did not return (this was theft). However, ten days later, she returned, disguised, with an accomplice. The wife was pushed and hit; and her purse snatched. They searched the room and left, stealing £300, papers and bank cards (this was robbery). Within a day, £1200 was withdrawn from the woman's bank account.

Second, the same woman befriended an 80-year old lady, for whom the woman's son had apparently done some work. The woman called at her home, and during a distraction, stole £400 from a wardrobe. Third, whilst at the chemist collecting her methadone prescription, she met a 90-year old woman and assisted her out of the shop, during which time she stole her purse. Fourth, an 88-year old man went to a bank to open an account, with £120 in his rear pocket. He was unsuccessful. The woman offered to help him open the account in another bank; she surreptitiously stole the £120. Fifth, she struck up a conversation with a 90-year old man on a street corner. Later that evening, he invited her in for a cup of tea; she stole £45 from a pair of trousers. Sixth, she approached a 79-year old lady, who was not feeling well and offered assistance. They had a cup of tea together. The lady put her handbag on the floor; her wallet, containing £70, was stolen. Lastly, an 83-year old man went to the Post Office to collect his pension and had difficulty getting to his feet. The woman helped him to the bus stop, where she and her son helped him fasten his coat; on getting home he discovered his pension book and £57 were missing.

She was convicted of robbery (in relation to the first episode described above) and of theft (for the others). The offences involved targeting vulnerable people, gaining their trust with a display of false sympathy. She was sentenced to five years for the robbery, with three years for the thefts to run concurrently (R v Moss).

An 84-year old woman lived alone in a flat in Plymouth. The perpetrator's mother was her carer and the perpetrator had previously been to her home to clean the windows. He visited her and stole her pension book and cash. He was arrested that evening, charged and released on bail. Four days later he returned, grabbed her, dragged her into the bedroom, where she ended up on the floor. He stole her purse, pension book and £90 in cash. He gave himself up the following day. He was sentenced to six years in prison (*R v Sowden*).

9.7 FRAUD

The offence of fraud is to be found in the Fraud Act 2006 (not Scotland). The three main offences are fraud by false representation, by failure to disclose information or by abuse of position (ss.1–4). Previous offences under ss.15, 15A and 16 of the Theft Act 1968, of obtaining property, money transfer or pecuniary advantage by deception, were repealed by the Fraud Act and are in substance subsumed now within the 2006 Act. Some of the cases cited below refer to these previous offences.

Abuse of position is perhaps particularly relevant to safeguarding adults concerns. The ingredients are that a person (a) occupies a position in which he is expected to safeguard, or not to act against, the financial interests of another person; (b) dishonestly abuses that position; and (c) intends, by means of the abuse of that position to make a gain for himself or another – or to cause loss to another or to expose another to a risk of loss. Abuse can be made out even if the conduct consists of an omission rather than an act (s.4).

In the following case, a fraud worth £500,000 was perpetrated on a man who at time of trial had Alzheimer's disease and terminal cancer:

Fraud perpetrated on former civil servant. The court described this case as the 'worst crime of deception of the elderly ever to be before the courts in Scotland.' A builder was convicted of fraud and sentenced to ten years in prison. He had tricked a retired, 77-year-old civil servant out if his life savings, almost £500,000 in cash – by pretending to lead a secret inquiry into police corruption, for which he required funds. The victim had been a former chief inspector of the pollution inspectorate. He had subsequently been forced to sell his home in order to pay for the care home in which he now lived, suffering from Alzheimer's disease and prostate cancer (Harris 2002; also *BBC News* 2002).

Being a person's fiancé does not mean that fraud may not take place. A woman, engaged to a lorry driver, pretended to be suffering from cancer and to be incurring high medical bills. She took £300,000 from him and spent it instead on a secret life of luxury with a lover. She was jailed for two years for fraud (*The Scotsman* 2008). In another case, two

Hampstead estate agents carried out a sophisticated fraud on a rich, vulnerable and mentally ill (schizophrenia), middle-aged man. They were convicted of conspiracy to defraud, two counts of theft and one of obtaining money by deception. The fraud involved persuading the man to give them £200,000 for investment in property, on the promise of a £500 billion return. In addition, they duped him into giving them gold, jewellery (including his mother's ring), and share certificates worth £600,000. They were sentenced to five years in prison (Osley 2008; Fletcher 2007).

A so-called investment adviser obtained £360,000 from vulnerable people (disabled, dying or bereaved), ostensibly to invest their money, but in fact to put into his own failing business. He was sentenced to four and a half years in prison for obtaining money by deception (Beattie 2008). A lawyer, Plaid Cymru parliamentary candidate and former head of administration for a county council, grossly abused the trust of two elderly sisters, obtaining some £50,000 from them by overcharging. For instance, he visited one of them in a nursing home, read poetry to her, and then charged her hundreds of pounds for the privilege. He was sentenced to three years in prison for obtaining property by deception and theft – and ordered to pay compensation (*BBC News* 2003c).

Another solicitor was sentenced to six years in prison for theft and obtaining property by deception. He had stolen money belonging to clients amounting to some £3 million, comprising sums from the estates of recently deceased clients – including £100,000 which was meant to provide income for the deceased client's son who had Down's Syndrome (*R v Shaw*). Thus, the fraud might be after a vulnerable adult has died, but not just necessarily from financial or legal professions. For instance, the carer of a woman with multiple sclerosis fraudulently obtained a £5000 loan by pretending to be the dead woman. She was also convicted of dishonestly obtaining money from the dead woman's estate, by pillaging her bank account after her death (*Wirral Globe* 1998).

In general, probate fraud is thought to be an increasing problem, with the Royal National Institute for the Blind estimating that it may amount to some £150 million a year, and often involving solicitors or legal advisers (*The Times* 2004). Thus, in 2005, two directors of a wills and probate service were sentenced to three years, nine months (subsequently reduced by 13 months) and four years, six months in prison respectively for fraudulent trading under s.458 of the Companies Act 1985. The client account deficiency stood at nearly £5 million (*R v Furr*).

The manager of a sheltered housing complex was sent to prison after defrauding a 78-year-old widower of nearly £4000. She admitted six counts of abusing her position to commit fraud; this included using the resident's bank card on shopping sprees in Castleford. She was found not guilty on three other fraud charges, which related to him changing his will in her favour and fraudulently obtaining cash withdrawals of £10,000 and £2000 from his account (*Pontefract and Castleford Express* 2008).

In the following case, the carer obtained thousands of pounds from two highly vulnerable women by deception:

Answering advertisements for carers in the *Lady Magazine*. A carer was employed to look after a 90-year old woman who had been discharged from hospital and required 24-hour care. The carer stole £3300 from a drawer, as well as blank cheques, on which she forged the woman's signature (she was unsuccessful in drawing money on them). She left this employment without notice a day later. She then answered an advertisement in the *Lady Magazine* and stared work two months later, caring for an 88-year old, immobile woman. The carer was allowed to withdraw £250 cash per week, to cover her wages and housekeeping expenses. On six occasions, the carer exceeded this limit until a total of £3300 had been obtained. The carer pleaded guilty to theft, obtaining pecuniary advantage by deception and obtaining property by deception; she was sentenced to 30 months' prison reduced on appeal to 18 months (*R v Donaldson*).

An agency carer cared for an 80-year old, housebound woman, unable to walk. The carer collected her pension, did a bit of shopping, went to the launderette, cleaned the home and paid bills. At the carer's request, the woman would sign blank cheques, purportedly so the carer could then fill them in to pay the water and electricity bills. In fact, over a two year period, she wrote out cheques to herself, amounting to £2875. She was convicted of obtaining a money transfer by deception and sentenced to 18 months in prison (*R v Roach*). The deception and fraud might be perpetrated by an opportunistic neighbour:

Opportunistic obtaining and concealing pass book from social worker. A 65-year old neighbour became friendly with an older woman. As the latter's mental health began to deteriorate the neighbour began to act as her carer and discovered that she had substantial sums of money in various building society accounts. The neighbour arranged the transfer of one of the accounts into joint names. When she later handed over the woman's documents to a social worker, she retained the pass book, withdrew £44,000 and closed the account. She also obtained a watch, valued between £1200 and £1500, that the woman had left at a jeweller's. She was convicted of theft and obtaining money by deception (*R v Starsmeare*).

In another case, three people were convicted of conspiracy to defraud. One of the conspirators had disguised herself as an 87-year old woman, had made a new will, forging the woman's signature on letters of instruction and drawing cash from her account. They had arranged for her instructions to be transferred away from her longstanding solicitors to a new firm of solicitors. The woman had died shortly afterwards. Those responsible were sentenced to seven, five and three years in prison respectively (*R v Spillman*).

9.8 FALSE ACCOUNTING

An offence of false accounting, in summary, requires dishonesty, with a view to gain or to cause loss to somebody else. It is about destruction, defacing, concealing or falsifying accounts, records or documents – or making use of these, when the person knows they may be misleading, false or deceptive. The maximum penalty attached to it is imprisonment for seven years (Theft Act 1968, s.17).

For instance, when a care home owner was convicted of stealing money from residents with learning disabilities, by withdrawing money from their bank accounts, she concealed the theft by false accounting (*Community Care* 2007f). And when a social services manager took £4000 from elderly women in her care, she was convicted of forgery and of seven counts of false accounting (*Isle of Thanet Gazette* 2002). Likewise, a solicitor was convicted of more than 50 offences of false accounting, having stolen more than £1 million compensation money which had been awarded to his client, who had been paralysed in a road accident. The solicitor was jailed for ten years (*Solicitors' Journal* 2008).

A Barclays Bank customer adviser was sent to prison for 15 months, after pleading guilty to 23 offences of false accounting over a period of three and a half years, and involving £58,000. She had transferred money from customer accounts to her own, often via another account first. The four customers were elderly and infirm, including an elderly priest; none had noticed the missing money (*Bradford Telegraph and Argus* 2008). A solicitor was imprisoned for two years, having stolen money in his capacity as trustee of large sums of clients' money or of money belonging to the estates of dead clients, and as holding power of attorney in relation to clients' affairs. For example, he deprived a Weymouth-based charity, which operated an older persons' care home, of £168,000 (Serious Fraud Office 2000). A nursing home manager was convicted of false accounting, theft and obtaining property by deception from the home's severely disabled residents:

False accounting: care home manager taking over £100,000 from severely disabled residents. The manager of a nursing home had obtained well over £100,000 from sick and dying residents in order to fund an extravagant lifestyle, including six luxury holidays each year. She had access to residents' bank accounts, for example, as a signatory, as well as to residents' cash cards and PIN numbers. She was eventually ordered to pay some £134,000 compensation. The manager appealed her conviction to the Court of Appeal and lost.

The false accounting had involved using the care home's cheque book to obtain items for herself, but falsely writing on the stub that the cheque had been paid to someone doing work for the home. The theft counts typically involved her withdrawing money from residents' accounts, amounts that bore no relationship to the actual expenditure of those residents. Obtaining property by deception involved, for example, using the care home's Barclaycard purportedly for items for the home or for residents, but actually for herself (*R v Forbes*).

Another care home owner was convicted, when she withdrew money from the bank accounts of residents with learning disabilities and kept some of it, covering the theft with false accounting (*Community Care* 2007f).

9.9 FORGERY

A person is guilty of forgery if he or she makes a false document, intending that it be used to induce a second person to accept it as genuine and prejudicially to act (or not to act) in respect of that second person or somebody else (Forgery and Counterfeiting Act 1981, s.1).

When a Suffolk woman obtained more than £13,000 from her husband's vulnerable parents, she was jailed for six months for forgery. She had forged cheques and letters of authority to withdraw money from their bank account. She had started taking the money before her husband's father had died, and had continued when the latter's wife had gone into a care home (Hunt 2006). Even church ministers may be convicted of forgery:

Church minister forging powers of attorney and wills. A church minister befriended elderly parishioners before forging documents in order to inherit their property and possessions. He planned to wait until they were close to death before signing their properties over to himself. In one instance, he forged documents giving him power of attorney for a woman. When she moved into a nursing home, he gained control over her house. However, he was caught when one of the women involved made an unexpected recovery from a brain haemorrhage and stroke, after having received the last rites from the minister. She returned home from hospital to find that he had forged her will, which now left the house to him. He was sentenced to 240 hours' community service; one of his victims was appalled he had not been sent to prison (Britten 2006).

Social services managers may also commit forgery. Under pressure from her drug-taking husband, who was physically and mentally abusing her, the manager forged the signature of an 84-year-old client, so as to remove money from her saving account. She was convicted of forgery (and false accounting) but given a community sentence rather than prison because of her children (*Isle of Thanet Gazette* 2002).

Cheques may be forged for large amounts, for example, when the service user finds it difficult to read:

Carer of woman with multiple sclerosis forging a cheque for £8000. A care assistant employed by a care agency was caring for a woman with multiple sclerosis who found it difficult to read. The carer would open and read her mail for her. The victim received a statement from her building society concerning an £8000 withdrawal. It transpired that the carer had forged the victim's signature on a letter to the building society, in order to pay a finance company for a car. The carer was convicted and sentenced to 15 months in prison (*R v Ross-Goulding*).

Another carer for a nursing agency acquired the National Savings pass book of a 95-year old woman in her care. She forged the woman's signature twice, withdrawing a total of £5000. She was sentenced to 15 months in prison on appeal (*R v Mangham*). Not only carers, but also law enforcers may be involved. A policeman extracted some £280,000 from an 89-year old over a period of three years. He had gained her confidence, but was convicted of forgery and using a copy of a false instrument (this included selling her house) (*BBC News* 2006b). A financial adviser was convicted of forgery, false accounting, theft and money laundering. This included stealing £185,000 from an elderly woman, an £82,000 legacy bequeathed to a man with learning disabilities, and £31,000 from an 84-year old man's will (covered up by forged paperwork suggesting that the dead man had spent the money on foreign trips and double glazing) (Jenkins 2006).

9.10 COLD CALLING

Door-to-door cold calling may result in abuse and may typically be aimed at older, vulnerable people. Clearly capable of constituting abuse and causing substantial harm, it may result in criminal offences being committed.

For example, in one case, two 'roofers' called, sat for most of morning on the roof of an 86-year-old woman with dementia drinking tea, supplied less than £50 of labour and goods, and then charged her £600, escorting her to the bank to withdraw the money. In this case, the offenders were identified by CCTV at the bank and was convicted on the evidence of a neighbour and the police (Trading Standards Institute 2003).

It has been suggested that current legislation is inadequate to prevent the range of cold calling abuses, including:

- intimidation and persistence, false or no names and addresses being given
- token work being carried out so that the issue may be regarded as civil and contractual in nature, rather than criminal
- taking deposits and never returning
- starting work immediately before people have had a chance to read the small print, driving people to the bank, there to withdraw large amounts of money etc.

Relevant legislation includes the Pedlars Act 1871, Trade Descriptions Act 1968, and the Enterprise Act 2002. In addition, the *Cancellation of Contracts Made in Consumer's Home or Place of Work etc. Regulations 2008* create a seven-day cooling off period. But legislation may be ineffective when traders' names and addresses are rarely known, and large amounts of cash change hands on the spot. Fraud or deception might work, but the police may be reluctant to bring a case if at least some work has been carried out; they may characterise the issue as a civil, contractual, rather than a criminal, matter. It has been suggested by the Trading Standards Institute that cold calling for property services should be prohibited with a power of arrest attached (Trading Standards Institute 2003, pp.6–13, 40).

Apart from shortcomings in legislation, there is generally slow reporting of doorstep-selling offences, a lack of resources to devote to prevention and detection, reluctance or inability of complainants to give evidence, poor evidence given, and no agreed multi-agency approach. Alleged perpetrators may simply deny everything, and the police may then drop the criminal investigation and say instead that it is just a civil dispute (Office of Fair Trading 2004, pp.93–94).

That said, convictions are sometimes secured. For instance, a man purporting to sell stairlifts was successfully prosecuted by Devon County Council (trading standards). He pleaded guilty to breach of the Theft Act 1968, Consumer Protection Act 1987, and Forgery and Counterfeiting Act 1981. He had posed as a stairlift repairer and installer, and targeted vulnerable elderly and disabled people. He would advise that a stairlift was irreparable, show customers advertisements from two well known stairlift companies (he had no contract to supply their products nor permission to use the trademarks), take their money, take away their existing stairlift – and not deliver the new stairlift. He was an undischarged bankrupt and used a number of false names and adresses (Devon County Council Trading Standards 2007).

Also in Devon, a builder was sentenced to 100 hours community service under s.2 of the Fraud Act 2006 (false representation of the price of work) after carrying out roofing work for an 81-year old, vulnerable woman. He had called uninvited. The work he had carried out was worth £562 plus VAT; he had in fact charged £4240 (Devon County Council Trading Standards 2008). Likewise, when worthless damp proof services were supplied at extortionate prices to elderly and vulnerable customers, those responsible were found guilty of obtaining property by deception and sentenced to prison. They had obtained some £3 million from the scheme (*BBC News* 2008b). Sometimes the perpetrator gains the trust of a vulnerable person first, by carrying out a legitimate piece of work first and becoming known to the person:

Builder gaining trust of vulnerable person first. A builder used his business to target elderly people by charging a modest price for an initial piece of work, but then following up with subsequent works for which he charge excessive amounts. His customers were duped into parting with substantial sums of money. He was sentenced to five and a half years in prison for theft and a compensation order and a confiscation order were made against him, each for £141,000. It was not quite a cold calling case; he distributed leaflets to obtain work (*R v Williams*).

The cold calling for building work may turn into a full blooded and more extensive confidence trick. In 2008, a builder was sentenced to seven and a half years in prison for fraud; a vulnerable 76-year old man had been tricked into paying over £120,000 of his life savings. The builders had first approached him offering a free roof survey. They then carried out unnecessary and substandard building jobs for which they charged £66,000. The man then refused to pay for any more work; at which point, a bogus Customs and Excise officer visited, claiming that the man had inadvertently become part of a VAT 'scam' and would have to make payment s or go to prison. The man ended up paying a further £61,400 (Metropolitan Police 2008).

A related issue is that of doorstep, 'hard' selling of high value products, including assistive products for older, vulnerable people such as stairlifts, scooters and buggies, and digital hearing aids. Protection under consumer legislation extends only to cold calling, not if the visit is pre-planned and agreed with the consumer (Office of Fair Trading 2004, Chapter 5).

CHAPTER 10

Disclosure of personal information and confidentiality

KEY POINTS

The *No secrets* guidance refers to the importance of sharing of personal information between agencies (see 2.2). The Commission for Social Care Inspection's protocol on safeguarding adults refers, too, to its importance (CSCI 2007).

In summary, the law generally affecting the sharing of personal information between organisations consists of the common law of confidentiality, the Data Protection Act 1998 and article 8 of the European Convention on Human Rights. The Data Protection Act 1998 contains a number of specific rules relating to the processing of personal information. One issue that often arises in the context of adult protection and safeguarding is about striking the balance between the public and private interests of maintaining confidentiality and the public and private interests of disclosure. Proportionality is the key, in respect of relevant risks associated with disclosure or non-disclosure. From a legal point of view, an organisation's ability to justify its decision is all important.

In relation to safeguarding adults, information disclosure may arise in a number of different ways.

SHARING OF INFORMATION BETWEEN AGENCIES WITH OR WITHOUT CONSENT

In order to protect people disclosure may need to be made within and between agencies, even if consent has not, or cannot be, obtained from the persons whose personal information is being shared around. Typically, a vulnerable person, child or adult, may be inadequately protected from harm and abuse precisely because of a failure to share information. This may occur because of poor working arrangements between agencies, and sometimes because of misplaced notions about the law and confidentiality.

For instance, the serious case review into the murder of a man with learning disabilities in Cornwall highlighted the fact that a number of agencies gathered extensive information about the problems building up – but that cross-referral between those agencies did not occur. The agencies included the NHS, the police, the housing association and the local authority. Even within social services, adequate communication did not take place, with legal services not informing senior managers of a police request for information, and senior managers not even informing the director of adult social care of the man's murder (Cornwall County Council 2008). And, in Scotland, the Mental Welfare Commission reported on the failure by a local authority to protect a 67-year old woman (in the care of the authority from the age of eight) from serious sexual assaults over a prolonged period of time. Contributory was the fact that the housing association, in whose property she lived, had not been informed by the local authority of her vulnerability and the history of assaults (MWCS 2008, p.1).

SUBJECT ACCESS TO PERSONAL INFORMATION

Second, a vulnerable adult, somebody acting on their behalf, or perhaps a suspected perpetrator of harm or abuse, may wish to see what personal data are being held about them. Sometimes they may wish even to see the record and minutes of adult protection meetings. There are various rules under the Data Protection 1998 about such 'subject access' requests; disclosure may be refused on specific grounds.

ACCESS TO NON-PERSONAL INFORMATION

Access to non-personal information may also be directly relevant to the protection and safeguarding of vulnerable adults. For instance, concealment by NHS trusts of facts concerning outbreaks of infection arguably contributed to scores of deaths (see 4.2.8 above). Had these facts emerged earlier, and been put in the public domain, prevention of these deaths might have been facilitated. Such requests, involving non-personal information, come under the Freedom of Information Act 2000.

OTHER SPECIFIC LEGISLATION AFFECTING THE DISCLOSURE OF INFORMATION

There are other specific, relevant legislative provisions that affect the balance to be struck between disclosure and non-disclosure of personal information. For instance, the provision of both conviction and 'soft' non-conviction information by the police in the context of enhanced criminal record certificates is covered by the Police Act 1997. The courts have held that the common law presumption of non-disclosure is reversed in this Act to create a presumption of disclosure. Likewise, the Safeguarding Vulnerable Groups Act 2006 specifically provides for extensive information sharing in relation to the barring and monitoring of people working with vulnerable adults. And s.115 of the Crime and Disorder Act 1998 specifically confers additional legal power to share information.

10.1 COMMON LAW OF CONFIDENTIALITY AND HUMAN RIGHTS

A common law of confidentiality has in the past existed and in principle remains to the extent that any particular issue is not determined by other legislation. In summary, confidential information disclosure is – in any particular circumstances – about balancing the private and public interests of confidentiality against the private and public interests of disclosure. The following are illustrations of such balancing exercises which the courts have had to perform:

Breaching confidentiality to mental health patient. A consultant psychiatrist prepared a report for a patient prior to a mental health review tribunal hearing. The report was unfavourable and the patient withdrew his application. However, the consultant was so concerned about the potential danger that the man represented that he sent the report to both the Home Office and the hospital where the man was detained. The court held that the breach of confidentiality was justified in the public interest (*W v Edgell*).

In another case, the court pointed out that it was not known how, if at all, the relevant information would be recorded and thus whether the Data Protection Act 1998 applied at all. It therefore decided the case with reference to the common law of confidentiality (*R(A) v National Probation Service*; see 7.12). In the following case, the court found that the Data Protection Act 1998 did apply but was of limited assistance because of its generality. Instead the judge turned to article 8 of the European Convention on Human Rights (right to respect for privacy) and the common law of confidentiality. Both demanded that a balance be struck:

Disclosure of information to a mother. A mother was the nearest relative under the Mental Health Act 1983 to her adult son who was under the guardianship of the local authority. He lacked the capacity to take the relevant decisions for himself. She wished to gain access to her son's council files and to his medical records. The council was prepared to let experts appointed by the mother to have access, and for them to communicate information as they thought fit to the mother and her solicitors. The mother challenged this.

The court accepted that the Data Protection Act 1998 helped little; it generality meant that it did not prevent disclosure to the mother, but nor did it require the local authority positively to disclose. The judge turned to the common law of confidentiality and to human rights. Both required a balance to be struck between the 'public and private interests in maintaining the confidentiality of this information and the public and private interests in permitting, indeed requiring, its disclosure for certain purposes.'

The interests to be balanced consisted of the confidentiality of the information, the proper administration of justice and the mother's right of access to legal advice (relating to the guardianship, the mother's exercise of the nearest relative function, and her possible displacement as nearest relative by the local authority); the rights of the mother and son to respect for their family life and adequate involvement in decision-making processes; the son's right to respect for his private life; and the protection of the son's health and welfare.

The court held that the balance came down in favour of disclosure to the mother and her solicitors as well as the experts (*R v Plymouth CC, ex p Stevens*).

In another case, the courts similarly found that disclosure would breach neither confidentiality nor human rights:

Disclosure by local authority of personal details of social work student to university. A woman was known to social services, because of concerns and difficulties about the bringing up of her child. The woman subsequently wished to study to become a social worker. The local authority had concerns about her fitness for such a job; it disclosed its concerns to the university. The court held that in this instance the local authority's disclosure was lawful, even though it had not maintained confidentiality. The matter was one of public interest. Good practice would have involved the council informing the woman first, so that she could seek an injunction to prevent disclosure; however, breach of good practice did not equate to a breach of the duty of confidence. Likewise the claim failed under article 8 (right to respect for privacy); the means were proportionate and the purpose was to protect others from unsuitable social workers (*Maddock v Devon CC*).

Similarly, in a case concerning allegations surrounding the death of a resident in a nursing home, the courts found disclosure by the police to a regulatory body to be justified. Referring to article 8 of the European Convention on Human Rights, the court accepted the disclosure as necessary in a democratic society for the protection of health or morals or for the protection and rights of freedoms of others:

Nursing home death and disclosure. The matron of a nursing home was interviewed following the death of a resident alleged to have followed an overdose of diamorphine. The police concluded there was insufficient evidence to bring charges. The United Kingdom Central Council for Nursing, Midwifery and Health Visiting began an investigation. The police sought the matron's permission to disclose the statements she had made at police interview. The Royal College of Nursing, on behalf of the matron, refused that permission. The court ruled in this case that the police could in such circumstances pass on such confidential information in the interests of public health or safety. Nevertheless, generally, a balance had to be struck between competing public interests in such circumstances; the individual should be notified about the proposed disclosure; and in case of refusal, the court could be applied to (*Woolgar v Chief Constable of Sussex Police*).

In the past, the courts have pointed out that there is generally no presumption of disclosure. For example, even where there were suspicious deaths in the family and care proceedings under the Children Act 1989, the court cautioned against a presumption of disclosure to the police, but instead insisted that a balancing act be carried out (*Chief Constable v A County Council*). The courts have typically expected the disclosing organisation to carry out a 'pressing need' test, before any disclosure is made. The disclosure might be justified:

Disclosure to caravan site owner. A married couple was released from prison, where they served sentences for serious sexual offences against children. They went to live on a caravan site in the North of England. The local police asked them to move from the site before Easter, when many children would be visiting. The couple refused. The police disclosed their background to the caravan site owner. He asked them to leave. The couple claimed they had been treated unfairly and should have been shown the allegations. The court held that they should have been informed of the gist of the information held by the police, but that this would not have affected the conclusion. The police needed to apply a 'pressing need' test as to whether to disclose, on the basis of as much information as possible. The disclosure was lawful (*R v Chief Constable of North Wales, ex p AB*).

Alternatively, disclosure might be unjustified in the absence of a pressing need test being applied:

Failure to consider facts of particular case. An uncorroborated allegation was made that a man had abused a child at a hostel for vulnerable children. A few years later a further allegation that he had abused his daughter was made by the wife during acrimonious divorce proceedings. No action was taken, but the family was placed on the child protection register. He then set up his own bus company with a contract to run school bus services. The police and social services disclosed his background to the education department of the local authority. The latter terminated the contract. The court held that the disclosure by the police and by social services was unlawful because (a) disclosure should be the exception and not the rule and (b) there was no evidence that either agency had applied the pressing need test in terms of considering the facts of the particular case (*R v A local authority in the Midlands, ex p LM*).

The pressing need test was again brought into play concerning the issue of an NHS 'alert letter' (see: HSC 2002/011), to ensure that all NHS bodies were ware of allegations made against a medical doctor:

NHS alert letter: justification. An alert letter was issued containing details of allegations made about a medical doctor in relation to indecent assaults on female patients. Even after a decision had been taken that he would not be prosecuted, and the General Medical Council did not pursue the matter, the alert letter remained.

The Court of Appeal did not find this unlawful, noting that a balance had to be struck between the interests of the doctor and that of patients. The 'nature and strength of the allegations and the vulnerability of the class of persons to be protected are likely to be at the centre of the decision-maker's consideration.' In terms of human rights, under article 8 of the European Convention, the court accepted that the alert letter constituted an interference with respect for private life. But, such inter-ference could be justified if it was proportionate ('necessary in a democratic society') with a legiti-mate aim in mind (protection of patients). The question was effectively the same as that posed by the common law, namely whether there was a pressing need.

However, the court did emphasise that such alert letters needed to be reviewed at short inter-vals, with substantive consideration to be given to whether they should remain in circulation. This was because, in this particular case, a number of errors had been made, contrary to the Department of Health's guidance (*R(D) v Secretary of State for Health*).

In the following case, involving a local authority wishing to disclose information about a woman working in a care home in the area of a different local authority, the judge did approve disclosure but was meticulous in weighing up the relevant and competing factors which led to the court's decision:

Disclosure of information, about assault by mother on child, to a care home for older people where the mother was working. A mother had assaulted her eight-year-old daughter, who was subsequently removed from the mother after the local authority had applied for and obtained a care order. The mother still worked at a care home for older people in the area of a second local authority. The first local authority wished to inform both the second local authority and the woman's employer about the background to the care proceedings. The judge referred to the *No secrets* guidance and to its exhortation for inter-agency arrangements, as well as to the Protection of Vulnerable Adults list kept by the Secretary of State, and the statutory duty of care providers to refer care workers in case of misconduct causing harm (or risk of harm) to a vulnerable adult.

The first local authority believed that, whatever the Secretary of State decided, nonetheless the employer (and second local authority) needed to be able to discharge their statutory duties under the Care Standards Act 2000. They could only do that if the first local authority disclosed the informa-tion to them. The judge then set out the competing considerations.

Considerations against disclosure. Potentially militating against disclosure were (a) the impact of dis-closure on the child (there would be no benefit for the child in disclosure); (b) the consequences for the family (the woman might lose her job, she might not find easily other employment, the child might be upset if she became aware of the effect on her mother); (c) risk of publicity with potentially serious consequences for the child; and (d) importance of encouraging frankness in children's cases (fear of publicity may deter people revealing what is happening to children),

Considerations for disclosure. In favour of disclosure were: (a) the gravity of the conduct and risk to public if there were no disclosure (serious assault on child meant that there was a real and potent risk to vulnerable adults); (b) evidence of a pressing need for disclosure (there was both a right and a duty to disclose); (c) interest of other bodies in receiving the information (significant obligations on second local authority and employer to carry out statutory duties); and (d) public interest in disclosure (strong and potent – with the need for public safety outweighing the mother's right to respect for her privacy, under article 8 of the European Convention on Human Rights).

Balance in favour of disclosure but with safeguards. The judge was quite clear that disclosure was the proper course, but needed first to be satisfied that confidential discussions between the two local authorities and the employer could adequately address the question of avoiding publicity (*Brent LBC v SK*).

10.2 DATA PROTECTION ACT 1998

The Data Protection Act 1998 contains a number of key points that are relevant to the holding, sharing and destruction of information in the context of safeguarding adults. In particular, reference needs to be made to the data protection principles which include general rules and safeguards concerning the processing of information. There are various basic definitions contained within the Data Protection Act 1998:

- **Personal data**. The Act applies to data controllers in respect of personal data. This means data relating to a living individual who can be identified from those data alone, or from those data together with other information in the possession of, or likely to come into the possession of, the data controller. Personal data include any expression of opinion about the individual, as well as any indication of the intentions toward the individual of the data controller or any other person (s.1).

- **Sensitive personal data**. Sensitive personal data include information, among other things, about the person's racial or ethnic origin, physical or mental health or condition, sexual life, commission of an alleged offence, proceedings for any offence committed or allegedly committed, and court sentence in any such proceedings (s.1).

- **Processing**. Processing of information is defined very widely. It means obtaining, recording or holding it or carrying out any operation on it, including (a) its organisation, adaptation or alteration; (b) retrieval, consultation or use; (c) disclosure; and (d) alignment, combination, blocking, erasure or destruction (s.1).

- **Relevant filing system: manual information**. In addition to applying to automated, computerised information, the Act also applies to manual information held as part of a relevant filing system. This means a set of information structured so that specific information relating to a particular individual is readily accessible (s.1). However, from January 2005, the Freedom of Information Act 2000 (s.68) amends the definition of data in the Data Protection Act 1998 (s.1), so as to include in effect personal information held in unstructured manual filing systems by public authorities. However, personal health or social care information is anyway covered, because it counts as an 'accessible record'.

- **Accessible record**. This means a health record, educational record or accessible public record (s.68).

- **Health record**. This means any record which '(a) consists of information relating to the physical or mental health or condition of an individual; and (b) has been made by or on behalf of a health professional in connection with the care of that individual' (s.68).

- **Accessible public record**. This means a record kept by housing and social services authorities for the purpose respectively of any of the authority's tenancies or 'for any purpose of the authority's social services functions' (schedule 12).

10.2.1 DATA PROTECTION ACT PRINCIPLES

Data controllers must comply with data protection principles. All processing of personal data must comply with principles in Schedule 1 of the Act. These include:

- **fairness and lawfulness**: personal data must be processed fairly and lawfully and in particular the processing must meet (a) at least one condition in schedule 2 and (b) in the case of sensitive personal data at least one condition in schedule 3

- **purpose**: the data must be obtained for one or more specified purposes and should not be processed for another, incompatible purpose
- **relevance**: the data must be adequate, relevant and not excessive for the purpose
- **length of time**: data should be accurate and kept up to date, and not kept for longer than necessary for the purpose for which it had been processed
- **security**: appropriate technical and organisational measures should be taken in relation to the security of the data.

Following the conviction of Ian Huntley for the murder of two children, Jessica Chapman and Holly Wells, concerns were raised that the Act might have been to blame for some of the police and local authority failings to retain and share information. In which case, the principles set out above might have been deficient. However, the subsequent government enquiry concluded that the Act could not be blamed for the failure to retain relevant information (Bichard 2004, para 4.3).

Considerable latitude is given by the Act, so that terms such as adequacy, relevance, excessiveness and length of time can be interpreted depending on context and circumstances. Thus in contrast to the Huntley case, the Information Commissioner ordered in 2007 four police forces to delete old criminal convictions from the Police National Computer. The records included the details of the theft in 1984 of a packet of meat valued at £0.99 with a fine of £15; of an offence of attempted theft committed 25 years ago and involving a fine of £25; and of a person under 14 years old who was cautioned for a minor assault, had been told that the information would be deleted when she reached 18, but had now been informed that it would not in fact be deleted for 100 years (ICO 2007). Clearly, what the Information Commissioner is getting at, is that justification for the processing of information is closely linked to proportionality.

As to the purpose for which personal information is held, the Information Commissioner has issued a good practice note about the sharing of information between local authorities and local authority departments. First, the sharing of such information between two separate local authorities is clearly subject to the Act. Second, however, the sharing of personal information between two local authority departments is not subject to the Act, unless the second department will use the information for a different, 'secondary' purpose – in which case the principles of the Act do apply. In particular, under schedule 1, fair processing means that people must be informed about the purpose of processing the information, including any secondary uses. And, personal information should be obtained only for one or more 'specified' purposes – and not be used for any other incompatible purpose (ICO 2008).

10.2.2 DISCLOSURE OF SENSITIVE PERSONAL INFORMATION WITH OR WITHOUT A PERSON'S CONSENT

All personal data must be processed in accordance with at least one of the principles in Schedule 2 of the Act. These entail either that the data subject has consented or that various principles are satisfied including that the data processing is necessary; for example because of:

- **legal obligation**: to comply with a legal obligation
- **vital interests**: to safeguard the vital interests of the data subject
- **justice**: for the administration of justice
- **legislation**: for the administration of justice, for the exercise of any functions conferred on any person by or under any enactment (i.e. legislation)
- **Crown functions**: for the exercise of any functions of the Crown, a Minister of the Crown or a government department
- **public interest**: for the exercise of any other functions of a public nature exercised in the public interest by any person
- **legitimate interests**: for the purposes of legitimate interests pursued by the data controller or by a third party seeking disclosure – unless the disclosure is unwarranted because of prejudice to the 'rights and freedoms or legitimate interests of the data subject'.

In addition, in the case of sensitive personal data (particularly relevant to social care and health care), at least one of the principles in schedule 3 must be complied with. The person must have explicitly consented, otherwise the principles include that the processing is necessary, for example:

- **right or obligation**: for the purpose of exercising or performing a right or obligation conferred by law on the data controller in connection with employment
- **inability to consent, protection of others**: to protect the vital interests of the data subject, where either consent cannot be given by or on behalf of the data subject and the data controller cannot reasonably be expected to obtain the consent of the data subject – or to protect the vital interests of someone else, where consent by or on behalf of the data subject has been unreasonably withheld
- **public information**: the information contained in the personal data has been made public as result of steps taken deliberately by the data subject
- **legal proceedings**: for the purpose of legal proceedings, obtaining legal advice, or otherwise in connection with establishing, exercising or defending legal rights
- **justice**: for the administration of justice
- **legislation**: for the exercise of any functions conferred on any person by or under any enactment
- **Crown functions**: for the exercise of any functions of the Crown, a Minister of the Crown or a government department
- **medical purposes**: for medical purposes and is undertaken by a health professional – or by a person who in the circumstances owes a duty of confidentiality which is equivalent to that which would arise if that person were a health professional.

It will be noticed that under schedule 3, in the case of sensitive personal data, the fact that a person refuses consent to disclosure of personal information (second point above), such that he or she would thereby suffer harm, is not in itself sufficient to justify disclosure.

However, in such instances, protection of the vital interests of somebody else will justify disclosure. Equally disclosure may be justifiable under another point; for example, as part and parcel of the carrying out of statutory functions (e.g. social services functions, NHS functions, police functions etc). Thus, Department of Health guidance states that local social services authorities may disclose information in a number of circumstances in carrying out of their social services functions – without consent if necessary. For instance, information may be shared with line managers, other people caring for a client, such as a voluntary body or foster carers – and other departments or agencies including health, education, child protection, inspection teams, legal advisers, finance staff, police (DH 2000a, para 6.18).

Under schedule 3 also, in contrast to schedule 2, a person's consent must be explicit. Department of Health guidance states that the consent must therefore be absolutely clear and cover the specific detail of what is to be processed, as well as the purpose (DH 2000a, para 6.9).

In addition, an order has been passed allowing sensitive personal data to be processed if, amongst other things, the processing is in the substantial public interest; is necessary for the purposes of the prevention or detection of any unlawful act; and must necessarily be carried out without the explicit consent of the data subject being sought, so as not to prejudice those purposes. The schedule to the order refers to the processing being necessary for the exercise of any functions conferred on a constable by any rule of law (SI 2000/417).

Information passed between police forces and then to education authority. Non-conviction information was passed from one police force to another; the latter then informed the education authority with whom the person concerned had applied for a job that involved working with children (headship of an infants' school). The job offer was withdrawn.

The court pointed out that the Data Protection Act 1998 was not breached either when the information passed between the police forces, or from one police force to the education authority. This was because the information came under the 2000 order, which referred to the processing of sensitive personal data by a constable under any rule of law, and to the prevention or detection of unlawful acts (*R v Chief Constables of C and D, ex p A*).

In sum, it can be seen that the data protection principles are so broadly drawn that in case of disclosure matters the courts have sometimes held that the Act only gets one so far. It might both justify disclosure and non-disclosure. The balancing act has to be performed with reference to principles established in other areas of law such as human rights and the common law of confidentiality (*R v Plymouth CC, ex p Stevens*). The key point is that disclosure has to be justified; the Act by no means imports *carte blanche* for the sharing of information, willy nilly. Equally, it fully supports justified disclosure. It all depends.

10.2.3 SUBJECT ACCESS TO PERSONAL DATA

Under the Data Protection Act 1998, people (data subjects) have a general right to find out about and receive copies of personal data of which they are the subject. However, there are some provisos to this right of access.

One is where complying with a request for information would also mean disclosing information relating to somebody else. In this case, the data controller is not obliged to disclose, unless (a) the other person has consented; (b) it is nevertheless reasonable in all the circumstances to disclose without that consent; or (c) the other individual referred to is either a health professional who has compiled or contributed to the information or has been involved in caring for the data subject – or is a 'relevant person' (such as a social worker) who has supplied the information in an official capacity or in connection with provision of a service. However, the data controller could in any case communicate so much of the information as could be communicated without disclosing the identity of the other individual concerned (s.7 and SI 2000/413 and SI 2000/415).

This rule, together with the possibility of independent review by the Information Commissioner or by the courts, is to remedy the problem identified in *Gaskin v United Kingdom*, and which led to a breach of article 8 of the European Convention on Human Rights. Under the earlier Data Protection Act 1984, no process was specified for such disclosure in case of lack of consent of a third party, nor the possibility of independent review. The European Court on Human Rights has accepted that this aspect of the 1998 Act cures the previous defect (*MG v United Kingdom*).

10.2.3.1 Refusing subject access request on grounds relating to crime or harm

There are also specific exemptions relating to disclosure of data, in response to a subject access request, concerning the prevention or detection of crime, where this would be likely to be prejudiced by disclosure (s.29).

Likewise exemptions apply to information about a person's physical or mental health or condition or in relation to social services functions.

The exemption in the case of information about a person's physical or mental health, is when access by the data subject to the information would be likely to cause serious harm to the physical or mental health or condition of the data subject or of any other person. If the data controller is not a health professional, then the data controller must consult the appropriate health professional about whether the exemption applies (DPA 1998, s.30 and SI 2000/413).

In the case of information relating to social services functions, the exemption applies if disclosure would be likely to prejudice the carrying out of social work functions, because serious harm would be caused to the physical or mental health or condition of the data subject or of any other person (SI 2000/415). Department of Health guidance states that there is no general test of what constitutes serious harm, but that restriction on the right of access should be exceptional and restricted to serious harm, such as risk of harm to a child to the extent that a child protection plan is in place (DH 2000a, para 5.37).

10.2.3.2 Dead people

The Data Protection Act 1998 does not apply to information relating to dead people, since it covers personal data relating only to a living person (s.1). Thus request for information about a deceased person will come under the Freedom of Information Act 2000. In some circumstances, it may come under the Access to Health Records Act 1990.

10.2.3.3 People lacking capacity

The Mental Capacity Act 2005 Code of Practice states that, in the case of people lacking capacity, a person with a lasting power of attorney, enduring power of attorney or a court-appointed deputy could ask to see the information under the s.7 subject access provisions, so long as the information related to the decisions that representative had the legal power to make (Lord Chancellor 2007, chapter 16).

Regulations made under the Data Protection Act 1998 state that, in the case of information about the physical or mental health of the person lacking capacity – or information relating to social services functions – a person who has been appointed by the court to manage his or her affairs, can make a subject access request under s.7 of the Act. However, an exemption from disclosure would apply if (a) the information had been provided by the data subject in the expectation that it would not be disclosed to the person now making the request; (b) the information had been obtained as a result of any examination or investigation in the expectation that the information would not be disclosed; or (c) the data subject has expressly indicated that it should not be disclosed (SI 2000/413 and SI 2000/415).

Arguably, however, disclosure could still be made in a person's best interests in some other circumstances; in fact the Mental Capacity Act 2005 code of practice points out that in consulting about a person's best interests, health and social care staff may anyway need to disclose information about the person lacking capacity in order to make consultation meaningful (Lord Chancellor 2007, chapter 16).

10.3 PRESUMPTION OF NON-DISCLOSURE MODIFIED BY SPECIFIC LEGISLATION

The particular legislative context may alter or even reverse the common law presumption of non-disclosure of personal information. Certain legislation specifically contemplates disclosure and might affect the nature of any balancing test that the courts bring to bear.

For example, under s.115 of the Crime and Disorder Act 1998, any person who would not otherwise have the power to disclose information to a relevant authority or to a person acting on behalf of that authority (including the police, local authority, probation committee, health authority) shall have the power to do so in any case where the disclosure is necessary or expedient for the purposes of any provision of that Act.

The Court of Appeal has held that s.115 of the Police Act 1997 tends toward a presumption of disclosure by the police in response to information sought in respect of enhanced criminal record certificates (see 5.3.2 above). This decision overrules that of the

High Court, which had held that the (common law) presumption of non-disclosure still applied in the context of the Police Act (*R(X) v Chief Constable of West Midlands Police*).

Under the Criminal Justice Act 2003, what are termed Multi-Agency Public Protection Agency arrangements demand cooperation between different bodies, which may involve information sharing, referred to in the Criminal Justice Act 2003 (see section 7.12).

The Safeguarding Vulnerable Groups Act 2006 specifically provides for extensive information sharing between various organisations and agencies in relation to the barring and monitoring of people working with vulnerable adults (see 5.2 above).

10.4 DISCLOSURE OF NON-PERSONAL INFORMATION: FREEDOM OF INFORMATION

The Freedom of Information Act 2000 applies to public authorities including local authorities and the NHS. Public authorities must have a publication scheme (s.19) and provide information in response to requests (s.1). There are various exempted types of information including the following that are relevant in the context of health and social care. Some of the exemptions are as follows:

- information otherwise reasonably accessible to the applicant (s.21)
- information intended for future publication (s.22)
- information held in relation to:
  - security matters (s.23)
  - public authority investigations and proceedings (s.30)
  - law enforcement that would otherwise be prejudiced (s.31)
  - court records (s.32)
  - audit functions (s.33)
  - formulation of government policy (s.35)
  - conduct of public affairs that would otherwise be prejudiced (s.36)
  - health and safety (s.38)
  - personal information (s.40)
  - information provided in confidence (s.41)
  - legal professional privilege (s.42)
  - commercial interests (s.43)
- information, disclosure of which is prohibited by other legislation, is incompatible with any European Community obligation or would be a contempt of court (s.44).

Under s.50 of the Act, a complainant can apply to the Information Commissioner to make a decision about whether a request for information has been dealt with by a public body in accordance with the Act. The Commissioner must make a decision unless (a) the complainant has not exhausted any complaints procedure provided by the public body in conformity with the code of practice made under the 2000 Act; (b) there has been undue delay making the application to the Commissioner; (c) the application is frivolous or vexatious; or (d) the application has been withdrawn or abandoned. Appeal lies, for the public body or the complainant, to the Information Tribunal (s.57).

10.5 FREEDOM OF INFORMATION ACT: RELEVANCE TO ADULT PROTECTION

Requests are sometimes made to local authorities or the NHS to access information, which may sometimes have a bearing on adult protection and safeguarding issues. Depending on who is asking for the information, and what information is being requested, the request will give rise to different questions under the Freedom of Information Act 2000. In particular family members might be doing their own protection or safeguarding work, trying to find out what went, or what is going, wrong in the health or social care of a relative. This may involve trying to get hold of investigations, reports, meeting minutes, care plans, evidence of how adult protection or safeguarding procedures were followed, details about staff involved etc.

In some circumstances, the request will in fact legally come to rest under the Data Protection Act 1998, even though the person has made the request under the 2000 Act. On occasion, the request might also come, legally, under other legislation altogether, such as the Access to Health Records Act 1990. The following paragraphs consider in more detail certain provisions of the Freedom of Information Act 2000, and illustrate them with examples which are explicitly linked to adult protection and safeguarding issues or which at least involve relevant principles.

10.5.1 EXEMPTIONS FROM DISCLOSURE: ABSOLUTE OR QUALIFIED

The Freedom of Information Act 2000 Act effectively creates an expectation that public bodies will confirm or deny that they hold the information sought, and will disclose that information (s.1). This twofold duty is however subject to specified exemptions. Some of these exemptions are absolute, some are qualified. A qualified exemption means applying a test of whether in all the circumstances of the case, the public interest in maintaining the exemption outweighs the public interest in disclosure (s.2). The presumption of disclosure in relation to qualified exemptions is the reverse of the test traditionally applied in the common law of confidentiality – namely a presumption of non-disclosure which has to be outweighed by a public interest in disclosure.

10.5.2 INVESTIGATIONS AND PROCEEDINGS

A qualified exemption (i.e. subject to the public interest test) applies to investigations carried out by public bodies (under a duty) and which may lead to a person being charged with an offence or to ascertaining whether the person is guilty of an offence already charged – or may lead to the public body instituting criminal proceedings. Likewise there is a qualified exemption in respect of information obtained from confidential sources in the course of such (and some other) investigations (s.30).

For instance, s.30 could apply to investigations by the Health and Safety Executive (HSE). In one Information Commissioner case, the HSE disclosed its factual report about a potentially fatal accident, but not its analysis. In this particular case, the analysis did not contain obviously sensitive information, witness statements or information which would assist law breakers. The public interest in exemption was therefore was outweighed by that of disclosure (*Health and Safety Executive 2008*).

In addition, under s.31, qualified exemption applies for a variety of reasons including where disclosure would be likely to prejudice prevention or detection of crime, apprehension or prosecution of offenders, administration of justice etc. It applies also if a public authority is exercising various functions to determine failure to comply with the law, improper conduct, health and safety etc. Thus, a person requested details of records of a health and social services board investigation relating to the death of his mother. The board resisted disclosure under s.31, because the Northern Ireland ombudsman was investigating in response to separate complaints made. The Information Commissioner held that disclosure would prejudice the ombudsman's functions, and that the public interest fell on the side of non-disclosure (*Eastern Health and Social Services Board 2006*).

10.5.3 PREJUDICE TO CONDUCT OF PUBLIC AFFAIRS

A qualified exemption applies if disclosure by a public body would prejudice the effective conduct of public affairs and would be likely to inhibit free and frank provision of advice, or free and frank exchange of views for the purpose of deliberation (s.36).

For instance, in one case a person sought information about adult protection procedures in respect of the death of his mother. The local authority put up various arguments, including one under s.36. This was that there was an expectation of confidence between a client and social services and that clients would fear to provide appropriate information for fear of potential disclosure. This would arguably prejudice the conduct of public affairs. The Information Commissioner gave no view on this particular argument, finding instead that the information sought was anyway exempted from disclosure under ss.40 and 41 relating to personal information provided in confidence (*Trafford MBC 2007*).

In one case an NHS primary care trust argued s.36 in relation to the medical records of a woman's father. The Information Commissioner was unable to reach a decision on this point because the PCT had destroyed the notes of a panel meeting at which the original non-disclosure decision in relation to s.36 was taken. The Commissioner did not find a breach of s.77 of the 2000 Act – which creates an offence of destroying or otherwise tampering with information which the intention of preventing disclosure – but came perilously close to it. But he could not find sufficient evidence of deliberate intent (*Gloucestershire NHS Primary Care Trust 2007*).

However, under s.36, the Information Commissioner clearly accepted that a 'part 8' serious case review by the local Area Child Protection Committee (ACPC) under the Children Act 1989 was exempt from disclosure:

Disclosure of child protection serious case review: prejudicial to the conduct of public affairs. The Information Commissioner found that disclosure would inhibit the participation of professionals; this would reduce the effectiveness of the review and in turn have a detrimental impact on child protection. So, whilst there was a high public interest in accountability and scrutiny, there were persuasive arguments for non-disclosure. Furthermore the executive summary which was available provided a balanced and coherent overview, without disclosing sensitive information. In addition, non-disclosure was justified under s.40 because of the personal information inextricably linked to the dead child and surviving members of the family; and the Commissioner could find no condition met in either schedule 2 of 3 of the Data Protection Act which would justify disclosure. In which case, the first data protection principle would be breached (fairness and lawfulness). Likewise, the s.41 (duty of confidence) exemption would apply to the information about, or provided by, family members and their associates (*Plymouth City Council 2006*).

10.5.4 PERSONAL INFORMATION

An absolute exemption from disclosure under the 2000 Act applies to personal information on various grounds.

10.5.4.1 Personal information of which the applicant is the subject

An absolute exemption applies to personal information, of which the applicant is the data subject (s.40). Such a request should be dealt with under the Data Protection Act 1998. For instance:

Family seeking information about complaint made against them. The parents of a baby asked to see details of a complaint made against them, with a view to identifying the hospital staff who had made the complaint. The Information Tribunal held that the request fell under the Data Protection Act 1998 subject access provisions rather under than the 2000 Act (*Southampton University Hospitals NHS Trust 2007*). Thus, in terms of identification of the staff, the subject access rules under the 1998 Act, about third party information and about where that third party is a health professional, would apply (see 10.2.3 above).

10.5.4.2 Personal information of other people

If the request concerns the personal information of other people but not the data subject, then an absolute exemption applies in two cases (s.40).

First, the exemption applies if disclosure would contravene (a) any of the data protection principles; or (b) section 10 of the Data Protection Act. Section 10 concerns notification by the data subject to the data controller, requesting non-disclosure of his or her personal information because of the substantial damage or distress that would be caused (to him or her or anybody else) – and the response of the data controller as to whether it will comply with the request not to disclose.

Second, the exemption applies if any of the exemptions to subject access, under the Data Protection Act, apply (see 10.2.3 above).

The Information Commissioner has issued guidance about contravention of data protection principles under s.40. The guidance refers in particular to the principles of fairness and lawfulness, the first data protection principle. This states that at least one of the conditions in schedule 2 of the Act is met and, in the case of sensitive personal data, at least one in schedule 3 (see 10.2.1 above). One of the conditions in schedule 2 refers to processing (including disclosure) being necessary for the purposes of legitimate interests pursued by the data controller or by a third party seeking disclosure – unless the disclosure is unwarranted because of prejudice to the 'rights and freedoms or legitimate interests of the data subject'. In sum, the Information Tribunal has held that although s.40 represents an absolute exemption, this condition in schedule 2 of the 1998 Act actually imports a balance of competing interests comparable to that applied in the 2000 Act to qualified exemptions (*House of Commons v Information Commissioner 2007*). In other words, a public interest test by the back door.

Thus, according to the guidance, disclosure might concern personal health or social care information that was provided in confidence and so be exempt from disclosure. Fairness is referred to as harder to define and would involve questions about:

- whether disclosure would cause unjustified distress or damage
- whether the third party would expect the information to be disclosed
- whether that party been led to believe the information would be kept secret
- whether the third party had expressly refused consent to disclosure. In addition, it would be relevant to ask whether the information – for example, if staff were concerned – was about their private or public life.

Thus, taking account of damage or distress to the third party should be in connection with private life – and not used as an exemption from disclosure in order to spare 'officials embarrassment over poor administrative decisions' (IC 2000). The Commissioner has in practice also added in a fifth question as to whether the legitimate interest of a member of the public seeking information about a public authority, including personal information, outweigh the rights, freedoms and legitimate interests of the data subject (*Trafford MBC 2007*).

For instance, in relation to her mother's care, a woman wanted from the local authority copies of notes made by a social worker, written reports, copies of the minutes of a complaints panel meeting, and information about a subsequent complaint about the 'shoddy, superficial and seriously deficient investigation'. The Information Commissioner held that the s.40 exemption applied. The information was personal and release of it without the data subject's (the mother's) consent would breach the data protection principle of fairness and lawfulness. There was no evidence that the mother had given the daughter consent to access the information, or that the daughter had any right to act on her mother's behalf (*Worcestershire County Council 2006*).

In another case a woman sought information about what had happened to her mother and what adult protection procedures had been followed by the local authority. She found the information to be exempt from disclosure:

Information about adult protection procedures followed by a local authority. A woman sought information concerning adult protection matters and the course of action the local authority took following notification by a GP of injuries sustained by her now deceased mother, whilst in the care of a third party. In particular, she wanted to know how the vulnerable adult protection pathway procedure had been followed in this particular case, as well as the outcome of the enquiry and the documentation concerning the directions given by the GP. The local authority resisted disclosure under s.41 (information given in confidence), and s.44 (prohibitions on disclosure because of human rights), s.36 (prejudice to conduct of public affairs), and s.40 (personal information and data protection principles).

Exemption from disclosure under s.40: personal information of primary carer. Under s.40, the information included information about the woman's primary carer who provided virtually 24-hour care, as well as other social services and NHS employees. The information included opinions about the primary carer and references to the carer's personal circumstances, health and financial arrangements. The Information Commissioner accepted that disclosure of this information would be unfair under the data protection principles because the primary carer would have had a reasonable belief that her inter-action with the council was confidential – and access to the information did not outweigh her rights, freedoms and legitimate interests (under schedule 2 of the Data Protection Act 1998). Likewise, disclosure could be unlawful in terms of breach of confidence of the carer's personal information, some of it 'sensitive' (under the 1998 Act).

Exemption from disclosure under s.41 (duty of confidence). Under s.41, information had derived from the dead woman, the primary carer, the GP and the local health authority. The woman would have had an expectation of confidence, which was important if clients were to share private information with social services. The Information Commissioner held that the duty of confidence toward the deceased survived her death and that a breach would be actionable. Thus, the exemption under s.41 applied. The Commissioner disregarded the s.44 and human rights argument (*Trafford Metropolitan Borough Council 2007*).

Sometimes if things have gone wrong, a patient or family member might want the names of staff. Thus, when a woman wanted the names of a number of registrars who had worked for a particular hospital consultant, the NHS trust supplied her with the name of the registrar who had treated her but not others. The Information Commissioner found this justified under s.40, because while registrars might expect their current position to be disclosed, disclosure of past positions would, to a small degree, represent an infringement of privacy (*St George's Healthcare NHS Trust 2008*). The Information Commissioner has stated that normally, therefore, releasing the names of staff undertaking professional duties would not breach data protection principles, but would be unfair if the data subject (the staff member) were exposed to a risk of harassment as a result (*NHS Litigation Authority 2006*).

In the following case, a woman wanted information about an untoward incident involving her husband:

Exemption from disclosure: witness statements about untoward incident involving a patient. A woman sought witness statements that had been made about a serious untoward incident involving her late husband. The statements were given in the course of an internal investigation and staff were informed that their statements would be treated confidentially. The Information Commissioner held that disclosure would breach the first principle of the Data Protection Act – lawfulness and fairness – because of the expectations of the staff about confidentiality (*Central and North West London NHS Foundation Trust 2008*).

Information was sought from an NHS trust about five critical incident reports relating to the murder of a patient. The reports contained personal information about identifiable individuals – including patients or family members – who would not have expected that the information they provided be made public. This was particularly because such an internal review which gave rise to the reports was classed as confidential. Thus, under s.40, the Information Commissioner held it would be unfair, under the first data protection principle, for disclosure to take place (*Mersey Care NHS Trust 2008*).

Sometimes people may seek evidence of underpinning reasons for lapses in treatment or care. In the following case, even though it was her allegations that triggered an internal report, the person was unable to access the information:

Exempt from disclosure: internal report into alleged deficiencies in care on a ward. A former employee of an NHS trust requested a copy of an internal report, which had been triggered by allegations originally made by that employee – concerning supervision, management of medical staff and resource levels on a particular ward. The trust refused disclosure under s.40. The Information Commissioner upheld this decision; disclosure would have been unfair under the first data protection principle. This was because staff were likely to have expected confidentiality when interviewed as part of the investigation, and this had in fact been indicated to staff. Furthermore, critical comments made by the trust about individuals would have caused considerable distress and damaged their employment prospects, if entering the public domain. Undue inferences might be made even about those members of staff who were reluctant or unwilling to provide information during the investigation, if their names were disclosed (*University Hospital of North Staffordshire NHS Trust 2007*).

Likewise, the Commissioner held that an NHS trust could resist disclosure under s.40 of information concerning an internal investigation against two senior executives, which resulted in their departure. The disclosure of the information could have a harmful effect on the current and future employment prospects of both of them; they also had a reasonable expectation that the information would not be disclosed. Furthermore, the Commissioner was satisfied that the internal investigation had been thorough and independently verified. Thus, the public interest had largely been satisfied (*Nottinghamshire Healthcare Trust 2007*). Similar considerations arose about the departure of a chief executive from a public authority, following suspension. The NHS trust and executive had reached a compromise agreement, and not all the allegations were fully investigated. He would not have expected details to be disclosed and to do so would have been unfair (*George Eliot Hospital NHS Trust 2007*).

Other data protection principles may be considered in identifying an exemption. For instance, in one case information was sought from an NHS primary care trust about a doctor who had been investigated by the PCT in relation to alleged criminal offences. By the time a second set of requests had been made, he had appeared in court. The Information Commissioner noted that schedule 3 of the Data Protection Act 1998, concerning sensitive personal data clearly applied because the information concerned the commission or alleged commission of an offence. Therefore there was exemption from disclosure under s.40 of the 2000 Act, because it would not be fair or lawful (*Western Cheshire NHS Primary Care Trust 2007*).

There is a duty also under s.40 concerning a public body's refusal to confirm or deny that it holds the relevant information – irrespective of whether it will disclose. In one case a man and his partner sought the minutes of a meeting alleged to have taken place between the NHS, social services and the police. The NHS trust refused to confirm or deny that there were any such minutes; this was on the grounds that to do so would provide information about the individuals named in the request and that this would be contrary to the first data protection principle. The Information Commissioner disagreed, pointing out that he had been provided with no evidence that any individual would suffer unwarranted detriment; therefore the local authority should confirm or deny the exis-tence of the minutes (*Rotherham NHS Primary Care Trust 2007*).

10.5.5 INFORMATION PROVIDED IN CONFIDENCE

An absolute exemption from disclosure applies if the information requested was obtained by the public body from any other person – and if disclosure of that information to the public would constitute a breach of confidence actionable by that person (from whom it was obtained) or by anybody else (s.41). Although it is an absolute exemption, the common law involving breach of confidence contains its own public interest test. This means that disclosure will not constitute an actionable breach of confidence if there is a public interest in disclosure outweighing the public interest in confidentiality. This is the reverse of the public interest test applied generally under the Act to qualified exemption from disclosure; this assumes disclosure unless the public interest in confidentiality can be shown to outweigh the public interest in disclosure (*Hounslow Primary Care Trust 2008*). The following case concerned information about the death of a man in nursing home:

Exempt from disclosure: information provided by GP in relation to care and death of a man in a nursing home. A man sought information from an NHS primary care trust about the care of his late father-in-law and issues concerning a nursing home. It included correspondence between the nursing home, a doctor, the police and a coroner. A particular issue arose about the confidentiality of this information provided to the PCT by a GP. The Information Commissioner held that the public interest in the GP discussing issues of performance, with confidentiality assured, outweighed the public interest in disclosure. Likewise, the PCT was justified in withholding – under s.42, see below – five pieces of legal advice, on the basis of legal professional privilege (*Hounslow Primary Care Trust 2008*).

10.5.5.1 Information concerning dead people

Sometimes, family members or other people might be conducting their own 'adult pro-tection' investigations, albeit retrospectively, following a person's death in health or social care. The request for information does not come under the Data Protection Act, because that Act applies only to living persons. Consequently the Information Commis-sioner has considered a number of cases relating to whether the confidentiality exemption applies under s.41 of the Freedom of Information Act 2000. One such case reached the Information Tribunal. In sum, a duty of confidence does survive death.

Mother seeking information about daughter's death in hospital. A dead woman's mother sought information about her daughter's death. The NHS trust was not prepared to share the information without the consent of her widower, as next of kin. That consent was not forthcoming. The trust had, five years previously, admitted liability and reached a settlement with the widower. The trust argued that the s.41 exemption applied. The Tribunal established that the medical records had been compiled with information from somebody else, namely the dead woman. It then asked in particular a number of key questions.

Would the NHS have a defence to a breach of confidence claim? The first was whether the trust would have a defence to a breach of confidence claim, were it to disclose the information, because the public interest in disclosure would outweigh the public interest in maintaining confidence. The Tribunal stated that patient confidentiality outweighed by some distance the interests in disclosure.

Another was whether an action for breach of confidence would be defeated because neither the dead woman nor her estate would suffer detriment by disclosure. The Tribunal concluded that it would not necessarily be defeated – since there needed to be no detriment beyond an invasion of privacy, which there would be, given the private information involved.

Did the duty of confidence survive death? A third question was whether the duty of confidence survived the woman's death. The Tribunal was in no doubt that it did. If it did not, doctor and patient trust would be undermined if patients believed that information would be disclosed after death.

Bringing a claim for breach of confidence. Fourth was whether the dead woman's personal representatives would be able to bring a claim for breach of confidence. The answer was yes; and the duty of confidence would last until either the information became public or the public interest in disclosure outweighed that of confidentiality.

Human rights. Fifth, the trust argued that s.44 of the Act (legal prohibitions), the Human Rights Act 1998 and European Convention on Human Rights (article 8 concerning the right to respect for privacy) prevented disclosure. The Tribunal did not regard article 8 as a directly enforceable legal prohibition. But, if it was wrong about that, disclosure would not be consistent in this case with article 8, and so would be exempt under s.44 (*Bluck v Information Commissioner and Epsom and St Helier University NHS Trust 2007*).

In another case, the applicant, a professional writer, sought information about a dead person who had been under the care and supervision of a hospital. He initially applied under the Access to Health Records Act 1990 – unsuccessfully because, under s.3 of that Act, he was not the patient's personal representative or any person who might have a claim arising out of the patient's death. He then applied under the Freedom of Information Act 2000; the primary care trust (PCT) refused on the basis of survival of the duty of confidence and the possibility of an action for breach of confidence. Such an action would probably not result in damages, since there would no obvious financial loss at stake, but might lead to an injunction preventing publication. Thus, the Information Commissioner found the information exempt from disclosure under s.41 of the Act (*Walsall NHS Teaching PCT 2007*).

However, where a daughter sought her late father's medical records under the 2000 Act, the Information Commissioner ascertained that she was entitled to access under the Access to Health Records Act 1990; in which case it was an exempt disclosure under s.21

of the 2000 Act, because the information was otherwise reasonably accessible and held by a public authority which was obliged to provide it – under the 1990 Act (*Gloucestershire NHS Primary Care Trust 2007*). Likewise, a man sought a copy of a report by a hospital consultant about the care of his late mother. The trust stated it would disclose under the 1990 Act if he provided proof that he was his dead mother's personal representative; it asked to see a copy of his birth certificate as proof. He failed to produce this and gave no reasons for not doing so; he sought the information instead under the 2000 Act. The Information Commissioner held that the trust was exempt from disclosing under s.21. The request of proof by the trust, under the 1990 Act, was reasonable (*Liverpool Women's NHS Foundation Trust 2007*). In the following case the duty of confidence to a dead man and his family meant that the information about his death was exempt from disclosure:

Internal reports about death of patient: exempt from disclosure. A request was made for internal reports into the circumstances surrounding the death of a patient. The information had come from medical records and interviews with relevant health professionals, from the police and from the coroner. Thus, under s.41, it had been obtained by a public body from somebody else. The Information Commissioner noted that the duty of confidence to the patient survived death, and that there was an obligation of confidence created by the patient/doctor relationship. A breach of confidence action would have been possible if disclosure took place. The exemption applied under s.41; and no public interest outweighed the duty of confidentiality in terms of (a) the confider consenting; (b) disclosure required by law; or (c) a public interest in disclosure overriding the duty of confidence. Exemption was also justified under s.40, because in the reports there was a small amount of information comprising personal information about the man's family. Because of the sensitivity of the information and the subject, it would have been unfair under the first data protection principle to disclose (*East London and The City Mental Health NHS Trust 2007*).

10.5.6 EXEMPTION ON BASIS OF LEGAL PRIVILEGE

A qualified exemption applies to information subject to legal professional privilege (s.42). Although this is not absolute, the Information Tribunal has noted that there is a strong element of public interest built into the privilege and that an equally strong consideration would be required to override it (*Bellamy v Information Commissioner 2006*). In a case involving social services and members of his family, the applicant sought disclosure records, transactions and memoranda. Following intervention by the Information Commissioner, these were disclosed, but not the barrister's advice given to the council. The Information Tribunal upheld this non-disclosure under s.42, noting that the powerful arguments in favour of legal privilege can be outweighed exceptionally in the public interest – but not in this case (*Kitchener v Information Commissioner and Derby City Council 2006*). However, identifying exactly to what the legal privilege attaches will not always be straightforward, as the following Information Tribunal case illustrates:

Solicitors' papers about suicide of an NHS patient: varied status. A woman sought information in relation to the death of her son, after he had jumped from a fourth floor window, having discharged himself from the care of an NHS trust earlier in the day. Amongst the information sought were papers lodged with three sets of solicitors. The trust resisted disclosure on the basis either of legal professional privilege – or that the papers held by the legal firms were not owned by, and held on behalf of, the trust, but were owned by the solicitors. In which case, they would not come under the Freedom of Information Act at all.

Of the three sets of papers, the Tribunal found that the first did not belong to the trust, the second were covered by legal professional privilege (the Tribunal emphasised the strength and public importance of this exemption, even though it is qualified rather than absolute) - and the third set of papers were not privileged (because they would have been made available to all parties at the inquest, in which case the privilege is waived), did belong to the trust and so should be disclosed (*Francis v Information Commissioner* 2008).

10.5.7 PROHIBITION ON DISCLOSURE

Under s.44 of the 2000 Act, there is an absolute exemption on certain grounds including prohibition by other legislation. So, in relation to a complaint about an NHS trust, information was sought from the health service ombudsman who had investigated the complaint, in particular transcripts of certain interviews. However, s.15 of the Health Service Commissioners Act 1993 contains a statutory bar on disclosure by the health service ombudsman of information obtained in an investigation, except in limited situations. Thus, the Information Tribunal held that the information was exempt from disclosure under s.44 of the 2000 Act because of this prohibition in the 1993 Act (*Parker v Information Commissioner and Health Service Ombudsman 2007*).

10.5.8 COMPLIANCE EXCEEDING COST LIMIT

Under s.12 of the Freedom of Information Act 2000, the public body does not have to comply with a request to disclose if the cost of complying would exceed the appropriate cost limit, which is set in regulations and is currently £600 (SI 2004/3244). Thus, the following request, relevant to adult protection and safeguarding matters, failed:

Mistreatment, abuse and neglect: compliance request for details of complaints made would exceed the appropriate cost limit. The information sought revolved around complaints of mistreatment, neglect and abuse on NHS trust premises. The request asked for details of complaints made by patients, relatives and staff involving such issues and in particular hydration, nutrition, inappropriate use of diamorphine or potassium chloride, 'do not resuscitate' and 'not for intensive therapy' instructions. The NHS trust declined to disclose arguing that to do so would mean exceeding the appropriate limit under s.12 (at that time, £450). It explained that complaints records were indexed alphabetically by patient, not by the nature of type of the complaint. The request would involve combing each complaints file for its contents. The Information Commissioner accepted the trust's argument; there were some 10,000 complaints files (*Swansea NHS Trust 2006*).

10.5.9 INFORMATION REASONABLY ACCESSIBLE BY OTHER MEANS

Under s.21 of the 2000 Act, an exemption applies if the information sought is reasonably accessible by other means, and from a public authority with an obligation to provide it. For instance, this exemption will sometimes apply to disclosure of medical records of deceased people under the Access to Health Records Act 1990 (see 10.5.5.1). It also applied when a man wanted to obtain the background, details and legal basis for removal of his mother from hospital to a residential home where she subsequently died. The local authority argued that it had already disclosed this information in previous correspondence and reports produced in response to the man's complaints. Both the Information Commissioner and then, on appeal, the Information Tribunal, agreed with the local authority and held that s.21 applied (*Prior v Information Commissioner 2006*).

10.5.10 VEXATIOUS REQUESTS

Under s.14 of the Freedom of Information Act 2000, a public body does not have to comply with a vexatious request. Guidance from the Information Commissioner refers to such a request having no serious purpose or value, designed to cause disruption and annoyance, harassing the public body, being obsessive or manifestly unreasonable (IC 2007).

So, when an Age Concern volunteer obsessively pursued information about a woman's care plan drawn up by a local authority and the charges she had paid for that care, the Information Commissioner held that the local authority had correctly refused on grounds of vexatiousness (*Norfolk County Council 2007*). The Information Tribunal upheld the decision but gave a few pointers about vexatiousness:

Information about alleged overcharging in respect of community care services. At the outset, the matters raised by the volunteer did show that the elderly woman was being overcharged, and the matter was rectified by the council. However, the volunteer believed that there were further irregularities. Overall, he went on to write to the local authority 73 letters and 17 postcards, and made twenty freedom of information requests. The allegations were investigated by an independent complaints investigator and the Commission for Social Care Inspection; the volunteer did not believe the veracity of these investigations. The police had also advised Age Concern that there was no evidence of dishonesty. At this point, the Tribunal noted, the volunteer should have let the matter drop.

However, the Tribunal did caution against over-simple application of the Information Commissioner's guidance on vexatiousness. For example, the Tribunal could imagine circumstances in which a request creates a significant burden and indeed harasses a public body – but nonetheless could have a serious and proper purpose and so should not be considered vexatious (*Coggins v Information Commissioner 2008*).

However, in another case, an NHS trust (which garnered notoriety later in 2007: see 4.2.3 above) wrongly dismissed as vexatious an information request concerning correspondence between the trust and the coroner, about the death of the man's wife. The man had to make a significant number of requests, partly because the trust's responses were confusing. The Information Commissioner held that the requests were not vexatious. However, the particular request for which the trust had wrongly cited s.14 was the coroner's report; by virtue of s.32 of the Act (documents held by the public body deriving from a court or inquiry), such disclosure was exempt (*Maidstone and Tunbridge Wells NHS Trust 2007*).

10.6 PROCESSING PERSONAL INFORMATION: CALDICOTT GUARDIANS

The Department of Health issued guidance to local social services authorities, expecting them to have appointed by April 2002 a 'Caldicott Guardian'. The function of this person is to safeguard and govern the use made of confidential information, particularly in respect of the requirements of the Data Protection Act 1998, including the processing, sharing and security of confidential information (LAC(2002)2). Caldicott Guardians had already been introduced to the NHS at an earlier date.

Adult protection: procedural aspects

KEY POINTS

Safeguarding adults inevitably involves many procedural aspects. It is beyond the scope of this book to consider these in detail, other than where they have a legal or quasi-legal association. This chapter gives a number of examples in relation to local authorities and the NHS.

These include, for instance, matters relating to failure to implement relevant procedures, failure to report incidents or allegations, failure to investigate, failure to investigate adequately, limits on local authority legal powers to intervene, fairness and even-handedness (in relation to alleged victims and alleged perpetrators), and having sufficient evidence in proportion to the intervention proposed or implemented. Whilst the safeguarding of adults clearly has to be taken extremely seriously, nonetheless disproportionate and unevidenced interventions have at the same time to be guarded against. This of course is not just to do with fairness to an alleged perpetrator, but also with the welfare of vulnerable adults – since an ill considered intervention may result in more harm than good.

Also outlined are some of the factors considered by the Crown Prosecution Service in deciding about prosecutions under criminal law, evidence-giving by vulnerable adults including those with doubtful capacity – as well as the special measures and assistance that in principle are available to vulnerable witnesses in criminal proceedings.

11.1 LOCAL AUTHORITIES AND THE NHS: SAFEGUARDING PROCEDURES AND INVESTIGATIONS

Clearly, effective investigations will be a crucial part of a local authority's safeguarding adults activity. The following local ombudsman cases illustrate failures in policies, procedures and such investigations. One concerned a gift to a carer and the question of whether undue influence had been exercised:

Bequest to council carer. In 1984, guidance on the receipt of gifts from service users was issued to its staff by a local authority; in 1990 a further instruction was issued. However, in the case of one particular carer (against whom the complaint of undue influence had been made), it could not be shown that she had received either the guidance or further instruction. She was not asked to sign a record that she had done so. This in itself was maladministration.

The carer was left a significant amount of money in the will of one of the service users for whom she provided care, and had also received £1000 as a lifetime gift. When the service user died, her grand-daughter complained to the council that the bequest and gift had been procured by undue influence.

The local ombudsman found maladministration on a number of grounds; one was that the local authority did not investigate the complaint for three years; when it did so, its response was inadequate since it sought no evidence from third parties who might have contributed the relevant evidence (*Suffolk CC 2001*).

A second case involved a failure to investigate the physical injuries received by a severely brain damaged woman at a local authority run centre:

Failure in investigation and response to abuse. The parents of a severely brain damaged 30-year-old woman complained that she had been injured on two occasions when receiving respite care at a facility run by the local authority.

The local ombudsman found maladministration in the council's response. On the first occasion, it did not consider whether to hold an investigation; on the second, it did investigate but did not identify the perpetrator – even though there was no doubt that the injuries were inflicted deliberately (although poor record-keeping and failure to communicate and implement the revised care plan were uncovered). The parents understandably withdrew their daughter from the centre. It was then maladministration for the authority not to have considered alternative respite care for the woman at an earlier date, even if this meant spending scarce extra resources; since it still had a statutory duty to meet her needs (*Bedfordshire CC 2003*).

In a third case, even a catalogue of injuries suffered by the service user, and assaults by staff, did not result in either the woman's father or police being informed:

Failure to report assaults. A woman had been placed by the local authority in a care home (owned by a housing association but staffed by council employees). She was blind, of partial hearing, had virtually no speech and had severe learning difficulties. She weighed six stone. Over a period of 18 months, she suffered a catalogue of injuries including a fractured skull, broken fingers, cuts and bruises. She was assaulted by two members of staff.

The local ombudsman found maladministration; the local authority had provided deficient care, delayed telling the father about his daughter's fractured skull, failed to tell the woman's father or the police about the assaults on her, and had amended the investigator's report without consulting the investigator (who stated that her integrity had been compromised, and that she could no longer work for the council) (*Southwark LBC 2001a*).

In a fourth case, gathering information (about alleged physical abuse) from council officers but not seeking the views of other people who had known the person concerned, and not gathering medical evidence, was maladministration (*Wakefield MDC 1997*). The consequence of not following adult protection procedures might simply result in people's needs not being met:

Staff failure to follow adult protection procedures. A complaint was made to the local ombudsman. A woman with learning disabilities was increasingly at loggerheads with her parents about her life. Despite awareness of this, the local authority had failed to complete a care plan that might have hit on a reasonable compromise between daughter and parents.

She now specifically alleged that her parents, with whom she lived, hit her, locked her in her room, and prevented her from seeing her friends. The local authority had a clear written policy and procedure for dealing with abuse allegations. The procedure required immediate action to determine the risk involved and to assess needs of both disabled person and carers. The policy was not followed; the consequence was that the woman left home in an unplanned and precipitous manner and ended up in unsuitable accommodation with someone who lacked the skill to meet her needs. This was maladministration (*Cumbria CC 2000a*).

When allegations of sexual assault were made by a woman with learning disabilities, the response of the primary care trust and the local authority betrayed a failure to take the allegations seriously:

Failure to respond to allegations of sexual assault at a respite facility. Allegations were made by a woman with Down's syndrome, epilepsy and scoliosis of the spine that she had been sexually assaulted at a respite facility run the by the local NHS primary care trust. The facility was unsupervised at the time. PCT staff did not contact social services until two weeks later. Neither agency contacted the police.

An investigation by a manager did not include an interview with the mother. His report referred to reports from other professionals, but there was no record of those on file, nor a record of how the investigation was conducted. There was no evidence as to how his report's conclusions were reached.

The complaints investigator, appointed later, did not consider the council had taken the incident seriously. The ombudsman agreed with this. In addition, the woman's behaviour had significantly changed and she could not tolerate meeting the other service user who had allegedly abused her. Yet the council failed to carry out a new community care assessment promptly. The ombudsman also had concerns that the woman's care managers had seen very little of the woman herself. All this was maladministration (*Bromley LBC 2004*).

Alternatively, the council might take matters too far without the safeguard of adequate procedures, as in the following case about alleged financial abuse:

Unsubstantiated allegations and information disclosure procedures. A local authority disclosed information to a woman's employer concerning unsubstantiated allegations made by a third party of financial abuse by the woman of a vulnerable adult. The local ombudsman investigated; the council agreed a settlement whereby it would send a letter of apology, make a token payment of £250, seek the woman's permission to send copies of the apology to her employer, review its policy and procedures on disclosure of information and inform her of the outcome. The local authority then delayed in changing its policy and procedures; and its failure to make any contact with the woman about this or with the ombudsman was inexcusable and maladministration (*Kirklees MBC 2002*).

The following case, investigated by the local government ombudsman, involved blatant failure by the council properly to investigate serious allegations. One of the reasons given by a council officer was that a full investigation did not take place because it was a council owned and managed scheme, as opposed to one run by the independent sector:

Bullying, harassment in sheltered housing scheme: failure of adult protection procedures. Two neighbours, living in council-owned sheltered accommodation, complained about their treatment by the warden. They alleged that they were being bullied, harassed, intimidated, humiliated and abused. In the end both felt forced to move away from their home town because the council failed to follow its adult protection procedures and sort the problem out.

The council did offer some help by changing the locks on their flat, putting in an additional employee, paying for washing machines in their flats (there had been problems about using the communal laundry room), giving out a senior manager's mobile phone number, temporarily moving them into a hotel and rehousing them. However, the ombudsman found this bizarre, because the local authority failed to investigate the serious allegations that had been made. The evidence was compelling; it included a tape of the threats the two residents had received from the warden's daughter; even the ombudsman's investigator found this harrowing and deeply distressing when listening to it.

The ombudsman found maladministration. The authority had failed to follow its own procedures and (a) to meet its timescale of 15 days to complete an investigation, (b) to retain the notification and outcome records, (c) construct an appropriate investigation team, (d) set the remit and give direction to the POVA meetings, and (e) ensure that monitoring and review arrangements were clearly identified. Worse than this procedural failing was the substantive failure to undertake a proper investigation into serious allegations about an employee (the warden) responsible for vulnerable people, in the face of very persuasive evidence. This was maladministration with 'potentially very serious consequence'.

The ombudsman made a long list of recommendations. These included giving the two complainants priority for rehousing if they wished to return to their home town, making and paying for any moving arrangements, paying all the costs incurred in moving out of the sheltered housing, paying each an additional £2500 for their time, trouble and distress. The council should also seek advice on staff disciplinary issues, review the role and job descriptions of wardens, examine why its adult protection procedures failed to work, consider whether to amend them, and report back to the ombudsman in six months (*South Tyneside MBC 2008*).

11.1.1 NHS: SAFEGUARDING PROCEDURES

Adult protection work is described in Department of Health guidance as being essentially multi-agency in nature; in the following case the health service ombudsman found fault with the NHS for inadequate procedures:

Rough handling. An elderly woman was admitted to hospital for repair of a fractured hip. She told her daughter that on Christmas Day a member of the night staff treated her roughly when attending to her because of vomiting and diarrhoea. Now she was frightened. The daughter made an oral complaint. The ward manager investigated and interviewed the staff member, but did not tell the daughter of the result of the investigation. The daughter then made a formal complaint; the trust apologised for not telling mother and daughter the outcome of the investigation.

The health service ombudsman found that the trust's complaints procedures and documentation were deficient; and that the trust had failed to realise that the mother and daughter viewed the incident as an assault. As such, the trust had not responded sufficiently robustly, and should review its complaints policy in the light of the Department of Health's guidance *No secrets* (DH 2000) (*Warrington Hospital NHS Trust 2001*).

Very much more major failings in procedures seemed to emerge from the findings of a serious case review of the murder of a man with learning disabilities in Cornwall. Noting the lack of statutory obligation on the NHS in respect of adult protection, the chair made a number of observations:

NHS failing to give adult protection alert. In this particular case, the vulnerable adult who was killed was an intensive user of emergency, primary care and mental health services. In addition, the man who would eventually commit the murder had moved into the vulnerable person's bedsit. The perpetrator himself had made 24 calls to ambulance services in the year before the vulnerable adult's death, eight visits to accident and emergency, seven visits to minor injury units, 15 GP consultations and 21 calls to out-of-hours doctors. Despite the perpetrator's close proximity to the vulnerable adult concerned, and the fact that the ambulance service knew he was dangerous and requested a police presence when it attended, nonetheless adult protection procedure were not triggered by the NHS.

After he had ceased contact with social services, the vulnerable adult's visits to primary care increased; even when he told NHS staff he had been assaulted, he went home alone and with no adult protection alert. NHS staff appeared not to regard themselves as 'alerters', even though they knew that he was drinking to excess – and despite the British Medical Association's guidelines that in the case of a vulnerable adult, protection should take precedence over confidentiality (Flynn 2008).

11.2 INTER-AUTHORITY PROTOCOL

The Association of Directors of Social Services published a protocol outlining the responsibilities of local authorities when cross-boundary issues arose in adult protection cases. In summary, it makes clear that the authority where abuse occurs (the host authority) will have overall responsibility for coordinating the adult protection arrangements. However, the placing authority will have a continuing duty of care to the vulnerable adult; should ensure that provider has arrangements in place to protect vulnerable adults; and will provide necessary support and information for the host authority to enable a prompt and thorough investigation to take place (ADSS 2004, para 3).

11.3 IDENTIFYING LIMITS TO INTERVENTION

When abuse (or simply neglect without accompanying abuse) is identified or suspected, there is sometimes uncertainty about what interventions might be appropriate to protect the person involved. The general position is that a statutory intervention must be used –

that is, an intervention based on a duty or power given in legislation. The intervention might be one grounded in social services legislation (e.g. advice, information, support, care services); it might alternatively be based elsewhere, for instance, in environmental health, criminal justice or family law.

If the person being abused is refusing assistance, further questions arise about which statutory interventions can be used irrespective of a person's wishes or ability to consent. For instance, in the case of a person lacking the capacity to decide, or consent to, the relevant matters, a possible intervention comes under the Mental Capacity Act 2005 (see Chapter 6).

In other circumstances, there may be limits to what a local authority can do, notwithstanding its leading role in adult protection. In the following case, concerning a prospective suicide, the judge set out in some detail what could be expected:

Assisted suicide and adult protection procedures. A woman was suffering from cerebellar ataxia; the condition was incurable and irreversible; it attacked that part of the brain controlling the body's motor functions. She had become increasingly disabled. She wished to be assisted to commit suicide; her family was initially opposed to this. Now, reluctantly, her family had decided to support her wishes. Her husband informed the local authority, which had been providing extensive support for his wife, that he was arranging to take her to Switzerland where assisted suicide is not a criminal offence.

The local authority applied to the courts for exercise of the inherent jurisdiction; an injunction was initially granted restraining the husband from removing his wife to Switzerland. The court then subsequently considered the situation. It concluded that the adult protection duties of the local authorities were as follows:

- to investigate the position of the vulnerable adult to consider her true position and intention
- to consider whether she was legally competent to make and carry out her decision and intention
- to consider whether (or what) influence may have been operating on her position and intention and to ensure that she had all the relevant information and knew all available options
- to consider whether to invoke the inherent jurisdiction of the courts to decide about the issue of her competence
- if she was not competent, to provide assistance in her best interests
- if she was competent, to allow her in any lawful way to give effect to her decision, although this should not preclude advice or assistance being given about what are perceived to be her best interests
- to inform the police if there were reasonable grounds for suspecting that a criminal offence would be involved
- in very exceptional circumstances only, to seek an injunction from the courts using s.222 of the Local Government Act 1972.

By the time of the hearing, it had become quite clear that the woman had legal competence to take the decision. The court concluded that the local authority's duties extended no further than the above list; and that the authority had no obligation to seek a continuation of an injunction under s.222; criminal justice agencies had all the powers. For its part, unless it was under an obligation, the local authority anyway did not wish to do so.

Nor would the court, of its own motion, continue the injunction where no-one else with the necessary standing was seeking such an order, where the criminal justice agencies had the requisite knowledge and power, and where the effect of the injunction would be to 'deny a right to a seriously disabled but competent person that cannot be exercised herself by reason only of her physical disability' (Re Z).

11.4 LOCAL AUTHORITY INVESTIGATIONS AND RESPONSES: STRIKING THE RIGHT BALANCE

Safeguarding and protecting vulnerable adults seem to be gaining a higher profile, certainly in the work that local social services authorities carry out. Nevertheless, as ever, a balance is required in a number of respects.

For instance, a court case (albeit prior to the implementation of the Protection of Vulnerable Adults list) showed the potential human and legal consequences of what the court regarded as an overreaction – leading to breach of the principle of good faith in employment contracts and to financial compensation payable for psychiatric personal injury to the member of staff concerned who had effectively been wrongly accused of abuse:

Suspension, and breach of employment contract. A residential social worker was suspended following potential allegations made by a child with learning and communication difficulties. Following a 'strategy meeting', a decision was taken to hold an investigation under s.47 of the Children Act 1989. The investigation concluded that the child had never disclosed any abuse in relation to any member of staff, and while in therapy had never said anything that could be construed as an allegation of abuse. The social worker was immediately reinstated; but by then she was ill and had by and large not worked since the suspension. She claimed loss of earnings and damages for personal injury caused by breach of contract; she now suffered from clinical depression caused by the suspension.

The court held that it was quite proper for the local authority to investigate and make inquiries; but it did not necessarily follow that a member of staff, who may have been implicated in the risk to the vulnerable person, had to be suspended. The question should be whether, in the individual circumstances, it was reasonable and proper to do so. The court thought not. The strategy meeting had itself recognised that the information was 'difficult to evaluate' and to describe it as an allegation of abuse was putting it 'far too high'. The court also asked whether there were not other alternatives, such as a short period of leave or a transfer to other useful work.

Instead there had been a 'knee-jerk' reaction. The local authority had seriously damaged the relationship of trust and confidence between employee and employer – a relationship implied into contracts of employment. The claimant was entitled to damages (Gogay v Hertfordshire CC).

Other examples, although not related to the adult POVA list, also serve as reminders that care must be taken not to act unfairly to the detriment of care workers. Sometimes libel proceedings might result:

Malicious actions of review team on child abuse. The two claimants were nursery nurses. They had been suspended and then dismissed for gross misconduct involving child abuse. They were acquitted at trial. The council investigated and set up an independent review. The review concluded the two were guilty of serious abuse; 743 copies of the report were distributed by the council. The claimants brought libel proceedings. The judge found that the review team had acted maliciously by making a number of claims it would have known were untrue. The terms of appointment, and the methodology, of the review team were wholly unsuited to the task in hand. Elementary safeguards for the accused had been omitted, and the principles of natural justice had been overlooked. The claim succeeded against the review team, but not against the council (*Lillie v Newcastle CC*).

The following local ombudsman case, involving legal action (for defamation), uncovered a situation whereby a relative who had raised adult protection issues, concerning his sister-in-law who had learning disabilities, was in turn made the subject of unsubstantiated allegations that the local authority too readily took at face value:

Unsubstantiated allegations. The sister and brother-in-law of a woman with learning disabilities complained that she had suffered abuse at two care homes. In the course of a long and protracted dispute, the owner of one of the care homes made unsubstantiated allegations about the behaviour of the brother-in-law – involving drunkenness, sexual misconduct and racist behaviour. A report by the council's registration and inspection unit repeated the allegations; the report came into the hands of members of another part of the family, which promptly ostracised the brother-in-law. The council wrote to the brother-in-law, repeating the allegations as if they were fact; he regarded the letter as defamatory.

The allegations were finally investigated and found to be without substance; subsequent legal action for defamation was settled by payment of a considerable sum of money, and agreement by the council to purge its records and to pay legal costs. In the end, the ombudsman found that abuse had not in fact been suffered by the sister, but he was appalled at the 'almost complete lack of planning' behind one placement, and the lack of reasonable social care work that went into it. It was more by luck than judgement that no harm befell her (*Bromley LBC 2003*).

However, the courts will not necessarily rush into finding libel. For instance, an NHS trust emailed another, in response to a request by the second trust, and raised concerns about a doctor's professionalism. The doctor brought a libel action, but a summary judgement was made against him, and the case never proceeded to trial. The judge found that the email was protected by 'qualified privilege' and was not malicious. Given that it was a serious issue of public safety, involving questions of competence, integrity and professionalism, it was not only relevant that the information had been provided, it had been positively called for (*Akinleye v East Sussex Hospitals NHS Trust*).

11.4.1 SUPPORTING EVIDENCE

In their eagerness to take safeguarding of adults seriously, local authorities still have to weigh up both the evidence, and also what would constitute a proportionate response in relation to the risk of harm involved.

For instance, the courts have sometimes been less than impressed with the evidence of abuse put forward by local authorities. In one case, it appeared that the local authority had come close to scraping the bottom of the barrel by dredging up old and largely unsubstantiated allegations concerning abuse by a father against his daughter with learning disabilities. The court largely discounted this evidence, finding most of it not made out. However, the order sought by the local authority (to accommodate the daughter elsewhere) was given – albeit on general welfare, rather than abuse, grounds (*Newham LBC v BS*).

In another case, in which a local authority sought an order preventing a woman interfering with her husband's removal to hospital in his best interests, it sought to bolster its
case with allegations that she abused him. The court criticised the local authority for
acting 'in breach of its duties of full disclosure and fairness'. It had failed to particularise
the allegations, to support them with evidence, and to give a more balanced account. For
instance, explanation was lacking about how the incidents were raised with the wife or
why they were not raised with her – and about why, if they had occurred, he had previously continued to be cared for at home. In addition, reference was not made to the good
aspects of her care of, and relationship with, her husband. Particularly in the light of this
unbalanced approach by the local authority, the court cautioned that without notice
orders – that is, not giving the other side a chance to dispute or respond at the time the
order is made – should be exceptional. The court gave the order but on general welfare
grounds, rather than on the allegations of abuse (*B Borough Council v Mrs S*).

The concern about such without notice orders arose more pointedly in a subsequent
case, in which the local authority went badly wrong with its evidence. This involved
another without notice application, with the local authority seeking an order to transfer a
78-year-old man with dementia out of the care of his daughter and grand-daughter into a
care home. He lacked capacity to decide for himself. The first court hearing had granted
the without notice order to this effect. At a second court hearing, the family challenged
the making of that without notice application in the first hearing. It transpired that virtually all the allegations, with which the local authority had justified its initial application,
were incorrect:

Without notice application lacking evidence. A local authority sought a without notice order
to transfer a man away from the care of his relatives (daughter and grand-daughter) into a care home.
They did so on the basis that (a) the relatives had obstructed a full 'mini-mental state examination'; (b)
his previous care home placement had been terminated by the care home because of the verbally
abusive and threatening behaviour of the two relatives; (c) he had been assessed during a hospital stay
as requiring 24-hour care in a nursing home; (d) the two relatives had removed him from hospital; (e)
the relatives lived in a one-bedroom flat in which it would clearly be unsuitable for him to stay; (f) he
had complex care needs; (g) his problematic diabetes required careful control but the relatives gave
him unsuitable food; and (h) he would be at serious risk of harm in the care of the relatives.

Allegations unfounded. The judge found virtually all of these grounds had not been made out. The
evidence did not support the claim about the mini-mental state examination. The evidence about the
behaviour in the care home might have been established but it was highly regrettable that the local
authority did not obtain first hand behaviour about the family's behaviour.

The assessment, concerning the need for 24-hour nursing home care, was found by the judge to
have fallen short of a 'genuine and reasonable attempt to carry out a full assessment of the capacity of
the family to meet the relative's needs in the community'. The authority had not in fact carried out
such an assessment. When a thorough assessment was finally carried out, it concluded that he could in
fact be cared for in the community by his relatives.

It also transpired that the relatives had not in fact removed him from hospital. He had instead
been discharged by the hospital itself, and this had followed the non-attendance by a social worker at a
case conference. The social worker had instead opted for court action.

The flat turned out not to have one bedroom; in fact it had two. The men clearly did have complex needs, but they did not necessarily rule out care in the community.

And, on the question of diet, the local authority had claimed that he was regularly fed inappropriately by the relatives. In fact no evidence was produced to the court about this. The relatives had received training and, by the time of the court case, when he was in the care of his relatives, his diabetes was now more stable than it had been in the care home.

Without notice application not justified. The judge concluded that given the standoff with the family at the relevant time, a period in the care home might have been justified had the application been made by means of an 'on notice' order. However, a without notice process was not justified. The judge also noted that although a without notice order gives 'liberty to apply' to the other party, for relatives this may mean little. It should be spelt out to the other party that they can challenge the order.

Local authority's change of view about the man's bests interests. Finally, the judge pointed out that the final allegation, that he would be at serious risk of harm in the care of his relatives, was nonsense – given that by the time of the second court hearing, all were agreed (even the local authority) that his best interests would be served by living with his relatives. The judge pinpointed the core issue as being lack of communication on the part of the local authority, and the failure by the relatives to make themselves physically and emotionally available to receive any communication (*LLBC v TG*).

11.4.2 PROPORTIONATE RESPONSE

Local authorities may have to judge what constitutes a proportionate response in relation to the risk of harm involved. Sometimes matters may become more complicated when competing risks are in issue.

Thus, when councils act decisively in relation to adult protection, they need to be careful to ensure that they keep in focus the overall welfare of the service user. For instance, in the local ombudsman investigation immediately below, safeguarding concerns were responded to swiftly but in such a way that arguably placed the woman's welfare at risk, and might or might not have contributed to her death three days later. The case is worth summarising at some length, since it is illustrative of the difficult decisions sometimes facing local authority staff:

Judging a proportionate response to alleged abuse. A severely physically disabled woman of 26 years lived with her parents. She suffered from spinal muscular atrophy, had severe curvature of the spine and was unable to use her legs. Her mother (and father) had always been her main carer. She had specialist equipment and adaptations including a special ripple mattress, a customised electric wheelchair, a special alarm system, a wheelchair accessible bathroom, a bath cushion, and an adapted toilet seat. She was liable to chest infections, and care had to be taken with her posture both during the day in the wheelchair and during the night; sometimes her mother adjusted her position (but did not turn her over) in bed several times a night.

Alleged taking of money and slap. The woman attended a day centre run by a voluntary body on behalf of social services. This particular day she was upset and explained to the manager of the centre that her mother had taken money from her bank account without her permission; and that when she had found out she had an argument with her mother who had slapped her legs.

Emergency placement organised. The centre manager contacted a social worker who knew the woman. The woman was adamant that she did not want to return home. The mother arrived to collect her daughter but was told that the latter did not want to return home, although not about the allegations. The mother went away and subsequently refused to return to the centre. The social worker talked to his manager and decided to arrange an emergency residential placement. A care home was identified that provided for people with severe physical disabilities.

Transport arrangements. The centre arranged transport to the home, though there was not an escort in the van; the social worker drove behind most of the way. On the way, they collected various belongings from the woman's home; the mother said she was not asked about any equipment her daughter might need or about her care needs. The journey lasted much longer than expected (some two hours) because of traffic jams on the M25.

First night in care home, sickness and death three days later. The woman spent her first night in the care home. She did not have a ripple mattress; a baby alarm was fixed up for her because she could not operate the emergency buzzer system. The notes stated that she needed turning several times a night. In the morning she felt uncomfortable, felt sick, frail and unwell and wanted to go home. Her parents arrived to collect her. She died of bronchial pneumonia three days later.

Making enquiries before the placement. The local ombudsman pointed out that the mother had given unstinting care and love to her daughter all her life; that the daughter had been upset and that the local authority staff had been right to take her distress seriously. However, it was maladministration not to make proper enquiries before the placement and before deciding that the woman should travel without an escort. In particular the woman's general practitioner and occupational therapist should have been consulted. This might have resulted in the placement going ahead, an alternative placement, or her going back home. In any event the ombudsman was not satisfied that she might still not have contracted the chest infection; thus he could not blame the council for her death.

Considering a complicated case at a 'deep level'. The ombudsman also agreed with the view expressed by the local authority manager who had led the investigation into the events, that the staff involved had failed to recognise at a 'deep level' that the woman's case was 'problematic'. They should have realised that only her parents had ever looked after her, and that despite her being articulate and intellectually able, they should have talked to the GP and occupational therapist. They had also taken the woman's statements as 'absolute' without attempting to verify what had been said. The care home should have been checked for appropriate equipment, and also for its ability to assess the woman's needs, given that the local authority staff involved on the day knew little about her needs. Staff should have sensed that the case was 'more complicated than most'. Furthermore, he felt that the woman should have been accompanied in the vehicle during the trip to the care home (*Kent CC 1999*).

Likewise, in the next case, the local ombudsman recognised the importance of adult protection policies, but reminded the local authority not to forget the needs and welfare of individual service users – which might call for exceptions to be made to an otherwise sensible policy:

Blanket policy on visits to staff's homes. A local authority implemented a new policy, debarring social services staff from taking clients to their homes. The ombudsman recognised the persuasive arguments in favour of such a policy. However, it meant that a woman with learning difficulties could no longer spend seven hours a week with a family aide, employed by social services. Her parents complained that this arrangement had always worked well and was an essential part of meeting their daughter's needs; furthermore the change had now made her unhappy. The ombudsman concluded that the council fettered its discretion by applying the policy so rigidly that it gave no consideration to the individual circumstances of the case. Furthermore, before making the change, the local authority had failed to reassess the woman's needs and to consult with her parents. All this was maladministration (*Carmarthenshire CC 1999*).

In the following case, the Care Standards Tribunal considered the reaction of the Commission for Social Care Inspection (CSCI) and three local authorities to adult protection concerns at a care home. It found CSCI's reaction to have been disproportionate, and that the local authorities who had placed residents in the home were excessively influenced by CSCI. The result was that the rights and welfare of the residents of the care home were not given sufficient attention, and they ended up being removed from the home without due procedure and not in their best interests. The case is worth summarising in greater detail, illustrating the fine line between protection and over-reaction and also to illustrate the apparently sometimes unsatisfactory interaction between local authorities and the CSCI:

Over-reaction to adult protection concerns at care home. A number of issues had arisen concerning the registration of a care home, in particular about the varying of registration conditions in relation to the category type of resident permitted to be admitted to the home. Amongst the matters raised by the CSCI were adult protection concerns.

These concerns related to a member of staff who had answered the door to an unannounced inspection, but who at the time was provisionally included on the POVA list and so was barred from working with vulnerable adults. The care worker explained that she had been told that she could do administrative work as long as she did not have contact with residents (i.e. in a non-care position). The provider of the home (the appellant), who was on holiday in Nigeria (a) claimed he did not know of the provisional listing before he went on holiday, and (b) that the care worker had told him that she was unwell, and so he had anyway not expected her to be at work that week.

On that occasion, the inspector noted that there was no significant risk to residents but that management cover was needed. Six days later, another CSCI visit took place to check compliance with this, and took the view that the management cover, in the form of an agency member of staff, was inadequate.

Adult protection meetings convened: factual inaccuracies; CSCI trawling for bizarre letters. The inspector on the second visit noted that a number of requirements from the last inspection report had still not been complied with (although the deadline set had not yet been reached). She also had concerns about management of the money of two of the residents (although the local authority's auditors were subsequently satisfied). As a result of this second visit, the CSCI initiated adult protection strategy meetings and recorded neglect and inappropriate financial management. (The Tribunal noted that the recorded assertion that 'neglect was evident' was factually inaccurate). The appellant was not informed of what was happening (this was normal practice).

The CSCI inspector also told the meeting that it would be helpful if each of the three local authorities (with placed residents) could provide copies of any 'bizarre letters' the appellant had sent, so that CSCI could use them as evidence to get him deregistered. Subsequently, CSCI admitted that it had expected all the local authorities to remove their residents and for the home to be closed.

Local authorities deeply influenced by CSCI; removal of residents without assessment of risk; residents and relatives not consulted; removal not in residents' best interests. The three local authorities concerned had had a good relationship with the home for some ten years. But once the adult protection procedures had been initiated, they reassessed their residents at the home to determine where it would be suitable to move them. However, these reassessments seemed just to be based on an assumption that that the residents needed to be moved; the Tribunal found no evidence that the local authorities had made their own assessment of the risk to their residents; the CSCI's concerns, as recorded in the minutes (with inaccuracies), were taken as read and acted on.

The Tribunal noted: 'There is no justification to move a resident against their will, as happened here, unless the placing local authority has determined for itself that the person for whom they have responsibility is at significant risk'. The placing authorities had been deeply influenced by the CSCI.

Furthermore, well-settled residents were removed by social workers without adequate consultation with the residents or their relatives. The Tribunal believed that, on the balance of probability, it was not in their best interests to have been moved.

Refusal of one resident to move and diversion of another. One resident in fact refused to move, although the local authority had removed and then kept his belongings for two months. It did not return these for two months, until asked by the manager of the home – who had been criticised by CSCI for the absence of these personal possessions. Also, at the time of the removals, one of the residents had had to attend a routine hospital appointment; on finding this out, the social worker involved stated that she would not be returning to the care home, and she was simply taken to another home on the spot.

Disproportionate reaction by the CSCI. On the adult protection issue, the Tribunal did 'not accept that there was sufficient cause or risk to commence an adult protection procedure'. To initiate it had been a 'disproportionate response" in relation to the risk posed to residents at the time. Overall, the Tribunal considered that the appellant displayed some management failings but that his record with carers and residents was good, as was his delivery of care. He had improved the home and engaged an experienced manager. The Tribunal held that the conditions of registration should be varied to admit one category, but not the other two categories of service user, sought by the appellant (*Onyerindu v Commission for Social Care Inspection*).

11.5 DECISION WHETHER TO PROSECUTE

The decision whether to prosecute under criminal law is one for the Crown Prosecution Service (CPS) to make. The CPS code refers to an evidential test, that is, whether there is enough evidence to provide a realistic prospect of conviction. The more serious the offence, the more likely will a prosecution be needed in the public interest. A number of factors make prosecution more likely including (a) whether the victim of the offence was vulnerable, and was put in considerable fear, or suffered personal attack, damage or disturbance; (b) whether the offence was motivated by any form of discrimination, including disability, ethnic or national origin; and (c) whether there was a marked difference between the actual or mental ages of the defendant and the victim, or if there was any element of corruption. However, prosecution may be less likely if:

- a nominal penalty only would be imposed
- the offence was on the basis of a genuine misunderstanding
- the loss or harm was minor and the result of a single incident (especially if caused by misjudgement)
- the prosecution is likely to have a bad effect on the victim's physical or mental health always bearing in mind the seriousness of the offence, or
- the defendant is elderly or is, or was at the time of the offence, suffering from significant mental or physical ill health, unless the offence is serious or there is a real possibility that it may be repeated.

The code also points out that the CPS prosecutes on behalf of the public and not just the victim; however, the consequences for the victim, of a decision to prosecute or not, should be taken into account, together with any views expressed by the victim, or the victim's family (CPS 2004, chapter 5).

Under s.146 of the Criminal Justice Act 2003, it is an aggravating feature of an offence – i.e. makes it more serious – if the offender showed hostility toward the victim based on the latter's disability, or if the offence was motivated by hostility toward people who have a disability. However, the CPS has pointed out that for s.146 to apply there does need to be that hostility. It applies where the offender assumes a person is disabled, even if that assumption is false. There is no statutory definition of a disability-related incident, but the Crown Prosecution Service takes it to mean 'any incident, which is perceived to be based upon prejudice towards or hatred of the victim because of their disability or so perceived by the victim or any other person' (CPS 2007a, para 2.2). Picking on a disabled person because he or she is an easy target would not in itself trigger s.146 (CPS 2007a, para 2.5.2; JCHR 2007, para 206).

Alternatively, under s.143 of the Criminal Justice Act 2003, the court must – in considering the seriousness of any offence – assess the offender's culpability in committing the offence and any harm which the offence caused, was intended to cause, or might foreseeably have caused. The Sentencing Guidelines Council notes that culpability will be greater where a vulnerable victim has been targeted because of age, youth, disability or the job they do. Relevant factors would also include abuse of power and abuse of a position of trust (SGC 2004, pp.5-6). In late 2007, the CPS published a draft document about prosecuting crimes against older people, proposing that a prosecution is likely to be in the public interest if:

- the offence is serious
- the defendant is in a position of trust or authority
- the offence is likely to be continued or repeated, the victim is vulnerable
- the victim is injured, the defendant was motivated by prejudice or discrimination based on the victim's age
- the defendant used a weapon
- the defendant made threats before or after the attack
- the defendant planned the attack
- there is a continuing threat to the health or safety of the victim or anyone else involved, or
- the defendant has a criminal history (CPS 2007, para 4.7).

In the following case the judge questioned whether the prosecution was in the public interest; there was also some implied criticism of social services:

Prosecution of elderly man for attempted murder of wife with Alzheimer's following dispute with social services. A distressed elderly man attempted to kill both himself and his wife following a dispute with a local authority over home care arrangements and manual handling. His wife suffered from Alzheimer's disease, was doubly incontinent and immobile. A prosecution for attempted murder was brought; the judge criticised the CPS for bringing the case, questioning whether it had been in the public interest to do so (R v Bouldstridge).

Evidence for a criminal prosecution or conviction may be lacking, but other measures might nonetheless be taken. For example, because of lack of evidence a care worker was both cleared of rape at trial and not prosecuted for a separate indecent assault. The alleged victims were elderly women at a mental health unit; however, following an investigation, the NHS trust employer still dismissed him for gross misconduct (Dayani 2004s).

Furthermore, although witnesses can be compelled to give evidence, the CPS might weigh up, in individual cases, whether such compulsion is likely to succeed. For example, some reluctant prosecution witnesses, particularly in cases of domestic abuse (e.g. wife and husband, father and son), may change their story at the last moment and become in effect witnesses hostile to the prosecution. The police may drop the investigation if the key witness (and alleged victim) simply refuses to cooperate – as was reported extensively in the case of a very disabled famous physicist and allegations about ill-treatment at the hands of his wife:

Allegations of cruelty not pursued because of non-cooperation of alleged victim. Statements were made by at least ten nurses or carers that a famous physicist, suffering from motor neurone disease, was subjected to cruelty by his wife. However, the police dropped the investigation, three years after the first allegations had been made. Most recently, he had been left in his wheelchair in the garden on the hottest day of the year and suffered severe heatstroke and sunburn. He had refused to answer any questions and threatened to sue the police for harassment. Consideration had been given to calling him to give evidence as a hostile witness, if medical evidence corroborated the allegations from the nurses and carers (Peek 2004; Fresco 2004; Peek 2004a).

11.6 CRIMINAL JUSTICE PROCEDURE: VULNERABLE WITNESSES AND SUSPECTS

A number of specialist rules and provisions apply to vulnerable adults, whether as suspects or witnesses. These include the 'appropriate adult' and other rules under the Police and Criminal Evidence Act 1984 in relation to suspects; special measures under the Youth Justice and Criminal Evidence Act 1999; and guidance on achieving 'best evidence' from witnesses.

In late 2007, the government consulted about improving access to health services and support for people in police custody who have physical and mental health needs (DH 2007). In the case of alleged perpetrators of a crime, a number of matters may have to be considered including mental disorder or vulnerability at time of interview, fitness to stand trial at the time of trial (Criminal Procedure (Insanity) Act 1964), the question of insanity at the time of the alleged offence (*M'Naghten's Case*) or at least of diminished responsibility (Homicide Act 1957, s.2), or mental disorder at the time of conviction (and the making of a hospital order under the Mental Health Act 1983).

11.6.1 POLICE AND CRIMINAL EVIDENCE ACT: PROVISION OF APPROPRIATE ADULT
The detention, treatment and questioning of suspects, who are vulnerable, by police officers is governed by special provisions, in particular the provision of an appropriate adult under Code of Practice C, made under the Police and Criminal Evidence Act 1984.

In summary only, if a police officer suspects or is told in good faith that a suspect of any age may be mentally disordered or mentally vulnerable – or mentally incapable of understanding the significance of questions or their replies – then the appropriate adult, and other protective provisions, apply.

In relation to a mentally disordered or vulnerable adult suspect, an appropriate adult means (a) a relative, guardian or somebody else responsible for their care or custody; or (b) someone who is experienced in dealing with mentally disordered or mentally vulnerable people; or (c) some other responsible adult over 18 who is not a police officer or employed by the police. (Guidance notes to the Code state that it may be more satisfactory if the appropriate adult is someone experienced or trained in the care of mentally disordered or mentally vulnerable adults; but if the detainee prefers a relative to a better qualified stranger, his or her wishes should, if practicable, be respected.)

Custody officers must inform the appropriate adult of the grounds for the detention, the whereabouts of the person, and ask the adult to come to the police station.

The custody officer must ensure a person receives appropriate clinical attention as soon as reasonably practicable if the person appears to be suffering from a mental disorder. It is imperative that a mentally disordered person detained under s.136 of the Mental Health Act 1983 be assessed as soon as possible.

If the person is cautioned in the absence of the appropriate adult, it must be repeated in the presence of the latter. The person must not be interviewed or asked to sign a written statement in the absence of the appropriate adult, unless the delay would be likely to lead to (a) interference with, or harm to, evidence connected with an offence; (b) interference with, or physical harm to, other people; (c) serious loss of, or damage to, property; (d) the alerting of other people suspected of an offence but not yet arrested; or (e) a hindering of the recovery of property related to an offence.

Present at the interview, appropriate adults must be informed that they are not expected to act simply as observer but are there to advise the interviewee, to observe whether the interview is being conducted properly and fairly, and to facilitate communication with the interviewee.

If the custody officer charges the person, this must be done in the presence of the appropriate adult. Particular care must be taken in deciding whether to use any form of approved restraint (Home Office 2008).

For example, in one case, the local government ombudsman found fault with the council when one of its service users in supported housing was interviewed by the police in respect of a theft he was alleged to have carried out. No appropriate adult was present, even though he was a vulnerable adult. The council conceded that he should have been treated as such and provided with support during the interview (*Stockport MBC 2006*).

11.6.2 VULNERABLE WITNESSES: SPECIAL ASSISTIVE MEASURES

Both legislation and guidance are aimed at providing assistance for vulnerable witnesses as well.

The Youth Justice and Criminal Evidence Act 1999 provides for special measures to be taken in the case of both vulnerable and intimidated witnesses. A vulnerable adult witness is defined as a person whose quality of evidence the court believes will be diminished by reason of (a) mental disorder or significant impairment of intelligence and social functioning; or (b) has a physical disability or is suffering from a physical disorder (Youth Justice and Criminal Evidence Act 1999, s.16).

The special measures listed include screening the witness from the accused, evidence by live link, evidence given in private, removal of wigs and gowns, video-recorded evidence in chief, video-recorded cross-examination or re-examination, examination of witness through intermediary, and aids to communication (ss.23–30; see also the rules on special measures directions in respect of magistrates' courts and crown courts: SI 2002/1687 and SI 2002/1688). The need for special measures should be investigated at the earliest stage by the police, the prosecutor and maybe by the witness care officer of the Crown Prosecution Service; but it is for the court to grant special measures (CPS 2007, para 8.7).

For instance, live link evidence was given in the following theft case by two women from their living room:

Giving live video link evidence from the living room. Two elderly women aged 72 and 91, whose carer had stolen cash from their homes, were able to give evidence by live link under s.24 of the 1999 Act. Real time sound and images were relayed to the courtroom using a mobile video conferencing kit set up in their living room. The jury convicted the carer for theft; she was sentenced to 18 months in prison (*R v Atkins*).

In addition, the Home Office has published a set of guidance as part of its 'achieving best evidence' policy covering vulnerable or intimidated witnesses, including children. Various aspects are covered for vulnerable adults. These include a definition and identification of vulnerable witnesses, and support for the witness in terms of planning for an interview, at interview, during the investigation, pre-court hearing, during the court hearing and after the hearing. As well, court-based intermediaries are referred to, and issues around capacity (and oath taking) discussed (CJS 2007). An intermediary might come, for example, from the social work, speech and language therapy or social work professions – and assist the witness to understand questions put to them and to be understood (CPS 2007, para 8.5).

Clinical psychologist as intermediary. At an appeal hearing, a man convicted of murdering Jill Dando (the television presenter) was assisted throughout the hearing by a clinical psychologist. Her role was to help him follow the progress of the case. He had learning disabilities. His intellectual functioning was in the borderline range, he suffered from epilepsy and had severe cognitive impairment (O'Neill 2007).

Separate guidance has been issued on the use of therapy in relation to the welfare of the witness, and on precautions to be taken so that the therapy does not unnecessarily contaminate the evidence to be given by the vulnerable witness. The guidance does emphasise though that 'priority must be given to the best interests of the vulnerable or intimidated witness' (Home Office 2002a, p.19).

This cautionary reminder is because witness training for criminal trials is prohibited, although this is not the same as pre-trial familiarisation arrangements which do not include discussion about proposed or intended evidence (*R v Momodu*). In one case, concerning the prosecution of an NHS nurse for attempted murder, witness training was given to other staff, but the judge concluded that it did not give the prosecution an unfair advantage. It had been an attempt to familiarise the witnesses with the giving of evidence coherently, rather than to orchestrate the evidence (*R v Salisbury*).

The following court case shows the importance of a basic recognition of a person's ability to give evidence in the light of a disability:

Making allowances for a vulnerable witness who had suffered a stroke. A man was conducting his own defence in respect of an alleged offence of failing to comply with a statutory notice under the Housing Act 1985. He had suffered a stroke, which had caused brain damage and affected his ability to work, concentrate and remember things. He waited all day in court before the hearing was held. He said to the judge that he was therefore physically and mentally unable to conduct his case due to the medical problems arising from the stroke. The judge insisted on proceeding. The Court of Appeal held that the man had not been given a fair hearing; the consequences of stress and fatigue on a person who had suffered a stroke had not been taken into account; the case would have to be reheard (*R v Isleworth Crown Court, ex p King*).

In related vein, a conviction of a man with learning disabilities was quashed after it became clear that at the time of the trial he suffered from a verbal memory impairment which affected his ability to put forward a proper defence, to instruct his lawyer and to follow the evidence. However, for various reasons, his lawyer was not aware of the extent of his disability. There was a reasonable explanation for this unawareness, and there was no blame to be attached to the man himself (*R v Silcock*).

11.6.3 GIVING AND ADMISSIBILITY OF EVIDENCE

The question of the giving, and admissibility, of evidence by people with some form of mental impairment or disorder has been considered by the courts on a number of occasions. Some of these cases have involved in particular:

- **(video-recorded evidence):** Section 27 of the Youth Justice and Criminal Evidence Act 1999. This allows for video-recorded evidence in chief in respect of vulnerable or intimidated witnesses. But any such recording does not have to be admitted by the court in certain circumstances, for example if it is not in the interests of justice, or the witness would not be available for cross examination
- **(presumption of competence to give evidence):** Section 53 of the Youth Justice and Criminal Evidence Act 1999. This creates a presumption that at all stages of criminal proceedings, a person of whatever age is competent to give evidence, unless

it appears to the court that he or she is unable to understand questions put to him or her as a witness, or to give answers to those questions which can be understood

- **(fairness of admitting evidence):** Section 78 of the Police and Criminal Evidence Act 1984. This is about whether in all the circumstances, including how the evidence was obtained, it would be unfair to admit the evidence
- **(hearsay evidence):** Section 114 of the Criminal Justice Act 2003. Concerns admissibility of hearsay evidence, including whether it is in the interests of justice
- **(admissibility of evidence not made orally in the proceedings):** Section 116 of the Criminal Justice Act 2003. Concerns admissibility of evidence not made in oral evidence in the proceedings, if certain conditions are satisfied, including that the person is unfit to be a witness because of his or her bodily or mental condition.

In the following case, the court disentangled a number of potentially complex issues surrounding these legal provisions. Having done so, it then questioned whether the case should have been brought to court at all, given the learning disabilities of both alleged victim and alleged perpetrator:

Two children with severe learning disabilities: alleged indecent assault by one on the other. The accused and the alleged victim were both 13 years old at the time of the alleged offence. Both were pupils at the same special school, and both had severe learning disabilities. The boy was accused of having indecently touched the girl.

Initial interviews and evidence. Shortly after the initial complaint, the girl was interviewed on police camera. She gave an intelligible account. The boy was then interviewed under caution, with a solicitor and appropriate adult present. He appeared to admit he had touched the girl indecently.

Girl unable to remember events by the time of trial. By the time of the trial, the girl could not remember anything and could rely only on what she had said on the video-recorded original interview.

Boy unable to give meaningful evidence: s.53 of 1999 Act. The boy had subsequently been examined by a consultant clinical psychologist, who concluded that the boy was severely handicapped, such that he was in the bottom 0.1 of the population according to the Wechsler test. He could not remember why he was being brought to court. He was highly suggestible; a variation in voice intonation of the same question would elicit directly contradictory answers. The psychologist believed that the boy could give no meaningful evidence, either as a witness in court, or at the time of the original interview. The case reached the High Court, where a number of points were clarified.

Competence to give evidence under s.53 of 1999 Act: to be considered both at interview and throughout trial. Under the Youth Justice and Criminal Evidence Act, the test of competence contained in s.53 should be addressed both when consideration is given as to whether to admit a video-recorded interview, and also throughout the trial.

Admitting or excluding video interview under s.27 of 1999 Act. If it appeared that the witness was not competent at the time of the video interview, it would be a reason for declining to make a special measures direction under s.27 of the Act, and thus declining to admit the video interview. However, in this case, the question about the girl's competence had arisen only at time of trial. If it was clear that the witness was not competent immediately before the trial, then the video interview would normally not be admitted, because the witness would not be available for cross examination. However, if the competence issue only arises after the video interview has been admitted, then it is open to the court to place little or no weight on it, precisely because it cannot be tested in cross examination.

Lack of memory not to be equated with lack of competence: sections 53 and 27 of 1999 Act. In this case, the issue that had arisen at trial had not, in fact, been the girl's competence but her memory. Lack of memory was not the same as incompetence, even if it meant she could not give useful evidence. Her answers were intelligible ('I can't remember'), but were just of no use. However, this still meant that the video interview, though admitted, might be of little value because it could not be tested by cross examination. This was an assessment for the court to make.

Admission of statement not made in oral evidence in the proceedings: section 116 of the 2003 Act. If s.116 of the Criminal Justice Act 2003 applies (statement not made in oral evidence in the proceedings because, for example, the person is unfit to be a witness because of bodily or mental condition), then the evidence is admissible (subject only to s.78 of the Police and Criminal Evidence Act).

Admission of hearsay under section 114 of 2003 Act. If s.114 applies (admission of hearsay), the admissibility is not automatic and the court has to make a judgment whether admissibility is in the interests of justice. The court thought, however, that in almost every case in which the witness is incompetent at the time of the trial, s.116 would apply in respect of the person being unfit because of bodily or mental condition.

Unfair to admit boy's evidence under s.78 of the 1978 Act. The court was entitled to apply s.78 of the Police and Criminal Evidence Act 1978. It would result in exclusion of the boy's interview, because it had no value, in the light of his severe disability and high degree of suggestibility. But the court could in any case, with or without s.78, simply say that the interview had no value (*Director of Public Prosecutions v R*).

Thus, the boy's offence could not be proved given his inability to give evidence and the loss of memory of the girl. The court pointed out that: 'where very young, or very handicapped, children are concerned there may often be better ways of dealing with inappropriate behaviour than the full panoply of a criminal trial. Even where the complaint is of sexual misbehaviour, it ought not to be thought that it is invariably in the public interest for it to be investigated by means of a criminal trial, rather than by inter-disciplinary action and co-operation between those who are experienced in dealing with children of this age and handicap' (*Director of Public Prosecutions v R*).

Two other earlier court cases each concerned the alleged rape of an elderly woman suffering from Alzheimer's disease and whether their video evidence should be admitted to court.

Admissibility of video evidence given by woman with Alzheimer's disease in rape trial. The defendant was accused of attempting to rape and of indecently assaulting an 81-year-old woman who had longstanding delusional problems associated with early Alzheimer's disease. He attempted to have video testimony given by the woman excluded from the trial – partly on the grounds that the woman lacked capacity to give evidence. The Court of Appeal upheld the judge's decision to admit the video, and confirmed that, though relevant, the woman's capacity was not decisive as to whether the video should at least be admitted as evidence. Its reliability could then be challenged by the defendant, through medical evidence as to the woman's capacity when the video was made (*R v D*).

A similar outcome was reached in the following case.

Admissibility of video interview given by woman with Alzheimer's disease in rape case. A minicab driver had been convicted of raping an 81-year-old woman suffering from Alzheimer's disease. He appealed. The main issue was whether a video-tape of an interview carried out by the police with her should have been admissible as evidence.

Mental state, unreliability, suggestibility. The Court of Appeal summarised the doubts about her evidence: 'As to her mental state, [the expert] evidence was at one. At the material time she was suffering from moderate to severe Alzheimer's disease, which, as is well known, is a dementia that affects the functioning of the brain, including the memory… Both experts expressed the view that, at the time when she gave the video-taped interview and thereafter, she was not fit to give evidence in court owing to her dementia. They acknowledged that, in the interview, the video-tape of which they had both viewed, she was clearly speaking of a sexual incident that appeared to have been unpleasant and unwelcome to her. But they agreed that she was unreliable on the details and seemingly did not appreciate that she was being interviewed by the police as distinct from having a social conversation. They were both of the view that, given her condition, she was likely to have been suggestible to at least some of the leading questions put to her.'

Nonetheless, it was for the jury to decide about the reliability of this evidence; it was right that the judge had admitted it. The appeal failed (*R v Ali Sed*).

In a third, unusual, case, it was one of the defendants who wanted the video evidence, given by a severely disabled man, admitted – whilst her co-defendant sought its exclusion:

Admissibility of transcript made by social worker. An elderly man, living with his disabled son, had shown kindness to a female heroin addict. She went round to his flat with an acquaintance; they stole money, a television set and video-recorder. The elderly man was punched and kicked such that he died 16 days later. The woman was convicted of robbery and manslaughter. However, she denied this, arguing that she had not inflicted any injuries, that there had been no agreement about using violence, and that she had acted under duress from her companion.

Her version of events was supported by the elderly man's son (since deceased), whose interview had been video-taped. The son had been severely disabled, though with unimpaired mental faculties. He suffered from cerebral palsy, epilepsy, Parkinson's disease, severe speech difficulties and was confined to a wheelchair. He had acute difficulties in making himself understood, quite apart from a reluctance to speak to strangers. Only the social worker could understand what he was saying in what had been supposed to be a police interview; in fact the man did not answer the police officers, so the social worker asked all the questions. The social worker then made a transcript record of what the man had been trying to say. The court concluded that the video and transcript could be admitted; the question would then be to decide at trial how much weight to place on them (*R v Duffy*).

References

Legal cases
Care Standards Tribunal cases
Information Commissioner cases (Freedom of Information Act 2000)
Information Tribunal cases
Employment Tribunal cases
Local government ombudsman cases
Health service ombudsman cases
Professional regulatory body cases
Statutory instruments
Other references

LEGAL CASES

A v A health authority [2001] EWHC Fam/Admin 18.
A local authority v E [2007] EWHC 2396 Fam.
A primary care trust v P [2008] EWHC 1403 (Fam).
Airedale Trust v Bland [1993] AC 789 (House of Lords).
Akinleye v East Sussex Hospitals NHS Trust [2008] EWHC 68.
Alcard v Skinner 36 Ch D 145.
An Hospital Trust v S [2003] EWHC Admin 365.
An NHS Trust v Ms T [2004] EWHC Fam 1279.
Ashingdane v UK (1985) 7 EHRR 528, European Court of Human Rights.
B Borough Council v Mrs S [2006] EWHC 2584 Fam.
Baigent v BBC (1999) unreported, Court of Session, Outer House (Scotland).
Bamgbala v Commission for Social Care Inspection [2008] EWHC 629 (Admin).
Banks v Banks (1999) FLR 726.
Banks v Goodfellow (1870) LR 5 QB 549.
Barrett v Enfield LBC [1999] 3 WLR 79, House of Lords.
Barrett v Kasprzyk (2000) unreported, High Court (Chancery).
Bicknell v HM Coroner for Birmingham/Solihull [2007] EWHC 2547 Admin.
Blackman v Kim Sing Man (2007) Case no. HC050C01190, 7 December 2007, High Court (Chancery).
Brent LBC v SK [2007] EWHC 1250, Fam.
Brown v Mott (2002) unreported, High Court (Chancery).
Burke v General Medical Council [2005] EWCA Civ 1003.
Campbell v Griffin [2001] EWCA Civ 990.
Chief Constable v A county council [2002] EWHC Fam 2198.
Chief Constable of Hertfordshire v Van Colle; Smith v Chief Constable of Sussex [2008] UKHL 50.
City of Sunderland v PS [2007] EWHC 623 Fam.

Clancy v Clancy [2003] EWHC 1885.

Clunis v Camden and Islington Health Authority [1998] 3 All ER 180, Court of Appeal.

Conn v Sunderland CC [2007] EWCA 1492.

Daniel v Drew [2005] EWCA Civ 507.

Director of Public Prosecutions v R [2007] EWHC 1842 Admin.

Dodov v Bulgaria (2008) European Court of Human Rights, case no. 59548/00.

Doncaster & Bassetlaw Hospitals NHS Trust & Anor v C [2004] EWHC 1657 (Fam).

Ealing London Borough Council v KS [2008] EWHC 636 (Fam).

Edwards v Edwards [2007] EWHC 119 (Chancery).

Faulkner v Talbot [1981] 3 All ER 468 (Court of Appeal).

Finsbury Park Mortgage Funding v Burrows and Pegram Heron (2002), Brighton County Court, 22 February 2002 and 3 May 2002.

Glanville v Glanville [2002] EWHC 1271 (Chancery).

Glass v United Kingdom (2004) Application 61827/00 (European Court of Human Rights).

Gogay v Hertfordshire County Council (2001) 1 FLR 280 (Court of Appeal).

Goodchild v Bradbury [2006] EWCA Civ 1868.

Governor & Company of the Bank of Scotland v Bennett [1997] 1 FLR 801.

Gull v Gull [2007] EWCA Civ 900.

Hammond v Osborne [2002] EWCA Civ 885.

Harris v Harris (1999) unreported (Court of Appeal).

HE v A Hospital NHS Trust [2003] EWHC Fam 1017.

Health and Safety Executive v London Borough of Barnet (1997) unreported, Crown Court.

Hipgrave v Jones [2004] EWHC 2901 QB.

HL v United Kingdom (2004) 40 EHRR 761 (European Court of Human Rights).

HM v Switzerland (2002) Application 39187/98 (European Court of Human Rights).

Hodson v Hodson [2006] EWHC 2878 Chancery.

Hoff, Beagan, Wiechulla v Atherton [2004] EWHC 177 (Chancery); [2004] EWCA Civ 1554 (Court of Appeal).

Hulme v Director of Public Prosecutions [2006] EWHC 1347 Admin.

Hutty v Hutty [2005] EWCA Civ 1026.

Jain v Trent Strategic Health Authority [2007] EWCA Civ 1186.

JD v East Berkshire NHS Trust [2005] UKHL 23.

JE v DE and Surrey County Council [2006] EWHC Fam 3459.

Jennings v Rice [2002] EWCA Civ 159.

Jennings and Lewis v Cairns [2003] EWCA Civ 1935.

Jones v National Care Standards Commission [2004] EWHC Admin 918 (High Court); [2004] EWHC Civ 1713 (Court of Appeal).

Joyce v Secretary of State for Health [2008] EWHC 1891 (Admin).

JT (Adult: refusal of medical treatment) [1998] FLR 48.

K v Central and North West London Mental Health NHS Trust, and Kensington and Chelsea Royal London Borough Council [2008] EWHC 1217 QB.

KC v City of Westminster Social and Community Services Department [2008] EWCA Civ 198.

Kenward v Adams (1975), The Times Law Reports, 28 November 1975.

Kostic v Chaplin [2007] EWHC 2298 Ch.

Lewis v Gibson [2005] EWCA Civ 587.

Lillie v Newcastle City Council [2002] EWHC 1600 (QBD).

Lindsay v Wood [2006] EWHC 2895 QB.

Lister v Hesley Hall [2001] UKHL 22.

LLBC v TG [2007] EWHC Fam 2640.

Local Authority X v MM [2007] EWHC Fam 2003.

M v B [2005] EWHC Fam 1681.

Maddock v Devon County Council (2003) unreported, case Ex190052, Exeter District Registry, High Court (QBD).

Majrowski v Guy's and St Thomas' NHS Trust [2006] UKHL 34.

Manchester City Council v Romano; Manchester City Council v Samari [2004] EWCA Civ 384.

Masterman-Lister v Brutton [2002] EWHC QBD 417 (High Court); [2002] EWCA Civ 1889 (Court of Appeal).

McGlinchey v United Kingdom (2003) Application 50390/99, European Court of Human Rights.

M'Naghten's Case (1843) 10 Cl & Fin 200.

Munjaz v Mersey Care NHS Trust [2003] EWCA Civ 1036.

Nel v Kean [2003] EWHC 190 (QB).

Newham London Borough Council v BS [2003] EWHC Fam 1909.

Page v Page (1999) 2 FLR 897 (Fam), Court of Appeal.

Pesticcio v Huet [2004] EWCA Civ 372.

Phelps v Hillingdon LBC (2000) 3 WLR 776 (House of Lords).

Pluck v Pluck [2007] EWCA Civ 1250.

Pretty v United Kingdom [2002] 2 FCR 97, European Court of Human Rights.

Price v United Kingdom (2001) Application 33394/96 (European Court of Human Rights).

R v A local authority in the Midlands, ex p LM (2000) 1 FLR 612.

R v Adomako [1994] 3 All ER 79 (House of Lords).

R v Ali Sed [2004] EWCA Crim 1295.

R v Allison [2003] EWCA Crim 2452.

R v Atkins (2004) Reported in: Humberside Crown Prosecution Services (2004) Humberside Annual Report 2003–04, p.5.

R v Bouldstridge (2000) unreported (but see Kelso, P. (2000) 'He only wanted to end his wife's pain. He ended up in court, at 84', *Guardian*, 7 June 2000, p.1.

R v Bournewood Community and Mental Health NHS Trust, ex p L [1998] 1 CCLR 390 (House of Lords).

R v Bowles (Lewis) and Bowles (Christine) [2004] EWCA Crim 1608.

R v C [2008] EWCA Crim 1155; Times Law Reports, 9 June 2008; and [2008] EWCA Crim 1856.

R v Carter (2005) Reported in Wiltshire Police News (2005). 'Chippenham woman sentenced for theft from elderly male relative.' Available at http://wiltshire.police.uk/news/newsview.asp?id=644, accessed 20 October 2007.

R v Cawley [2007] EWCA Crim 2030.

R v Charles [2007] EWCA Crim 2266.

R v Chief Constable of NorthWales, ex p AB [1998] 3 WLR 57 (Court of Appeal).

R v Chief Constables of C and D, ex p A [2001] 2 FCR Admin 431 (High Court).

R v Clarke [2003] EWCA Crim 1764.

R v Collins, Pathfinder Mental Health Services NHS Trust and St George's Healthcare NHS Trust, ex p S (1998) 1 CCLR 578 (Court of Appeal).

R v Collins, Pathfinder Mental Health Services NHS Trust and St George's Healthcare NHS Trust, ex p S (no.2) (1998) 3 WLR 936 (Court of Appeal).

R v D [2002] EWCA Crim 990.

R v Donaldson [2001] EWCA Crim 2854.

R v Duffy (1998) 3 WLR 1060 (Court of Appeal).

R v Forbes [2007] EWCA Crim 621. (See also: 'Nursing home matron jailed after stealing £100,000 from dying patients', *Daily Mail*, 21 August 2006. Available at www.dailymail.co.uk/news/article-401506/Nursing-home-matron-jailed-stealing-100-000-dying-patients.html, accessed 23 October 2008. Also: 'Matron ordered to pay compensation', *Worcester News*, 11 May, 2007. Available at http://archive.worcesternews.co.uk/2007/5/11/464267.html, accessed 23 October 2008.)

R v Furr [2007] EWCA Crim 191.

R v Hardwick [2006] EWCA Crim 969.

R v Hinks (2001) 2 AC 241 (House of Lords).

R v Isleworth Crown Court, ex p King [2001] EWCA Admin 22.

R v Islington London Borough Council, ex p Rixon [1997] 1 ELR 477.

R v Johnson (2001) 1 Criminal Appeal Reports (S) 123.

R v Kelly (1997), Court of Appeal, 14 November 1997.

R v Kendrick [1997] 2 Cr App 524.

R v Kent County Council, ex p Marston (1997) unreported, High Court.

R v Lennon [2005] EWCA Crim 3530.

R v Lidar (1999), Court of Appeal, 11 November 1999.

R v Manchester City Council, ex p Stennett (1999) [2002] UKHL 34.

R v Mangham (1998) 2 Criminal Appeal Reports (S) 344.

R v Mazo [1997] 2 Cr App R 518.

R v McInerney [2002] EWCA Crim 3003.

R v Misra [2004] EWCA Crim 2375.

R v Momodu [2005] EWCA Crim 177.

R v Moss [2005] EWCA Crim 133.

R v Newington [1990] 91 Criminal Appeal Reports 247.

R v North and East Devon Health Authority, ex p Coughlan (1999) 2 CCLR 285.

R v Plymouth City Council, ex p Stevens [2002] EWCA Civ 388.

R v Poderis (2007) Chester Crown Court, 2007 (reported in McKeever 2007).

R v Randall (2005) 1 Criminal Appeal Reports (S) 60.

R v Roach [2001] EWCA Crim 992.

R v Ross-Goulding (1997) 2 Criminal Appeal Reports (S) 348.

R v Salisbury (2004). Crown Court, Chester, 18 June 2004.

R v Savage and Parmenter [1991] AC 699 (House of Lords).

R v Shaw (1996) 2 Criminal Appeal Reports (S) 278.

R v Silcock [2007] EWCA Crim 2283.

R v Singh (2007). Reported in London Borough of Hounslow News (2007). 'Callous carer jailed for theft from 89-year-old woman', 14 September 2007. Available at http://www.hounslow.gov.uk/ news_mod_home/news_mod_year/news_mod_month/news_mod_show?year1=2007&month1=9&Ne wsID=30078, accessed 23 October 2008.

R v Sowden (2000) Criminal Law Reports 500, Court of Appeal.

R v Spedding [2001] EWCA Crim 2190.

R v Spillman (2001) 1 Criminal Appeal Reports (S) 139.

R v Starsmeare [2003] EWCA Crim 577.

R v Stockdale (1994) 15 Criminal Appeal Reports (S) 48.

R v Stone (1977) 64 Cr App R 186.

R v TS [2008] EWCA Crim 6.

R v Webster [2007] EWCA Crim 619.

R v Williams (2001) 1 Criminal Appeal Reports 23.

R(A) v National Probation Service [2003] EWHC Admin 2910.

R(B) v Dr Haddock [2005] EWHC 921 Admin.

R(B) v Dr SS & Ors [2005] EWHC 86 (Admin).

R(Bernard) v Enfield London Borough Council [2002] EWHC Admin 2282.

R(D) v Secretary of State for Health [2006] EWCA 989.

R(G) v Chief Constable of Staffordshire [2006] EWHC 482 Admin.

R(Goldsmith) v Wandsworth London Borough Council [2004] EWCA Civ 1170.

R(Graham) v Secretary of State for Justice [2007] EWHC 2940 Admin.

R(Grogan) v Bexley NHS Care Trust [2006] EWHC 44, High Court.

R(L) v Commissioner of Police for the Metropolis [2007] EWCA Civ 168.

R(M) v Birmingham City Council [2008] EWHC 949 (Admin).

R(McCann) v Manchester Crown Court [2002] UKHL 39.

R(N) v Mental Health Review Tribunal (Northern Region) [2006] 4 All ER 194.

R(Pinnington) v Chief Constable of Thames Valley [2008] EWHC 1870 (Admin).

R(Wright) v Secretary of State for Health [2006] EWHC 2886 Admin (High Court); [2007] EWCA 999 Civ (Court of Appeal).

R(X) v Chief Constable of West Midlands Police [2004] EWHC Admin 61 (High Court); [2004] EWCA Civ 1068 (Court of Appeal).

Randall v Randall [2004] EWHC 2258 (Chancery).

Re a power given by Mrs W, a donor (1999), Chancery (Court of Protection).

Re B (Adult: refusal of treatment) [2002] EWHC 429.

Re Beaney (deceased) [1978] 1 WLR 770.

Re C (Adult: refusal of treatment) [1994] 1 WLR 290.

Re Craig [1970] 2 All ER 390 (High Court).

Re D (Evidence: facilitated communication) [2001] 1 FLR.

Re Ethel Mary Good [2002] EWHC 640 (Chancery).

Re F (A child) (1999) 2 CCLR 445 (Court of Appeal).

Re F (Adult patient) (2000) 3 CCLR 210 (Court of Appeal).

Re K [1988] 2 FLR 15.

Re MB (Adult: caesarian section) [1997] 2 FCR 541.

Re S (Adult patient) [2002] EWHC Fam 2278.

Re S (Hospital patient: court's jurisdiction) [1995] 1 FLR 1075 (Court of Appeal).

Re SA [2005] EWHC 2942 Fam.

Re SK [2004] EWHCD 3202 Fam.

Re W(Adult: refusal of treatment) [2002] EWHC Fam 901.

Re Y (Mental incapacity: bone marrow transplant) [1996] 2 FLR 787.

Re Z [2004] EWHC Fam 2817.

Richards v Allan (2000) unreported (Chancery).

Rowley v Director of Public Prosecutions [2003] EWHC Admin 693.

Royal Bank of Scotland v Etridge (no.2) [2001] UKHL 44.

RP v Nottingham City Council [2008] EWCA Civ 462.

Saulle v Nouvet [2007] EWHC 2902 (QB).

Savage v South Essex Partnership NHS Foundation Trust [2007] EWCA Civ 1375.

Scammell v Scammell [2008] EWHC 1100 (Ch).

Sheffield CC v E [2004] EWHC Fam 2808.

SL v SL (2000) 3 WLR 1288 (Court of Appeal).

Special Trustees of Great Ormond Street Hospital v Rushin (1997) unreported (Chancery).

St Helens BC v PE [2006] EWHC Fam 3460.

Tait v Wedgwood [2002] EWHC 2594, High Court (Chancery).

Tchilingirian v Ouzounian [2003] EWHC 1220 (Chancery).

Three Rivers District Council v Bank of England [2003] 2 AC 1.

Trust A v H (An Adult Patient [2006] EWHC 1230 Fam. Special Trustees of Great Ormond Street Hospital v Rushin (1997) unreported, High Court (Chancery).

Vaughan v Vaughan [2002] EWHC 699 Chancery.

W v Edgell [1990] 1 All ER 835 (Court of Appeal).

Welsh Ministers v Care Standards Tribunal [2008] EWHC 49 Admin.

Wookey v Wookey [1991] 3 WLR 135 Court of Appeal.

Woolgar v Chief Constable of Sussex Police (2000) 1 WLR 25 (Court of Appeal).

X City Council v MB & Ors [2006] EWHC 168 (Fam).

X,Y v Hounslow London Borough Council [2008] EWHC 1168 (QB).

YL v Birmingham City Council [2007] UKHL 27.

CARE STANDARDS TRIBUNAL CASES

AB v Secretary of State for Education and Skills [2007] 0948.PVA.

Bradford v General Social Care Council [2006] 792 SW-SUS.

Brown v Secretary of State for Health [2005] 580 PVA/581 PC.

Close v Secretary of State for Health [2006] 852.PVA.

Del Mundo v Secretary of State for Health [2005] 557 PVA/558 PC.

DG v Secretary of State [2006] 824 PVA.

Dixon v Secretary of State for Health [2005] 621 PVA.

DSH v General Social Care Council [2007] 1098.SW.

EK v Secretary of State [2006] 0716 PVA/0717 PC.

Hillier v Commission for Social Care Inspection [2003] 0187 NC.

Jackson v Secretary of State for Health [2005] 623 PVA/624 PC.

JF v Secretary of State [2005] 591 PVA/592 PC.

Johnston v Secretary of State for Health [2007] 1064.PC.

Kalchev v Secretary of State for Education and Skills [2005] 589 PVA/590 PC.

LLM v Secretary of State [2006] 832 PVA.

LU and DH v Secretary of State for Health [2007] 1092 PVA.

Matswairo v Secretary of State for Health [2007] 0937.PVA.

McNish v Secretary of State for Health [2006] 0646 PVA.

Mrs P v Secretary of State for Education and Skills [2005] 562 PVA/563 PC.

Mwaura v Secretary of State for Health [2006] 687 PVA/688 PC.

NJ v Secretary of State for Health [2006] 727.PVA.

Nkala v Secretary of State for Health [2007] 1015.PVA.

Onyerindu v Commission for Social Care Inspection [2007] 1041.EA, [2008] 1268.EA.

Pain v Secretary of State [2006] 636 PVA.

PHH v Secretary of State for Education and Skills [2006] 876.PVA.

Rathbone v Secretary of State [2007] 975.PVA.

Simpson v National Care Standards Commission [2004] 255 EA.

SM v Secretary of State [2007] 1006 PVA.

Smith v Secretary of State for Health [2007] 1174 PVA.

SP v Secretary of State [2006] 725 PVA/726 PC.

TM v Secretary of State for Health [2007] 1118.PVA.

Wilkinson v National Care Standards Commission [2003] 231 EA.

INFORMATION COMMISSIONER CASES (FREEDOM OF INFORMATION ACT 2000)

Bellamy v Information Commissioner (2006) 27 March 2006.

Central and North West London NHS Foundation Trust (2008) 17 March 2008.

East London and the City Mental Health NHS Trust (2007) 3 December 2007.

Eastern Health and Social Services Board (2006) 10 July 2006.

George Eliot Hospital NHS Trust (2007) 7 June 2007.

Gloucestershire NHS Primary Care Trust (2007) 12 November 2007.

Health and Safety Executive (2008) 18 February 2007.

Hounslow Primary Care Trust (2008) 19 March 2008.
LiverpoolWomen's NHS Foundation Trust (2007) 19 February 2007.
Maidstone and Tunbridge Wells NHS Trust (2007) 19 April 2007.
Mersey Care NHS Trust (2008) 14 January 2008.
NHS Litigation Authority (2006) 27 September 2006.
Nottinghamshire Healthcare Trust (2007) 13 August 2007.
Norfolk County Council (2007) 7 November 2007.
Plymouth City Council (2006) 23 August 2006.
Rotherham NHS Primary Care Trust (2007) 23 April 2007.
Southampton University Hospitals NHS Trust (2007) 2 July 2007.
St George's Healthcare NHS Trust (2008) 19 March 2008.
Swansea NHS Trust (2006) 5 December 2006.
Trafford Metropolitan Borough Council (2007) 27 November 2007.
University Hospital of North Staffordshire NHS Trust (2007) 30 August 2007.
Walsall NHS Teaching Primary Care Trust (2007) 13 December 2007.
Western Cheshire NHS Primary Care Trust (2007) 25 June 2007.
Worcestershire County Council (2006) 31 May 2006.

INFORMATION TRIBUNAL CASES

Bluck v Information Commisioner and Epsom and St Helier University NHS Trust (2007), 17 September 2007.
Coggins v Information Commissioner (2008), 13 May 2008
Francis v Information Commissioner (2008), 21 July 2008.
House of Commons v Information Commissioner and Norman Baker, MP (2007), 16 January 2007.
Kitchener v Information Commissioner and Derby City Council (2006) 20 December 2006.
Parker v Information Commissioner and Health Service Ombudsman (2007) 15 October 2007.
Prior v Information Commissioner (2006) 27 April 2006.

EMPLOYMENT TRIBUNAL CASES

Kay v Northumbria Healthcare NHS Trust. Employment Tribunal case no. 6405617/00, 29 November 2001 (Newcastle upon Tyne). Summarised in: Bowers, J. et al. (2007) *Whistleblowing: law and practice.* Oxford: Oxford University Press, p.575.

LOCAL GOVERNMENT OMBUDSMAN CASES

Bath and North East Somerset Council 2007 (06/B/16774).
Bedfordshire County Council 2003 (02/B/16654).
Bexley London Borough Council 1998 (97/A/2021).
Birmingham City Council 2008 (05/C/18474).
Blackpool Borough Council 2006 (03/C/17141).
Bolton Metropolitan Borough Council 2004 (02/C/17068).
Bromley London Borough Council 2003 (01/B/17272).
Bromley London Borough Council 2004 (03/B/18884).
Bury Metropolitan Borough Council 2000 (97/C/3668).
Carmarthenshire County Council 1999 (99/0117/CM/210).
Clwyd County Council 1997 (97/0177, 97/0755).
Cumbria County Council 2000 (98/C/0002).
Ealing London Borough Council 2004 (03/A/17640).
Hertfordshire County Council 2003 (00/B/16833).
Kent County Council 1999 (98/A/1612).

Kirklees Metropolitan Borough Council 2002 (01/C/02370).
Leicestershire County Council 2001 (00/B/08307).
North Somerset Council 1999 (98/C/4033).
North Yorkshire County Council 2007 (05/C/13158).
Sheffield City Council 2001 (00/C/10708).
Sheffield City Council 2007 (05/C/06420).
South Tyneside Metropolitan Borough Council 2008 (O6/C/18619 and 07/C/01489).
Southend-on-Sea Borough Council 2005 (04/A/10159).
Southwark London Borough Council 2001 (99/A/4226).
Stockport Metropolitan Borough Council 2006 (05/C/07774).
Suffolk County Council 2001 (99/B/1651).
Wakefield Metropolitan District Council 1997 (95/C/3584).
Wakefield Metropolitan District Council 2003 (01/C/15652).
Wiltshire County Council 1999 (98/B/0341).
York City Council 2006 (04/B/01280).

HEALTH SERVICE OMBUDSMAN CASES

HSO (1999) Health Service Ombudsman. HC 497. *Investigations completed October 1998–March 1999.* London: TSO.
HSO (2001) Health Service Ombudsman. HC 4–I. *Selected investigations completed December 2000–March 2001.* London: TSO.
HSO (2003) Health Service Ombudsman. *NHS funding for long term care.* London: TSO.
Oldham NHS Trust 1999 (E.1780/97–98 in HSO 1999).
Preston Acute Hospitals NHS Trust 2001 (E.743/99–00 in HSO 2001).
Warrington Hospital NHS Trust 2001 (E.1846/99–00 in HSO 2001).

PROFESSIONAL REGULATORY BODY CASES

NMC 2007: L71Y1288E, 12 July 2007 (Nursing and Midwifery Council).
NMC 2007: 01G2069O, 4 October 2007 (Nursing and Midwifery Council).
NMC 2007: 68IO223N, 10 October 2007 (Nursing and Midwifery Council).
NMC 2007: 72A0213S, 18 October 2007 (Nursing and Midwifery Council).
NMC 2007: 79K0365E, 16 July 2007 (Nursing and Midwifery Council).
NMC 2007: 87H01616E, 26 July 2007 (Nursing and Midwifery Council).
NMC 2007: 8711737E, 17 October 2007 (Nursing and Midwifery Council).
NMC 2007: 89H0066H, 12 September 2007 (Nursing and Midwifery Council).
NMC 2008: 02H12440, 8 January 2008 (Nursing and Midwifery Council).
NMC 2008: 712h2138E, 28 March 2008 (Nursing and Midwifery Council).
NMC 2008: 75U6681E, 27–28 March 2008 (Nursing and Midwifery Council).
NMC 2008: 83A0008E, 27 March 2008 (Nursing and Midwifery Council).
NMC 2008: 83Y0105W, 6 March 2008 (Nursing and Midwifery Council).

STATUTORY INSTRUMENTS

SI 1975/1023. *Rehabilitation of Offenders Act 1974 (Exceptions) Order 1975.*
SI 1987/1968. *Social Security (Claims and Payments) Regulations 1987.*
SI 2000/413. *Data Protection (Subject Access Modification) (Health) Order 2000.*
SI 2000/415. *Data Protection (Subject Access Modification) (Social Work) Order 2000.*
SI 2000/417. *Data Protection (Processing of Sensitive Personal Data) Order 2000.*

SI 2001/3441. *National Assistance (Residential Accommodation) (Additional Payments and Assessment of Resources) (Amendment) (England) Regulations 2001.*

SI 2001/3965. *Care Homes Regulations 2001.*

SI 2002/233. *The Police Act 1997 (Criminal Records) Regulations 2002.*

SI 2002/446. *The Police Act 1997 (Enhanced Criminal Record Certificates) (Protection of Vulnerable Adults) Regulations 2002.*

SI 2002/1687. *Magistrates' Courts (Special Measures Directions) Rules 2002.*

SI 2002/1688. *Crown Court (Special Measures Directions and Directions Prohibiting Cross-examination) Rules 2002.*

SI 2002/3214. *Domiciliary Care Agencies Regulations 2002.*

SI 2004/2070. *Adult Placement Schemes (England) Regulations 2004.*

SI 2006/750. *The Police Act 1997 (Criminal Records) (Registration) Regulations 2006.*

SI 2006/1832. *The Mental Capacity Act 2005 (Independent Mental Capacity Advocates) (General) Regulations 2006.*

SI 2006/2883. *The Mental Capacity Act 2005 (Independent Mental Capacity Advocates) (Expansion of Role) Regulations 2006.*

SI 2007/1744. *Court of Protection Rules.*

SI 2007/1745. *Court of Protection Fees Order.*

SI 2007/1898. *The Mental Capacity Act 2005 (Transitional and Consequential Provisions) Order 2007.*

SI 2007/1899. *The Mental Capacity Act 2005 (Transfer Of Proceedings) Order 2007.*

SI 2008/16. *Safeguarding Vulnerable Groups Act 2006 (Barred List Prescribed Information) Regulations 2008.*

SI 2008/473. *Safeguarding Vulnerable Groups Act 2006 (Transitional Provisions) Order 2008.*

SI 2008/474. *Safeguarding Vulnerable Groups Act 2006 (Barring Procedure) Regulations 2008.*

SI 2008/1062. *Safeguarding Vulnerable Groups Act 2006 (Prescribed Criteria) (Transitional Provisions) Regulations 2008.*

SI 2008/1315. *Mental Capacity (Deprivation of Liberty: Appointment of Relevant Person's Representative) Regulations 2008.*

SI 2008/1858. *Mental Capacity (Deprivation of Liberty: Standard Authorisations, Assessments and Ordinary Residence)Regulations 2008.*

OTHER REFERENCES

24dash.com (2007). 'Council admits safety breaches over man's care home death', 22 November 2007. Available at http://www.24dash.com/news, accessed 17 October 2008.

Action on Elder Abuse (2004) 'Hidden voices: older people's experience of abuse.' London: Action on Elder Abuse.

Action on Elder Abuse (2007) '£Millions stolen, defrauded or conned from older people by their own sons and daughters each year.' News release, 30 January 2007.

ADSS (2004) Association of Directors of Social Services. *Protocol for inter-authority investigation of vulnerable adult abuse.* London: ADSS.

ADSS (2005) Association of Directors of Social Services. *Safeguarding adults: a national framework of standards for good practice and outcomes in adult protection work.* London: ADSS.

ADASS (2007) Association of Directors of Adult Social Services; *Local Government Association. Commentary and advice for local authorities on the national framework for NHS continuing healthcare and NHS-funded nursing care.* London: ADASS, LGA.

Age Concern England (2006) *Hungry to be heard: the scandal of malnourished older people in hospital.* London: Age Concern England.

Alder, A. (2007) 'Suspended sentence for money-grabbing carer', *Bedfordshire on Sunday,* 6 October.

Barkham, P. (2003) 'Fraudster that fluttered inside a suburban banker', *The Times,* 3 September.

Barnes, J. (2006) *Making referrals to the Protection of Vulnerable Adults (POVA) list.* London: SCIE.

Barnes, J. (2007) 'Hospital bed shortages revealed', *East Anglian Daily Times,* 13 April.

Batchelor, W. (2007) 'Man guilty of murdering wife in assisted euthanasia', *The Independent,* 10 May.

Bateman, N. (2001) 'The dangers of being appointed.' *Community Care*, 7–13 June 2001, p.29.

BBC News (1998) 'Former Saudi nurse guilty of theft.' (21 December 1998). Available at http://news.bbc.co.uk/1/hi/uk/239703.stm, accessed 17 October 2008.

BBC News (2001) 'Nurse convicted of murder.' (19 June 2001). Available at http://news.bbc.co.uk/1/hi/health/1396950.stm, accessed 17 October 208.

BBC News (2001a) 'Care home bosses guilty of abuse.' (28 June 2001). Available at http://news.bbc.co.uk/1/hi/wales/1412595.stm, accessed 17 October 2008.

BBC News (2002) 'Conman jailed for 10 years.' (22 March 2002). Available at http://news.bbc.co.uk/1/hi/scotland/1887420.stm, accessed 17 October 2008.

BBC News (2003) 'Nurses guilty of neglect by death.' (27 October 2003). Available at http://news.bbc.co.uk/1/hi/england/3218847.stm, accessed 17 October 2008.

BBC News (2003a) 'Patient abuse: nurse struck off.' (30 April 2003). Available at http://news.bbc.co.uk/1/hi/wales/2989241.stm, accessed 17 October 2008.

BBC News (2003b) 'Banker stole to buy parrots.' (2 September 2003). Available at http://news.bbc.co.uk/1/hi/england/kent/3201135.stm, accessed 17 October.

BBC News (2003c). 'Lawyer stole from elderly sisters.' (3 October 2003). Available at http://news.bbc.co.uk/1/hi/wales/north_west/3159442.stm, accessed 17 October 2008.

BBC News (2004) 'Settlement over pensioner's death.' (3 March 2004). Available at http://news.bbc.co.uk/1/hi/england/west_midlands/3530283.stm, accessed 17 October 2008.

BBC News (2004a) 'Patient theft nurse is struck off.' (17 December 2004). Available at http://news.bbc.co.uk/1/hi/england/leicestershire/4106257.stm, accessed 17 October 2008.

BBC News (2004b). 'Care home pair guilty of neglect.' (26 April 2004). Available at http://news.bbc.co.uk/1/hi/england/norfolk/3660605.stm, accessed 17 October 2008.

BBC News (2005) 'Probe following GP murder trial.' (15 December 2005). Available at http://news.bbc.co.uk/1/hi/england/4530842.stm, accessed 17 October 2008.

BBC News (2005a) 'Matron not guilty of manslaughter.' (9 March 2005). Available at http://news.bbc.co.uk/1/hi/wales/4333015.stm,accessed 17 October 2008.

BBC News (2006) 'Murder terms increased by judges.' (16 February 2006). Available at http://news.bbc.co.uk/1/hi/england/tees/4720642.stm, accessed 17 October 2008.

BBC News (2006a) 'Safeguards follow care home theft.' (14 February 2006). Available at http://news.bbc.co.uk/1/hi/world/europe/isle_of_man/4713286.stm, accessed 17 October 2008.

BBC News (2006b). 'Ex-PC conned victim out of home.' (5 April 2006). Available at http://news.bbc.co.uk/1/hi/england/essex/4880720.stm, accessed 17 October 2008.

BBC News (2007) 'Care homes under closure threat.' (18 July 2007). Available at http://news.bbc.co.uk/1/hi/england/devon/6904593.stm, accessed 17 October 2008.

BBC News (2007a) 'Hillside murderers get life terms.' (4 May 2007). Available at http://news.bbc.co.uk/1/hi/wales/south_east/6624515.stm, accessed 17 October 2008.

BBC News (2008) 'Woman, 84, discharged in nightie.' (6 January 2008). Available at http://news.bbc.co.uk/1/hi/england/shropshire/7174066.stm, accessed 17 October 2008.

BBC News (2008a) 'Boy convicted of '£5 bet' murder.' (22 January 2008). Available at http://news.bbc.co.uk/1/hi/england/wear/7202351.stm, accessed 17 October 2008.

BBC News (2008b) 'Family jailed for damp-proof scam.' (18 March 2008). Available at http://news.bbc.co.uk/1/hi/england/lancashire/7303648.stm, accessed 17 October 2008.

BBC News (2008c). 'Carer guilty of sadistic attack.' (9 July 2008). Available at http://news.bbc.co.uk/1/hi/wales/mid/7498574.stm, accessed 17 October 2008.

BBC News (2008d). 'Neglect case tragic for nurse.' (22 May 2008). Available at http://news.bbc.co.uk/1/hi/wales/south_east/7414850.stm, accessed 17 October 2008.

BBC News (2008e) 'Closure appeal won by care home.' (5 September 2008). Available at http://news.bbc.co.uk/1/hi/england/northamptonshire/7601358.stm, accessed 17 October 2008.

Beattie, S. (2008). 'Conman jailed for £360,000 fraud', *Teeside Evening Gazette*, 31 May.

Bichard, M. (2004) *The Bichard inquiry report*. London: TSO.

Bird, S. (2003) 'Conman jailed for 600 raids in just 18 months', *The Times*, 8 February.

Bond, A. (2007) 'Hospital hit by bed crisis', *East Anglian Daily Times*, 22 December.

'Boss jailed for fraud at home', *The Argus*, 3 March 2005.

Bowen, P. (2007) *Blackstone's guide to the Mental Health Act 2007*. Oxford: Oxford University Press.

Britten, N. (2006) 'Trusted minister who fleeced his flock', *Daily Telegraph*, 9 September.

Brody, S. (2006) 'Council seeks stronger safeguards after killing at Surrey home.' *Community Care*, 12–18 January 2006.

Burstow, P. (2008) *Keep taking the medicine 4: the scandal of inappropriate medication of older people in care*. London: P. Burstow.

Card, R. (2006) *Card, Cross & Jones Criminal Law, 17th ed.* Oxford: Oxford University Press.

'Care home death is reopened', *Bolton Evening News*, 12 April 2004.

'Care worker jailed for theft', *Dorset Echo*, 12 December 2001.

'Care worker slapped patient', *The Independent*, 3 January 2002.

'Carer, 42, sentenced over theft', *Shropshire Star*, 12 March 2008.

'Carer convicted on theft charges', *Swindon Advertiser*, 15 June 2001.

'Carer found guilty of fraud on dead woman's estate', *Wirral Globe*, 1 April 1998.

'Carer is jailed for theft of £5000', *Northern Echo*, 6 November 2004.

'Carer jailed for nine months after stealing cash', *Oxford Mail*, 14 January 2006.

'Carer jailed for theft from elderly widower', *Wiltshire Gazette and Herald*, 24 March 2005.

'Carer jailed over £1,150 theft', *Lancashire Evening Telegraph*, 10 August 1999.

'Carer stole antiques from war veteran', *Daily Telegraph*, 28 November 2007.

'Carer who stole is spared prison', *Sudbury Mercury*, 28 August 2008.

'Carer's theft from the sick', *The Echo*, 6 January 2006.

Carter, H. (2007) 'He couldn't say "no"', *Guardian (Society)*, 15 August.

Carvel, J. (2006) 'Hospital's focus on waiting time targets led to 41 superbug deaths', *Guardian*, 25 July.

Carvel, J. (2006a) '£10,000 for widow, 89, "fed talcum powder" by carers', *Guardian (Society)*, 12 July.

CCC (2007) Continuing Care Conference. *Paying for care: third party top-ups and cross-subsidies*. London: CCC.

Chartered Institute of Personnel and Development (CIPD) (undated) *Employing ex-offenders: a practical guide*. London: CRB.

CHI (2000) Commission for Health Improvement. *Investigation into the North Lakeland NHS Trust*. London: CHI.

CHI (2002) Commission for Health Improvement. *Clinical performance review: East Kent Hospitals NHS Trust*. London: CHI.

CHI (2002a) Commission for Health Improvement. *Investigation: Portsmouth Healthcare NHS Trust at Gosport War Memorial Hospital*. London: CHI.

CHI (2003) Commission for Healthcare Improvement. *Investigation into matters arising from care on Rowan Ward, Manchester Mental Health & Social Care Trust*. London: CHI.

CJS (2007) *Achieving best evidence in criminal proceedings: guidance for vulnerable or intimidated witnesses, including children*. London: CJS.

CLAE (2004) Commission for Local Administration in England. *Local Government Ombudsman: annual report 2003/4*. London: CLAE.

Clements, A., Halton, K., Graves, N., Pettitt, A., Morton, A., Looke, D. and Whitby, M. (2008). 'Overcrowding and understaffing in modern healthcare systems: key determinants in methicillin resistant Staphylococcus aureus transmission.' *Lancet Infectious Diseases 2008*, 8, 427–434.

Community Care (1998) 'News.' *Community Care*, 25 June–1 July 1998.

Community Care (2007) 'Suspicious death care home closed.' *Community Care*, 22–28 March 2007.

Community Care (2007a) 'Social worker warned over tax fraud.' *Community Care*, 19 February 2007.

Community Care (2007b) 'Social worker struck off for catalogue of fraud.' *Community Care*, 21 June 2007.

Community Care (2007c) 'Social worker banned after child pornography conviction.' *Community Care*, 31 May 2007.

Community Care (2007d) 'Whistleblowers win payout.' *Community Care*, 23 August 2007, p.7.

Community Care (2007e) 'Improved staff checks came too late to prevent abuse.' *Community Care*, 30 August 2007.

Community Care (2007f) 'Care home owner guilty of stealing from residents.' *Community Care*, 5 July 2007.

Community Care (2008) 'Relationships dominate GSCC caseload.' *Community Care*, 17 April 2008.

Community Care (2008a). 'Care home closed due to serious risk to residents.' *Community Care*, 14 August 2008, p.6.

Cornwall Adult Protection Committee (2007) *The murder of Steven Hoskin: serious case review.* Truro: Cornwall County Council.

Cornwall County Council (2008) *Findings of serious case review: Steven Hoskins.* Health and Adult Social Care Overview and Scrutiny Committee. Truro: Cornwall County Council.

Cox, C. (2007) 'Carer stole disabled man's cash for cocaine', *Macclesfield Express*, 5 December 2007.

CPS/1 (undated) Crown Prosecution Service. *Offences against the person, incorporating charging standard: guidance.* Available at http://213.121.214.241/legal/l_to_o/offences_against_the_person/, accessed 24 March 2008.

CPS/2 (undated) Crown Prosecution Service. *Homicide: murder, guidance.* Available at http://213.121.214.241/legal/h_to_k/homicide_murder_and_manslaughter/, accessed 24 March 2008.

CPS (2004) Crown Prosecution Service. *The Code for Crown Prosecutors.* London: CPS.

CPS (2007) Crown Prosecution Service. *Policy for prosecuting crimes against the older person: draft.* London: CPS.

CPS (2007a) Crown Prosecution Service. *Policy for prosecuting disability hate crime.* London: CPS.

'Care home worker jailed for theft', *Craven Herald*, 20 December 2007.

Cretney, S. and Lush, D. (2001) *Cretney and Lush on enduring powers of attorney, 5th edn.* Bristol: Jordan.

CSCI (2005) Commission for Social Care Inspection. *News: Solihull care agency prosecuted by CSCI*, 3 May 2005. Available at www.csci.org.uk, accessed 24 March 2008.

CSCI (2007) Commission for Social Care and Inspection. *Safeguarding adults protocol and guidance.* London: CSCI.

CSCI (2007a) Commission for Social Care Inspection. *A fair contract with older people?* London: CSCI.

CSCI (2007b) Commission for Social Care Inspection. *Annual report and accounts 2006–07.* HC 794. London: TSO.

CSCI (2007c) Commission for Social Care Inspection. *Rights, risk and restraints.* London: CSCI.

CSCI (2008) Commission for Social Care Inspection. *The state of social care in England 2006–07.* London: CSCI.

CSCI (2008a) Commission for Social Care Inspection. *Raising voices: views on safeguarding adults.* London: CSCI.

Cumming, J. (2006) 'Man aided his ailing wife's suicide', *The Scotsman*, 15 September.

Davidson, C. (2007) 'Nurse jailed for abuse of care home patients', *The Scotsman*, 18 May.

Dayani, A. (2004) 'Ban them for life', *Birmingham Evening Mail*, 4 February.

Dayani, A. (2004a) 'Sex probe carer sacked', *Birmingham Evening Mail*, 5 February.

de Bruxelles, S. (2007) 'Couple held on suspicion of 5 murders at care home', *The Times*, 11 December.

de Bruxelles, S. (2007a) 'Three tortured shed captive until he died', *The Times*, 10 July.

Devon County Council Trading Standards (2007) *Devon Trading Standards successfully prosecutes stairlift fraudster.* Press release, 16 April 2007. Exeter: Devon County Council.

Devon County Council Trading Standards (2008) *Builder sentenced for defrauding elderly resident.* Press release, 16 July 2008. Exeter: Devon County Council.

DFES (2007) Department for Education and Skills. *Safeguarding Vulnerable Groups Act 2006: barring consultation document.* London: DFES.

DH (1999) Department of Health. *Mental Health Act Code of Practice.* London: DH.

DH (2000) Department of Health. *No secrets.* London: DH.

DH (2000a) Department of Health. *Data Protection Act 1998: guidance to social services.* London: DH.

DH (2001) Department of Health. *Valuing people: a new strategy for learning disability for the 21st century.* London: Stationery Office.

DH (2002) Department of Health. *Guidance on physically restrictive interventions for people with learning disability and austistic spectrum disorder in health, education and social care settings.* London: DH.

DH (2003) Department of Health. *Care homes for older people: national minimum standards*. London: TSO.

DH (2003a) Department of Health. *Domiciliary care: national minimum standards*. London: TSO.

DH (2003b) Department of Health. *Fair access to care services: practice guidance*. London: DH.

DH (2004) Department of Health. *Protection of vulnerable adults scheme in England and Wales for care home and domiciliary care agencies: a practical guide*. London: DH.

DH (2004a) Department of Health. *Advice on the decision of the European Court of Human Rights in the case of HL v UK (the 'Bournewood' case)*. London: DH.

DH (2007) Department of Health. *Improving health, supporting justice: a consultation document*. London: DH.

DH (2008). Department of Health. *Draft regulations. Community Care, Services for Carers and Children's Services (Direct Payments) (England) Regulations 2009*. London: DH.

DH (2008a) Department of Health. *Code of practice: Mental Health Act 1983*. London: DH.

DH, MJ, Home Office (2008) Department of Health, Ministry of Justice, Home Office. *Safeguarding Adults: a consultation on the review of the 'No secrets' guidance*. London: DH, MJ, Home Office.

Disability Now (2003) 'A punishment to fit the crime.' *Disability Now*, December 2003.

'Dishonest carer told to pay up', *Sunderland Echo*, 6 November 2007.

'Ex-care home boss cleared of 15 abuse charges', *Cheshire Guardian*, 20 May 2004.

File on Four: *Care homes*, BBC radio programme, Radio Four, 18 September 2007.

Fleming, N. (2007) 'MRSA risk rising in crowded hospitals', *Daily Telegraph*, 17 April.

Fletcher, H. (2007) 'Estate agents "swindled £m out of schizophrenic man"', *The Times*, 9 November.

Fletcher, H. (2008) 'Husband is spared jail for suffocating sick wife who wanted to die', *The Times*, 2 February.

Flynn, M. (2007) The murder of Steven Hoskin: a serious case review. Truro: Cornwall Adult Protection Committee.

Flynn, M. (2008) 'How the NHS is failing vulnerable adults.' *Health Service Journal*, 8 April 2008.

FON (2005) *Financial Ombudsman News*, Issue 50, November/December 2005, case 50/5.

FON (2005a) *Financial Ombudsman News*, Issue 50, November/December 2005, case 50/4.

Ford, R. (2007) 'Police told to erase irrelevant crime records', *The Times*, 1 November, p.14.

Ford, R. (2008) 'Care home workers go unchecked, police warn', *The Times*, 2 June.

Forder, J. (2007) *Self-funded care for older people: an analysis of eligibility, variations and future projections*. London: CSCI.

'Fraud carer jailed', *Pontefract and Castleford Times*, 17 April 2008.

'Fraud robs bereaved of £150 million', *The Times*, 25 July 2004.

Fresco, A. (2004) 'Hawking may be called as hostile witness in "brutality" case', *The Times*, 4 February.

Gadelrab, R. (2006) 'Patients abused at care home', *Islington Tribune*, 22 December.

Gorczynska, T. and Thompson, D. (2007) 'Role of the independent mental capacity advocate in adult protection.' *Journal of Adult Protection*, November 2007, p.38.

GSCC (2007) General Social Care Council. *Social worker admonished following conduct hearing in Blackpool*. News, 18 December 2007. Available at http://www.gscc.org.uk/News+and+events/Media+releases/2007+archive/Social+worker+admonished+following+conduct+hearing+in+Blackpool.htm, accessed 23 October 2008.

GSCC (2008) General Social Care Council. *Rotherham social worker found guilty of misconduct and removed from register*. News, 6 March 2008. Available at http://www.gscc.org.uk/News+and+events/Media+releases/Rotherham+social+worker+found+guilty+of+misconduct+and+removed+from+register.htm, accessed 23 October 2008.

GSCC (2008a) General Social Care Council. *Social worker removed from register following relationship with vulnerable client*. News, 28 March 2008. Available at http://www.gscc.org.uk/News+and+events/Media+releases/Social+worker+removed+from+Register+following+relationship+with+vulnerable+client.htm, accessed 23 October 2008.

GSCC (2008b) General Social Care Council. *Social worker suspended from register after inappropriate relationship*. News, 21/2/2008. Available at http://www.gscc.org.uk/News+and+events/

Media+releases/Social+worker+suspended+from+register+after+inappropriate+relationship.htm, accessed 23 October 2008.

Hamilton, S. (2005) 'Loophole that let killers off is finally closed', *The Times*, 15 March.

Harris, G. (2002) 'Builder cons man out of £450,000', *The Times*, 2 March.

HC (2006) Healthcare Commission. *Investigation into outbreaks of Clostridium difficile at Stoke Mandeville Hospital, Buckinghamshire Hospitals NHS Trust.* London: HC.

HC (2006a) Healthcare Commission (2006) *Investigation into Mid Cheshire Hospitals NHS Trust.* London: HC.

HC (2007) Healthcare Commission. *Caring for dignity.* London: HC.

HC (2007a) Healthcare Commission. *Investigation into outbreaks of Clostridium difficile at Maidstone and Tunbridge Wells NHS Trust.* London: HC.

HC (2007b) Healthcare Commission 2007. *A life like no other.* London: HC.

HC (2007c) Healthcare Commission. *Investigation into the service for people with learning disabilities provided by Sutton and Merton Primary Care Trust.* London: HC.

HC (2007d) Healthcare Commission. *Caring for dignity: a national report on dignity on care for older people while in hospital.* London: HC.

HC (2008) Healthcare Commission. *Spotlight on complaints, April 2008.* London: HC.

HC (2008a) Healthcare Commission. *Healthcare Commission publishes results of survey of staff at every NHS trust in England.* Press release. London: HSC.

HC, AC, CSCI (2006) Healthcare Commission, Audit Commission, Commission for Social Care Inspection. *Living well in later life.* London: HC, AC, CSCI.

HC, CSCI (2006) Healthcare Commission, Commission for Social Care Inspection. *Joint investigation into the provision of services for people with learning disabilities at Cornwall Partnership NHS Trust.* London: HC, CSCI.

HCHC (2004) House of Commons Health Committee. *Elder abuse.* HC 111–1. London: TSO.

Hemsley, A. (2008) 'Heartless care worker stole from elderly Winchelsea couple', *Hastings and St Leonards Observer*, 22 August.

Henwood, M. and Hudson, B. (2008) *Lost to the system? The impact of Fair Access to Care.* London: Commission for Social Care Inspection.

'Heroin death mother and sister jailed', *The Times*, 20 May 2008.

Hester, M., Westmarland, N., Pearce, J. and Williamson, E. (2008) *Early evaluation of the Domestic Violence, Crime and Victims Act 2004.* London: Ministry of Justice.

Hill, A. (2001) 'Tide of cruelty sweeps through our care homes', *The Observer*, 18 February.

Hills, S. (2008) 'Sex offender waiting to be deported', *Kent Messenger*, 25 July.

HMG (2007) Her Majesty's Government. *Putting people first: a shared vision and commitment to the transformation of adult social care.* London: HMG.

Hogg, D. (2006) 'Architect fined over deadly outbreak of disease', *Yorkshire Post*, 1 August.

Home Office (2002a) *Provision of therapy for vulnerable adults or intimidated witnesses prior to a criminal trial: practice guidance.* London: Home Office.

Home Office (2004) *Young people and vulnerable adults facing forced marriage: practice guidance for social workers.* London: Home Office.

Home Office (2008) *Police and Criminal Evidence Act 1984 (PACE) Code C: Code of Practice for the detention, treatment and questioning of persons by police officers.* London: Home Office.

Horsnell, M. (2001) 'Fluids force fed to elderly in care', *The Times*, 20 October.

Hotopf, M. (2005) 'The assessment of mental capacity.' *Clinical Medicine*, November/December 2005, p.580.

HSC 2000/3; LAC(2000)3. Department of Health. *After-care under the Mental Health Act 1983.* London: DH.

HSC 2002/011. Department of Health. *Issue of Alert Letters for health professionals in England.* London: DH.

HSJ (2008) 'Gibb sues former employer.' *Health Service Journal*, 10 April 2008.

Hudson, C. (2006) 'Carer stole from patients', *Macclesfield Express*, 22 November.

Hull, L. (2008) 'Camera hidden in a teddy bear catches carer stealing £100 from terminally ill pensioner', *Daily Mail*, 18 August.

Hunt, J. (2006) 'Elderly couple victims of theft', *East Anglian Daily Times*, 24 January.

Hunt, K. (2008) 'Social worker faces judge after stealing from vulnerable patients', *Medway Messenger*, 11 July.

'I resent her for still being alive', *The Times (Times 2)*, 14 November 2007.

IC (2001) Information Commissioner. *Freedom of Information Act awareness guidance, no.1: personal information.* Wilmslow: Information Commissioner.

IC (2007) Information Commissioner. *Freedom of Information Act awareness guidance, no.22: vexatious and repeated requests.* Wilmslow: Information Commissioner.

IC Wales (2007) 'No jail for mother who stole £20,000 plus from neighbour.' 16 August 2007. Available at http://icwales.icnetwork.co.uk, accessed 20 August 2007.

IC Wales (2007a) 'Theft shame nurse struck off.' 5 August 2007. Available at http://icwales.icnetwork.co.uk, accessed 20 August 2007.

ICO (2007) Information Commissioner's Office. *Police told to delete old criminal conviction records.* Press release, 1 November 2007. Wilmslow: ICO.

ICO (2008) Information Commissioner's Office. *Data sharing between different local authority departments.* Wilmslow: ICO.

'Inquest results in neglect verdict', *Westmoreland Gazette*, 21st December 2001.

'Jail after theft spree revealed', *Bromsgrove Advertiser*, 10 August 2006.

'Jail for care home assault deputy', *South Wales Guardian*, 1 December 2004.

JCHR (2007) Joint Committee on Human Rights (House of Lords and House of Commons) (2007) *The human rights of older people in healthcare. HL 156–1.* London: TSO.

JCHR (2007a) Joint Committee on Human Rights (House of Lords and House of Commons). *A life like any other? Human rights of adults with learning disabilities. HL 40–1.* London: TSO.

Jenkins, R. (2005) 'Nurse found dead may have killed 23 patients', *The Times*, 31 August.

Jenkins, R. (2006) 'Financier stole from elderly clients', *The Times*, 13 September.

Jenkins, R. (2008) 'Killer nurse must serve at least 30 years', *The Times*, 5 March.

Jenkins, R. (2008a) 'Women face prison for ignoring a murder under their own roof', *The Times*, 6 February.

Jones, R. (2004) *Encyclopaedia of social services and child care law.* London: Sweet and Maxwell.

Journal Live (2007) 'Carer facing jail for theft from patient.' 16 November 2007. Available at www.journallive.co.uk, accessed 23 October 2008.

Kalaga, H. and Kingston, P. (2007) *Review of literature on effective interventions that prevent and respond to harm against adults.* Edinburgh: Scottish Government Social Research.

Kelly, K. (2008). 'Pregnant carer jailed for theft from OAP', *The Shields Gazette*, 9 May.

Kelso, P. (2000) 'Woman who killed disabled sons is freed', *Guardian*, 24 June.

LAC(92)27. Department of Health. *National Assistance Act 1948 (Choice of Accommodation) Directions 1992.* London: DH.

LAC(2002)2. Department of Health. *Implementing the Caldicott standard in social care: appointment of 'Caldicott Guardians'.* London: DH.

LAC(2002)13. Department of Health. *Fair access to care services: guidance on eligibility criteria for adult social care.* London: DH.

LAC(2004)20. Department of Health. *Guidance on National Assistance Act 1948 (Choice of Accommodation) Directions 1992.* London: DH.

LAC(DH)(2008)1. Department of Health. *Transforming social care.* London: DH.

LASSL(2004)3. Department of Health. *Multi-agency public protection arrangements (MAPPA) and the duty to cooperate.* London: DH.

Laurance, J. (2007) 'Targets blamed as hospital infection deaths rise 59%', *Belfast Telegraph*, 23 February.

Laville, S. (2005) 'Mother who killed son with Down's syndrome gets suspended sentence', *Guardian*, 3 November.

Law Commission (1995) *Mental Incapacity Law.* Law Com. no.231. London: HMSO.

Levenson, R. (2007) *The challenge of dignity in care.* London: Help the Aged.

LGA (2007) Local Government Association. *Council crackdown on 'cold callers' see doorstep crime plummet.* News release, 20 August 2007. London: LGA.

London Borough of Hounslow News (2007) 'Callous carer jailed for theft from 89-year-old woman', 14 September. Available at http://www.hounslow.gov.uk/news_mod_home/news_mod_year/news_mod_month/news_mod_show?year1=2007&month1=9&NewsID=30078, accessed 23 October 2008.

Lord Chancellor (2007) *Mental Capacity Act 2005: code of practice.* London: TSO.

Manthorpe, J., Tinker, A., McCreadie, C., Biggs, S., Doyle, M., Erens, B. and Hills, A. (2008). 'Number and nuances: the implications for adult protection coordinators and committees of the UK national prevalence study of abuse and neglect of older people.' *Journal of Adult Protection,* volume 10, issue 1, February 2008.

Mark, D. (2005) 'Care home firm which failed to act on abuse claims is fined £100,000', *Yorkshire Post,* 28 October.

Marriott, H. (2003) *The selfish pig's guide to caring.* Clifton-upon-Teme: Polperro Heritage Press.

'Matron ordered to pay compensation', *Worcester News,* 11 May 2007. Available at http://archive.worcesternews.co.uk/2007/5/11/464267.html, accessed 23 october 2008.

McKeever, K. (2007) 'Cruel carer is guilty in landmark court case', *Wilmslow Express,* 15 August. Available at http://www.wilmslowexpress.co.uk/news/s/531/531529_cruel_carer_is_guilty_in_landmark_court_case.html, accessed 23 October 2008.

Metropolitan Police Service (2008). *Male imprisoned for seven and a half years for fraud.* July 2008. Available at http://cms.met.police.uk/met/boroughs/enfield/04how_are_we_doing/news/male_imprisoned_for_7_and_a_half_years_for_fraud, accessed 23 October 2008.

MHAC (2008) Mental Health Act Commission. *Risk, rights, recovery: twelfth biennial report, 2005–2007.* London: MHAC.

Ministry of Justice (2008) *Deprivation of liberty safeguards.* London: TSO.

Moffat, K. (a pseudonym) (2006) 'Nurses can't walk away', *Guardian,* 28 April.

Moore, A. (2008) 'Trusts warned C diff probe decision sets no precedent.' *Health Service Journal,* 7 August 2008.

Morris, S. (2007) 'Tortured, drugged and killed a month after the care visits were stopped', *Guardian,* 4 August.

Morris, S. and Brindle, D. (2008). 'Carers accused of faking log of home visits to woman, 83', *Guardian,* 12 March.

'Mother stole £58,000 from bank to pay school fees', *Bradford Telegraph and Argus,* 21 August 2008.

MWCS (2008) Mental Welfare Commission for Scotland. *Summary of our investigation into the care and treatment of Ms A.* Edinburgh: MHWC.

NAFWC 9/02; WHC(2002)32. National Assembly for Wales. *Health and social care for adults: creating a unified and fair system for assessing and managing care.* Cardiff: NAFW.

Narain, J. (2008) 'Care home boss jailed after wilful neglect killed Alzheimer's patient', *Daily Mail,* 21 May.

Newell, C. (2007) 'Exposed: filth and abuse in care home', *Sunday Times,* 4 November.

Newell, C. (2007a) 'Inspectors order nursing firm to raise standards', *Sunday Times,* 4 November.

Norfolk, A. (2003) 'Coroner who stole £155,000 from the dead', *The Times,* 8 February.

Norfolk, A. (2005) 'Care home killer, 82, was violent psychopath', *The Times,* 10 June.

Nowaczyk, W. (2008) 'Carer's reputation is ruined after theft' *Walesonline,* 3 July 2008. Available at http://www.walesonline.co.uk/news/south-wales-news/pontypridd-llantrisant/2008/07/03/carer-s-reputation-is-ruined-after-theft-91466-21209746/, accessed 23 October 2008.

NPS 54/2004/ National Probation Service. *MAPPA guidance.* London: NPS.

NPSA (2006) National Patient Safety Agency. *With safety in mind.* London: NPSA.

'Nurse is struck off over thefts', *Telegraph and Argus,* 23 March 2005.

'Nurse stole card from dying man', *The Times,* 3 October 2007.

'Nurse struck off', The Times, 9 January 2002.

'Nurse who left man lying in own vomit is struck off', *South Manchester Reporter,* 29 January 2004.

'Nurse who slapped patient is struck off', *Bury Times,* 2 November 2006.

Nursing Standard (2005) 'Act used to show "shocking" care.' *Nursing Standard*, 13 April 2005.

Nursing Standard (2005a) 'Dementia patients were not starved, inquest finds.' *Nursing Standard*, 30 March 2005.

Nursing Times (2005) 'NMC to monitor elder abuse after high rates revealed in misconduct case figures.' *Nursing Times*, 15 November 2005.

O'Keefe, M., Hills, A., Doyle, M., McCreadie, C. *et al.* (2007) *UK Study of abuse and neglect of older people*. London: Comic Relief and Department of Health.

O'Neill, S. (2007) 'Gunshot particle that helped to convict Dando's murderer should be discounted', *The Times*, 6 November.

'OAP falls prey to "wicked and mean" thefts by Sudbury carer', *Sudbury Free Press*, 28 August 2008.

Office of Fair Trading (2004) *Doorstep selling*. London: Office of Fair Trading.

Osley, R. (2008) 'Facing prison for £500,000 fraud', *Camden New Journal*, 10 January.

Pannone (2006) *Pannone wins care home negligence settlement of £45,000*. Press release. Manchester: Pannone.

Peek, L. (2004) 'Hawking assaulted by wife, claim nurses', *The Times*, 23 January.

Peek, L. (2004a) 'Police drop Hawking assault case', *The Times*, 30 March.

Persaud, R. (2003) *From the edge of the couch*. London: Bantam Press.

Rayner, G. and Smith, R. (2007) 'Superbug boss has record of dirty hospitals', *Daily Telegraph*, 12 October.

Rose, D. (2007) 'Deaths scandal NHS chief quits with attack on "target culture"', *The Times*, 16 October.

Rose, D. (2007a) 'Hospital ordered to halt pay off to chief after superbug scandal', *The Times*, 12 October.

Sanderson, D. (2008) 'Leslie Ash gets £5m payout from hospital where she caught MRSA', *The Times*, 17 January.

Santry, C. (2008) 'Chiefs and managers at odds on safety.' *Health Service Journal*, 22 May 2008, p.4.

Scorer, R. (2008) 'Assisting death.' *New Law Journal*, 4 July 2008.

Scott, M. (2008) 'Nurse plunders £300k from dying patient', *Sunday Mail*, 16 March.

Scottish Executive (2008) *Adult Support and Protection (Scotland) Act 2007: code of practice*. Edinburgh: Scottish Executive.

Serious Fraud Office (2000) *Former solicitor admits to plundering clients' accounts*. Press release, 6 June 2000. London: Serious Fraud Office.

SGC (2004) Sentencing Guidelines Council. *Overarching principles: seriousness*. London: SGC.

'Shed captive was unlawfully killed', *Metro Newspaper*, 28 February 2008.

Skills for Care (2008) *Common core principles to support self care*. London: Skills for Care (foreword written by two government ministers).

Smith, L. (2001) 'Father who suffocated sick daughter is freed', *The Times*, 9 June.

'Social services manager stole from elderly', *Isle of Thanet Gazette News*, 8 February 2002.

Solicitors' Journal (2003) '£1m compensation for abused care home residents.' *Solicitors' Journal,* 17 October 2003.

Solicitors' Journal (2008) 'Ten year jail sentence for solicitor who stole over £1m compensation from paralysed client.' *Solicitors' Journal,* 15 April 2008.

SSI (1992) Social Services Inspectorate. *Confronting elder abuse*. London: DH.

Steel, M. (2007) 'You can't go round telling people you've been sacked', *Independent*, 14 November, p.37.

Stephens, A. (2008) '£75,000 pay-off too little, says woman in charge of worst superbug outbreak', *Evening Standard*, 1 February.

SWSI (2004) Social Work Services Inspectorate. *Report of the inspection of Scottish Borders Council social work services for people affected by learning disabilities*. Edinburgh: Scottish Executive.

Taylor, A. (2007) 'The war on the wards.' *Community Care*, 13 December 2007, p.12.

This is Cornwall (2008) 'Care home employs nurse cautioned for patient attack.' Available at www.thisiscornwall.co.uk, accessed 23 October 2008.

Tozer, J. (2007) 'Why was my mum sent home from hospital to die alone?', *Daily Mail*, 9 February.

Trading Standards Institute (2003) *Door to door cold calling of property repairs, maintenance and improvements: long overdue for statutory control.* Basildon: Trading Standards Institute.

Traynor, L. (2008) 'Law says "sorry" after theft leaves Mary £2000 in debt – and crook gets only 4 months', *Liverpool Echo,* 18 February.

Vaughan, V. (2007) 'Dishonesty and disingenuousness.' *Health Service Journal,* 1 March 2007, p.7.

Vinter, P. (2007) 'Killer preyed on "kind Sean"', *Oxford Mail,* 20 April.

'Vulnerable patients locked in car for three hours while carers went to the bookies', *Daily Mail,* 21 January 2008.

Wainwright, M. (2005) 'GP deliberately killed three patients, court told', *The Times,* 26 October.

Ward, D. (2006) 'Nurse who put patient's glass eye in drink is struck off', *Guardian,* 17 February.

'We just want to clear our names'. *Norwich Evening News,* 26 May 2006.

Williams, J. (2008) 'OPA told to get bus home after op', *Wiltshire Times & Chippenham News,* 28 March.

'Woman in two-year cancer con on fiancé sent to jail', *The Scotsman,* 24 June 2008.

Wood, A. (2005) 'Cruel care home abusers are jailed', *Yorkshire Post,* 22 March.

Woolcock, N. (2002) 'Widow, 91, sued over nursing home fees', *Daily Telegraph,* 1 October.

Womack, S. (2008) 'Elderly care blunders cost NHS £180m', *Daily Telegraph,* 13 February.

Wood, A. (2008) 'Daughter spared jail over attempted "mercy killing"', *Yorkshire Post,* 21 December.

Wright, O. and Carson, V. (2002) '86-year-old is killed by hospital's cruel neglect', *The Times,* 8 August.

Yourcanterbury (2008) 'Carer sentenced for theft from 91-year-old woman', 22 March 2008. Available at www.yourcanterbury.co.uk, accessed 23 October 2008.

Index